Pragmatics of Uncertainty

CHAPMAN & HALL/CRC
Texts in Statistical Science Series

Series Editors

Francesca Dominici, *Harvard School of Public Health, USA*
Julian J. Faraway, *University of Bath, UK*
Martin Tanner, *Northwestern University, USA*
Jim Zidek, *University of British Columbia, Canada*

Texts in Statistical Science

Pragmatics of Uncertainty

Joseph B. Kadane

Carnegie Mellon University,
Pittsburgh, Pennsylvania, USA

CRC Press
Taylor & Francis Group
Boca Raton London New York

CRC Press is an imprint of the
Taylor & Francis Group, an **informa** business

A CHAPMAN & HALL BOOK

CRC Press
Taylor & Francis Group
6000 Broken Sound Parkway NW, Suite 300
Boca Raton, FL 33487-2742

First issued in paperback 2020

© 2017 by Taylor & Francis Group, LLC
CRC Press is an imprint of Taylor & Francis Group, an Informa business

No claim to original U.S. Government works

ISBN-13: 978-1-4987-1984-1 (hbk)
ISBN-13: 978-0-367-73681-1 (pbk)

Library of Congress Cataloging-in-Publication Data

Names: Kadane, Joseph B.
Title: Pragmatics of uncertainty / Joseph B. Kadane.
Description: Boca Raton : CRC Press, 2017. | Series: Chapman & Hall/CRC texts in statistical science | Includes bibliographical references and index.
Identifiers: LCCN 2016022982 | ISBN 9781498719841 (alk. paper)
Subjects: LCSH: Measurement uncertainty (Statistics)
Classification: LCC T50 .K38 2017 | DDC 519.5/42--dc23
LC record available at https://lccn.loc.gov/2016022982

Visit the Taylor & Francis Web site at
http://www.taylorandfrancis.com

and the CRC Press Web site at
http://www.crcpress.com

Dedication

To my family:

My wife, Caroline, my daughter, Mary, and my grandchildren.

My sister, Kay, and her extended family.

My sisters-in-law, brother-in-law, and their families.

And to my assistant, Heidi Rhodes Sestrich, who has contributed so much to my productivity for all these years.

Contents

Foreword

In **Principle of Uncertainty** (2011), I proposed

1. "Applications of statistics and probability is where the center of the subject is" (p. 447).

2. The issue for applied work is "persuading a reader of the reasonableness of the beliefs expressed." (ibid)

The purpose of this volume, then, is to allow the reader to examine the extent to which my applied work has made good on that promise.

Preface

The subjective Bayesian viewpoint leads to a theory with "clean lines," in that, having declared a likelihood and prior distribution, only computational error would lead to different posterior distributions. Similarly, having declared a utility or loss function, again only computational error would lead to a decision that failed to maximize expected utility or minimize expected loss.

So attention has to be focused on where the likelihood, prior distribution and utility or loss "come from." The subjective view holds that the specification of these is the responsibility of the author. If the author wishes others to read and take seriously the results of the computations, those specifications have to be explained and justified in the context of the application. While it is all very well to say that the judgments required are subjective and context dependent, these observations do not help to offer useful guidance to others attracted by the conceptual elegance and computational availability of subjective Bayesianism.

A fair question to ask, then, of an advocate of subjective Bayesianism (which I am) is, "How would you do it?". Not knowing the context of your problem, I cannot answer that. But I can write about how I have done it in the past, and offer additional comments about the context in which I was working. Thus this book.

The papers discussed in this volume span twenty-five years of statistical practice. With each paper, I explain the context and give further thoughts on the specifications involved. I also offer an epilogue with my (admittedly biased) assessment of how well I think I did in adhering to the standard I set.

The papers are presented chronologically, with two thoughts in mind: to allow a reader to see whether and how my ideas have developed over time, and to observe how the increasing availability of computation has changed how I approach applied problems. The papers themselves reflect my interests and opportunities at the time, and address a broad variety of subjects.

In the Statistics Department at Carnegie Mellon, one of the requirements for a Ph.D. degree is to do a year-long Advanced Data Analysis (ADA) project, on data that has not been analyzed before, with a client outside the department and a statistical advisor. Typically, the way I handle this is that, once the project is set up, I do not contact the client. Instead, I ask the student many questions, which requires the student to discuss the project in depth with the client. These projects also introduce students to the issues that attend real data, including missing data, recording errors, modeling and computation. Papers 6, 9, 10, 11 and 14 in this volume were ADA projects.

How to read this book:

Much of the space in this book is occupied by reprints of 15 papers, most of which one can download from the Web. But the purpose of the book is philosophical, to address, with specific examples, the question of whether Bayesian statistics is ready for prime time. Can it be used in a variety of applied settings to address real applied problems? What are the issues that arise in choosing likelihoods and priors? Are the conclusions convincing? Have the data been properly handled; neither over, nor under, enthusiastically? To help the reader address these questions, I have added a Foreword to each paper explaining the context in which it was written, and an epilogue giving my assessment of the paper.

How might this book be used in teaching? In a course that mainly emphasizes applications, there are exercises at the end of each chapter. To assist students with theoretical ideas they may need help with, I have added references, principally but not solely, to the companion volume, *Principles of Uncertainty*.

In a course principally aimed at theory, I offer an index of topics. Thus, if one needs an example of a particular topic, the index tells you where to find it.

I thank Oxford University Press, J. Wiley & Sons, Taylor & Francis, the American Statistical Association, and SAGE Publishers for permission to reproduce articles. I especially thank the Institute of Mathematical Statistics, the Royal Statistical Society and the International Society for Bayesian Analysis for not requiring such permission.

Chapter 1

Bayesian Paleoethnobotany (1988)

Foreword

I met Christine Hastorf in 1986 when we were both at the Center for Advanced Study in the Behavioral Sciences at Stanford. She is an archeologist, and had been on an excavation project in Peru in 1982. One of her specialities is the use of botanical remains as evidence of social behavior in ancient sites. Because botanical remains deteriorate over time, only burnt seeds tend to survive to be studied. Typically a bag of dirt would be dug at specific points in the site being studied. The dirt would be placed in water, so the soil would fall to the bottom, while the burnt seeds would float on top. These would be skimmed off, packaged, and sent to a laboratory for species identification. Christine's question was how she could persuade her fellow archeologists that the botanical evidence she was finding would add to their understanding of the social issues of the site.

From all their other sources of information, the archeologists already knew a lot. To find information that duplicated what they already knew would not justify paying attention to botanical evidence. Hence the emphasis is on the *additional* power that botanical evidence might have.

To model this, we took all the non-botanical evidence as prior information. The botanicals would contribute the likelihood, and the comparison between prior and posterior would show the extent to which the botanical evidence had added to knowledge.

The site easily divided into areas within structures, and patio areas between structures. Within structures, we defined four categories of use: hearth, storage against walls, living quarters and midden. Outside of structures, we defined storage against the wall, midden, and activity center. The digging notes were used (by Christine) to give prior probabilities for each possible use at each spot where botanical evidence was gathered. In some of these, there was the possibility of more than one use of the spot. Our treatment of this issue is described in Section 1.4.

The likelihood is the probability of the data given the parameters, viewed as a function of the parameters. Here the data are the numbers of seeds of each species observed at a particular spot, and the parameters are indicators of the use, whether in a structure or in a patio. To divide the questions into meaningful chunks, we distinguished what may have been present in AD 1460, when the site was abandoned, from what was found in 1982, when the samples were taken. The second step was to divide the gross categories of use into subcategories, with numbers indicating the proportion of burnt botanicals expected from each subactivity, as given in Table 1.4. For each subactivity, Table 1.3 gives numbers proportional to the expected number of burnt botanicals by species. At first, I asked Christine for numbers that added up to 100. Then she realized that she had neglected some kinds of seeds she thought were possible. Should she rejigger the numbers to make them add up, once again, to 100? I saw that this was unnecessary, so we relaxed the constraint that the numbers had to add to 100. Together, Tables 1.3 and 1.4 yield numbers proportional to the expected number of burnt botanicals by species for each activity, as of 1460.

There are two additional steps to creating the likelihood. The first, addressed in

Table 1.5, is the expected number of seeds, by activity, expected to have been deposited in 1460. Together with Tables 1.3 and 1.4, this permits calculation of the expected numbers of burnt botanical remains, by species, for each activity as of 1460. This is given in Table 1.6 (unfortunately the original printing of this paper recorded this as Table 1.7).

The final step is to address the preservation probabilities by species. Some species, like tubers (think potatoes) would be unlikely to survive from 1460 to 1982, while others, such as Chenopodium, are small, hard and tough, and much more likely to survive. The first column of Table 1.7 (unfortunately, again, Table 1.6 in the original version) gives Christine's preservation probabilities. The result is the remainder of Table 1.7, which gives the expected number of botanical remains, by species, for each activity, as of 1982. The observed number of burnt botanicals by species in 1982 is taken to have a Poisson distribution with means specified in Table 1.7.

It is difficult to recall just how rudimentary the computers were at this time. I think they were done on a Tandy-80 (known at the time as a Trash-80), probably in Fortran. I remember the computer working for hours to do the integrals involved.

There were two observations worthy of special note. Float number 284 had 17,465 Chenopodium seeds, while the expected numbers were 17.60 for a hearth, 16.14 for midden, and 7.72 for indoor storage as given in Table 1.7. As a result, the posterior put probability 1 on a hearth. But such a huge number of Chenopodium seeds really suggests that this is an outlying observation deserving of special treatment. The second observation worthy of special comment is float 299, where 66 Scirpus seeds were found. The likelihood put the expected number of Scirpus seeds in a hearth at 0, but the prior put probability 1 on this location being a hearth. When asked about it, Christine was still sure this location was a hearth. Hence, the issue here was the likelihood, not the prior. We made the decision to leave this in the paper as is, rather than to adjust the 0 expected number of Scirpus seeds in a hearth to make everything look nicer.

So what is to be learned from this exercise? First, the posterior distributions on the activities in many of the locations were different than the priors, substantiating Christine's belief in the informativeness of botanical remains for archeologists. Second, our analysis is entirely transparent, in that all of the assumptions are stated and available for critique. It took courage, I think, for Christine to put numbers on her views so publicly, but the payoff is to make archeology more transparent. Of course their interpretations are influenced by their beliefs as well as what they find at the site. Bayesian methods offer them a way of communicating what those beliefs are, and allow dissenting archeologists to see whether alternative beliefs lead to importantly different conclusions.

Philosophically, this is an example in which the likelihood is obviously subjective, and in which the probabilistic statements are personal beliefs.

At the time, the dominant understanding of probability was through the concept of relative frequency, for example, by associating the probability that a flipped coin would come up heads with the fraction of times it would come up heads in many (independent) flips. In this paper, the probabilities are avowedly subjective, and there is not a useful sense of many independent trials. Thus working this problem requires a more general understanding of probability, in which relative frequency is a special case.

This paper was originally published by Oxford University Press in *Bayesian Statistics III*, edited by J. Bernardo, M. DeGroot, D.V. Lindley and A.F.M. Smith, pp. 243–259. Reproduction in this volume by permission of Oxford University Press.

Christine Hastorf is Professor of Archeology at the University of California, Berkeley.

Published Paper

J.B. Kadane and C.A. Hastorf[1]

Abstract

Paleoethnobotany is the use of burnt plant remains to investigate certain types of activity at archaeological sites. Ethnographic studies are used to inform opinion on the various points in the processing, storing, and cooking of grains at which the plants might come into contact with fire. Combined with opinions about the relative decay rates of different species, botanical remains are thus used to update an archaeologist's opinion of the activities carried out in various places at a prehistoric house in a large settlement. The extent of the shift from prior to posterior is a measure of the importance of botanical evidence in archaeological interpretation.

The methods are applied to excavations at a prehistoric site in Perú.

Keywords: archaeology; botany; burnt botanical remains; Cromwell's Rule; patio; Perú

1.1 Styles of Data Analysis

There are many styles of data analysis and interpretation. The goal of all is to make the data more meaningful and interpretable. To illustrate how Bayesian analysis can help with meaningful interpretation, we have chosen to apply it to the archaeological problem of determining prehistoric household activities.

For the record, and so that other data analysts may compare their methods to the one used here, the full data set discussed in this paper is reported in Table 1.1. The columns in that table are seed-types, the rows are specific excavated locations (proveniences), and the entries are the number of burnt seeds found in soil from each place.

The method of analysis pursued here, is to set out in detail both the way the data came into being and what else is known or believed about the data by archaeologists who study this cultural area (section 1.2). In this case, these data are part of a larger archaeological research project and database. We then discuss the kinds of questions that paleobotanical data, such as those reported in the table, are collected to answer. For greater specificity, we choose one archaeological question to address in detail, namely, what daily life activities might have been conducted at each provenience or location within one prehistoric household (section 1.3). We report priors for activities based on the field notes of the archaeologists digging at each provenience (section 1.4) The botanical data yield a likelihood on activities (section 1.5), which is used to update the priors to posteriors (section 1.6). All these specifications must be regarded as tentative, as they represent our first attempt to quantify paleoethnobotanical beliefs in this manner. Our conclusions are reported in section 1.7.

1.2 The Data

The archaeological data in this paper come from a region around the modern town of Jauja in the central Andes of Perú. This region is approximately 250 km east of Lima, between the two mountain ranges that run parallel to the west coast of South America. The specific

---

[1]The authors are members of the Center for Advanced Study in the Behavioral Sciences, Stanford.

region of study is the northern portion of the Wanka ethnic territory. The Wanka have lived in the area since approximately 200 B.C. In 1977, a research team, the Upper Mantaro Archaeological Research Project (UMARP, directed by T. Earle, T. D'Altroy, C. Hastorf, and C. Scott), began investigating the economy and political organization of this local group, throughout prehistory, until the arrival of the Spanish *conquistadores* in A.D. 1532. This temporal sequence has been divided into cultural periods characterized by changes in the political organization and settlement pattern. The Wanka, living between 10,000 and 12,0000 feet above sea level, farmed locally adapted crops: potato (*Solanum tuberosum L.*); maize (*Zea mays L.*); quinoa (*Chenopodium quinoa* Wild.), a grain; lupine (*Lupinus mutabilis* Sweet), a legume; and a series of Andean tubers. They also herded camelids, the llama (*Llama glama* Linnæus 1758) and the alpaca (*Llama pacos* Linnæus 1758), and raised guinea pigs (*cavia cf. porcellus* Linnæus 1759) in their house (Hastorf, 1983).

This project is based on data collected during the 1982 field season, during which the excavations studied the organization of the Wanka economy during the late prehistoric periods: the Late Intermediate Period (A.D. 1350–1460), called the Wanka II Period and the Late Horizon-Inca Period (1460–1532) called the Wanka III Period (Earle et al., 1987).

During the Wanka II era the local population was organized into chiefdoms composed of groups numbering in the thousands. This organization is inferred from the settlement-pattern and artifact distribution at centers and small associated satellites. Large towns, such as Tunánmarca (label J7 in Figure 1.1), comprised habitation structures numbering in the thousands. These were associated with smaller nearby settlements. Sites occupied in this time period were located on high, rocky knolls, overlooking the small valleys and rolling countryside (Figure 1.1). Within stone defensive walls, these sites were filled with hundreds of household residences called patio areas (an example of which is shown in Figure 1.2). Each patio area was composed of one or more circular structures that opened onto an enclosed space and were joined together by stone walls. These patio areas were linked by narrow winding pathways that wove through the settlement. From the artifacts found at the site and this architectural layout, we believe that each patio area housed a family, either nuclear or extended.

The archaeological evidence suggests that local political units competed with each other for control of land and other resources. Within a polity, a large community appears to have dominated smaller nearby villages. These polities had leaders who were especially important in warfare (LeBlanc, 1981).

During Late Horizon, the Wanka society was transformed through imperial conquest (D'Altroy, 1981, 1987). As the region was pacified and organized under Inca rule, the settlement locations changed radically. The Wanka population was moved into smaller, unfortified settlements at lower elevations.

To understand the overall Wanka economy, UMARP began by investigating the domestic household economy. The researchers wanted to understand the daily tasks and occupations of household groups, and consequently were interested in the activities that took place in patios. In the 1982 field season UMARP excavated patios at four different sites. In that year, six patios were excavated totally to retrieve data on a complete distribution of artifacts within individual households. In 1983 23 more patios were sampled to improve the patio sample size. Patio selection was based on a series of architectural and spatial criterial that were used to define two economic statuses within the society: elites and commoners. In each patio, excavators divided the space into units no bigger than 2×2 m. In each of these units, they tried to collect all cultural material: ceramic fragments (sherds), stone tools (lithics), animal bone, plant remains, metal, shell, and other miscellaneous objects that the Wanka managed to bring home. However, not all objects that were used and deposited in the past are still present in the soil. Erosion, scavenging by later people, and decomposition all affect the artifact assemblage of an archaeological site.

Of major interest to archaeologists, therefore, are (1) the relationship (spatial, temporal, or social) of the excavated objects to each other; (2) the conjectural recreation of the original deposited assemblage from the incomplete record that is actually excavated; and (3) the differential preservation of various types of artifacts. To understand the economics and politics

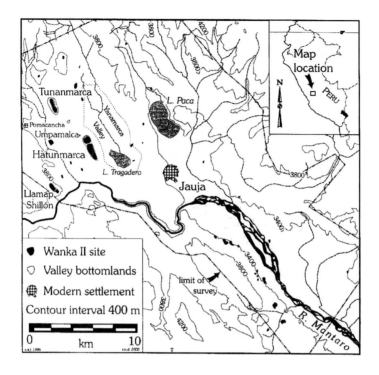

Figure 1.1: Wanka II Period settlement pattern in the archaeological study area.

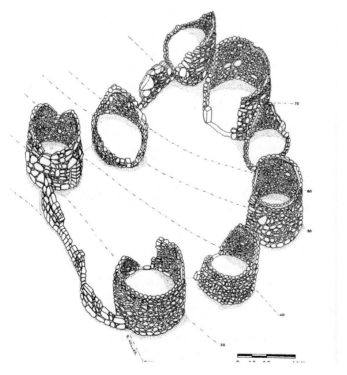

Figure 1.2: A patio at Tunánmarca: An Axiometric view of $J7 = 2$ patio.

of a group, we must begin with a reconstruction of the activities that occurred in the excavated areas. Once we know something about the activities, we can consider the causes of change.

Commonly, the excavated artifacts are divided by type and analyzed by specialists (e.g., a ceramic specialist, an osteological specialist). Each artifact type can inform us about certain aspects of the prehistoric past. For example, ceramic sherds are often used to infer trade relations between villages and groups; lithic tools tell us about a group's complexity and type of technology.

Of special interest here are the botanical remains collected from the patios, because their information is rarely applied in archaeological research and they offer an important window into the past. Because plants and plant use in the past have a direct link with their collection and agricultural production, they should be able to give us a unique perspective on agricultural activities and the related economics (Hastorf, 1988). Because of the long time between deposition and excavation (over 500 years for the Wanka II samples), and the weathering process, only charred botanical remains survive. Such remains are quite fragile, and require special procedures. When, as here, these procedures are utilized, however, the analysis results in a viable archaeological data set. In the past, botanical remains have not been considered important in archaeology both because of the difficulty of the procedures and because of the special assumptions that need to be made, particularly concerning the differential preservation between plant taxa. We address this issue below.

1.3   Research Plan

How much can archaeological data inform us about prehistoric activities? Toward this general question, we have chosen to focus on the more specific question, what were the activities in different places within a Wanka household patio? Even more specifically, what can botanical data tell us about these activities? The purpose of this paper is to see how much paleoethnobotanical data can inform us about the past in one prehistoric location. The steps in the study are:

1. Conversion of the archaeological field notes into probabilities, here treated as prior probabilities, for the activities at each location.

2. Development of a model for the botanical remains conditional on each activity, which plays the role of the likelihood.

3. Computation of posterior probabilities given the actual botanical data.

4. Comparison of prior to posterior probabilities as an indication of the extent to which botanical remains are useful in informing the archaeologists about activities at sites.

We have chosen one household patio $J7 = 2$ (the second patio excavated on site J7), as our test case in this exploratory study. It was excavated in 1982. It was the dwelling of an elite family on the central site of Tunánmarca and included six structures and a large inner patio space (Figure 1.3). The excavation units divide the patio into manageable areas. The excavation procedure included two sampling strategies. First, within each of 88 excavation sub-units (determined by location and depth) a bag of soil, 6 kg in weight, was collected. The specific soil collection locations are shown by pie charts in Figures 1.3 and 1.4, which are discussed in detail later. This soil then was processed by a mechanical water flotation system (Watson, 1976) that gently separated the plant remains from the soil matrix. Charred or carbonized plant remains have a lighter specific gravity than water, and as the soil is lightly agitated by moving water, the plant fragments float to the surface and can be skimmed off. This procedure also collects a systematic subsample of the very small artifacts at the site.

In the second data collection strategy, all the remaining excavated soil was processed through $\frac{1}{4}$" screens. This allowed the artifacts greater than $\frac{1}{4}$" to be collected and placed in coded bags. Naturally, most seeds are too small to be recovered by this sifting procedure, although occasional wood or tuber fragments are collected. Systematically retrieved botanical remains come from the equal-sized bags of soil processed by water flotation, and are the data reported in Table 1.1.

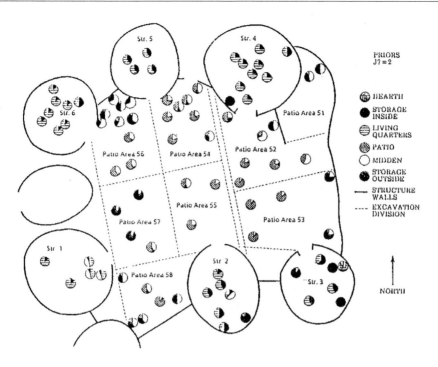

Figure 1.3: Plan of patio $J7 = 2$. Structures and excavation units labeled by number. Soil sample flotation locations indicated by pie charts representing the prior probabilities.

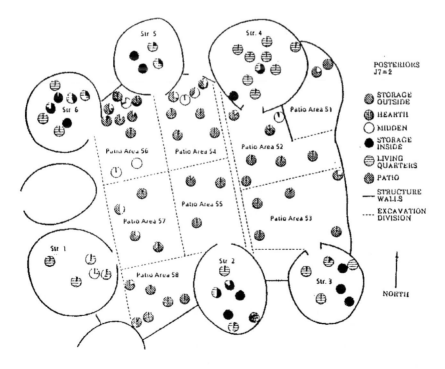

Figure 1.4: Plan of patio $J7 = 2$. Structures and excavation units labeled by number. Soil sample flotation locations indicated by pie charts representing their posterior probabilities.

The cultural description of each of provenience at $J7 = 2$ is based on the excavation notes, the soil changes, and the artifacts that came from the screening. The observations we are comparing to the prior descriptions are the identified plants from the individual samples of bagged and floated soil. What can the botanical data tell us about the cultural activities in this prehistoric elite patio compound? Let us now turn to the construction of the prior probabilities.

1.4 Prior Probabilities of Activities

The first step in determining the prior probabilities of prehistoric activities is to be specific about the categories used. For this paper we have chosen a rather coarse division of activities. We are treating the inside of the circular structures differently from the patio space. Within a structure, the activity areas we recognize are hearths, storage against the walls, living quarters, and midden. In the patio outside of the structures, we divide the activity areas into storage against the wall, midden, and activity center. These activities and their locations are defined by modern daily life activities, recorded from observing the Wanka who live in the region today. A hearth (A) is a place where food is cooked and heat is generated. It is a very localized spot, identified by dense carbon and *in situ* burning of the soil. Storage inside the structure (F) is located against the walls of the house structure. It is where fuel and food are stored. Living quarters (G) within the structure are where the residents eat, sleep, and socialize; the guinea pigs also reside there and eat the food scraps dropped on the floor. Midden (E) is a localized place, often near a wall, where objects and refuse are discarded. The activity of storage in the patio area (H) remains the same, with more emphasis on storing fuel, ash, and wild collectables. Midden (E) in the patio has the same use as in the structure. An activity center (I) is an area where many tasks are performed. The most common are food processing, such as winnowing, sorting, drying, bagging; household goods construction or repair, such as wool carding, dyeing, weaving; tool construction, such as digging-stick making, mat weaving, pottery making, leather working, etc. A particular spot may or may not have been used for only one of these categories. Thus we must consider the possibility of mixed usage, where appropriate.

For each provenience, the notes of the archaeologist who excavated it provide the basis for an opinion about use of the location where the soil sample was collected. The notes incorporate evidence other than the botanical specimens recovered by flotation, of which the excavating archaeologist would have no knowledge. For each provenience, the archaeologist on our team (Hastorf) gave her opinion of the prior probabilities of usage, based on the notes and ethnographic knowledge. These probabilities are given in Table 1.2.

The probabilities given in Table 1.2 are incomplete, as the following example demonstrates. Consider provenience #283, a sample recovered from inside a structure. The prior probabilities given in Table 1.2 are:

$$P(\overline{AEF}G) = 0.25$$
$$P(\overline{AE}F\overline{G}) = 0.25$$
$$P(\overline{AE}FG) = 0.50$$

Thus Hastorf is sure provenience 283 was *not* used as hearth (A) or midden (E). It might have been used solely as storage (F) (probability $\frac{1}{4}$) solely as living quarters (G) (probability $\frac{1}{4}$), or both (probability $\frac{1}{2}$). If it had been used as both, what is the probability that a given deposited botanical specimen came from a storage area or from living quarters?

We have chosen to treat this as a beta distribution, and here in particular a uniform distribution. In general we choose the hyper parameters α and β of this beta distribution as follows: The mean of the beta distribution is chosen to be the same as the mean of the distribution of uses conditional on the provenience being used for

Table 1.1: Burnt Botanical remains by Provenience as found. (1982). *Paleoethnobotanical data by flotation number from J7 = 2*

OBS	FLOTNO	MZKERNEL	CUPCOBS	CHENOPOD	AMARANTH	SCIRPUS	TLEGUME	VERBENA	PLANTAGO	MALVALST	COMPOST	WOOD	GRSSTKS	COCA	PAPAVER	GALIUM	VITAC	SYSRINC	RELBUN	POLYGON	CYPERS	GRASS	TUBER	LEGUMES
1	275			133																				1
2	276	13		56								2										1	2	24
3	264	7		25		3	1					4									3	9	2	14
4	288	41		45		2	2					7									2	1	21	1
5	290	3		33		1						1									1			2
6	314	1	1	3	1																1	6		
7	299			20		66	2					14									66	2		9
8	191		1																					
9	302			51		1						4									1	11	6	2
10	337			14																		5		
11	284		2	17465								26	3									3	90	
12	283					1						6									1			
13	273	1	1	29	1	2	1					4									2	12		
14	175			14								7											2	
15	174	1		22	1	1						4									1	2		
16	407			7								6		47						1		1		2
17	342											1												
18	204			2								44												
19	300			1		3	1					9									3	1		
20	396			22					1			2												
21	164					1						5									1	1	3	
22	170			2		1															1	3		
23	172											7												
24	165	1		3																		1	1	
25	181			5								1										1		
26	185											4										1		
27	159			7		1						2									1	7		
28	167																					1		
29	160			1						1		1										4		
30	171		48	13	1		7	8	2			1	7		1	1						200	5	
31	184	1		5								2										5	2	
32	169			1								3										5		
33	182	4		26								41											15	24
34	155	3		10								37											4	6
35	157			2								3											14	
36	301		2	8		1						10									1	5	5	3
37	156		1	4								13										2	50	
38	423		1	79		63						24									63	61	989	
39	177			1																			4	
40	419			32		11	1					17			44						11	13	37	1
41	158			2								1											9	
42	279			10				1				10	7									3	25	
43	310			1																				
44	322			5		2						2									2	4	7	
45	144											5										1	5	3
46	326			3								24											1	6
47	292			48		6						31									6	8		1
48	154			1								1												
49	148	1							1															
50	289			3								7										1		

Table 1.1: (continued) Burnt Botanical remains by Provenience as found. (1982). *Paleoethnobotanical data by flotation number from J7 = 2*

OBS	FLOTNO	MZKERNEL	CUPCOBS	CHENOPOD	AMARANTH	SCIRPUS	TLEGUME	VERBENA	PLANTAGO	MALVALST	COMPOST	WOOD	GRSSTKS	COCA	PAPAVER	GALIUM	VITAC	SYSRINC	RELBUN	POLYGON	CYPERS	GRASS	TUBER	LEGUMES
51	291			3								9												
52	319																							
53	321											1												
54	327											3												3
55	325			13	1							3									1	1		
56	333			3								4												
57	142			2								1										1		
58	336											3												
59	340																							
60	305			1								1												
61	285		2	45								2											4	
62	149			2	1							161											1	
63	312	1										16									1			
64	139			14	1							13									1	3		1
65	168			2										42										
66	161											9											1	
67	146											2												
68	152											1												
69	188	1		2								6											4	1
70	186			12								9									5			
71	187	21		18	8	1						9									1	3	10	3
72	282			12	1							20									1	4		
73	147			1																				
74	145			4								4											2	3
75	281			10	5	1						4									5	4		
76	286	1		9							1	13											4	29
77	287	210	15	5	1							47									1			
78	330	47	18	3	2							15						2			2			
79	339			38	1							2									1	1		
80	324			2								3										1	1	
81	303											25												
82	422			20								5									1			
83	280			1								2		26										
84	329	1	1	9								6										3		
85	313											1												
86	332	2		1								2												
87	274			0								2												
88	277	1		1																			4	

only one purpose. Thus if in general

$$P(\overline{A}E\overline{F}G) = p_1$$
$$P(\overline{A}E F\overline{G}) = p_2$$

then α and β would be chosen so that

$$\frac{\alpha}{\alpha + \beta} = \frac{p_1}{p_1 + p_2}.$$

The sum $\alpha + \beta$ is an indication of how much total information is available in a beta distribution. (The variance of a beta distribution is $E(p)E(1 - p)(1/(\alpha + \beta + 1))$.) We chose $\alpha + \beta$ to indicate considerable uncertainty about the mixture. In fact, we chose

Proveniences Inside Structures
Key A: Hearth; F: Storage(I): G: Living quarters, E: Midden
(all no Act Area, no midden, no storage (O))

FLOTATION SAMPLE NUMBER	$P(\overline{A}F\overline{G})$	$P(\overline{A}\,\overline{F}G)$	$P(\overline{A}FG)$
283	0.25	0.25	0.50
273	0.33	0.33	0.34
172	0.25	0.25	0.50
156	0.25	0.25	0.50
175	0.80	0.10	0.10
275	0.70	0.10	0.20
290	0.70	0.10	0.20
174	0.20	0.30	0.50
314	0.30	0.20	0.50
302	0.30	0.20	0.50
297	0.30	0.20	0.50
396	0.30	0.20	0.50
164	0.60	0.20	0.20
170	0.60	0.20	0.20
165	0.60	0.20	0.20
181	0.60	0.20	0.20
185	0.60	0.20	0.20
159	0.60	0.20	0.20
167	0.60	0.20	0.20
160	0.60	0.20	0.20
184	0.50	0.30	0.20
169	0.50	0.30	0.20
182	0.50	0.30	0.20
155	0.50	0.30	0.20
157	0.70	0.10	0.20
177	0.70	0.10	0.20
301	0.70	0.10	0.20
158	0.70	0.10	0.20
423	0.70	0.10	0.20
419	0.70	0.10	0.20
279	0.70	0.10	0.20

FLOTATION SAMPLE NUMBER   FLOTATION SAMPLE NUMBER

$\left.\begin{array}{l} 283 \\ 273 \\ 172 \\ 288 \\ 264 \\ 276 \end{array}\right\}$

$P(E\overline{F}G) = 0.50$
$P(EF\overline{G}) = 0.05$
$P(EFG) = 0.05$
$P(E\overline{F}\overline{G}) = 0.15$
$P(EFG) = 0.15$
$P(\overline{E}FG) = 0.05$
$P(\overline{E}FG) = 0.05$

407

$P(A\overline{F}G) = 0.8$
$P(AF\overline{G}) = 0.1$
$P(\overline{A}F\overline{G}) = 0.1$

$P(A\overline{F}G) = 0.05$
$P(AF\overline{G}) = 0.10$
284   $P(AFG) = 0.10$
$P(\overline{A}FG) = 0.05$
$P(\overline{A}F\overline{G}) = 0.65$
$P(AFG) = 0.05$

191

$P(A\overline{F}G) = 0.05$
$P(AF\overline{G}) = 0.05$
$P(AFG) = 0.20$
$P(\overline{A}FG) = 0.40$
$P(\overline{A}F\overline{G}) = 0.10$
$P(\overline{A}FG) = 0.20$

337

$P(A\overline{E}F) = 0.05$
$P(AE\overline{F}) = 0.20$
$P(\overline{A}EF) = 0.10$
$P(A\overline{E}\overline{F}) = 0.10$
$P(AEF) = 0.20$

299   $P(A\overline{F}G) = 1.0$

$\left.\begin{array}{l} 300 \\ 342 \\ 172 \end{array}\right\}$ $P(\overline{A}F\overline{G}) = 1.0$

Table 1.2: Priors of Activities by Flotation Sample Number

Proveniences Outside Structures
Key I: Activity Area in Patio; H: Storage (O); E: Midden
(all no Hearth, no storage (I), no Living Quarters)

FLOTATION SAMPLE NUMBER	$P(\bar{I}\bar{H}\bar{E})$	$P(\bar{I}\bar{H}E)$	$P(I\bar{H}\bar{E})$	$P(IH\bar{E})$	$P(\bar{I}H\bar{E})$	$P(\bar{I}H\bar{E})$	$P(\bar{I}HE)$
310	0.02	0.02	0.02	0.05	0.33	0.33	0.23
325	0.05	0.05	0.07	0.10	0.15	0.43	0.15
285 149	0.20	0.20	0.80	0.17	0.15	0.50	0.15
139	0.30	0.35	0.05	0.10	0.10	0.05	0.50
332	0.03	0.07	0.10	0.10	0.30	0.20	0.20
292	0.01	0.01	0.01	0.09	0.19	0.19	0.50
187 281	0.01	0.01	0.01	0.10	0.47	0.20	0.20
289	0.50	0.10	0.05	0.10	0.10	0.05	0.10
291	0.50	0.15	0.05	0.10	0.10	0.05	0.55
319	0.63	0.10	0.05	0.10	0.05	0.05	0.02
321	0.63	0.10	0.05	0.10	0.05	0.05	0.02
327	0.60	0.15	0.05	0.05	0.10	0.05	0.02
142	0.63	0.10	0.05	0.10	0.05	0.05	0.02
340	0.10	0.10	0.10	0.10	0.20	0.10	0.30
305	0.55	0.15	0.04	0.05	0.10	0.01	0.10
312	0.55	0.15	0.04	0. 05	0.10	0.01	0.10
161	0.20	0.20	0.10	0.15	0.20	0.05	0.10
152	0.50	0.15	0.05	0.05	0.15	0.05	0.05
339	0.80	0.10	0.00	0.00	0.10	0.0	0.00
324	0.80	0.10	0.00	0.00	0.10	0.0	0.00
329	0.05	0.10	0.05	0.10	0.20	0.20	0.30
277	0.10	0.10	0.10	0.10	0.20	0.20	0.20
154	0.20	0.35	0.04	0.05	0.30	0.02	0.04
336	0.30	0.30	0.10	0.10	0.10	0.05	0.05
147 287	0.30	0.30	0.05	0.10	0.15	0.05	0.05
330 303	0.30	0.30	0.05	0.05	0.20	0.05	0.05
144	0.20	0.30	0.10	0.10	0.10	0.10	0.10
326	0.10	0.20	0.05	0.10	0.30	05	0.20
188	0.10	0.10	0.10	0.10	0.30	0.20	0.30
186 286	0.05	0.05	0.05	0.10	0.25	0.20	0.30
148	0.01	0.01	0.04	0.04	0.40	0.20	0.30
168	0.15	0.20	0.50	0.20	0.20	0.05	0.05
146	0.55	0.20	0.05	0.10	0.10	0.0	0.0
282	0.02	0.02	0.02	0.05	0.50	0.19	0.20
145	0.05	0.02	0.05	0.10	0.25	0.28	0.30
422	0.80	0.10	0.00	0.00	0.10	0.0	0.0
280	0.20	0.25	0.10	0.15	0.15	0.05	0.10
274	0.10	0.10	0.10	0.10	0.20	0.20	0.20
322	0.05	0.05	0.05	0.15	0.15	0.15	0.40
333	0.05	0.05	0.05	0.10	0.15	0.20	0.40
313	0.60	0.20	0.05	0.05	0.05	0.05	0.0

it so that it is the same as it would be for a uniform distribution, i.e., $\alpha + \beta = 2$. These choices imply $\alpha = 2p_1/(p_1 + p_2)$ and $\beta = 2p_2/(p_1 + p_2)$. This specifies the prior in all cases in which only two uses were given positive probability.

These ideas can be extended easily to cases of three or more possible activities. First, the prior probability on each combination of two activities is specified using the principles above. If k activities are possible, that they individually have probabilities, respectively, of $p_1, \ldots, p_k$. Then, analogous to the work before, a Dirichlet prior would be imposed, with parameters $\alpha, \ldots, \alpha_k$. These hyper parameters α_i would be chosen to satisfy

$$\frac{\alpha_i}{\sum_{j=1}^{k} \alpha_j} = \frac{p_i}{\sum_{j=1}^{k} p_j} \quad i = 1, \ldots, k.$$

Also, to make the uniform distribution a possibility, $(\alpha_1 = \cdots = \alpha_k = 1)$, the sum of the alphas is constrained by

$$\sum_{i=1}^{k} \alpha_i = k.$$

These equations have the solution

$$\alpha_i = \frac{kp_i}{\sum_{j=1}^{k} p_j},$$

which defines the prior on each k-dimensional space. This assumes each $p_i > 0, i = 1, \ldots, k$.

1.5   Botanical Remains: The Likelihood Function

For convenience, we accept a Poisson model for the number X of burnt botanical remains believed to have been at a provenience at the time of site abandonment (*ca.* A.D. 1460, when the Inca conquered and relocated the population). Suppose the X has mean λ. If the process determining whether the seed survives until 1982 is binomial with probability p, then the number of botanical remains found in 1982, Y, is Poisson with mean λp. For each kind of possible botanical specimen, then the probability p must be specified. In addition, for each activity and specimen the mean λ (as of 1460) must be specified.

Leaving aside for the moment the issue of preservation, it is necessary to elicit Poisson rates λ for botanical remains expected by use of the provenience as, of A.D. 1460. As a first step, the group of subactivities was identified, and botanical remains were associated with each. Points were then distributed, sometimes on the basis of 100, but sometimes with other totals. The totals were chosen only for convenience, and are not regarded as having archaeological meaning. The results are listed in Table 1.3.

The next step was to subdivide the six activities into subactivities. These decompositions are given in Table 1.4. Again the totals are not regarded as meaningful, but simply as devices to get the proportions of botanical remains internal to each activity correct. Finally, we considered how many botanical remains would be expected (as of A.D. 1460) were the provenience used for each activity or combination of activities. These expectations are given in Table 1.5. The information in Tables 1.3, 1.4 and 1.5 jointly implies Poisson rates by activity in A.D. 1460, as reported in Table 1.6.

With respect to preservation, our first step was to rank botanical remains by how likely they are to survive. The ranking was as follows, from most to least likely to survive; small seeds, wood, *Zea mays* kernels, legume cotyledons, grass stalks, animal dung, and tubers. After that the archaeologist chose probabilities for the survival of each kind of botanical specimen. Those are reported in column 1 of Table 1.7. Finally

Table 1.3: Botanical Remains by Subactivity (1460)

Food		Sweepings		Tool Construction	
Zea mays kernels	3	Chenopodium spp.	20	wood	4
Chenopodium spp.	11	Amaranthus	8.3		
tubers	4	Scirpus	2.5	Scirpus	1
domestic legumes	2	wild legumes	8.3		
	20	Verbena	8.3	Polygonum	1
Hearth Misc.		Plantago	2.5		
Amaranthus	11	Malvastrum	2.5	Cyperaceae	1
wild legumes	11	Asteraceae	8.3		
Verbena sp.	11	wood	2.5	grass	1
Piantago sp.	11	grass stalks	2.5		8
Asteraceae	11	Papaveraceae	2.5		
Erthroxylum coca	1	Galium	2.5		
Vitaceae	1	Vitaceae	2.5		
Sisyrinchium	11	Sysrinchium	2.5		
Polygonum	11	Relbunium	0.5		
Cyperaceae	11	Polygonum	8.3		
grass	11	Cyperaceae	8.3		
	101	grass	2.5		
Medicinals		tubers	2.5		
Verbena sp.	3	domestic legumes	2.5		
Plantago sp.	3	animal dung	4.0		
Sysrinchium	1		104.3		
orgiga colorado	1	Winnowing			
Vaccinium sp.	1	Zea mays kernels	10		
Valeriana sp.	1	Chenopodium spp.	30		
	10	Amaranthus	15		
Fuel		Scirpus spp.	15		
Zea mays cobs & cupules	5	Malvastrum sp.	15		
wood	30	Asteraceae	15		
grass stalks	10	domestic legume pods	10		
grass	20		110		
animal dung	30	Stored Food			
	95	Zea mays kernels	3		
Household Good Fabrication		Chenopodium spp.	11		
Verbena	10	Scirpus	2		
Asteraceae	2.5	Asteraceae	2		
wood	60	Cyperaceae	2		
grass stalks	2.5	grass	4		
Relbunium	2.5	tubers	4		
Polygonum	10	domestic legumes	2		
Cyperaceae	10	Minthostachys sp.	4		
grass	2.5		34		
	100				

Table 1.4: Activities Partitioned into Subactivities

Hearth		*Storage (outside)*	
food	20	fuel	1
fuel	70	sweepings	1
hearth misc.	5	household good fabrication	1
medicinals	5		3
	100	*Open Area in Patio*	
Midden		household good fabrication	4
hearth misc.	70	tools	4
sweepings	30	winnowing	1
	10		9
Storage (inside)		*Living Quarters*	
stored food	30	food	6
fuel	20	sweepings	6
sweepings	50	medicinals	0.5
	100	tools	1
			13.5

the other columns of Table 1.7 report the expected Poisson rates of botanical remains as found in 1982, and are the rates in Table 1.6 multiplied by the probabilities in column 1 of Table 1.7. This specifies the likelihood for the problem.

It is perhaps noteworthy that the likelihood in this problem is just as subjective as the prior. That such might be the case has been remarked many times in the Bayesian literature, and is consistent with the view of Bayarri et al. (1987) that only the product of likelihood and prior has unique status from a Bayesian perspective. We have taken extra space to report the reasoning that leads to this specification because we think it might be interesting in its own right.

1.6   Computation of Posterior Distributions

The problem as posed is not a convenient family to report a conjugate posterior distribution. We have chosen to report it in terms of the predictive probability of each activity. For convenience of comparison, the prior has been reformulated that way as well.

This computation distinguished each subset of possible activities. These subsets contained one to three activities each. First, each subset was checked to see if a botanical specimen, believed impossible for some of its constituents, has been found there. If so, this subset was eliminated. For the others, a computation was done: in the subsets of size one, a simple calculation of Poisson probability, for the subsets of size two, a 1-dimensional integral, and finally for subsets of size 3, a 2-dimensional integral.

The posteriors were calculated for 1-dimensional integrals using a 10-point grid, and for the 2-dimensional problems with a truncated 10×10 grid. Although these methods were adequate for such low-dimensional integrals, we would anticipate moving

Table 1.5: Expected Total Botanical Remains (in 1460) by Activity

Hearth	200	Living Quarters	30
Midden	150	Storage (0)	50
Storage (I)	50	Open Area in Patio	10

Table 1.6: Preservation Probabilities and Expected Botanical Remains by Usage as of 1982.

	Preservation Probability	HEARTH	MIDDEN	INDOOR STORE	LIVING QTR	OUTDOOR STORE	ACTIVITY CENTER
Mzkernels	0.50	3.00	1.58	0.66	1.00	0.00	0.05
cupcobs	0.40	2.95	1.55	0.21	0.00	0.35	0.00
Chenopodium	0.80	17.60	16.14	7.72	7.91	2.56	0.24
Amaranthus	0.80	0.87	3.32	1.59	0.85	1.06	0.12
Scirpus	0.80	0.00	0.86	1.19	0.48	1.65	0.92
wild legumes	0.80	0.87	3.32	1.59	0.85	1.06	0.00
Verbena	0.80	3.27	4.58	1.59	1.12	1.06	0.00
Plantago	0.80	3.27	2.58	0.48	0.52	0.32	0.00
Malvalstrum	0.80	0.00	0.86	0.48	0.26	0.32	0.12
Asteraceae	0.80	0.87	3.32	2.30	0.85	1.39	0.21
wood	0.60	26.53	14.57	2.25	0.86	9.40	2.93
grass stalks	0.30	14.74	8.82	1.65	0.32	2.57	0.11
Coca	0.30	0.03	0.02	0.00	0.00	0.00	0.00
Papaveraceae	0.80	0.00	0.86	0.48	0.26	0.32	0.00
Galium	0.80	0.00	0.86	0.48	0.26	0.32	0.00
Vitaceae	0.80	0.08	0.90	0.48	0.26	0.32	0.00
Sisyrinchium	0.80	1.67	1.74	0.48	0.34	0.32	0.00
Relbunium	0.80	0.00	0.17	0.10	0.05	0.40	0.09
Polygonum	0.80	0.87	3.32	1.59	1.07	2.39	0.80
Cyperaceae	0.80	0.87	3.32	2.30	1.07	2.39	0.80
grass	0.80	24.45	13.70	3.58	0.48	3.46	0.53
tubers	0.10	0.80	0.53	0.24	0.30	0.04	0.00
dom. legumes	0.30	1.20	0.95	0.44	0.50	0.12	0.00
dung	0.30	13.26	7.48	1.24	0.15	1.77	0.00
Minthostachys	0.80	0.00	0.00	1.41	0.00	0.00	0.00
ortiga	0.80	0.80	0.42	0.00	0.09	0.00	0.00
Vaccinium	0.80	0.80	0.42	0.00	0.09	0.00	0.00
Valeriana	0.80	0.80	0.42	0.00	009	0.00	0.00
Legume pods	0.40	0.00	0.00	0.00	0.00	0.00	0.04
TOTAL		119.60	96.61	34.53	20.03	33.59	6.96

to more sophisticated methods (Smith et al., 1985; Tierney and Kadane, 1986) as the dimensionality of the integrals grows.

Several proveniences posed special computational difficulty. In an earlier draft of this paper, numerical problems of overflow and underflow prevented calculation of posteriors in proveniences 275, 284, 171, 423, 292, 148, 149, 188, 286, 287, 330, and 329. However, careful study of these proveniences showed that multiplying the Poisson probabilities by a well-chosen constant made it possible to calculate all of the posteriors. Some of the difficulty that appears to be numerical is perhaps better thought of as being a modeling problem. For example, float number 284, the observation of more than 17,000 *Chenopodium* seeds is astonishing given the likelihoods here, or anything close to them. That the posterior puts probability 1 on float number 284 being a hearth is an artifact of the huge number of *Chenopodium* seeds observed and the fact that hearths have the highest expected number of *Chenopodium* seeds among activities given positive prior weight.

A second difficulty caused one provenience (299) not to be computable. The prior puts probability one on its being a hearth. But 66 *Scirpus* seeds were found there, an impossible event because the expected number of *Scirpus* seeds found in a hearth is zero according to Table 1.7. This problem is a straight issue of beliefs incompatible with the data. The difficulty is due to disregard of "Cromwell's Rule" (Lindley, 1985, p. 104), which says to avoid putting zero probabilities on anything. Provenience 299 is still regarded by Hastorf as a hearth, so the problem lies in the expected numbers of seeds (Tables 1.6 and 1.7), and not in the priors (Table 1.2). As more experience is jointly gained in this kind of analysis, we expect this problem not to recur.

Table 1.7: Expected Botanical Remains by Usage as of 1460.

	HEARTH	MIDDEN	INDOOR STORE	LIVING QTR	OUTDOOR STORE	ACTIVITY CENTER
Mzkernels	6.00	3.15	1.32	2.00	0.00	0.10
cupcobs	7.37	3.87	0.53	0.00	0.88	0.00
Chenopodium	22.00	20.18	9.65	9.89	3.20	0.30
Amaranthus	1.09	4.15	1.99	1.06	1.33	0.15
Scirpus	0.00	1.08	1.48	0.60	2.07	1.15
wild legumes	1.09	4.15	1.99	1.06	1.33	0.00
Verbena	4.09	5.73	1.99	1.39	1.33	0.00
Plantago	4.09	3.23	0.60	0.65	0.40	0.00
Malvalstrum	0.00	1.08	0.60	0.32	0.40	0.15
Asteraceae	1.09	4.15	2.87	1.06	1.74	0.26
wood	44.21	24.29	3.76	1.43	15.66	4.89
grass stalks	14.74	8.82	1.65	0.32	2.57	0.11
Coca	0.10	0.05	0.00	0.00	0.00	0.00
Papaveraceae	0.00	1.08	0.60	0.32	0.40	0.00
Galium	0.00	1.08	0.60	0.32	0.40	0.00
Vitaceae	0.10	1.13	0.60	0.32	0.40	0.00
Sisyrinchium	2.09	2.18	0.60	0.43	0.40	0.00
Relbunium	0.00	0.22	0.12	0.06	0.50	0.11
Polygonum	1.09	4.15	1.99	1.34	2.99	1.00
Cyperaceae	1.09	4.15	2.87	1.34	2.99	1.00
grass	30.56	17.12	4.47	0.60	4.32	0.67
tubers	8.00	5.28	2.36	2.99	0.40	0.00
dom. legumes	4.00	3.18	1.48	1.65	0.40	0.00
dung	44.21	29.94	4.12	0.51	5.90	0.00
Minthostachys	0.00	0.00	1.76	0.00	0.00	0.00
ortiga	1.00	0.53	0.00	0.11	0.00	0.00
Vaccinium	1.00	0.53	0.00	0.11	0.00	0.00
Valeriana	1.00	0.53	0.00	0.11	0.00	0.00
Legume pods	0.00	0.00	0.00	0.00	0.00	0.10
TOTAL	200.00	150.00	50.00	30.00	50.00	10.00

1.7 Conclusion

The most significant aspects of our study are (1) the new method by which paleoethnobotany can shed light on prehistoric behaviors, (2) the usefulness of botanical data to prehistoric interpretation generally, and (3) an application of Bayesian statistics.

Culturally, the botanical remains help us interpret the structures more explicitly. Each structure of Patio $J7 = 2$ now reveals a new pattern of use activity that had not been identified before our analysis. Figures 1.3 and 1.4 have presented the priors and posteriors for each flotation sample respectively. Glancing between these two figures one can begin to see the amount of information the botanical remains contribute to the priors.

In general, our statistical exercise shifted the posterior of some proveniences systematically toward one activity. Specifically, samples that produced few seeds tended to be identified with more certainty as either living quarters (inside structures) or patios-activity areas (outside). In a cultural interpretation that shift makes intuitive sense. Both in and outside the structures, the posterior pattern is quite strongly changed from the priors. The reinterpretation is notable in the proveniences against the walls in the open patio, with a dominance in patio use over midden or storage. Within the structures there is a shift toward living quarters with less storage. In the structures, the posteriors shifted the storage areas into more discrete locations, seen in five of the six structures. All six structures increased their probabilities for being living quarters with a bit of storage.

Both the priors and the posteriors define the patio use areas less clearly than the structures. The patio areas were probably used for many more amorphous and diverse activities. These activities were probably not as constrained to specific locations as those within the structures. Overall each location was used for many more activities,

Table 1.8: Prior and Posterior Means and Standard Deviations by Flotation Number and Use (probabilities multiplied by 1000)

		Hearth	Midden	Storage Inside	Living Quarters	Storage Outside	Patio Activity Center	Structure
		Mean SD	Mean SD	Mean SD	Mean SD	Mean SD	Mean SD	
Float Number								
275	PRIOR			125 (331)	875 (331)			1
	POST			003 (016)	997 (016)			
276	PRIOR		459 (494)	082 (275)	459 (198)			*
	POST		424 (131)	001 (010)	574 (132)			
264	PRIOR		459 (498)	082 (275)	459 (198)			*
	POST		391 (099)	006 (032)	603 (103)			
288	PRIOR		459 (498)	082 (275)	459 (498)			*
	POST		731 (158)	001 (009)	267 (158)			
290	PRIOR			125 (331)	875 (331)			*
	POST		005 (022)	995 (022)				
314	PRIOR		400 (490)	600 (490)				2
	POST		502 (229)	498 (229)				
299*								*
191	PRIOR	074(261)		176 (301)	750 (433)			*
	POST	000 (002)		006 (024)	993 (024)			
302	PRIOR			400 (490)	600(490)			*
	POST			805 (206)	195 (206)			
337	PRIOR	387 (487)	480 (500)	133(340)				*
	POST	000 (004)		1000 (004)				
284	PRIOR	064 (244)		876 (330)	060 (238)			*
	POST	1000 (000)		000 (000)	000 (0000)			
283	PRIOR			500 (500)	500 (500)			*
	POST			069 (136)	931 (136)			
273	PRIOR			5000 (500)	500 (500)			*
	POST			973 (075)	027 (075)			
175	PRIOR			111 (314)	889 (314)			3
	POST			006 (031)	994 (031)			
174	PRIOR			600 (490)	400 (490)			*
	POST			182 (221)	618 (221)			
407	PRIOR	889 (314)			111 (314)			*
	POST	000 (004)			1000 (004)			
342	PRIOR			1000 (000)				*
	POST			1000 (000)				
294	PRIOR			400 (490)	600 (490)			*
	POST			993 (028)	007 (028)			
300	PRIOR			1000 (000)				*
	POST			1000 (000)				
396	PRIOR			400 (490)	600 (490)			*
	POST			016 (047)	984 (047)			
164	PRIOR			250 (133)	750 (433)			*
	POST			028 (083)	972 (083)			
170	PRIOR			250 (433)	750 (433)			*
	POST			035 (090)	965 (090)			

with only limited midden areas and minor evidence of storage than was supposed in the priors. Storage in the patio occupied two corners, areas 56 and 58. Patio midden was only along the north wall of the patio.

Both inside and outside the structures, the botanical data provided more exact information about the proveniences than we had from the field notes. Doubtless, more precision in the priors is a critical exercise, but it is clear nevertheless that the botanical data have aided our interpretation of prehistoric activities in this specific example and are likely to do so in other investigations.

Interpreting the posteriors generated by Bayesian analysis, structure 1 was used for

Table 1.8: (continued) Prior and Posterior Means and Standard Deviations by Flotation Number and Use

		Hearth	Midden	Storage Inside	Living Quarters	Storage Outside	Patio Activity Center	Structure
	Samples Inside Structures (continued)							
Float Number		Mean SD	Mean SD	Mean SD	Mean SD	Mean SD	Mean SD	
172	PRIOR			500 (500)	500 (500)			4
	POST			055 (118)	945 (118)			
165	PRIOR			250 (433)	750 (433)			*
	POST			006 (027)	994 (027)			
181	PRIOR			250 (433)	750 (433)			*
	POST			008 (032)	992 (032)			
185	PRIOR			250 (433)	750 (433)			*
	POST			015 (053)	985 (053)			
159	PRIOR			250 (433)	750 (433)			*
	POST			643 (313)	357 (313)			
167	PRIOR			250 (433)	750 (433)			*
	POST			007 (028)	993 (028)			
160	PRIOR			250 (433)	750 (433)			*
	POST			055 (116)	945 (116)			
171	PRIOR			1000 (000)				*
	POST			10000 (000)				
184	PRIOR			375 (484)	625 (484)			5
	POST			179 (221)	821 (221)			
169	PRIOR			375 (484)	625 (484)			*
	POST			311 (294)	689 (294)			
182	PRIOR			375 (484)	625 (484)			*
	POST			988 (054)	012 (054)			
155	PRIOR			375 (484)	625 (484)			*
	POST			994 (035)	006 (035)			
157	PRIOR			125 (331)	875 (331)			6
	POST			005 (021)	995 (021)			
301	PRIOR			125 (331)	875 (331)			*
	POST			929 (162)	071 (162)			
156	PRIOR			500 (500)	500 (500)			*
	POST			295 (146)	705 (146)			
423	PRIOR			125 (331)	875 (331)			*
	POST			434 (054)	566 (054)			
177	PRIOR			125 (331)	875 (311)			*
	POST			004 (018)	996 (018)			
419	PRIOR			125 (331)	875 (331)			*
	POST			1000 (003)	000 (003)			
158	PRIOR			125 (331)	875 (331)			*
	POST			004 (019)	996 (019)			
279	PRIOR			125 (331)	875 (331)			*
	POST			791 (255)	209 (255)			

living quarters but shows some midden deposit near the entrance. This is supported by a disturbed human burial toward the front of structure. Structure 2 data show storage use in the center, with some daily living activities evident, supported by a hearth. Structure 3 was used mainly for living activities with some storage in the eastern half. Structure 4 was used predominantly for living activities, with a bit of storage in the western part near the entrance. Structure 5 was used for both storage and living quarters. Structure 6, like 3 and 5, also had living quarters, a hearth (not illustrated), and some storage areas. Evidently only structure 1 was used predominantly for living quarters throughout its life history, without evidence of storage. As mentioned above, this structure has additional artifactual data suggesting that it was abandoned while the patio was still occupied. This supports the lack of storage in the structure, and

Table 1.8: (continued) Prior and Posterior Means and Standard Deviations by Flotation Number and Use

		Hearth Mean SD	Midden Mean SD	Storage Inside Mean SD	Living Quarters Mean SD	Storage Outside Mean SD	Patio Activity Center Mean SD	Patio Area
				Samples Outside Structures				
Float Number								
310	PRIOR		488 (500)			488(500)	.024 (152)	51
	POST		000 (001)			000 (005)	1000 (005)	
322	PRIOR		452 (193)			452 (498)	096 (295)	*
	POST		209 (059)			060 (106)	731 (108)	
144	PRIOR		215 (117)			208 (406)	517 (500)	52
	POST		117 (037)			008 (035)	845 (017)	
326	PRIOR		(603 (163)			106 (308)	206 (104)	*
	POST		078 (118)			766 (361)	156 (261)	
292	PRIOR		493 (500)			493 (500)	013 (115)	*
	POST		919 (090)			059 (089)	002 (013)	
154	PRIOR		576 (491)			028 (465)	396 (489)	*
	POST		000 (002)			002 (010)	998 (010)	
159	PRIOR		199 (.499)			098 (294)	706 (456)	*
	POST		027 (028)			029 (064)	944 (069)	
291	PRIOR		174 (379)			079 (270)	747 (435)	*
	POST		024 (028)			028 (066)	948 (070)	
319	PRIOR		074 (262)			071 (256)	855 (352)	*
	POST		000 (002)			001 (006)	999 (007)	
321	PRIOR		074 (262)			071 (256)	855 (352)	53
	POST		000 (002)			001 (007)	999 (007)	
327	PRIOR		144 (351)			079 (194)	817 (386)	*
	POST		079 (012)			011 (034)	910 (030)	
325	PRIOR		250 (433)			672 (469)	078 (268)	*
	POST		172 (064)			084 (203)	714 (173)	
333	PRIOR		250 (433)			672 (469)	078 (268)	*
	POST		003 (012)			010 (049)	988 (051)	
142	PRIOR		074 (262)			071 (256)	855 (352)	*
	POST		004 (013)			003 (017)	993 (023)	
336	PRIOR		231 (121)			092 (289)	677 (467)	54
	POST		000 (005)			003 (015)	996 (015)	
340	PRIOR		517 (500)			275 (447)	208 (406)	*
	POST		000 (001)			002 (012)	998 (012)	
305	PRIOR		222 (415)			021 (442)	758 (428)	*
	POST		000 (005)			001 (009)	998 (010)	
289	PRIOR		412 (492)			125 (330)	463 (499)	*
	POST		620 (090)			018 (041)	362 (099)	
149	PRIOR		412 (492)			125 (330)	463 (199)	*
	POST		966 (069)			014 (069)	000 (004)	
312	PRIOR		222 (115)			021 (142)	758 (128)	*
	POST		010 (023)			024 (069)	966 (074)	
139	PRIOR		243 (129)			085 (279)	672 (469)	*
	POST		285 (070)			038 (117)	677 (110)	
168	PRIOR		454 (498)			122 (328)	423 (494)	*
	POST		194 (197)			719 (316)	087 (145)	

Table 1.8: (continued) Prior and Posterior Means and Standard Deviations by Flotation Number and Use

		Hearth	Midden	Storage Inside	Living Quarters	Storage Outside	Patio Activity Center	Patio Area
Float Number		Mean SD	Mean SD	Mean SD	Mean SD	Mean SD	Mean SD	
161	PRIOR		447 (197)			107(389)	447 (497)	55
	POST		068 (042)			029 (072)	904 (074)	
146	PRIOR		165 (371)			028 (166)	806 (395)	*
	POST		000 (003)			001 (008)	999 (009)	
152	PRIOR		233 (123)			071 (256)	697 (160)	*
	POST		000 (002)			001 (007)	999 (008)	
188	PRIOR		585 (493)			220 (414)	195 (196)	56
	POST		143 (041)			018 (019)	838 (053)	
186	PRIOR		508 (500)			413 (492)	078 (269)	*
	POST		242 (096)			240 (319)	518 (252)	
148	PRIOR		636 (481)			351 (477)	013 (112)	*
	POST		001 (014)			100 (072)	896 (063)	
282	PRIOR		699 (159)			277 (417)	024 (151)	*
	POST		050 (096)			923 (170)	027 (098)	
147	PRIOR		318 (166)			080 (271)	603 (189)	*
	POST		001 (006)			002 (011)	997 (013)	
145	PRIOR		379 (485)			550 (497)	071 (257)	*
	POST		101 (062)			165 (203)	734 (173)	
281	PRIOR		689 (463)			299 (458)	012 (110)	*
	POST		025 (065)			914 (228)	061 (171)	
286	PRIOR		508 (500)			411 (492)	078 (269)	*
	POST		677 (113)			072 (116)	250 (146)	
287	PRIOR		318 (166)			080 (271)	603 (189)	*
	POST		1000 (000)			000 (000)	000 (000)	
330	PRIOR		318 (466)			080 (271)	603 (189)	*
	POST		985 (042)			003 (015)	011 (099)	
339	PRIOR		111 (314)				839 (314)	57
	POST		488 (075)				512 (075)	
324	PRIOR		111 (311)				889 (311)	*
	POST		051 (009)				949 (009)	
303	PRIOR		378 (485)			072 (258)	550 (497)	*
	POST		002 (011)			631 (317)	368 (315)	
422	PRIOR		111 (311)				889 (311)	*
	POST		267 (057)				713 (057)	
280	PRIOR		388 (187)			114 (318)	498 (500)	58
	POST		007 (036)			978 (099)	016 (071)	
329	PRIOR		474 (499)			414 (496)	091 (233)	*
	POST		193 (059)			049 (115)	758 (112)	
313	PRIOR		069 (253)			057 (233)	874 (332)	*
	POST		000 (003)			001 (007)	999 (007)	
332	PRIOR		540 (498)			405 (491)	055 (228)	*
	POST		000 (004)			001 (013)	998 (014)	
274	PRIOR		407 (491)			407 (491)	187 (390)	*
	POST		000 (001)			001 (010)	999 (010)	
277	PRIOR		407 (491)			407 (491)	187 (390)	*
	POST		061 (031)			008 (080)	929 (014)	

also its use as a garbage dump. Over all, the priors and posteriors reflect multiple usage in all structures, either sequentially or simultaneously.

In general, our analysis supports the usefulness of botanical remains in the interpretation of prehistoric dwelling patterns by a method that has not previously been tested or even applied to archaeological research. This type of analysis offers great potential for the refinement of in-field data collection and location description.

This paper suggests an approach to archaeological data interpretation not often taken. The ramifications may be several. First, our work may encourage other archaeologists to be more explicit and precise about operating assumptions in their data analysis and interpretations. Second, it may influence the way archaeological data will be analyzed. Third, it may influence the way archaeological field notes are recorded. The review of the field dig notes revealed that often they were not as informative as one might have hoped. Perhaps in a future excavation, the archaeologists will record their probabilities by provenience as part of their field recordings.

The posteriors suggest that in many proveniences the botanical data are strong enough to affect radically the archaeologist's opinion of the activities conducted there. The results of this paper thus affirm both the usefulness of botanical evidence in archaeology and the usefulness of Bayesian methods to analyze such data.

We look forward to future successful collaboration between Bayesian statisticians and paleoethnobotanists.

Acknowledgements

The authors are grateful to the Center for Advanced Study in the Behavioral Sciences which provided the opportunity for the work. The staff gave us a lot of help along the way, especially Deanna Knickerbocker and Kathleen Much. Jill Larkin provided valuable computing advice at critical points. Our research was supported in part by the Office of Naval Research under Contract N00014-85-K-0539 (JBK) and by the National Science Foundation under Grants DMS-850319 (JBK), BNS 82-03723 (CAH), and BNS 84-11738 (both).

REFERENCES

Bayarri, M., DeGroot, M., and Kadane, J. (1987). "What is the Likelihood Function?" In *Statistical Decision Theory and Related Topics*, eds. S. Gupta and J. Berger. New York: Springer. 15

D'Altroy, T. (1981). *Empire Growth and Consolidation: The Xauxa Region of Perú under the Incas*. Ann Arbor: University Microfilms. 4

— (1987). "Transitions to power: Centralization of Wanka political organization under Inca rule." *Ethnohistory*, 34, 1, 78–102. 4

Earle, T., D'Altroy, T., Hastof, C., Scott, C., Costin, C., Russell, G., and Sandefur, E. (1987). *The Effects of Inca Conquest on the Wanka Domestic Economy*. Los Angeles: UCLA Insitute of Archaeology. 4

Hastorf, C. (1983). *Prehistoric Agricultural Intensification and Political Development in the Jauja Region of Perú*. Ann Arbor: University Microfilms. 4

— (1988). *Current Paleoethnobotany (to appear)*, chap. The study of paleoethnobotanical data in prehistoric crop production, processing, and consumption. University of Chicago Press. 6

LeBlanc, C. (1981). *Late Prehispanic Settlement Patterns in the Yanamarca Valley, Perú*. Ann Arbor: University Microfilms. 4

Lindley, D. (1985). *Making Decisions*. 2nd ed. New York: Wiley. 16

Smith, A., Skene, A., Shaw, J., Naylor, J., and Dransfield, M. (1985). "The Implementation of the Bayesian Paradigm." *Commun. Statist. Theory and Meth.*, 14, 5, 1079–1102. 16

Tierney, L. and Kadane, J. (1986). "Accurate Approximations for Posterior Moments and Marginal Densities." *J. Amer. Statist. Assoc.*, 81, 82–86. 16

Watson, P. (1976). "In pursuit of prehistoric subsistence: A comparative account of some contemporary flotation techniques." *Midcontinental Journal of Archaeology*, 1, 77–100. 6

DISCUSSION

I.POLI (*Universita di Bologna*)

This paper is to be welcomed for providing a clear illustration of the Bayesian predictive approach to a special topic such as applied archaeological research. It is original in proposing new methodology which performs well, and in investigating a type of data (burnt botanical remains) rarely considered in this area of research.

The main question that the authors consider deals with the possible activities, that might have been carried out by the Wanka people at a particular site up to 1460, to infer, subsequently, something about their economic and political system. Such problems in quantitative archaeology are often described by models that suppose a preferential distribution of archaeological items assuming that certain activities took place. Literature on this topic is mainly concerned with taxonomy procedures, factor and principal components analysis and sometimes with spatial point or lattice processes, and is mostly related to distributional patterns of artifacts (H. J. Hietala 1984, and C.R. Orton 1982).

The research described here is developed from a Bayesian point of view. The archaeologist with her own beliefs, derived from field notes, is asked to quantify such beliefs in the form of prior probabilities for a set of excavated sites. The likelihood function is thus defined, noting however that the likelihood is to be for activities occurring in 1460 while the data refers to burnt botanical remains found in 1982. A time dimension is therefore introduced into the model and subjective elements enter into both the definition of activities with respect to the plants involved and in the assessment of the survival probability of each plant. In general we can then see that the posterior probabilities of activities in each provenience show the relevance of plant remains in studying prehistorical activity patterns and the adequacy of the Bayes procedures in investigating such special areas of applied research. However it should be noticed that comments on the results are developed on aggregates of locations, namely structures and patio areas, which apparently have not been considered in the development of the research. In fact, the analysis has been conducted with respect to each single provenience, spread over all the area of interest, with no consideration of their location. Inside each provenience an hypothesis of space independence is assumed (e.g. the Poisson model) but inside the patio no hypothesis on the space distribution of data is considered. This could have undesirable consequences.

In fact, the authors mention the serious problems which arise in evaluating posterior distributions of activities because the observation of botanical remains is sometime in conflict with the definition of activity areas given by the archaeologist. These problems are related both to the number of remains (e.g. Chenopodia seeds, or the mixture assumed for the hearth activity) and to the type of remains (e.g. seeds extraneous to the activity area defined). Finding remains on a provenience could, of course, be the direct result of the location of human activities, but there could also be the effects of wind and water disturbance, differential erosion or simple reorganization of the sites. Actually, the authors seem to tackle this problem by assigning zero prior probability to those activities which they regard as most uncertain in a specific archaeological site. In this way, however, they prevent the data from ever influencing prior beliefs, thus denying any evidential value for the remains found in the site. This represents a violation of the well-known "Cromwell's Rule" and seems not to be a satisfactory answer to the problem. I wonder, instead, whether the archaeological mechanism which governs the preferential distributions of botanical remains in activity areas might not be more adequately described by a random process that accounts explicitly for the space dimension of each provenience. The whole patio has to be regarded, therefore, as a random field in which the structures and the patio areas (see Figure 1.3) that contains proveniences, enter into the model analysis. Specifically, structure and patio areas are clusters of proveniences that seem defined by archaeological remains such as the wall around the areas or specific patterns of artifacts which receive no mention in the paper. The spatial distribution of the proveniences could then be analysed by first identifying some form of nearest neighbor structure characterizing them; afterwards, the distribution of plant remains, given the locations of sites, can be considered. In this way, we could derive a likelihood function for the problem which accounts both for the time and the spatial dimensions of data and respects Cromwell's Rule by assigning strictly positive probability to each activity. This seems to me a more flexible and useful way of learning from the data, taking into due account all of its special features.

D.A. BERRY (*University of Minnesota*)

This is a terrific application of Bayesian ideas and was a high point of the conference for me. There is, however, one small aspect of the approach that I think could be improved. An explanation being considered as part of a universe of models should seldom (if ever!) be assigned zero probability. I would have placed a positive lower bound on all prior probabilities (people are notoriously bad at assessing small probabilities). It does no harm to carry along improbable explanations whose likelihoods also turn out to be small. On the other hand, I would have been interested to see how many of these "impossible" events became the most likely of all a posteriori!

W. POLASEK (*University of Basel*)

I think the paper is a good example demonstrating the subjective nature of likelihoods and priors. Instead of listing long tables with prior-posterior probabilities, I would recommend some graphical summaries in order to facilitate the reporting process.

REPLY TO THE DISCUSSION

We welcome the comments of Poli, Berry, Polasek, and have no fundamental disagreements with any of them.

To Professor Berry:
Berry proposes that a small positive lower on prior probability be routinely used in connection with each of the models. This is an interesting suggestion. However, we doubt that it would have helped with our problem proveniences. With respect to provenience 284, the prior did put positive probability on hearth, indoor storage, and living quarters. The only conceivable addition would have been midden. But adding midden would not have saved us from the embarrassment of a truly huge number of

Chenopodium seeds, far more than were to be expected under any prior. Our second kind of problem provenience was number 299, where we observed an impossible result: Scirpus seeds in a hearth. Had Berry's suggestion been followed in this instance, and we had put positive probability on storage and living quarters, the computed posterior would have eliminated hearths as a possibility. Since Hastorf is still sure that provenience 299 was a hearth, this would have led the computed posteriors to be far from the believed posterior, and would not have given the warning we got when we discovered our violation of Cromwell's rule. Perhaps extending Berry's suggestion to the likelihood as well would be a good idea. This would help with provenience 299, but not with 284.

To Professor Polasek:

We agree entirely with Polasek about the usefulness of graphical methods for displaying priors and posteriors. Figures 1.3 and 1.4 were added to the paper after the Valencia meeting to address this concern. A second method of graphical display for these priors and posteriors is given in Larkin (1989).

To Professor Poli:

Poli suggests the use of random field models to take better account of the spatial aspect of the problem. We think this would be a promising direction for future research. One aspect that would have to be considered is elicitation, both of priors and of likelihoods.

We believe that our assumptions about preservations are the strongest and most questionable. We regard with skepticism the idea that the events of each of two burnt botanical remains from the same provenience surviving for five hundred years are independent events with a probability known to us. This would be our first priority to relax in further work on this problem.

REFERENCES

Hietala, H.J. (1984). *Intersite Spatial Analysis in Archaeology.* Cambridge: University Press.

Larkin, J. (1989). Display based problem solving, (D. Klahr and K. Kotovsky eds.), *Complex Information Processing: Essays in Honor of Herbert A. Simon* Hillsdale, N.J.: Lawrence Erlbaum Associates, in press.

Orton, C.R. (1982). Stochastic Processes and Archaeological Mechanism in Spatial Analysis. *Journal of Archaeological Science* **9**, 1–23.

Epilogue

What is the scientific issue addressed?

Whether analysis of burnt seeds add substantially to an archeologist's understanding of the use of particular places in an archeology dig.

Is justification given for

a) the use of the data?

The data here were the burnt botanical remains. The data are directly relevant to the scientific question.

b) the use of the likelihood and prior?

The likelihood (Poisson with spatial independence) was chosen principally for tractability. The prior on the proveniences was informed by the digging notes, but the archeologist found those less informative than hoped. The preservation probabilities were elicited as known constants (which surely exaggerates the lack of uncertainty of what was, and is, known).

What robustness checks were conducted?

Such robustness checks as were computed had mainly to do with aberrant proveniences. There were no overall checks.

How was the computing done?

By a grid.

If I were doing the problem today, how would I change the approach?

I certainly would relax the assumption that the preservation probabilities are known with certainty. This would mean that I would no longer have the convenient relationship between the Poisson (for the number of burnt seeds on site in 1460) and the binomial (with known preservation probabilities). A second possible relaxation would be to allow for possible spatial association (positive or negative) between proveniences. Finally, I could also imagine allowing a more general count distribution that the Poisson, for example, the Conway-Maxwell generalization of the Poisson distribution (Shmueli et al., 2004). Each of these extensions would require computational methods (such as Markov chain Monte Carlo) that were unavailable at the time.

What do I see as the contributions of the paper?

1. It addresses and answers the scientific question posed. The finding is that the burnt seeds add important information for archeology.

2. Philosophically, it is an example of the use of statistics in a context in which repetition is not available. There is no natural or useful way to think of frequentism in this context.

Was Bayesian analysis useful in this problem?

My answer is "yes."

REFERENCES

Shmueli, G., Minka, T.P., Kadane, J.B., Borle, S. and Boatwright, P. (2004). "A useful distribution for fitting discrete data: Revival of the COM-Poisson," *Journal of the Royal Statistical Society C*, 54, 127–142.

TEACHING SUGGESTIONS

References for theoretical ideas:

1. Poisson Distribution: *Principles* Section 3.9

2. Independence: *Principles* Section 2.5

Exercises

1. Suppose X counts items, and has a Poisson distribution with mean λ, but is unobserved. Suppose that each item, independently, is observed with probability p, and that, in total, Y are observed. Prove that Y has a Poisson distribution with mean λp.

2. How is the result you prove in Exercise 1 used in Chapter 1? What does X represent and what does Y represent?

3. Find each of the ways in which independence is assumed in Chapter 1. Which are least plausible, in your opinion? Explain why.

4. How could a frequentist address the issue of whether burnt botanical remains are useful to an archeologist? What sequence of cases would you find most plausible?

Chapter 2

Statistical Sampling in Tax Audits (1988)

Foreword

This paper arose from the effort of the Pennsylvania Department of Revenue to audit a retailer's collection of sales taxes. In Pennsylvania, food, clothing and medicine are not subject to sales tax. Thus, for example, Scope, a mouthwash with no medication is taxed, but Listerine, a mouthwash with medication, is not taxed. It is even the case that the identity of the item purchased may not be sufficient to establish whether the purchase is subject to sales tax. Thus wool sold to someone to knit socks or a sweater is not taxed, but the same wool sold to someone to make a wall-hanging is taxed.

The rules concerning collection of sales tax are as follows: if the retailer fails to collect sales tax it should have collected, the retailer owes the tax to the state. On the other hand, if the retailer collects sales tax it should not have collected, it owes that money to the state. (Is it clear who makes the rules?)

Furthermore, there is an underlying principle in taxation that if the taxpayer offers records to the taxing authority, it has the right to have those records examined in establishing how much tax is owed. Yet in some situations it is infeasible to look at all the records, and sampling seems like a cost-effective alternative. What constraints on the taxing authority are reasonable to ensure the rights of the taxpayer in such a circumstance?

In the audit in question, the accountant arrived at the retailer's office on Friday, and announced that, although he had never done a sample before, he would read a book on sampling on the weekend and begin his audit on Monday. The retailer had the right to have a witness observe the audit. On Monday the auditor told his team to choose paper tapes to audit, and to be sure to include any tapes they found that included a purchase of Scope. Proceeding on that basis, the audit team found some $4.84 of tax owed in the tapes they examined, and extrapolated that to some $300,000 they thought the taxpayer owed.

I was hired as an expert by the taxpayer. I testified that I thought the taxpayer did owe the $4.84 found by the team, but not the extrapolation to $300,000, because the latter was based on a biased and unrandom sample. (Later the state redid the audit with a proper random sample, and still later, the retailer went bankrupt).

After the tax matter was resolved, I discussed it with Daniel Nagin, whom I had taught when he was a graduate student, and was later a colleague. At the time, Daniel was Deputy Secretary of Revenue for the state, and had overseen the audit. We realized that the most that could be learned from a sample was a probability distribution for how much is owed. But that is a difficult amount to write a check for. What principles should guide the determination of the amount owed? We saw that there were legal issues involved, and at Dan's suggestion reached out to Joe Bright, who had been the Legal Counsel for the Department of Revenue. This paper is the result of our discussions.

There are two considerations to take into account in recommending a policy about how much is owed. The first is pragmatic. Suppose the retailer delivered to the Department of Revenue a huge truckload of paper tapes of all the transactions made by its stores in Pennsylvania in a given year. It is absurd to contemplate going through each tape by hand to find errors that would benefit the state. A random sample leaps to mind as an efficient way to get a reasonable gauge on the amount owed.

On the other hand, the law favors the taxpayer by requiring the examination of the taxpayer's records, perhaps *all* the taxpayer's records. The issue, then, is to find a reasonable compromise.

In the paper we review the fundamentals of statistical sampling and the legal precedent cases on sampling in the context of taxation. We then argue on efficiency grounds that sampling may be in the interests of both the taxpayer and the government. But we also argue that the taxpayer should be compensated for the risk of over-assessment that sampling implies. Additionally, the state relies on voluntary compliance with taxation, and hence cannot put itself in the position where over-collection is likely. These considerations lead us to ask how many dollars of under-collection has the same consequence to the state as a single dollar of over-collection. We denote this number "k".

In practice, we could identify audits assessed at the mean ($k = 1$), at the .025 level ($k = 39$), and the 0.05 level ($k = 19$). (The latter is the policy of the federal Internal Revenue Service). We argue that the choice is really a legislative matter, and suggest that k's between 2 and 4 strike us as reasonable. To my knowledge, no legislature has yet taken up the issue we address.

This paper uses Bayesian analysis to address a question of public policy. Interestingly, the issue comes down to the question of what the public's loss (or utility) function is or ought to be.

This paper was originally published in the *Journal of Law and Social Inquiry*, **13**, pp. 305–338. Republished by permission of J. Wiley & Sons.

Where are they now? Joseph C. Bright, Jr., is an attorney with Cozen O'Connor in their Business Law Department in Philadelphia. Daniel S. Nagin is Teresa and H. John Heinz III University Professor of Public Policy and Statistics at Carnegie Mellon University.

Published Paper

Joseph C. Bright, Jr., J.B. Kadane and Daniel S. Nagin

Abstract

The courts, with some important qualifications, have been reluctant to uphold tax assessments based on a review of only a sample of all transactions. In this article we argue that audit assessments based on appropriately drawn and analyzed statistical samples do not suffer from the defects that the courts have correctly concluded mar assessments based on nonstatistical samples. We do, however, argue that because of the inherent imprecision of assessments based on a less-than-complete review of all records, the calculation of the assessment should include a factor to take into account the risk that the taxpayer has been overassessed. We suggest an assessment rule that does just this and also recommend guidelines for the use of statistical sampling in tax audits.

2.1   Introduction

Consider the following situation: A large department store is notified by a state revenue agency that it has been selected for a sales and use tax audit. The auditors conclude that it would be prohibitively time consuming to audit all the store's transactions. Instead they review only a sample of the transactions and estimate the total deficiency based on the sample. Is this a sufficient basis for determining the taxpayer's unpaid liability or must the state review all the transactions to determine the exact amount of tax owed? While the courts with some important qualifications have come down on the side of a complete review, this article suggests a different answer. We argue that audit assessments based on appropriately drawn and analyzed statistical samples do not suffer from the defects that the courts have concluded mar assessments based on nonstatistical samples. We do argue, however, that because of the inherent imprecision of an assessment based on less than a complete review of all records, the calculation of the assessment should include a factor to take into account the risk that the taxpayer has been overassessed. The article suggests an assessment rule that does just this.

The cases and data we rely on involve consumption taxes, primarily sales and use taxes. Such taxes are typically imposed on high-volume, recurring transactions for which sampling is an appropriate tool of analysis. The conclusions we draw, however, are applicable to other taxes, such as the income tax. Indeed, unlike most state and local governments, the Internal Revenue Service has the general authority to use

Joseph C. Bright is a partner in the law firm of Drinker Biddle and Reath, Philadelphia. J.D. 1970, University of Pennsylvania Law School

Joseph B. Kadane is Leonard J. Savage Professor of Statistics and Social Sciences, Carnegie Mellon University. Ph.D. 1966, Stanford University

Daniel S. Nagin is associate professor of management, Carnegie Mellon University, Ph.D. 1976, Carnegie Mellon University

The authors wish to thank Ms. Kristin Johnston and several anonymous reviewers for helpful comments and editorial assistance.

statistical sampling in the conduct of audits of all taxes that it is responsible for administering.[1]

The article is organized as follows. In section 2.1 we discuss some key concepts in statistical theory that distinguish statistical estimates from informal, nonstatistical inferences. In section 2.2 we review and analyze certain judicial decisions that have involved the use of sampling in tax audits. In section 2.3 we argue that the legal objections to sampling can be addressed if the sampling and analysis are based on well established and routinely applied statistical procedures. In section 2.4 we present a model that provides an analytic basis for translating sample findings into an overall audit assessment. In section 2.5 we make some concluding remarks.

2.2   The Theory of Statistical Sampling: An Overview

Every day of our lives we make decisions, both trivial and significant, based on inference from a sample. We choose from a luncheon menu based on experience from prior outings to the restaurant, decide what route to take home based on previous experience with travel times at different times of day, pick among potential employees based on experience with individuals with similar backgrounds and personalities, and make important business decisions based on prior experience with comparable products in similar markets. We may not think of this as sampling, but it is. We are drawing inferences based on a limited sample of information we deem relevant to the issue at hand. Occasionally we are wrong, but mostly we are right, which is why we keep doing it.

Statistical sampling is distinguished from casual inference both by method and consequence. The method requires a sampling frame, a random sampling mechanism that is independent of influence by either the taxpayer or the auditor, a sampling plan, and an appropriate analysis. The consequence is that, unlike their counterparts based on casual inferences, conclusions based on statistical samples can be rigorously evaluated in terms of reliability.

A sample frame is a group of items from which a sample is chosen. In the case of a tax audit, the sample frame is the universe of documented transactions available for audit. Generalization from statistical samples extends only to the sampling frame. Thus the application discussed below, in which a tax auditor sampled a taxpayer's inadequate records, is an example of statistical sampling, but the statistical conclusions extend only to the sampling frame – to those records available for examination. The extrapolation of results from records kept to records unkept is made by the courts on legal principles, not statistical ones.

A hallmark of a careful statistical sample is the proper choice of a sample frame. For example, in determining sales tax deficiencies, an auditor might choose to exclude certain untaxed transactions, such as sales of food, if the total food sales are known. However, it is not legitimate to change sampling frames in the midst of an audit.

The second key to adequate statistical sampling is that the items from the frame must be chosen by a random mechanism with known probabilistic properties. The items must be chosen without knowledge of or regard for their tax or other consequences. Failure to observe this principle can invalidate the statistical inference. For example, auditors are often asked to examine records to check certain facts. If they have preconceived ideas about where the problems might be, and exploit either their ideas or their initial findings in deciding where to look further, they are surely entitled to report the discrepancies they find. Nonetheless, they are not entitled to treat the

---

[1]It is our understanding, however, that as a matter of practice the IRS typically restricts its use of statistical sampling to audits of large corporate taxpayers.

cases they examined as a statistical sample, since they chose them purposely. Proper statistical sampling is a skill distinct from auditing.

The third key to successful statistical sampling is a sampling plan, determined before the process begins, that specifies the frame, the random mechanism to be employed and the probability of selection of each item or set of items, and the rule to be used to decide when to stop sampling. The sampling plan should be so explicit that two auditors with the same plan and the same random number generator for selecting transactions to be included in the sample should report the same results. Deviations from the sampling plan should be avoided.

The simplest sampling plan is called "simple random sampling." In this plan each item has the same chance of appearing in the sample as any other, and items appear or do not appear independently of each other. Another sampling plan is stratified sampling.[2] Here the sampling frame is divided into strata, each of which has its own separate sampling plan. For example, examining all transactions above one million dollars and randomly sampling the others can be thought of as a stratified sampling plan. Preconceived ideas about where problems might exist can be an excellent basis for stratification.

The use of "test periods" as a sampling plan is common in tax audits and requires special comment. In a test period analysis, a few time periods are selected and audit findings are extrapolated to the entire audit period. For this discussion, assume that the test periods are chosen by a random mechanism, even though in practice they are not. As explained above, if they are not randomly chosen, the sample is not a statistical sample. It is typical of a test period design that all the transactions in the selected months are analyzed, while none of those in unselected months are examined. The design is inefficient because a simple random sample among all transactions will provide a more precise estimate of the deficiency, as would a design stratified by month. Furthermore, either alternative design will permit estimation of the reliability of the tax assessment, as discussed later.

Consider the implications of the typical practice of purposely choosing test periods. After long discussions with management, market analysts, and other experts, one might be able to mount a strong argument that the estimated deficiency extrapolated from the test period audit is plausible. Nonetheless, it is important to distinguish inferences based on statistical sampling from the everyday notion of plausibility. Statistical sampling imposes rigorous standards, and a fundamental pillar of those standards is that the sample not be purposely chosen.

The final key element of statistical sampling is an analysis appropriate to the chosen design. For even a moderately complex statistical design, the services of a statistical expert or special training for the auditors may be required.

Four elements, then, constitute a statistical sample: (1) the sampling frame, (2) the random sampling mechanism, (3) the sampling plan, and (4) appropriate analysis.

The benefit of conducting a statistical sample is that the samplers can address the following technical questions: (1) What is the probability that the estimate deviates from the true value sought by some specific amount? The question concerns the reliability of the estimate. (2) How large a sample must be drawn for the estimate to reach a desired level of precision? This question concerns the sample size necessary to reach a particular level of reliability. We will discuss each of these concepts in turn.

---

[2]See W. G. Cochran, Sampling Techniques (3d ed. John Wiley & Sons, 1977).

Reliability

Reliability refers to the precision of the estimate. In formal statistical terms, an estimate may meet the standards for making statistical inferences but still be highly unreliable. For example, consider again the problem of estimating a sales tax deficiency based on a random sample of transactions from one month. Suppose that over the course of the month 1,000,000 transactions occurred. Random samples of 10, 100, 1,000, or 10,000 of these transactions will all provide a basis for estimating the deficiency. However, intuition suggests, and statistical theory confirms, that an estimate based on 10 or even 100 transactions may be so imprecise – or in formal statistical terms unreliable – that the sample is useless for assessing taxes.

What statistics adds to intuition is a formal analytical method for quantifying the degree of precision of a specified estimate – such as tax due – computed from a sample of some specific size and having some particular sample characteristics. Concretely, statistical theory provides the ability to make statements about the likely precision of an estimate. Returning to our sales tax auditing sample, suppose that from a sample of 1,000 transactions we estimate a tax deficiency of $500,000. Statistical theory allows us to quantify the imprecision of this estimate with such statements as: There is a 95% chance that the deficiency is as little as $450,000 or as much as $550,000.[3] In short, statistics tells the auditor how likely he is to have erred, and by how much.

Sample Size

Statistical theory not only allows ex post facto quantification of the reliability of an estimate based on a specific sample size, it also provides the basis for determining the sample size required to achieve a desired level of reliability. This capability has practical importance; it provides the tax administrator with an opportunity to control the level of precision of an audit assessment based on a statistical sample. Auditors can draw an initial sample, analyze the sample characteristics, and determine from their analysis the sample size required to meet a specified level of precision. Thus, unlike assessments based on an extrapolation of a test period, audit assessments based on statistical sampling may be tested against formal standards of reliability.

2.3   Judicial Decisions

In this section, we review judicial decisions on the use of samples to project audit findings. The principal issues raised are (1) the adequacy of taxpayer records, (2) the statutory authority for auditing, (3) whether the taxpayer consented to the sample, (4) the administrative burden of a complete audit, and (5) the reliability of an assessment based on a statistical sample.

By now, it is incontrovertible that a tax administrator may use sampling to project a tax assessment in the absence of accurate and reliable records kept by the taxpayer. While there was at least one false start when a statute did not require that records be

---

[3] For clarity, it is necessary to discuss some fine points of statistical theory. From the point of view of classical statistical theory, a 95% confidence interval means that if the same procedure is used many times, 95% of the uses will include the true tax deficiency. Confidence intervals do not purport to apply to any specific instance. By contrast, a 95% credible interval means that the probability is 95% that the true tax deficiency is in the interval specified in the given instance. Such intervals require added assumptions and a different, Bayesian statistical framework. Thus a confidence interval tells you what proportion of times you will bracket the right amount if you follow a set procedure and a credible interval tells you what the chances are that you bracketed the right amount this time. See L. J. Savage, The Foundations of Statistical Inference (New York: John Wiley & Sons, 1962), for a general discussion of the distinction. The relation between classical and Bayesian inference is treated in more detail in sec. 4.

kept,[4] the cases are now legion in which assessments based on samples are enforced against taxpayers who, in one way or another, failed to keep proper records.[5] Even when the lack of records has not been the taxpayer's fault, the courts have permitted sampling by auditors.[6] The cases are bottomed on the common sense premise that a taxpayer cannot escape tax liability through his own failures or even his own misfortunes.

It is equally clear that sampling may be used with a taxpayer's consent, even if implicitly given.[7] Indeed, taxpayer consent is the rule, not the exception. The willingness of most taxpayers to accept sampling suggests not only an interest in keeping the expense and disruption of an audit to a tolerable level but also a reasonable level of confidence in the process itself.

What is not clear, however, is whether, absent statutory authority or taxpayer consent, a tax examiner may assess a liability from a sample when the taxpayer's records are sufficient to determine a liability by a 100% audit. It has been suggested that a 100% audit is not always required when complete records are available,[8] but where the issue has been directly confronted, it has been decided in favor of the taxpayer.

An early and particularly well articulated case was decided by New York's Appellate Division in 1957. In In re Babylon Milk & Cream Co.,[9] the taxpayer successfully challenged the extrapolation of the results of a fuel tax audit of four "test months" to the remaining eight months of a one-year audit period in which the taxpayer had records. The company, however, failed in challenging an assessment based on a projection over a period for which the taxpayer did not have records.

With respect to the first issue, the taxpayer did not dispute the audit findings for the four months actually examined; rather the question was whether the findings could be projected over the period of an entire year. The court held for the taxpayer, ruling that as a matter of law the tax commissioner had no authority to project the results of a sample if complete records were available. The court stated:

> The records of the petitioner were all available for year 1953 and the exact amount of the understatement of mileage could have been determined for the remaining eight months in the same manner in which it was determined for the four months chosen for the test months. The only reason given for not determining the understatement in this manner was that it would have required additional work.... The use of the average method, at best, produced only an approximation of the amount of the tax owing.[10]

Thus the court took comfort in its conclusion from the observations that there did not

---

[4]State ex rel. Foster v. Evatt, 144 Ohio 65, 56 N.E.2d 265 (1944).

[5]E.g., Schwegmann Bros. Giant Supermarkets, Inc. v. Mouton, 309 S.2d 686 (La. 1975); Bouchard v. Johnson, 170 A.2d 372 (Me. 1961); Ridolfi v. Director, 1 N.J. Tax 198 (1980); In re Babylon Milk & Cream Co., 5 A.D.2d 712, 169 N.Y.S.2d 124 (1957); King Drug of Dayton v. Bowers, 171 Ohio 461, 172 N.E.2d 3 (1961). Other cases are cited in H. Leib, Using Sampling Techniques to Assess State Taxes, 3 J. St. Tax (1985) and L. Fournier & W. Raabe, Statistical Sampling Methods in State Tax Audits, 2 J. St. Tax 115 (1983).

[6]In re Grecian Square, Inc., 119 A.D.2d 948, 501 N.Y.S.2d 219 (1986); Pato Foods, Inc. v. Lindley, 7 Ohio App. 3d 22, 453 N.E.2d 1274 (1982); Torridge Corp. v. Commissioner of Revenue, 84 N.M. 610, 506 P.2d 354 (1972).

[7]E.g., Mitchell Bros. Truck Lines v. Hill, 363 P.2d 49 (Ore. 1961) (fuel use tax case); W. T. Grant Co. v. Joseph, 2 N.Y.2d 196, 140 N.E.2d 244 (1957). Compare In re Hard Face Welding & Machine Co., 81 A.D.2d 967, N.Y.S.2d 744 (1981).

[8]E.G., Yonkers Plumbing & Heating Supply Corp. v. Tully, 62 A.D.2d 18, 402 N.Y.S.2d 792 (1978). 674 P.2d 785 (Abs.1983).

[9]5 A.D.2d 712, 169 N.Y.S.2d 124 (1957).

[10]Id.

seem to be any reason for projecting a sample other than to avoid work and that the projection would result only in an approximation or even, perhaps, a guess.

However, on the second issue the court held for the tax commission, sustaining an assessment based on a projection over 27 months of an examination of two-week records. No doubt because the two-week records were the only ones available to the tax commission, the court did not disparage use of the projection. Rather the court stated: "The result reached by the auditors was consistent with other findings made when the trucks and loads were weighed in 1954 and 1955. The method used by the auditors was a reasonable one in view of the petitioner's failure to keep any records. The petitioner has not demonstrated that the amount of the assessment was to any extent unjustified."[11]

Babylon Milk is a microcosm of many cases that followed it. If a taxpayer fails to keep adequate records, courts usually approve the projection of a sample, often reinforcing the result by pointing out factors supporting the accuracy of the projection. Historically, judges have not often criticized the reliability of a sample when a taxpayer has failed to keep adequate records. A high-water mark of judicial tolerance occurred in New York in *Markowitz v. State Tax Commission.*[12] Three of five judges approved projecting the results of an audit of one day's cash register tapes over a three-year period. With remarkable understatement, the majority observed, "Although it is probably true that cash register tapes of several days would give a better picture of the business of the petitioner and thus his tax liability, exactness is not required where the party's own failure to maintain the proper records prevents it."[13]

A more balanced approach was taken by an Ohio court in McDonald's of Springfield, Ohio v. Kosydar.[14] The taxpayer did not have adequate records, and the tax examiner made two assessments based on statutorily authorized spot checks. Pointing to certain statutory language, the court sustained one assessment but struck down the other on the grounds that the second sample was not representative.[15]

Recently, New York judges have become more critical than they were in Markowitz. In In re Grecian Square, Inc.,[16] a taxpayer did not keep adequate records and an assessment was made on a sample. However, the court held:

> Here, respondent's auditor found petitioner sales figures to be much lower than other establishments which he audited. Accordingly, he increased petitioner's estimated sales figure by 200%. However, the record does not disclose any specific information concerning the bars which McKenna [the auditor] had audited and found to have been comparable to petitioner's. As best as we can determine, no such information was given petitioner in advance of the hearing. At the hearing, McKenna merely stated that he had estimated sales by calling upon his wide experience in auditing other bars. Considerable latitude is given an auditor's method of estimating sales under such circumstances as exist in this case.... Nevertheless, there was insufficient evidence for the auditor's computation. By the same token, without some information about the size, location, number of employees and nature of the operation, this court is unable to make a determination as to the existence of a rationale [sic] basis.

---

[11]Id.

[12]54 A.D.2d 1023, 38 N.Y.S.2d 176, 177 (1976), aff'd, 44 N.Y.2d 684, 405 N.Y.S.2d 454, 376 N.E.2d 927.

[13]Id.

[14]43 Ohio 2d 5, 330 N.E.2d 699 (1975).

[15]See also Zapitelli v. Lindley, 1981 Westlaw 4376 (Ohio App. N.E.2d 1981).

[16]119 A.D.2d 948, 501 N.Y.S.2d 219 (1986) (citation omitted).

> Hence, the matter must be remitted to respondent for further testimony of McKenna in accordance with this decision.[17]

Whatever may be the latitude given to auditors when proper records are not kept, as a general rule sampling has not been permitted in the absence of consent if adequate records are kept. Various reasons are given why sampling is not authorized in such cases, but invariably the reasons are accompanied, as in Babylon, by judicial comments on the unreliability of the sampling procedure.

For example, in a 1965 Maine case,[18] the records of a wholesaler and retailer of automotive parts and supplies were examined for a four-month period. The examination showed that the tax liability was understated. From their review of the four-month period, the auditors calculated what was described as a margin of error - that is, a ratio of understated liability to reported liability. An assessment was based on a projection of the margin of error over a 23-month period. The court struck down the projected assessment. After observing that the taxpayer had kept adequate records as required by the statute, the court observed: "The legislature required an audit based upon an examination of the taxpayers records and *not the establishment of tax liability by surmise and conjecture*" (emphasis added).[19] The court added: "We understand and appreciate the problem faced by the auditors in such a time-consuming task as they were confronted with but according to our analysis of the sales and use tax statute in its entirety, we find no alternative. This may constitute a serious administrative problem time-wise for the Tax Assessor's Department but it is one for the Legislature to consider and not the Courts."[20]

The court's decision was expressly based on the conclusion that the revenue agency had no statutory authority to base a tax liability on estimates, except in the limited circumstances "where a taxpayer fails to make a report, or where the departure from the State of a taxpayer is imminent." Nonetheless, it is evident from the opinion that the court was driven to its conclusion by anxieties about the reliability of sampling procedures and by a suspicion that governmental advocacy of the efficiency of sampling might be an excuse for laziness.

Such reservations were repeated in a 1978 New York case.[21] The taxpayer argued that a sample should not have been used to project liability because his records were adequate to determine any deficiency. Without expressly commenting on the adequacy of the records, the court held for the petitioner and stated: "There is no inflexible rule that an item-by-item audit be made whenever it is possible, but it should be utilized if the records are available and the test check method is insufficient to afford a reasonable calculation of the taxes due."[22]

In 1980, the same court in *Names in the News v. New York State Tax Commission*[23] held:

> According to the testimony of an Associate Sales Tax Examiner for the State, the test period approach was utilized by the Tax Bureau because petitioners records were "too voluminous" and it was the bureau's normal auditing procedure to use a trial period. This same examiner conceded, however, that petitioner's general ledger, purchase invoices, sales invoices and Federal tax returns were available to the bureau and that no request for information or documents was refused or rejected by petitioners, and

---

[17]Id.

[18]Farrar Brown Co. v. Johnson, 207 A.2d 406 (Me. 1965).

[19]Id.

[20]Id.

[21]Yonkers Plumbing & Heating Supply Corp. v. Tully, 62 A.D.2d 18, 402 N.Y.S.2d 792 (1978).

[22]Id.

[23]429 N.Y.S.2d 755 (App. Div. 1980).

upon the present record it can only be concluded that the State's auditors had access to petitioner's detailed records for the whole three year period, a vastly different situation from that encountered in *Matter of Meyer v. State Tax Comm.*, [61 A.D.2d 223, 402 N.Y.S.2d 74 (1978),] . . . where the court approved an analysis of purchases and that in the matter of *Markowitz v. State Tax Comm.*, [54 A.D.2d 1023, 38 N.Y.S.2d 176, 177 (1976), *aff'd*, 44 N.Y.2d 684, 405 N.Y.S.2d 454, 376 N.E.2d 927,] ... where we approved a test period or spot check only because of the inadequacies in methods and procedures and failure to maintain proper records... Under these circumstances, the bureau's use of the test period to compute petitioner's tax liability was plainly *unnecessary, arbitrary and capricious*, and petitioners were entitled to have their tax assessment calculated based upon a detailed audit of their records for the three-year period under consideration. [Mohawk Airlines v. Tully, 429 N.Y.S.2d 759 (App. Div. 1980) [emphasis added]; *In re* Chartair, Inc. v. State Tax Comm., 65 A.D.2d 44, 411 N.Y.S.2d 41 (App. Div. 1978).][24]

Recently, the law of New York was summarized in In re *Christ Cella, Inc.*:[25]

Section 1138 ... of the Tax Law governs when external indices tests may be used. The statute provides that: "if a return when filed is incorrect or insufficient, the amount of tax due shall be determined by the tax commission from such information as may be available. If necessary, the tax may be estimated on the basis of external indices, such as stock on hand, purchases, rental paid, number of rooms, location, scale of rents or charges, comparable rents or charges, type of accommodations and service, number of employees or other factors." The department, however, may not use such external indices unless it is "virtually impossible to verify taxable sales receipts and conduct a complete audit" with available records ....[26] Petitioner's contention that the department violated this rule by not requesting the records covering the three-year period, but rather proceeding directly to the markup test, has merit. The auditors testified that, "We do markup tests in approximately every restaurant to determine whether the particular restaurant has the proper records or not." This procedure violates *Chartair*, where this court stated: "The honest and conscientious taxpayer who maintains comprehensive records as required has a right to expect that they will be used in any audit to determine his ultimate tax liability." Consequently, the markup test could not be used unless petitioner's records were so insufficient that its sales could not be verified or such records were unavailable.[27]

What authority there is on the subject indicates that the same rules are applied in the case of a claim by a taxpayer for a refund. In an early case, a court determined that where adequate records were available, a petitioner could not claim a refund calculated from a sample, even when the sampling was apparently done on a statistically sound basis.[28] The court therefore directed a complete audit, which yielded a number very close to the result of the statistical sample.

---

[24]Names in the News v. New York State Tax Comm., 429 N.Y.S.2d 755 (App. Div. 1980) (emphasis added).

[25]102 A.D.2d 352, 477 N.Y.S.2d (1984).

[26]*In re* Korba, 84 A.D.2d 655, 444 N.Y.S.2d 312 (1981), *appeal denied* 56 N.Y.2d 502, 435 N.E.2d 1099; *In re* Chartair, Inc., 65 A.D.2d 44, 411 N.Y.S.2d 41 (App. Div. 1978).

[27]*Id.*

[28]Sears, Roebuck & Co. v. City of Inglewood (Los Angeles Super. Ct. 1955), discussed in Sprowls, Admissibility of Sample Data into a Court of Law, 4 U.C.L.A. L. Rev. 222, 226 (1957).

Conversely, a taxpayer without required records was entitled to a refund based on a sample, albeit with assistance from certain statutory language. In *Belgrade Gardens, Inc. v. Koysdar,*[29] a restaurant incorrectly determined the amount of sales tax collected and therefore overpaid the tax. A tax examiner made a "test check" of guests' checks and determined that an overpayment had been made, but the tax commissioner denied the refund claim on the grounds that the taxpayer had not maintained the required records. The court held for the taxpayer, holding that the absence of records does not, in itself, preclude a refund. The court stated:

> The audit period herein exceeded three years. There is no question that a test check conducted to determine the appropriate tax liability for that period could provide an accurate figure for the amount of overpayment. An audit of guest checks and cash register tapes maintained by the taxpayer for the period would provide a more accurate figure than the calculated approximation provided by a test check. However, adequate records were not available in this case, and the Tax Commissioner conducted a test check to fulfill his mandatory duty to investigate the facts in connection with the taxpayer's claim. Neither party has contested the accuracy of the test check.... However, the Tax Commissioner proposes that a valid test check conducted by him cannot be used to the advantage of the taxpayer.... This court has never held that any specific burden of proof attaches to a taxpayer who claims to have made an erroneous overpayment of sales tax. Indeed, [state law] places the duty of ascertaining the amount of overpayment upon the Tax Commissioner.[30]

Perhaps the closest a court has come to an unconditional authorization of sampling was in *Underwood v. Fairbanks North Star Borough.*[31] After lengthy procedural litigation, the taxpayer agreed to a sales tax audit by the borough, and a judgment was entered in favor of the borough. Shortly thereafter, the borough moved to amend the judgment to correct a clerical mistake in favor of the taxpayer. The taxpayer in response attacked the audit that led to the judgment in the first place. The court stated:

> Underwood argues that the sampling method was unreasonable because a better method of determining tax liability existed, namely, audit all the records. We agree that the figures a full-scale audit would have produced would have been more accurate than the estimate on which the Borough relies, but we see no reason to force the Borough to bear the expense of interpreting all the records Underwood has surrendered. The difference between the deficiency figure a statistically valid estimate produces and the deficiency a full-scale audit suggests will usually be far less than the added expense of conducting a full audit. If courts force a taxing authority to bear this additional cost even though a taxpayer's miscalculations have caused the problem, they rob it of resources with which it could be providing services.... The parties stipulated that Underwood "shall produce for [the Borough] for purpose of audit by [the Borough], all of the documents and records requested to be produced." . . . After the material is produced, how any tax arrearages are to be proven in court is a matter properly committed to the appropriate rules of evidence. Samples are generally receivable in evidence "to show the quality or condition of the entire lot or mass from which" they are taken. 2 J. Wigmore, Evidence 439, at 522 (Chadbourn rev. ed. 1979). The question becomes whether

---

[29] 38 Ohio 2d 135, 311 N.E.2d 1 (1974).
[30] *Id.* at 141-43.
[31] 26 174 P.2d 785 (Alaska 1983).

the sample used was large enough to be statistically reliable and, if so, whether there is something about the sample period that makes it atypical. These questions can go to both the admissibility and to the weight of the evidence. Here the evidence has been stipulated as admissible, and thus the only question is what weight should be given it. Underwood has not contended that the sample is too short a period to be reliable, or that the period was atypical. Therefore, we conclude that the trial court did not err in relying on the evidence presented on the grounds that it was a sample.[32]

The Alaska court perhaps for the first time addressed policy issues that we believe should be at the core of any discussion of the use of statistical sampling. Nonetheless, the unique procedural posture and the effect of the prior court settlement on the decision cloud any claim that the case is reliable precedent for nonconsensual statistical sampling cases.

The judicial responses are not surprising. The courts have not been provided with standards for balancing the interests of tax administrators against the concerns of taxpayers about the reliability of an assessment based on a sample. In this vacuum of standards, the courts have given the benefit of the doubt to the citizen, not to the state. Only where the taxpayer has failed to keep adequate records have the courts generally rejected challenges to the tax administrator's authority to use samples and other analytical methods to make plausible estimates of the taxpayer's liability. The reason has simply been that if the tax is to be enforceable, there is no choice.

When there is a choice – that is, when records are available – the authority has not been found. Probably it could be found if the judges were willing. The no-records cases support the use of sampling on the grounds that the taxpayer failed to comply with a statutory requirement to keep accurate records. However, the tax statutes also require that an accurate return be filed, and in every case in which sampling has not been approved, the sample has determined *definitively* that with respect to the sample the return was not accurate, and by likely inference that the returns for the balance of the period were not accurate either. As a matter of logic, there is no reason why the failure to file an accurate return could not justify the use of sampling. Statistical sampling is a specialized form of circumstantial evidence. As in other cases involving circumstantial evidence, there is no reason per se why it should not be used with appropriate safeguards. Yet no court has so held when complete records are available.

We believe the reason for the failure to approve audits using statistical sampling is that once the facts move beyond a no-choice situation, the courts are quite at sea about how the balance should be struck between administrability and reliability and have been given no help by any legislature or litigant. No statute provides even minimal guidance for sampling – when it may be used by a tax administrator and with what required degree of accuracy. Neither does it appear that any tax administrator has ever argued the case for sampling using well-established statistical theory. Perhaps the only statistically sound presentation was made 30 years ago by the taxpayer in the *Sears Roebuck* refund case noted above – but unsuccessfully. It is no wonder courts have refused to wade in alone.

If statistical sampling is to be used in a nonconsensual situation in which records are available, the guidance gap will have to be filled. The lines must be drawn with an eye to the concerns of both administrators and taxpayers. What are the relevant concerns?

The tax administrator is responsible for collecting the maximum amount of taxes legally due as equitably and efficiently as possible. Sampling techniques properly ap-

---

[32] *Id.*

plied can advance this objective, principally because they allow improved economies in the use of government resources.[33] But the taxpayer's concerns are equally real. Tax assessments based on statistical samples are always estimates and therefore are inherently imprecise. Although we do not believe that the imprecision should be fatal, the taxpayer does have the right to know the magnitude of the uncertainty; he should be protected by appropriate standards requiring a minimum level of precision; and arguably some accommodation should be made in the assessment to compensate for the risk that it exceeds the true liability. For both parties, there are some common objectives. Audits are disruptive, time-consuming, and inherently confrontational. Like the administrator, the taxpayer has an interest in minimizing their duration. Sampling can contribute to achieving this goal.

In the next section, we discuss how properly conducted statistical sampling, combined with well established procedures for extrapolating results, can provide the analytical basis for balancing the competing concerns of tax administrators and taxpayers.

2.4   The Case for Statistical Samples

In this section we draw upon the concepts developed in section 2.1 and apply them to the judicial concerns discussed in section 2.2. The judicial cases have expressed three principal concerns: (1) sampling may be used as a device to rationalize bureaucratic indolence; (2) assessments projected from sample results may be distorted by unobserved or unique factors and, therefore, the sample results are of unknown reliability; and (3) there is no statutory authority for the use of samples where records are complete.

The first objection is that sampling may be used as a rationalization for avoiding a thorough audit or, in the extreme, as a ruse to camouflage laziness. Certainly sampling, like almost all well-established procedures for improving efficiency can be abused. But statistical theory provides formal quality standards for detecting and insuring against such abuses. Moreover, sampling may be the tax administrator's only effective remedy if a taxpayer files an inaccurate return and simply insists that the tax assessor correct it. Although the practice of filing inaccurate returns may be only a minor nuisance that is adequately dealt with by penalties for understatement, the authority to use statistical sampling in the conduct of an audit can be tactically important when dealing with a taxpayer who conducts a large volume of transactions. Without sampling, it may be literally impossible for a tax examiner with a limited staff to audit an entire period before the statute of limitations runs. With proper safeguards, a tax examiner ought to be entitled to use statistical sampling to avoid such a result. Otherwise, not only will the state's fiscal position be injured, but tax equity will suffer by a shifting of the tax burden from noncomplying to complying taxpayers.

The second judicial concern is whether, in the words of one court, sampling is

---

[33]While the courts have placed tight constraints on its use, sampling is routinely used in sales and use tax audits. The reasons are that taxpayers without complete records are prime audit targets and that many taxpayers with complete records consent to the use of sampling. To illustrate sampling's contribution to efficient enforcement, consider the case of Pennsylvania's Department of Revenue. In fiscal year 1984-85, the department conducted about 6,500 sales and use tax audits that identified over $44 million in assessed deficiencies. The total direct personnel commitment charged to these audits was nearly 150 person years. In about 85% of these audits, some sort of test-period procedure was used. A restriction of test period auditing to instances where taxpayer records were incomplete would have required a 15-fold increase in auditors at an annual cost of about $75 million-a commitment of 2,500 additional auditors, which is more than the department's entire personnel complement. Alternatively, the no-sampling audit strategy would require a reduction in the number of audits of about 85%, resulting in a direct revenue loss of about $35 million. The direct reduction in audit productivity would have resulted in deficits for the Commonwealth in four of the past eight fiscal years.

"plainly unnecessary, arbitrary and capricious."[34] Although perhaps overstated, the criticism goes to the heart of judicial discomfort with sampling. We believe that *statistical* sampling is none of those things. In every taxpayer challenge of sampling we have identified, the sampling procedure did not meet the requirements necessary for drawing formal statistical inferences. In every case, the taxpayer was challenging the extrapolation of findings from a 100% sample of one or more purposely chosen test periods to an entire audit period.

The use of test periods to extrapolate tax assessments is a routine practice in state revenue agencies. Despite the high probability of a successful legal challenge to a test period audit assessment in most jurisdictions, few such challenges are made. The reasons, we believe, are threefold. First, as a general rule, taxpayers have reasonable confidence in the procedure. If the audits are conducted carefully and a sufficient number of test periods are examined, the projected assessments will pass the reasonable person's test of plausibility. Second, the taxpayer has an interest in shortening the duration of the auditor's unpleasant visit. Among other risks, the auditor might turn up some other problem. Third, legal challenges are costly.

If the test period approach to audit sampling has met with general acceptance, why has it failed to pass judicial muster when challenged by the nonconsenting taxpayer? The reason, we believe, is that it is impossible to defend the estimate's reliability in a formal statistical sense. Since test period samples fail to meet the requirements of a random sample, the tax administrator can make no formal quantitative evaluation of the precision of the projected assessment. Thus even a sympathetic court is placed in an awkward position: The taxpayer argues that the estimate may over-state his liability and that records are available for determining the true deficiency, and the tax administrator has no effective rebuttal.

As our discussion in section 2.1 states, appropriately drawn and analyzed statistical samples provide a basis for clearing the hurdles in the way of quantitative statements about the reliability of an estimate. We believe that if a tax administrator is armed with proper statistical procedures, the courtroom result might be different but for one missing ingredient: guidance on the minimum standards of reliability. As our prior discussion indicates, statistical theory cannot accomplish the impossible. It cannot eliminate the uncertainties inherent in projections. However, it can provide a basis for quantifying the imprecision and for developing strategies to reduce the imprecision to an acceptable level. Even so, what is an "acceptable" level of reliability is a normative issue about which statistical theory is mute. The issue requires the kind of judgment a legislature is particularly well situated to exercise. Among the questions that should be considered are:

Since sampling inherently results in an imprecise finding, should the assessment be adjusted to reflect the risk of overassessment? That is, should the lowest "reasonable" number be chosen for the assessment?

Where sampling is used, what minimum standard of reliability should be required? Perhaps a 10% chance of an error in excess of 5%?

Should sampling be permitted in all circumstances? Or should it be limited to circumstances where a minimum sales volume or transaction threshold is exceeded?

We address these issues in the next section.

---

[34] *Names in the News v. New York State Tax Comm.*, 429 N.Y.S.2d 755 (App. Div. 1980).

2.5   Statutory Standards for the Use of Statistical Sampling

Statistical sampling cannot provide an exact determination of tax owed. Only an examination of every item in the sample frame will do that – but that is not sampling. In recognition of the inherent imprecision of assessments based on the findings of a statistical sample, three of the revenue agencies we have identified as using statistical sampling – the IRS and the revenue departments in New York and Pennsylvania – adjust the assessment to provide the taxpayer with a considerable degree of protection from the risk of overassessment. The IRS and New York assess the taxpayer an amount designed to reduce the probability of overassessment to .05, and Pennsylvania on at least one occasion reduced the probability to .025. We believe that in concept the practice of these revenue agencies is sound. We will argue below that an audit assessment based on a less than exhaustive sample should reflect the risk of overassessment. We will also develop a formal assessment rule to accommodate the risk and show that the assessment rule of the three revenue agencies is a special case of the more general rule.

Derivation of the rule requires a formal mathematical characterization of both the uncertainty accompanying nonexhaustive sampling and the relative cost of overassessment versus underassessment of the true tax liability. The former is called a probability distribution and the latter a loss function.

In the following paragraphs, we elaborate on what a probability distribution is. We then discuss the central limit theorem – a theorem that gives conditions under which averages tend to have a normal distribution as the sample size increases. In combination, these ideas justify the use of the normal distribution as a representation of the uncertainty about the true tax deficiency, and thus provide the first ingredient for the derivation of an assessment rule. We note, however, that although this brief explanation of statistical ideas should be adequate to understand this article, it cannot substitute for a statistical text, such as DeGroot's, *Probability and Statistics*, to which the reader is referred for a more thorough discussion.[35]

Nonexhaustive sampling provides only a probability distribution on the tax owed. The distribution, which is based on the findings of the audited sample, permits us to calculate the probability that the true tax deficiency falls within any specified interval. For example, consider an audit based on a 15% random sample. A probability distribution provides the basis for making such statements as: "There is only a 10% chance that the total deficiency is less than \$4,500 or more than \$5,500."

The curve in figure 2.1 is the probability density of the normal distribution; it has the familiar bell shape. This distribution is characterized by two parameters: the mean, μ, and the standard deviation, σ. The mean is at the top of the bell. It is the average of the distribution; and, because of the symmetry of the normal distribution, it is also the median – that is, half the probability is above μ and half is below. The standard deviation σ measures how peaked or spread out the bell is.

The interpretation of the two parameters can be illustrated with a nonauditing example. Consider the distribution of heights in the population. The average height is measured by μ and the variability in heights is captured by σ. The shaded area under the curve measures the proportion of the population whose height is between A and B feet tall. Alternatively, this proportion can be interpreted as the probability that the height of a randomly chosen individual is between A and B feet.

More peaked normal curves correspond to those with smaller standard deviations-that is, to curves depicting populations with less variability. For example, a probability

---

[35] M. DeGroot, Probability and Statistics (Reading, Mass.: Addison-Wesley, 1978).

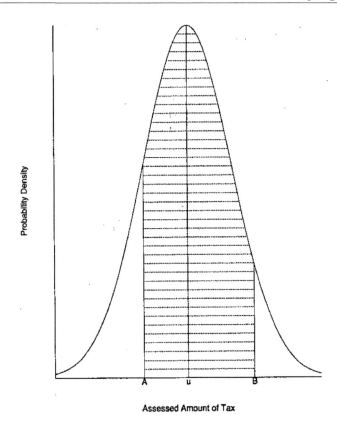

Figure 2.1: The normal probability density functions

distribution for the height of women only would be more peaked (i.e., have a smaller standard deviation) than for the population of both sexes.

The central limit theorem is a remarkable result of probability theory. It states that under a very general set of conditions, the distribution of averages of observations tends to become more and more like the normal distribution as the number of observations gets larger. The requirements for a random sample discussed in section 2.2 are sufficient to ensure that the central limit theorem applies. If the observations are transactions, and the datum is the amount of tax deficiency in the transaction, the average of the observed tax deficiencies will tend to have a normal distribution, with some mean and some standard deviation that can be estimated from the audit data. What is remarkable is that this result holds true even if the probability distribution of transaction deficiencies is not even remotely characterized by the normal distribution.

To illustrate the power of the central limit theorem, consider the following stylized example. Assume that a retailer sells only two items, both of which are taxable. One item costs $1, the other $2. Assume further that the tax rate is 5% and that for any given transaction, the retailer either collects all the tax due or fails to collect any tax. Thus an audit of any particular transaction will reveal one of three outcomes: (1) no tax due; (2) 5 cents due; or (3) 10 cents due. Obviously, a plot of the amount due per transaction will not correspond to the bell-shaped normal distribution depicted in figure 2.1. Instead, all observations will cluster at three points. According to the central limit theorem, however, the average deficiency across transactions will tend to be distributed normally as the sample size becomes large. Specifically, if successive samples of equal size are drawn and the average deficiency computed, a plot of these averages will approximate the bell-shaped normal distribution depicted in figure 2.1.

The reader may observe, however, that the distribution we have – the distribution of the average of the data – is not the distribution we need – the distribution of the tax deficiency. The central limit theorem provides the basis for calculating the probability that another estimate of the average deficiency calculated from still another independent sample of transactions will fall within a specified range. But this is not what we want. Instead, we want to be able to make some probabilistic pronouncements, based on the audit findings, about the true total tax deficiency. After all, that is why the audit was conducted.

The Bayesian school of statistics provides a remedy using a result in probability theory called Bayes' theorem. Bayes' theorem provides the basis for converting probability statements about the size of the deficiency in the sample to probability statements about the true deficiency in the population, given the value of the deficiency actually observed in the sample. A key concept is the prior distribution. In the case at hand, the distribution measures prior opinion about the amount of the tax deficiency. Although the audit may have been prompted by a strong opinion that a substantial deficiency exists, such a surmise will have no standing in substantiating a deficiency to a court. The case for the deficiency must be built from the audit findings. Thus for our purpose, the prior distribution must be characterized by substantial uncertainty. One way to characterize such uncertainty is by a normal distribution with a very large standard deviation.

Bayes' theorem provides a formal mechanism for updating the prior distribution to take account of data – in our case the audit findings from the sampled transactions. The resulting "updated" prior distribution, called the posterior distribution, measures precisely what we desire: the uncertainty about the true deficiency given the results of the audited sample. Further, when both the prior distribution and the distribution of the data are normal, then the posterior distribution is normal. In addition, when the standard deviation of the prior distribution is very large, as has been supposed above, the mean and standard deviation of the posterior normal distribution are, respectively, the mean and standard deviation of the data distribution. Hence, with these assumptions, the posterior distribution is well approximated by a normal distribution whose mean is the average of the sampled observations and whose standard deviation can also be calculated from the sample data.

In conclusion, Bayesian statistics combined with the central limit theorem provides the technical machinery for concluding that the uncertainty about the true deficiency can be reasonably characterized by a normal distribution with a mean equal to the average deficiency per transaction audited times the number of transactions in the universe, and a standard deviation, which can also be estimated from the audited sample.

The standard deviation will be affected by two factors. First, the standard deviation decreases as n increases. This result is intuitively appealing; as more transactions are audited, we expect our uncertainty about the true amount owed to decrease. Indeed, in the extreme case, where all transactions are audited, the standard deviation equals zero – that is, there is no uncertainty about the true tax deficiency. A second factor affecting the magnitude of the standard deviation is the inherent variation of the tax owed among individual transactions. For example, consider two different taxpayers. One is a retailer who specializes in selling inexpensive toys, all of which are taxable. The other is a general merchandise retailer who sells items of widely different values, only some of which are taxable. Further assume that the chance that either merchant does not collect the appropriate tax on any given transaction is equal. Statistics confirms the intuition that for any given non-exhaustive sample, the standard deviation on the taxes owed will be less for the first retailer than for the second.

Our first question is how much the taxpayer should be assessed in light of the uncertainty about the exact amount owed. One obvious candidate is the average of the observations multiplied by the number of transactions in the frame. If this rule is used, however, some taxpayers will pay more than they actually owe, and others will pay less. Moreover, it is not possible to tell which is which without doing a complete audit of every taxpayer. The probabilities of overassessment and underassessment are equal, but that gives little solace to the taxpayer who believes he or she has been overassessed.

For several reasons, we submit that the rule for balancing the two possible errors should build from the premise that overassessing is worse than underassessing. First, a cornerstone of tax jurisprudence is that statutes will be strictly interpreted against the state. One of the roots of this principle is that taxpayers need protection from overaggressive tax administrators attempting to collect taxes that the legislature did not intend to be levied. Second, since the burden of proof is on the taxpayer to prove that an assessment, once levied, is invalid, the taxpayer deserves some consideration for taking the risk that an audit assessment based on a statistical sample may overstate his liability. We say this because the taxpayer will have no basis for arguing that he in particular has been overassessed, beyond the observation that there is some chance the assessment is too high. Third, and perhaps most important, we believe that an assessment rule that fails to place greater emphasis on the cost of overassessment compared to underassessment may injure voluntary compliance and taxpayer perceptions of the equity of tax administration. Audited taxpayers will correctly conclude that 50% of their number are being overassessed by an amount equal to the underassessment of the remaining 50%. Such an assessment rule might appear to be more like a lottery than an appropriate system of tax administration.

Our argument that overassessments are worse than underassessments can be mathematically characterized in terms of the "loss function" depicted in figure 2.2. If the taxpayer is assessed an amount precisely equal to u, then as shown in figure 2.2, no underassessment or overassessment costs are incurred. This point is the minimum of the loss function. The line to the left of u measures the loss caused by underassessment and that to the right, the loss due to overassessment. Consider a deviation from u of some specified amount x. Consistent with our argument that overassessment is worse than underassessment, the value of the loss function for an assessment $u + x$ exceeds that for an assessment $u - x$. The result is guaranteed by requiring that the line measuring the overassessment cost be steeper (i.e., its slope be greater) than that measuring underassessment cost.

The ratio, k, of the slopes of these two lines measures the cost ratio of an overassessment versus underassessment of a given amount. Thus we suppose that k must necessarily be some number greater than one. Or, stated differently, the loss due to an overassessment of any given amount will always be greater than the loss from an underassessment of that same amount.

In light of the inherent uncertainty in the true amount owed, as illustrated by the probability density function in figure 2.1 and the relative losses from overassessment and underassessment as depicted by figure 2.2, the problem is to derive an assessment rule that, on average, minimizes the overall cost of under- and overassessment across all audits where statistical sampling is employed. The required assessment rule, which is derived in appendix A, is that the taxpayer should be assessed an amount equal to $\bar{x} - \rho\hat{s}$, where $\bar{x}$ is the average deficiency per sampled transaction times the number of transactions in the universe, ρ is a mathematical function of k, and $\hat{s}$ is the estimate of σ based on the sample audit findings. Table 2.1 gives ρ for various values of k. It shows

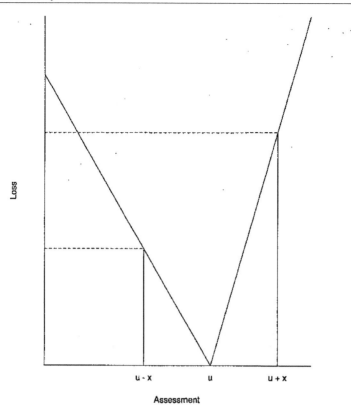

Figure 2.2: The costs of overassessment and underassessment: illustrative loss function

that the larger the value of k, the larger the resulting value of ρ. This is reasonable, since as k gets larger the relative consequence of collecting too much is worse, and hence the assessment should decline. To illustrate the application of the rule, consider again a tax deficiency of \$100,000 projected from a sample of 5,000 transactions. Assume further that $\hat{s}$ – the estimate of σ based on the audited sample – is \$10,000. If the cost of overassessment is judged to be twice that of an underassessment of the same amount-that is, $k = 2$–then $\rho = .46$, and in this example, the taxpayer would be assessed \$95,400 (= \$100,000 - [.46 × 10,000]). Alternatively, if overassessment were regarded as four times worse than underassessment, $k = 4$, and the corresponding $\rho = .84$. In this case, the adjustment for uncertainty is larger than for $k = 2$ (because there is an even higher cost attached to overestimating the tax liability), and the taxpayer would be assessed \$91,600 (= \$100,000 - [.84 × \$10,000]).

The last column of table 2.1 shows P, the probability that too much tax is collected. Observe that the probability declines as k increases. For example, if $k = 2$, the probability is 1 in 3, but if $k = 4$, it is 1 in 5. Again, the result is reasonable, since as k increases, the adverse consequences of overassessment are greater and the assessment rule should provide the taxpayer with greater protection.

Some further intuition into the mechanics of the rule are revealed by the fact that $k \times P$ equals the probability of underassessment, $1 - P$. Intuitively, this expresses a balance between the probability and relative cost of overassessment (kP) and the cost of underassessment ($1 - P$).

The rule, we submit, is fair to both the state and the taxpayer. It allows the state to collect an amount of tax equal to the mean of taxes owed, with a reduction equal to

Table 2.1: The Choice of k and the Resulting Values of p and P

Choice of k	p	Probability That Too Much Tax Is Collected
1	0	0.5
1.5	0.25	0.4
2	0.46	0.333
2.5	0.55	0.29
3	0.68	0.25
4	0.84	0.20
5	0.96	0.17
6	1.08	0.14
9	1.28	0.10
19	1.67	0.05
39	1.96	0.025

$\rho\hat{s}$ for the uncertainty that the state imposes on the taxpayer. The magnitude of the reduction can be controlled by the state. Recall from the previous discussion that one of the factors affecting the magnitude of $\hat{s}$ is sample size. This parameter decreases with sample size; in the extreme, where all transactions are sampled, it equals zero. Thus, if the state concludes that the uncertainty adjustment is sacrificing too much revenue, it has the option of drawing larger samples at its own cost.

Similarly, we believe the rule is fair to the taxpayer. Observe that the adjustment for uncertainty, $p\hat{s}$ increases in proportion to $\hat{s}$. Thus, as the imprecision of $\overline{x}$, as measured by $\hat{s}$, increases, the adjustment for uncertainty increases. This, we submit, is fair to the taxpayer because the magnitude of the uncertainty adjustment can be controlled by the state in its selection of sample size. If for whatever reason the state chooses to draw a sample that can provide only a highly imprecise estimate of the true deficiency, the taxpayer should not be required to bear all the risk that the assessment may substantially overstate the deficiency. Also observe that for any given value of k there is a *fixed* probability that the taxpayer will be overassessed which is independent of $\hat{s}$. This means that the uncertainty adjustment is always just large enough to maintain a constant probability of overassessment. Thus, as measured by the probability of overassessment, taxpayers are being treated uniformly.

Implementation of the assessment rule requires the choice of a specific value of k, which we believe should be made by the legislature. We will briefly discuss some of the considerations we believe the legislature should take into account and hazard a preliminary suggestion on an appropriate value. One consideration involves balancing the social cost to society, in marginally less funding for government-supported programs, versus the cost to the individual of having to pay marginally more tax than he owes. Another consideration is the extent to which the benefit of the doubt should be given to taxpayers in the exercise of the coercive power of the state. Here it should be kept in mind that what is at stake is money, not the individual's basic civil freedoms. A final consideration is the magnitude of imprecision in the assessment. For reasons that will be discussed below, we believe that minimum standards for precision should be tight.

Some might object to our proposed assessment rule on two grounds: that the choice of k is arbitrary and that on a practical level it would be difficult to implement. We address these two issues in turn.

As we previously noted, when statistical sampling is used, the IRS[36]and the New York State Department of Tax and Finance[37] assess the taxpayer an amount calculated to reduce the risk of overassessment to .05. Inspection of table 1 reveals that such an overassessment probability corresponds to a k of 19. What is the rationale for .05? The use of .05 dates back to R. A. Fisher in his exposition of significance testing.[38] As Raiffa and Schlaiffer put it, "decisions are actually made by treating the numbers .05 and .95 with the same superstitious awe that is usually reserved for the number 13."[39] There is no analysis we know of that supports the use of .05 in the context of tax collection.

Pennsylvania has used varying rules for calculating assessments based on statistical samples. As previously indicated, on at least one occasion, the assessment was calculated to reduce the risk of overassessment to .025.[40] This corresponds to a k of 39. On at least one other occasion Pennsylvania has assessed at the mean, which implies a probability of over- assessment of 0.5, and a k of 1.[41] We know of no analysis to support either of these rules.

Thus all three agencies, IRS and the revenue departments in New York and Pennsylvania (with both its rules), have already implicitly adopted our assessment rule but without apparent consideration of the relative costs of over- versus underassessment. While we acknowledge that the choice of k involves a subjective weighing of competing considerations, surely it is better to consider the tradeoffs explicitly. While the assessment rules of the IRS, New York and Pennsylvania appear to be objective, beneath the surface each of them constitutes a probably instinctive choice of k.

We believe that the choice of $k = 19$ is too high and $k = 1$ is too low. In our judgment, the cost of overassessing a taxpayer by a given amount is not, in most cases, 19 times worse than underassessing him by the same amount. Nor, in our judgment, is the cost of overassessing a taxpayer by a given amount equal to the cost of underassessing him by the same amount. We think that the appropriate value for k is in the range of 2 to 4.

Would our proposed rule be difficult to implement? Given a policy establishing a value for k, implementation would depend solely on correctly calculating a mean and a standard deviation for the amount of tax owed. The auditors could mechanically apply the rule in calculating the assessment, just as they now do for the IRS and in New York and sometimes in Pennsylvania. The greater difficulty will be in conducting a sampling audit competently, so that the items selected are a random sample chosen from a proper sampling frame.

We now consider whether the legislature should establish any minimum standard of reliability. An argument can be made that no such minimum standard is necessary. On one hand, the taxpayer is protected by an adjustment for uncertainty that increases with the imprecision of the estimate of u. On the other hand, the tax administrator can control the magnitude of this adjustment and thus the resulting loss in assessment revenue by the choice of sample size. Thus the problem reduces to a tradeoff between the cost of sampling and foregone revenue collections.

We reject this argument and urge a legislated floor on precision. First, from a purely technical perspective, our proposed assessment rule builds from the assump-

---

[36]See W. L. Felix & R. Roussey, Statistical Inference and the IRS, 159 J. Accountancy 38 (1985).

[37] New York State Dep't of Tax. & Finance, EDP Systems Audit Bureau, letter to Pennsylvania Dep't of Revenue, Bureau of Audit, at 4.

[38]R. A. Fisher, Statistical Methods for Research Workers (14th ed. New York: Hafner Publishing Co., 1973).

[39]H. Raiffa & R. Schlaiffer, Applied Statistical Decision Theory viii (Cambridge, Mass.: MIT Press, 1961).

[40]Pa. Dep't of Revenue, Board of Appeals Docket #504817 SUT.

[41]Pa. Dep't of Revenue, Board of Appeals Docket #713816 SUT.

tion that the probability density function depicted in figure 2.1 follows the normal distribution. This assumption, which is based on the central limit theorem, may be violated if sample sizes are too small. For any minimum reliability standard we can imagine being enacted, the sample size requirement would be sufficient to provide good insurance against failure of the normality assumption. Second, the loss function depicted in figure 2.2 assumes that the relative costs of over- and underassessments are characterized by linear functional forms. Aside from simplifying analysis, we can provide no rationale for choosing the linear functional form over, say, a quadratic form. By requiring a minimum level of precision, we may keep within tolerable limits any perceived inequities in the magnitude of the uncertainty adjustment resulting from competing arguments on the appropriate functional form of the loss function. Moving beyond technical observations, there is a fundamental argument. Without a minimum standard for reliability, the raison d'etre for sampling – namely, that sampling provides a scientifically proven method for making a valid and reliable estimate of the true amount owed – may be jeopardized. If audit assessments were to build routinely from unreliable estimates of the tax deficiency, the perceived legitimacy of the auditing process would be at risk. Notwithstanding the adjustment for uncertainty, taxpayers might come to perceive the auditing process as a game of chance rather than as a legitimate, albeit unpleasant, exercise of the state's authority to enforce the tax laws. Stated differently, the adjustment for uncertainty can increase the perceived fairness of an audit assessment based on sampling only if the sampling itself is perceived as being thorough. We suggest that one dimension of "thoroughness" is a sample size sufficient to guarantee a minimum level of precision.

The considerations above lead us to believe that the minimum standard of precision should be tight, but not so tight as to be unaffordable. Some calculations should be done with typical cases and costs to determine appropriate sample sizes, from which may emerge an appropriate minimum standard. We intend to pursue this issue in a separate work.

Even with a minimum standard of precision and an adjustment for uncertainty, some taxpayers might still be reluctant about the use of sampling and desire either that a larger sample be drawn or that all transactions be audited. In such circumstances we suggest that the taxpayer have the option of requesting further auditing, with two important provisos: (1) the taxpayer will bear the expense of the additional work, and (2) the statute of limitations on the periods under review would toll. The tax authorities would not be bound to honor the request if the level of effort required for the additional work would be prohibitive or would unduly disrupt the completion of other audit assignments, if the request is only a delaying tactic, or if there is a reasonable basis for concluding that the expense for the additional work would not or could not be paid.

Finally, we ask whether the legislature should limit sampling to taxpayers of some minimum size (assuming records are complete). We believe that the answer is yes. Smaller taxpayers are less likely to have experience with sampling in other business contexts (and therefore to trust the method), to be able to evaluate the quality of the sampling procedures, or to have the resources to challenge an audit assessment if the adequacy of the sampling procedures is in question. Regardless of the soundness of the sampling procedures, such taxpayers might perceive the assessment as arbitrary or oppressive. Put simply, the burden that sampling imposes on the small business is probably too high, since with a little more effort, a 100% audit is possible.

2.6 Conclusions

Statistical sampling is a well-established technological tool of the modern world. Tax administration can be made more efficient, fairer, and less intrusive if the tax administrator's technologies for identifying and measuring tax deficiencies are expanded to include controlled use of statistical sampling. We have attempted to identify the major elements of a statutory prescription for "controlled" uses: (1) careful adherence to the requirements of statistical sampling – namely, having well-defined sampling frames, random sampling mechanisms, and sampling plans and using appropriate analyses; (2) an assessment rule that explicitly accounts for the uncertainty inherent in statistical sampling; (3) establishment of minimum standards for acceptable reliability, and (4) a policy that statistical sampling will not be used in audits of small taxpayers.

APPENDIX A

This appendix uses calculus to derive the form of the optimal assessment. Let u be the unknown correct assessment, which by the argument of section 2.4 is taken to have a normal distribution with mean $\bar{x}$ and standard deviation $\hat{s} = s/n^{1/2}$. If a is the assessment imposed, the loss function is

$$L(a, u) = \left[\begin{cases} u - a \text{ if } u > a & \text{(underassessment)} \\ k(a - u) \text{ if } a > u & \text{(overassessment)} \end{cases} \right].$$

Then a is to be chosen to minimize the expected value of L, where the expectation is taken over the unknown value of u, as follows.

The expected loss is

$$L^* = \int_{-\infty}^{a} k(a - u)f(u)du + \int_{a}^{\infty} (u - a)f(u)du,$$

where

$$f(u) = \frac{\exp\left(-\frac{1}{2}\left(\frac{x-\bar{x}}{\hat{s}}\right)^2\right)}{\hat{s}\sqrt{2\pi}}$$

is the normal density function.

Now taking the derivative of L^* with respect to a, we obtain

$$\frac{dL^*}{da} = -k(a - u)f(u)|_{su=a} + \int_{-\infty}^{a} kf(u)du - (u - a)f(u)|_{u=a} + \int_{a}^{\infty} -f(u)du \quad \text{(A.1)}$$

This equation can be simplified using the fact that $k(a - u)f(u)|_{u=a}$ and $(u - a)f(u)|_{u=a}$ are both zero. Let

$$F_u(x) = \int_{-\infty}^{x} f(u)du.$$

Then

$$\frac{dL^*}{da} = kF_u(a) - (1 - F_u(a)).$$

Setting the derivative equal to zero to find the minimum

$$F_u(a) = \frac{1}{k+1} \quad \text{(A.2)}$$

is the only solution, and hence the value of a that minimizes the expected loss satisfies[42]

$$a = F_u^{-1}\left(\frac{1}{k+1}\right). \tag{A.3}$$

Note that $P = F_u(a)$ is the probability of overassessment. Then (A.2) can be rewritten as

$$P = \frac{1}{k+1}, \text{ or } kP = 1 - P,$$

as discussed in section 2.4.

It is a property of the normal distribution that u can be written

$$u = \bar{x} + \epsilon\hat{s},$$

where ϵ has a standard normal distribution with mean 0 and standard deviation 1. Then

$$F_u(x) = F_\epsilon\left(\frac{x - \bar{x}}{\hat{s}}\right) \text{ for all } x.$$

Consequently,

$$\frac{1}{k+1} = F_u(a) = F_\epsilon\left(\frac{a - \bar{x}}{\hat{s}}\right).$$

Thus,

$$a = \bar{x} + \hat{s}F_\epsilon^{-1}\left(\frac{1}{k+1}\right), \text{ or, } a = \bar{x} - \rho\hat{s}, \text{ where } \rho = -F_\epsilon^{-1}\left(\frac{1}{k+1}\right).$$

The function $F_\epsilon^{-1}(\cdot)$ is called the normal ogive, and is tabulated in many books, among them *Probability and Statistics*.[43]

Epilogue

What is the issue addressed?
When a sample is used to ascertain the amount of tax owed, how should the resulting uncertainty be divided between the taxpayer and the government?
Since this is an issue of public policy, how does Bayesian analysis apply?
The heart of the paper is a loss function for the government, with a parameter that expresses how many dollars of undercollection are equivalent (to the government) to a single dollar of overcollection.
What are the considerations that apply?
Some considerations are legal, having to do with the legal rights of the parties. Some are economic, having to do with costs, efficiency and mutual interest.
What is the contribution of Bayesian analysis?
By proposing a simple loss function that expresses the trade-offs, it clarifies the public policy issue. The Bayesian minimization of posterior loss gives a simple form for the amount owed.
Is the paper successful?
In principle, it addresses the issue posed. In practice, it has had no discernible influence on public policy.

---

[42]See also M. DeGroot, Optimal Statistical Decisions 261 (New York McGraw-Hill Book Co., 1970).
[43]M.H. DeGroot, Probability and Statistics 577 (Reading, MA: Addison-Wesley Publishing Co., 1975).

TEACHING SUGGESTIONS

References for theoretical ideas:

1. Central Limit Theorem: *Principles* Chapter 6

2. Conjugate analysis for the normal-normal case: *Principles* Chapter 8, especially Section 8.1

3. Utility functions: *Principles* Chapter 7, especially Sections 7.1 to 7.3

4. This example: *Principles* Section 7.9

5. Normal distribution: *Principles* Section 6.9

Exercises

1. In your opinion, what are the strongest reasons for allowing random sampling for determining how much tax is owed? What are the weakest reasons?

2. The paper proposes that each dollar under-collected has the same consequence to the state, no matter how much is under-collected, and similarly for over-collection. Do you find this argument convincing? Why or why not?

3. Accepting, for the purpose of this exercise, the two straight lines with possibly different slopes suggested in the paper, what value of k (the ratio of the slopes) would you choose, and why?

Chapter 3

A Statistical Analysis of Adverse Impact of Employer Decisions (1990)

Foreword

I was hired by the plaintiff's attorney in an age discrimination case. The plaintiff was dismissed in the fourth of four firing waves. The law provides protection against adverse action against employees over 40. If data shows actions that disproportionately disadvantage persons over 40, the employer is then called upon to explain some non-discriminatory business reason or necessity for its actions.

The employer in this case was negatively affected by a cyclical downturn in demand. As a result, it decided to reduce its management workforce. It had the legal right to decide how many workers to fire. The question was whether in choosing which ones to fire it disproportionately targeted workers over 40. So a simple way to think about the results of a firing wave is a 2×2 table, in which one dimension is the age of the employee (over or under 40), and the other is whether the employee was fired. The ages of its employees going into a firing wave is not a legal issue in the case, nor is the number of employees fired. Hence a natural model is a 2×2 table with both margins fixed.

Such a model has been examined classically. Fisher's Exact Test (Fisher, 1958) calculates the probability of data as or more extreme than that observed under the null hypothesis of independence between the two margins, here age and being fired. Famously, Fisher used the test to deal with the data arising from the lady tasting tea. I wanted to see what a Bayesian treatment would look like.

It turns out that the likelihood function depends only on a single parameter, the log odds ratio (see the paper for details). This parameter is positive if being over 40 is positively associated with being fired. As a result, symmetric priors centered at zero are fair to both parties, as they put equal prior weight on action favorable or unfavorable to those over 40, to the same extent. Thus I used normal priors with zero mean, and studied the effect of different prior standard deviations. I report both the posterior mode and the probability that the log odds ratio (L) is positive for each firing wave, for each firing wave separately, and for all four waves together.

The results show that the combined analysis, and the first, second and fourth firing waves all show disproportionate disadvantage to older workers, while the third shows the opposite. (Is it an accident that the first age discrimination lawsuit against the company was filed between the second and third firing wave?).

The heart of the comparison between classical and Bayesian methods is given in my fantasy cross-examination of a classical statistician. I gave what I take to be the correct classical answers (after all, my graduate training was all classical, all the time). But the result is embarrassing. By the end, the classical statistician is about to admit that his analyses are all based on the assumption that his employer is innocent, and that his analyses are not relevant to the particular case in hand (but only to a hypothetical infinite sequence of such cases).

You might be interested in what actually happened in the case. On Friday the parties met in the judge's chambers and found they were not able to settle the case. However, a jury was chosen. That weekend, the plaintiff's attorney and I met and prepared for the coming trial. On Monday, the plaintiff noticed that the defendant's lawyers had come to court with no briefcases or documents. The attorneys were called into the judge's chambers, and the defendant's lawyers said they wanted to accept the plaintiff's Friday settlement demand offer. The plaintiff's attorney said that offer was no longer available, as we had worked on the case all weekend. She made a new, higher offer of settlement, which was immediately accepted.

How do I know all this? As it happened, after the case was over, she and I started going together. We married a year and a half later. I can't think of a happier conclusion to a paper than to find one's lifetime companion.

This paper was originally published in the *Journal of the American Statistical Association*, **85**, pp. 925–933. Republished by permission from Taylor & Francis.

Published Paper

J.B. Kadane

Abstract

Federal law prohibits discrimination in employment decisions against persons forty years old and older. This paper uses data from an actual case to illustrate several methods of showing adverse impact, a legal doctrine under which only the effects of the employer's acts are at issue, and not the motives with which they were done. The strengths and weaknesses of the Fisher exact test of significance, a Bayesian analysis, and a method of paired observations inspired by the Mann-Whitney-Wilcoxon statistic are assessed. One important conclusion from this analysis is that it is useful to have several different kinds of analysis bearing on the same issue. To the extent that the analyses agree, this adds credibility to each.

Key words: Age Discrimination, Bayesian Analysis, Cross-Classified Table, Fisher Exact Test, Mann-Whitney-Wilcoxon Statistic, Reference Prior.

3.1 Introduction

Federal Law (U.S. Code, Title 29, Chapter 14 §626) forbids discrimination against persons forty years of age and older with respect to employment decisions. Under the doctrine of adverse impact, statistics can be used to establish a prima facie case of discrimination. Under this doctrine it is not necessary to prove that the employer had discriminatory intent, but only to show that his actions had the actual effect of disadvantaging a disproportionate number of people of protected age or race. See United States v. Hazelwood School District, 433 U.S. 299 (1977) (race discrimination), Geller v. Markham, 635 F.2d 1027 (2d Cir. 1980). To overcome such a prima facie showing, an employer can demonstrate a non-discriminatory business reason for the decisions.

What must be shown statistically to demonstrate adverse impact? This question is analyzed using the data from a recent case, for which I served as an expert witness for the plaintiff, and which was settled just before testimony. In order to protect the privacy of the parties involved, the plaintiff will be referred to as the Employee, and the defendant as the Company.

The Company was adversely affected by the down-turn in the basic metals markets in the early 1980's. In that period, the Company reduced the size of its workforce in a series of moves that were the occasion for this lawsuit. The Employee is a union member who had received several promotions leading to a very responsible management position. In the fourth of four firing waves, his job was "abolished" (divided among his two former subordinates) and he used his union seniority rights to bump

Joseph B. Kadane is Leonard J. Savage Professor of Statistics and Social Sciences, Department of Statistics, Carnegie Mellon University, Pittsburgh, PA 15213. The author thanks Caroline Mitchell and the Employee for involving him in the case. He also thanks George Duncan, Stephen Fienberg, John Lehoczky, Michael Meyer, Allan Sampson, and Teddy Seidenfeld for helpful conversations, and most particularly Thomas Short, for computational assistance.

someone from a lower-paying union position. Because there was another aspect of his case, involving actions on the Employee's part in the nature of whistle-blowing, his suit was brought individually against the Company, and not as a class-action proceeding on behalf of all fired management employees. In the adverse impact portion of his lawsuit the Employee alleged that the Company had disproportionately fired people 40 and over (himself included). The case was a civil suit: such cases are decided on "the preponderance of the evidence."

In the remainder of this article, Section 3.2 describes issues concerning the database, Section 3.3 treats the analysis, and Section 3.4 contains my conclusions.

3.2 Database Issues

In civil litigation, each side is entitled to discovery, that is, to whatever records and analyses the other side intends to use in court and, additionally, all other "relevant" records. In this case, the plaintiff's preparation of the case was hampered by the poor state of the defendant's personnel records. The Employee's position after he was dismissed from his management job involved handling personnel records; he often knew of errors or incompleteness in the service record cards made available by the defendant. Ultimately it was possible for the plaintiff to assemble a list, alleged to be complete, of all management employees during the period in question, their birth dates, and the dates they left management, if they had. Where ambiguities or doubts arose, the benefit of the doubt was given to the service record cards, because they were the documentary evidence made available by the Company in discovery. In this way, errors in the data base, if any, would be the responsibility of the Company.

A cursory examination of the list revealed that many management employees had left management on four specific dates: 06/30/82, 11/30/82, 05/31/83 and 06/28/84. I was informed by the Employee's attorney that the Company had announced to these employees that their jobs were to be abolished, that unless they had union rights they would no longer be employed by the Company, and that they could choose to retire and receive a pension from the company if they were eligible. In view of the involuntary nature of these departures from management service, I refer to them as "firings" even though some, with union rights, might still have been employed by the Company in other positions.

As is natural in any human population, there were in addition, various other departures from service during the two-year period in question. One employee died, several retired, and some resigned to take positions with other firms. There were very few, but some, hirings during the period as well. I ignored these departures on other dates, because they were the results of decisions not by the Company, but rather, in the main, by employees. Thus to include them would be either to credit or to blame the Company for decisions it did not make. For more on this point, see Michelson (1986), who distinguishes between "situations" (which are not relevant for discrimination suits) and "events" (which are relevant).

The first step in my analysis was simply to count those retained and fired in each of the four firing waves, divided by whether the employee was older than 40 or not at the time. These counts are given in Table 3.1.

Shortly before the trial the Company submitted its own version of the data, and an analysis of that data by its own expert. The data were prepared by the Company's Director of Personnel and Public Relations, who alleged that the database used by Plaintiff was "inaccurate and incomplete." He presented his results in two data bases. In the first data base, he reports his counts of both voluntary and involuntary terminations, divided into four periods: 06/30/82, 07/01/82 through 11/30/82, 12/01/82 through 05/31/83, and 06/01/83 through 06/24/84. The second data base records his

Table 3.1: Ages of those Fired and Retained in Four Firing Waves by the Company

Age	Fired	Retained
	6/30/82 Firings	
40+	18	129
39-	0	102
	11/30/82 Firings	
40+	26	105
39-	10	83
	5/31/83 Firings	
40+	13	92
39-	14	66
	6/28/84 Firings	
40+	13	81
39-	2	52

version of involuntary terminations for those four periods. Both of these data bases were simply counts: he did not explain why, or on what basis, he disagreed with the Employee's categorization of the individual terminations. The latter data base did not coincide with the Employee's for several reasons:

1. There were several young employees who were permitted to hold management jobs for a short time, and then furloughed. I did not include these as involuntary terminations in my counts since the circumstances were that these furloughs occurred while the employees were still on probation. The question of whether the Company had discriminated against its older management employees seemed to me to be independent of whether it had also temporarily promoted several younger workers and then furloughed them back to union positions.

2. The Personnel Director alleged that the entire first wave consisted only of voluntary departures from service.

3. The Personnel Director alleged various other errors and omissions in the data base I had been furnished, without specifying what they were, or to which employee they attached.

The struggle over the data base would have been a major feature of the trial had it occurred. The Company's attorney would have tried to portray the Employee, who would have been presenting the data base on his own behalf, as an error-prone and biased witness. The Employee's attorney would have tried to portray the Personnel Director as disingenuous. That the Personnel Director's information had not been made available to the Employee in discovery would have been used in a legal effort to have his testimony quashed. If the Personnel Director's testimony had been allowed, he would have been asked to identify those departures that he claimed were voluntary. This would have permitted the Employee, in surrebuttal, to call those former employees as witnesses, to testify about the circumstances of their departure from the Company. It is difficult to guess what the effect of all this would have been on the jury.

3.3   Analyses

My expert's report presented three kinds of analyses: a Fisher exact test, a Bayesian analysis, and an analysis based on the Mann-Whitney-Wilcoxon statistic. I would have

put least weight on the Fisher exact test; in contrast, the Company's statistician would
have put virtually all his weight on Fisher's exact tests at the .05 level.

3.3.1   Fisher's Exact Tests

The significance levels for the one-tailed Fisher exact test for the four firing waves
reported in Table 3.1 are .0001, 0485, .8821 and .0407, respectively. Thus wave I is
highly significant, waves II and IV are marginally significant at the .05 level, and wave
III is not significant. The Company's statistician told me after the settlement that with
respect to wave I he would have relied in court on the Company's Personnel Director's
explanation that those departures were voluntary, and that with respect to waves II
and IV the shift of a single fired person from the over-40 to the under-40 group would
have changed the Fisher exact test significance levels to .0906 and .1193, respectively,
thus allowing him to say that the case rested on a single birth date in each group. See
Gastwirth (1988, pp. 226–227) for discussion of this argument in another case.

In rebuttal I would have pointed out that the shift of a single fired employee in
the other direction, from the under-40 to the over-40 group, would have changed the
significance levels to .0234 and .0091, respectively. I also would have said that I think
statisticians should analyze the data sets they have, not make up new ones whose
conclusions they like better. Nonetheless, his robustness argument probably would
have had some appeal, or would have made the jury abandon all hope of understanding
the statistics.

In general, tests of significance, including the Fisher's exact test, are vulnerable in
court to the following sort of fantasy cross-examination:

Q: In your analysis, you used 40 years of age as a threshold between young
people and old people. Why did you use 40 years, as opposed to 35 or 45, say?

A: It is my understanding that the law protects exactly persons 40 years of
age and older. Consequently to be relevant to the case I think that it is essential to
use 40 years of age as the threshold.

Q: So your use of 40 years of age and older is because you think the law
requires it?

A: Yes.

Q: You also use the number .05 as a threshold between data you call "significant" and data you do not call "significant." Why do you use the number .05?
Would .03 or .07 do as well?

A: I use .05 because it is a traditional number to use in statistics. The Federal Government Equal Employment Opportunities Commission uses it as a threshold
level of significance (29 C.F.R. §1607.4(D)).

Q: To the best of your knowledge, is the number .05 used in the written
law?

A: Not to the best of my knowledge. Court decisions that use it include the
Federal Supreme Court in Albemarle Paper Co. v. Moody (1975).

Q: What is the origin of the use of .05 as a significance level?

A: I believe it goes back to Sir Ronald Fisher, the same statistician who
invented the Fisher exact test.

Q: Why did Fisher use .05 rather than .03 or .07?

A: Fisher doesn't really say. He points out that .05 is one in twenty, but
similar equivalences could be found for .03 and .07.

Q: Do you agree with Raiffa and Schlaifer (1961, p. *vi*) when they write
"the numbers .05 and .01 [are treated] in statistics with the same superstitious awe
that is usually reserved for the number 13"?

A: I use the number .05 because it is the traditional number.

Q: But if you used .07 or .03 you would come to rather different results in this case, is that true?

A: Yes, it is.

Q: Now I want to ask you about the meaning of a significance test, perhaps using the Fisher exact test as an example. What does it mean to say that the data are significant at the .05 level?

A: There are two different meanings given to such a statement. According to Fisher (1959), the meaning is that, if the null hypothesis of independence between age and being fired is true, the probability of seeing data as or more discriminatory than the data observed is less than .05. According to Neyman and Pearson (1967), the number .05 is a property of the decision procedure. It says that if I use this procedure many times when the null hypothesis is true, in only .05 of the times will I make an error in rejecting the null hypothesis.

Q: Let's take each of these meanings in turn. Do I understand correctly that, with respect to the Fisher interpretation, the calculation assumes that the null hypothesis is true, that is, it assumes that the Company did not discriminate?

A: Yes, that is correct.

Q: Since your calculation assumes that the Company did not discriminate, how can it be used to shed light on whether the Company discriminated?

A: Fisher would say that with a significance test, one faces a disjunction. If significance is found, either something rather unusual has happened, or the Company discriminated against older people.

Q: Does the Fisher theory allow you to say which of these has occurred, given that one has?

A: No, it does not.

Q: Does it allow you to give a probability that the Company discriminated?

A: No, it does not.

Q: Does it allow you to say anything in the case that the data are not significant?

A: No, it does not.

Q: What would happen if you made the opposite assumption, that the Company does discriminate?

A: One could do that. It is called a "power analysis," and would depend on exactly what you assume about the extent to which the Company discriminates. This is really part of the Neyman-Pearson, as opposed to Fisher, view of significance tests. Neyman and Pearson refer to such tests as hypothesis tests to distinguish their interpretation from Fisher's.

Q: Then let's now turn to the Neyman-Pearson interpretation. When you say that the Neyman-Pearson view is that .05 is a property of a procedure, do I understand you to mean that it is not a property of any particular use of the procedure?

A: Yes, that is correct.

Q: So, under the Neyman-Pearson interpretation, .05 has to do with a long-run sequence of use and not with this particular use?

A: Yes.

Q: So, for example a procedure that accepted the null hypothesis .95 proportion of the time and rejected it .05 proportion of the time, without looking at the data, would be a valid .05 level test according to the Neyman-Pearson theory?

A: Yes, it would. Other criteria would be introduced to show that it is not very sensible, in particular it has poor power compared with some other tests.

Q: So, under the Neyman-Pearson theory, the hypothesis test tells us nothing about this particular use of it, but only about what would happen, hypothetically, if we used it in many cases?

A: Yes.

Q: Have you performed any analyses that do not assume the innocence of your client and that *are* relevant to this particular case?

What this line of questioning shows is that while the language of significance testing is wonderful (who in court wants his data sneered at because of alleged insignificance?), its philosophical underpinnings are weak. There has to be some doubt about how long statisticians can go to court to testify on significance tests using the justification of tradition, which comes down to the idea that many others in statistics make the same mistake.

3.3.2   A Bayesian Analysis

A Bayesian analysis is a formal procedure for modeling an opinion concerning the issue being decided and then showing how that opinion is changed in light of the data. Since Bayesian analyses measure the transformation of opinion brought about by the data, the first critical question is whose opinion is to be modeled. There are several possibilities: the Employee's, the Company's, the judge or jury's, or my own. Since the Employee and the Company are parties to the conflict, they are likely to have convinced themselves of the justice of their cause. Neither judge nor jury is available for probability elicitation. Furthermore, since in at least some sense they know what they think, presenting them with my model of their beliefs seems convoluted and probably insulting. While as an expert witness my opinions are admissible in court, it is not clear why anyone would or should particularly care about my private views, especially since, having had access only to the plaintiff's side of the case, I am no longer impartial. I would prefer to think that the opinions to be modeled are those of a neutral statistical arbitrator working for the court (see Coulom and Fienberg (1986) for a case study of one such referee). Thus I am modeling impartiality, which may not represent my real opinion.

The data are presented in Table 3.1 in the form of four 2×2 tables. Certainly going into each of the decision dates, it is reasonable to consider the age structure of the workforce as fixed, and thus to condition on the number of management workers over and under 40. Consideration of the other margin raises issues that once were, and sometimes still are, hotly debated in statistics. Fisher (1958, pp. 96, 97) took the position that both marginal totals were ancillary, and consequently contained no relevant information. Barnard (1946) shows that each of several sampling models might be appropriate, depending on the experimental situation. See also Seidenfeld (1979). While in general I agree with Barnard's argument, I think that in this instance the most useful way to treat the data is by conditioning on both margins. The right of the Company to fire management workers at a time of financial stringency is not being challenged in this lawsuit, only whom they chose to fire. While conceivably the number of employees fired and retained might depend on the extent of discrimination against persons over 40, the dependence is likely to be weak and masked by the legitimate right of the Company to reduce its management workforce. Consequently a neutral statistician referee would want, I think, to condition on the other margin as well, the number of management workers fired and retained.

An alternative model would be to think of the Company as wishing to reduce its salary bill by a fixed amount. This would lead to a different linear constraint on the persons fired. However, it is obvious that salary and age tend to be highly correlated. The case law [Metz v. Transit Mix, Inc., C.A. 7 (Ind.) 1987, 828 F. 2d 1202 on remand 692 F. Supp. 987; Leftwich vs Harris-Stowe State College Bd. of Regents, 540 F. Supp. 37 (1982 E.D. Mo.); Geller v. Markham, 635 F. 2d 1027, 1034 (2d Cir.

1980) *cert. denied* 451 U.S. 945, 101 S. Ct. 2028, 68 L.Ed.2d 332 (1981) (Rehnquist, J. dissenting); Marshall v. Arlene Knitwear, Inc., 454 F. Supp. 715, 728 (E.D. N.Y. 1978); Laugeson v. Anaconda Co., 510 F. 2d. 307, 316 (6th Cir. 1975)] holds that to fire the highest paid employees is not a sound business reason for having discriminated against workers over 40. A neutral statistician would wish to avoid a model that prejudices the case against the Company before the data are even considered.

Conditioning on both margins leads to consideration of four doubly constrained 2×2 tables. The likelihood for a single table is given (see Plackett (1981, p. 38)) by

$$\frac{\binom{n}{n_{11}, n_{1+} - n_{11}, n_{+1} - n_{11}, n - n_{1+} - n_{+1} + n_{11}} p_{11}^{n_{11}} p_{12}^{n_{1+} - n_{11}} p_{21}^{n_{+1} - n_{11}} p_{22}^{n - n_{+1} - n_{1+} + n_{11}}}{\sum_{j=\max\{0, n_{1+} + n_{+1} - n\}}^{\min\{n_{1+}, n_{+1}\}} \binom{n}{j, n_{1+} - j, n_{+1} - j, n - n_{1+} - n_{+1} + j} p_{11}^{j} p_{12}^{n_{1+} - j} p_{21}^{n_{+1} - j} p_{22}^{n - n_{1+} - n_{1+} + j}}$$

$$= \frac{\binom{n}{n_{11}, n_{1+} - n_{11}, n_{+1} - n_{11}, n - n_{1+} - n_{+1} + n_{11}} \lambda^{n_{11}}}{\sum_{j=\max\{0, n_{1+} + n_{+1} - n\}}^{\min\{n_{1+}, n_{+1}\}} \binom{n}{j, n_{1+} - j, n_{+1} - j, n - n_{1+} - n_{+1} + j} \lambda^{j}}$$

Here $n_{i,j}$ is the number of people in age group i whose employment fate is j. Age group 1 is over 40, and group 2 is under 40. Employment fate 1 is to be fired, and fate 2 is to be retained. Similarly $p_{i,j}$ is the probability that a person will fall in category (i, j) in a given firing wave, where $\sum_{i=1}^{2} \sum_{i=1}^{2} p_{ij} = 1$. Then $\lambda = p_{11}p_{22}/p_{12}p_{21}$. Finally $n_{+1} = n_{11} + n_{21}$ and $n_{1+} = n_{11} + n_{12}$.

Thus the likelihood, although formally a function of $\mathbf{p} = (p_{11}, p_{12}, p_{21}, p_{22})$, is a function only of $\lambda(\mathbf{p})$. Consequently the entire prior-to-posterior analysis can be conducted on λ, as the conditional distribution of $\mathbf{p}$ given λ will be unaffected by the data. See Kadane (1975) for discussion of a similar situation occurring in the Bayesian theory of simultaneous equations in econometrics.

The odds ratio λ is, in addition, a natural and convenient measure of the extent of discrimination against older workers. However, there is one inconvenience to the odds ratio. An odds ratio of 2 would be transformed into an odds ratio of $1/2$ by a relabeling of the rows (or of the columns). Thus to think properly about odds ratios requires attention to multiplicative symmetry around 1. It is far less awkward to transform to the log odds ratio L, and attend to additive symmetry around 0. Relabeling now merely changes the sign of the log odds ratio.

The point $L = 0$ corresponds to a policy of the Company that discriminates neither for nor against its older workers. Positive values for L correspond to discrimination against older workers, and negative values correspond to discrimination against younger workers. Thus it certainly seems reasonable for the prior of an impartial statistician to be centered at a log odds ratio L of 0. Furthermore, a log odds ratio of log 2, corresponding to the example discussed previously, is as discriminatory as a log odds ratio of $\log \frac{1}{2} = -\log 2$, so symmetry around 0 seems to be a natural condition. Additionally, it seems reasonable to me to require that the prior be unimodal, so that points closer to 0 have at least as high density as that for points far away. I use the normal family, not because I think normality has anything to do with impartiality in this problem, but because I think calculations done with normal priors are typical of what I would get with other shapes symmetric around 0.

Within the family of normal distributions centered at 0, the only parameter left is the variance. When the prior variance is zero, all the mass is at $L = 0$. But this would say that the impartial statistician is so sure that the company did not discriminate as to be uninterested in and uninfluenced by the data, which is unreasonable. Because the likelihood is positive and continuous at $L = 0$, as the prior variance approaches 0

Table 3.2: Combined Likelihood Summary

	Prior Standard Deviation				
	1	2	4	8	∞(reference)
Mode L	.68	.71	.71	.72	.72
Prob($L > 0$)	.999	.999	.999	.999	.999

the limiting probability that L is positive approaches $\frac{1}{2}$, regardless of the data. Again, this is not reasonable. Consequently I choose a "large" variance, by which I do not mean an infinite variance, but rather one large enough to allow the data to dominate in the calculation of the posterior. In practice, I use a variety of variances, and show that the choice among them does not materially affect the conclusions.

One could argue that newer workers, usually junior, are on a kind of probation for some period after their formal six-month probation has expired. Consequently one might expect a higher natural dismissal rate for junior than for senior employees, absent discrimination. If one ignores this phenomenon by using priors symmetric around 0, the Bayesian analyses given here may understate the extent of the Company's discrimination against people over 40.

There are alternative priors that I considered but did not use. One of them puts a lump of probability, say $\frac{1}{2}$, at $L = 0$ and spreads the rest, perhaps as a normal distribution, with a mean of 0. This would have the anomalous effect of placing $\frac{3}{4}$ prior probability on the innocence of the Company, which does not seem consonant with impartiality. Another possibility puts such a lump at 0, and perhaps a half-normal on positive L. Now there would be a $\frac{1}{2}$ prior probability on the innocence of the Company, which seems appropriate, but the expected amount of discrimination (L) in the prior is positive, which does not.

One could imagine using Bayesian analysis in another way. Suppose instead of thinking of a prior to posterior transformation by describing the posterior, one asks what characteristics of the prior would be implied by $Pr(L < 0) = \frac{1}{2}$. If the normal family is accepted, there would be a curve of prior means and variances such that the posterior would indicate a probability of discrimination of exactly .5. A similar contour could be found for .6, .7, etc. I chose not to do this here, because I wish to stress the idea of impartiality of the prior, but this is a legitimate alternative use of Bayesian ideas to express the import of the data.

The statistical arbitrator might first want to know whether there is a pattern of age discrimination in the firings, taken as a whole. This suggests using the sequence of priors specified above, and a likelihood consisting of the product of the likelihoods for each of the four periods. In addition to the posterior distribution in general, the amount of probability falling below 0 (corresponding to discrimination against people under 40), and above 0 (corresponding to discrimination against people over 40) are of special interest. The results are given in Table 3.2. They show overall a definite pattern of discrimination by the Company against people over 40. It is notable that this conclusion is not sensitive to the standard deviation chosen for the prior. The modal log odds ratio of .72 corresponds to an odds ratio of 2.05. Thus the odds of an over-40 employee being fired are roughly twice those of an employee under 40, indicating substantial discrimination.

It is also of interest to examine each firing wave individually. I consider them chronologically, taking the firing wave of 06/30/82 first. As shown in Table 3.3, the probability that the log odds ratio is positive is virtually 1, indicating a virtual certainty of discrimination against people 40 years old and older. Because all people fired in this wave were over 40, the data are consistent with arbitrarily large extents of discrimination L against people over 40. It is only the prior distribution that constrains L. As the prior variance on L increases, the posterior mode of L increases. If the prior variance increased without limit, so would the posterior mode of L. It is for this reason that Table 3.2 does not report results for a reference prior for the firing wave of 6/30/82. The data from this wave indicate a truly extraordinary degree of discrimination against employees over 40.

The rhetoric of various authors would suggest something canonical about a prior proportional to Lebesgue measure. Jeffreys (1961, p. 49) wants a "simplicity postulate...sufficiently precise to give exact prior probabilities to all laws." Box and Tiao (1973) support many of the same priors as Jeffreys on the ground that they are "data translated." Bernardo (1979) justifies priors on grounds of a connection with information theory. While I do not find appealing the arguments supporting these priors as canonically correct, often, but not always, such priors yield about the same conclusions as would many other, proper priors better grounded in reasonable opinion that is informed about the problem at hand. In the case of the firing wave of 6/30/82, however, because none of the employees fired was under 40, the likelihood function is ill suited to such a prior. Nonetheless, the inference important here, the probability of discrimination against people 40 and older, is not sensitive to the choice of prior variance, as Table 3.3 shows.

The second firing wave is that of 11/30/82. In Table 3.4 the probability of discrimination against persons older than 40 is again very high (96% to 97%). Again the log odds ratio is about .72, indicating an odds of 2.05. Thus, as in the combined case, this indicates that the odds of an over-40 employee being fired on 11/30/82 were twice those of a person under 40.

The third wave of firings, that of 5/31/83, shows a very different pattern. As shown in Table 3.5, the probability of discrimination against people older than 40 drops to about 16%, and the estimated log odds drops to −.40, which corresponds to an odds of .67. Thus for this wave of firings, the odds of an over-40 person's being fired are roughly $\frac{2}{3}$ of those of a person under 40. This wave therefore does not show evidence of discrimination against people over 40 in the allocation of firings.

Finally, I examine the fourth wave, that of 6/28/84 in Table 3.6. This firing wave may have special significance since this was the wave in which the Employee was fired, having survived the firing waves of 6/30/82, 11/30/82, and 5/31/83. Here the probability that there was discrimination against those over 40 was .987 (for the

Table 3.3: Firing Wave of 6/30/82

	Prior Standard Deviation			
	1	2	4	8
Mode L	1.88	2.91	4.01	5.16
Prob($L > 0$)	1.000	1.000	1.000	1.000

Table 3.4: Firing Wave of 11/30/82

	Prior Standard Deviation				
	1	2	4	8	∞(reference)
Mode L	.62	.69	.71	.72	.72
Prob($L > 0$)	.960	.967	.969	.970	.970

Table 3.5: Firing Wave of 5/31/83

	Prior Standard Deviation				
	1	2	4	8	∞(reference)
Mode L	.34	-.39	-.40	-.40	-.40
Prob($L > 0$)	.183	.169	.165	.164	.164

reference prior). The modal estimate for the log odds ratio is 1.42, corresponding to an odds ratio of 4.14. Thus in the firing wave that affected the Employee, the odds of his being dismissed were over four times as great as those of his co-workers under 40 years of age.

My conclusions from this Bayesian study are as follows;

1. As to overall pattern, the data show that the Company did engage in a pattern of discrimination in firing management employees aged 40 years and older.

2. The first firing wave of 6/30/82 shows extreme discrimination. The fourth wave, of 6/28/84, in which the Employee was fired, also shows very substantial discrimination. The second wave, of 11/30/82, shows substantial discrimination. Finally, the wave of 5/31/83 does not show much of a pattern in either direction, but there is perhaps a slight hint of discrimination the other way, against people under 40 years of age.

One might argue that if there were a consistent pattern of discrimination on the basis of age, especially if there were some continuing mechanism at work, all four firing waves should demonstrate the same pattern. The exception of firing wave III, then, casts doubt on this interpretation of events. To establish adverse impact, one should not be required to show that every act of the Company, or even its decisions about whom to fire in each wave, were discriminatory. If a general pattern of age discrimination is found, it should be considered sufficient to shift the burden of proof to the Company of explaining the pattern in a nondiscriminatory way. However, if the case were brought as a class-action suit on behalf of all over-40 employees fired in the four waves, the data might be sufficient to support exclusion from the class of those fired in the third wave. Excluding the one wave in which the Company appears not to have discriminated would only make the combination of the remaining waves look more discriminatory, of course.

How might the Bayesian analysis be criticized? A likely line of attack is through the data base. What would be the consequence of excluding firing wave I entirely, taking the view that all these departures from management ranks were voluntary retirements rather than involuntary retirements? The answers are given in Table 3.7. The probability that the Company discriminated against its older workers drops from .999 in Table 3.2, to .937 here, not nearly enough of a drop to disturb my conclusions under a standard of the preponderance of the evidence. What does change is the modal

Table 3.6: Firing Wave of 6/28/84

	Prior Standard Deviation				
	1	2	4	8	∞(reference)
Mode L	0.94	1.24	1.37	1.41	1.42
Prob($L > 0$)	0.965	0.981	0.985	0.986	0.987

Table 3.7: Combination of Waves II – IV

	Prior Standard Deviation				
	1	2	4	8	∞(reference)
Mode L	.360	.380	.390	.390	.390
Prob($L > 0$)	.930	.935	.936	.937	.937

Table 3.8: Combination of Waves II – IV (Altered Data)

	Prior Standard Deviation				
	1	2	4	8	∞(reference)
Mode L	.260	.270	.270	.270	.270
Prob($L > 0$)	.853	.859	.860	.861	.861

log odds ratio, which drops from .72 in Table 3.2 to .39 here, corresponding to a drop in the odds ratio from 2.05 to 1.48.

Finally one could ask what the effect would be of changing one fired worker in each of waves II and IV from over 40 to under 40. The results are given in Table 3.8, and indicate a modest further shift in the results. Remembering that no evidence supports this alteration of the data, these calculations suggest reasonable robustness of the Bayesian analysis.

Faced with two methods of analyzing the same data set, one may naturally want to compare them, both in principle and numerically. Altham (1969) showed an equivalence between the Fisher exact test and a Bayesian analysis. However, the Bayesian analysis in Altham's equivalence has only one margin fixed, (hence two independent binomial populations), and independent beta priors with parameters (0,1) on each. This is quite an astonishing result, since the Fisher calculation is a summation over the sample space, while the Bayesian calculation is an integration over the parameter space. Because the Bayesian model used by Altham differs from the one used here both in likelihood and in prior, it is useful to compare the results numerically, as is done in Table 3.9.

The first four rows are the data from the four firing waves. The fifth and sixth rows result from shifting one fired person from the over-40 to the under-40 group in firing waves II and IV. Conversely, the seventh and eighth result from shifting one

Table 3.9: Fisher Exact Test Significance Levels and Bayesian Probabilities of Discrimination

Data	Fisher Exact Test	Bayes (ref. prior) Pr($L < 0$)
(18,0,129,102)	.0001	.000
(26,10,105,83)	.0485	.030
(13,14,92,66)	.8821	.846
(13,2,81,52)	.0407	.013
(25,11,105,83)	.0906	.061
(12,3,81,52)	.1193	.056
(27,9,105,83)	.0234	.013
(14,1,81,52)	.0091	.002

Table 3.10: Paired Analysis

Firing	Probability older person fired		
wave	Probability	Log odds	Odds
I	0.983	4.053	57.57
II	0.625	0.512	1.689
III	0.479	−0.085	0.919
IV	0.711	0.902	2.465
Combined	0.685	0.778	2.178

fired person from the under-40 to the over-40 group in those firing waves. Generally the Bayesian and Fisher results are parallel, but not the same.

The strength of a Bayesian analysis in this context, it seems to me, is that it answers the relevant legal question, namely what the probability is that the Company's policy (L) discriminated against people over 40. Unlike the classical analysis, it does not assume that either side is correct, and it is relevant to the particular case.

3.3.3 Paired Observations

The preceding analysis convinces me that my hypothetical neutral statistical arbitrator would find that the Employee has met the requirement of showing disparate impact of the Company's decisions against people 40 and older, thus placing the burden of proof on the Company to show sound, nondiscriminatory business reasons for its actions. However, it leaves open the question of whether the effects observed truly reflect age discrimination or are an artifact of defining the protected group to be people aged 40 and older. One way of looking at that question would be to perform analyses similar to those of Sections 3.3.1 and 3.3.2, varying the age cutoff. However, this does not deal with the question in a continuous way.

I think a more natural analysis of this question would proceed as follows: Suppose we form, conceptually, all pairs of employees, one of whom is fired and one of whom is not, in a given firing wave. If we picked one such pair at random, what is the probability that the older would be the one fired? This proportion is the Mann-Whitney-Wilcoxon statistic, thought of as an estimate of the probability that a member of the fired population is older than a member of the retained population (see Hoeffding (1948)). In this application, however, the entire population of management employees is available for analysis, so it seems wrong to conceive of the data as a random sample from some larger population.

The results are given in Table 3.10, for probabilities, log odds and odds. Exact non-discrimination corresponds to probability of $\frac{1}{2}$, log odds of 0, and odds of 1.

There are several ways of conceiving the combined analysis. The method used in Table 3.10 (and also Table 3.11) is to constrain the pairs of employees, whose ages are being compared, so that one was fired and one was retained in the same firing wave. This seems most consonant with an urn conception of the probability process (pour the four urns together and draw again). Also, it maintains the legal interpretation that age comparisons between fired and retained workers are limited to the same firing waves.

Again, the results of Table 3.10 confirm the earlier analysis: Wave I was very discriminating against older people, waves II and IV were substantially discriminatory, and wave III was not discriminatory. Overall, a pattern of discrimination against older people in these firings is confirmed.

These probabilities, log odds, and odds do not have uncertainty measures attached because every pair of employees, one of whom was fired and the other not, is considered. Consequently these are exactly the probabilities, log odds, and the odds, up to limits of numerical rounding.

Perhaps because of the absence of uncertainty, an analysis of this sort has an appeal. Might it be reformulated so as to respect, once again, the age 40 and over restriction of the protected class? One way to do this is to limit the pairs to those in which one employee is over 40 and one under 40. So now the question is, of all pairs of employees, one under 40 and one over, one fired and one not, what is the proportion of pairs in which the person fired is over 40? The results are given in Table 3.11.

Thus the results are quite similar to those in Table 3.10. Again there are no uncertainty measures here, for the same reason as in Table 3.10.

Let C be the proportion of pairs of employees, one under 40 and one over, one fired and one not, in which the person fired is over 40. Then

$$C = \frac{n_{11}n_{22}}{n_{11}n_{22} + n_{12}n_{21}}.$$

The odds of C are

$$0(C) = \frac{C}{1-C} = \frac{n_{11}n_{22}}{n_{12}n_{21}} = \frac{\frac{n_{11}n_{22}}{n}}{\frac{n_{12}n_{21}}{n}},$$

which is the Mantel and Haenszel (1959) statistic. However, for several tables combined,

$$C = \frac{\Sigma_k n_{11k}n_{22k}}{\Sigma_k n_{11k}n_{22k} + \Sigma_k n_{12k}n_{21k}},$$

where k indexes tables. Here the odds of C are

$$0(C) = \frac{C}{1-C} = \frac{\Sigma_k n_{11k}n_{22k}}{\Sigma_k n_{12k}n_{21k}},$$

which is not in general equal to the Mantel-Haenzel statistic

$$\frac{\Sigma_k (n_{11k}n_{22k}/n_k)}{\Sigma_k (n_{12k}n_{21k}/n_k)}$$

The Mantel-Haenzel statistic is used in articles discussing discrimination in hiring under a model of two or more independent populations (Gastwirth and Greenhouse, 1987; Louv and Little, 1986).

Table 3.11: Restricted Paired Analysis

| Firing | Probability older person fired | | |
wave	Probability	Log odds	Odds
I	1.00	∞	∞
II	0.672	0.72	2.055
III	0.400	−0.41	0.667
IV	0.806	1.43	4.173
Combined	0.689	0.794	2.211

3.4 Conclusions

What are the appropriate responsibilities of a statistician in a legal setting with respect to the data base used? It is interesting to note that I and the statistician working for the Company took different approaches to this question. The Company produced the 2 × 2 tables for analysis by the statistician. Thus the conclusions he could have reached would have been limited to the accuracy of those tables. In contrast, I based my choice of analysis on a list of employees, their birth dates, hiring dates, and firing or departure dates. This might have exposed me to cross examination about conditions in the Company, about which I would not be very knowledgeable. I do not know what is the best policy for a statistician in such an environment.

If I had been acting as a neutral statistical arbitrator, the Court would have been asked whether the evidence suffices to establish a prima facie case. If so, the Company would have been asked to give an accounting of its policy on firing. The Court would then have been asked whether the explanation offered would, or might, suffice as a sound business reason if sustained by the data. If the answer to this question were positive, then, and only then, would it make sense to consider covariates with a view toward examining the extent to which the Company's explanation is supported by the data.

I find it interesting that the legal context impinges on the data analysis in several places. While it is to be expected that the application would have a strong influence in every applied problem, it is somewhat surprising that an analysis done in a legal context might be substantially different from an analysis done with a solely scientific aim.

It is certainly a fortunate feature of this data set that several different analyses lead to very similar substantive conclusions. To the extent that different substantive conclusions are reached by different analyses, this only serves to sharpen the debate over the meaning of the analyses. It should not be a surprise that a legal case would confront statisticians with deep problems about the meaning of the various techniques proposed, because the adversary structure leads to sharper questioning than statisticians generally confront.

REFERENCES

Altham, P. (1969). "Exact Bayesian Analysis of a 2 × 2 Contingency Table, and Fisher's 'Exact Significance Test'." *Journal of the Royal Statistical Society Series B*, 31, 261–269. 65

Barnard, G. (1946). "Significance Test for 2 × 2 Tables." *Biometrika*, 34, 123–138. 60

Bernardo, J. (1979). "Reference Posterior Distributions for Bayesian Inference." *Journal of the Royal Statistical Society Series B*, 41, 113–148. 63

Box, G. and Tiao, G. (1973). *Bayesian Inference in Statistical Analysis*. Reading, MA: Addison-Wesley. 63

Coulom, R. and Fienberg, S. (1986). "The Use of Court Appointed Statistical Experts." In *Statistics and the Law*, eds. M. DeGroot, S. Fienberg, and J. Kadane, 305–332. New York: John Wiley. 60

Fisher, R. (1958). *Statistical Methods for Research Workers*. 13th ed. New York: Hafner Press. 53, 60

Gastwirth, J. (1988). *Statistical Reasoning in Law and Public Policy*. Boston: Academic Press. 58

Gastwirth, J. and Greenhouse, S. (1987). "Estimating a Common Relative Risk: Application in Equal Employment." *Journal of the American Statistical Association*, 82, 38–45. 67

Hoeffding, W. (1948). "A Class of Statistics with Asymptotically Normal Distribution." *Annals of Mathematical Statistics*, 19, 293–325. 66

Jeffreys, H. (1961). *Theory of Probability*. 3rd ed. Oxford, U.K.: Oxford University Press. 63

Kadane, J. (1975). "The Role of Identification in Bayesian Theory." In *L.J. Savage Memorial Volume Studies in Bayesian Statistics and Econometrics*, eds. S. Fienberg and A. Zellner, 175–191. Amsterdam: North Holland. 61

Louv, W. and Little, R. (1986). "Combining One-Sided Binomial Tests." *Journal of the American Statistical Association*, 81, 550–554. 67

Mantel, J. and Haenszel, W. (1959). "Statistical Aspects of the Analysis of Retrospective Sudies of Disease." *Journal of the National Cancer Institute*, 22, 719–748. 67

Michelson, S. (1986). "Comment." In *Statistics and the Law*, eds. M. DeGroot, S. Fienberg, and J. Kadane, 169–181. New York: John Wiley. 56

Neyman, J. and Pearson, E. (1967). *Joint Statistical Papers*. Cambridge, U.K.: Cambridge University Press. 59

Plackett, R. (1981). *The Analysis of Categorical Data*. New York: Macmillan. 61

Raiffa, H. and Schlaifer, R. (1961). *Applied Statistical Decision Theory*. Cambridge, MA: MIT Press. 58

Seidenfeld, T. (1979). *Philosophical Problems of Statistical Inference: Learning from R.A. Fisher*. Dordrecht: D. Reidel. 60

Epilogue

What is the scientific issue addressed?

Do the data support the legal allegation that older employees were fired at disproportionate rates?

Is justification given for

a) the use of the data?

Various aspects of the data collection would have been in dispute had this case gone to trial.

b) the use of the likelihood and prior?

The main issue in the likelihood is whether one should regard one or both margins as fixed in these 2×2 tables. There seems to be little doubt that the ages (over or under 40) of the employees should be regarded as fixed. But should the number of employees fired/retained also be regarded as fixed? The paper argues that the answer is "yes," largely on legal grounds.

The prior family for the log-odds ratio is taken to be normal (for convenience) centered at zero (for legal reasons) with a robustness analysis of the choice of standard deviation. The upshot is that in general, the same results are obtained for all reasonable standard deviation values.

How were the calculations done?

By a grid.

If I were doing the problem today, how would I change the approach?

I am satisfied with the approach, and would do the same now.

What do I see as the contributions of this paper?

1. It addresses and answers the scientific question posed. The finding is that fir-

ing waves I, II and IV show disproportionate firing of workers over 40, as does the amalgamation of all four firing waves. Firing wave III does not show the same pattern.

2. At the time, there were not a lot of examples of Bayesian analyses proposed for use in court. Although this analysis was not presented in court because the case settled, it was ready to go.

Further reading:

Kadane, J.B., Moreno, E., Perez, M.E. and Pericchi, .R. (2002). "Applying Non-parametric Robust Bayesian Analysis to Judicial Neutrality." *Journal of Statistical Planning and Inference*, 102, 425–439.

TEACHING SUGGESTIONS

References for theoretical ideas:

1. Prior to posterior transformation: *Principles* Section 7.7

2. Computation using a grid: *Principles* Section 10.2

Exercises

1. What are the arguments for and against treating both margins in these 2×2 tables as fixed? What arguments do you find most compelling, and why?

2. If one treated only the age margin as fixed, but not the margin specifying the number of employees fired, how would the analysis differ?

3. Write a program in R to calculate the likelihood on page 59. Use it together with the normal priors specified to verify the posterior calculations in the paper.

4. The paper gives results for each firing wave, and for an amalgamation of all four firing waves. Which calculations do you find most useful, and why?

Chapter 4

Subjective Bayesian Analysis for Surveys with Missing Data (1993)

Foreword

Social surveys typically have missing data, because the intended recipients cannot be reached or refuse to respond. How should such data be analyzed?

One response, all too common, I fear, is simply to ignore the issue, and assume that those who answered are typical of those who did not. There is usually no warrant for this belief, and indeed it is rarely even broached, let along discussed. Another extreme might be to refuse to extend the claims from the population that responded to the population to whom the survey was made available. Neither of these extremes seems adequate to the needs of social science.

This paper explores this issue in the context of a study of jurors' attitudes toward the death penalty. Jurors who served 57 non-capital trials in Wake County, North Carolina, were asked to disclose what the charges were, how they voted in the first jury vote, and the distribution of votes in the first jury vote. They were also asked for their telephone numbers so they could be further interviewed. The telephone interview ascertained their views on the death penalty, specifically whether they could fairly and impartially decide on guilt or innocence in a death penalty case and whether to impose the death penalty. These are includable jurors (I). A second group could decide guilt or innocence impartially, but not whether to impose the death penalty (these are excludable jurors (E)). A third group could not fairly and impartially decide guilt or innocence, the unfair jurors (U). The scientific question is whether includable jurors (I) are more likely to vote for guilt than are excludable jurors (E). The problem is that only 298 of the $12 \times 57 = 684$ jurors in the study were willing to do the telephone interview to ascertain their attitude toward the death penalty.

The paper conducts a sensitivity analysis to examine how much the results vary according to what one assumes about the relationship between attitudes toward the death penalty and refusal to participate in the telephone survey.

There's a very interesting issue that arises in the second half of the paper. About 40% of the cases the jurors heard were drunk driving cases. While the priors used in the previous analysis did not anticipate distinguishing drunk driving from other cases, I looked at it anyway. It turns out that the excludables (E) were much more prone to vote guilty in such cases than were the includeables (E). There is a question of how one should regard such an unexpected finding using an unanticipated covariate.

My friend Jim Dickey posed the question to me of what I would think if I plotted the residuals of a regression and saw a smiling face. I would think that the data had been falsified by someone as a joke. His point is that the likelihood and prior we assume are vast simplifications of a much more complicated belief structure we carry with us when we look at data.

In the instance of this data set, Wake County is split between an urban, largely Democratic-leaning population and a more rural, largely Republican-leaning population. The former is more likely to have qualms about the death penalty and to take an unforgiving attitude toward drunk driving than do the latter. So these findings are understandable in terms of what's reasonable to think of the Wake County population.

In this case, while we did not have data to illuminate further whether the urban/rural hypothesis is correct, it is certainly plausible, and could be examined in further study.

But to excuse this kind of additional analysis too enthusiastically is to come close to endorsing data dredging by pharmaceutical companies who may desperately try to find some subset of patients that can be argued to have benefit from a drug being tested.

There is a difference here, in that the differing social attitudes of urban Democrats and rural Republicans is hardly news to students of the American political and social scene. Often there is not an equally plausible theory for why only some subset of patients defined after the data are collected would benefit from the treatment in question. But admittedly both explanations are thought of after the data analysis, so there is peril in interpreting the data as confirming such an explanation.

Perhaps the fundamental difference between these examples is that the hypothetical pharmaceutical company would like to use the results not so much as the basis for further investigation, but rather as a basis to show that there are patients helped by the drug, and hence that the FDA should allow the drug to be marketed.

There's a balance to be found here. I feel comfortable with the drunk driving analysis of the Wake County data, but not with pharmaceutical data dredging. How far to go with data mining is an issue of some subtlety.

This paper was originally published in *The Statistician (Journal of the Royal Statistical Society, Series D)*, **42**, pp. 415–426. Correction: **45**, 539. Permission to republish not required.

Published Paper

J.B. Kadane

Abstract

Almost every survey has missing data, sometimes because of inadequacy of the sampling frame, sometimes because of the unwillingness of persons in the frame to participate, sometimes because of the inability of the surveyors to find everyone in the frame, and usually because of an unknown mixture of all these reasons and others. The analyses of surveys often ignore the missing data, treating it as a complete sample of those who responded. However, to do this is often to assume away the principal source of uncertainty, rendering statements of uncertainty conditioned on that assumption problematic. One solution is the assumption of 'ignorability', as discussed by Don Rubin. This approach essentially states in conditional probability terms what one must assume to get away with an analysis that does not take into account the missing data. The purpose of this paper is to explore a second approach, in which differing beliefs about what the missing data would have been had they been collected are explored to see how robust the results of the survey are. What is reasonable to assume depends on subjective judgments of the analyst. These ideas are considered in the context of a survey on juror death penalty attitudes and behavior.

4.1   Introduction

The comparison of subjectivist Bayesian and objectivist frequentistic methods applied to practical problems is very important to the advancement of both methodological positions. This paper is devoted to the consideration of a type of data in which one would have thought that the frequentists would be at their best.

The frequency argument is based on viewing a given instance or sample as a member of an infinite stream of independent and identically distributed such instances, and associating the probability of the instance with the relative frequency in the infinite stream. Of course there are data situations that are very awkward from this stance. Consider, for example, the probability that it will rain in Nottingham sometime tomorrow. Suppose that many years of past data are available. With what subset of this data should I associate tomorrow's rain? Should I choose only those in which the wind, rain and temperature conditions in Dublin match those of today? In making such choices the subjectivity of the associated 'infinite' stream is apparent, and is an embarrassment to a frequentist seeking objectivity.

Thus to explore the possible usefulness of frequentistic ideas one must choose an example more carefully, in the hope of finding one more congenial to their approach. Surely sampling from a fixed population comes to mind as a candidate. There are two possible senses of sampling that then come to mind: that the individuals in the sample are a random sample from a frame of such individuals, and that the sample itself is random from a frame of subsets, perhaps subsets of the same size. Since the latter results in a sample of size one, it seems very weak in a frequentistic sense. Consequently the first interpretation is concentrated on here.

In a practical implementation of sampling from a human population, not everyone responds. People move, are busy, don't bother, and find the questions objectionable. In a reasonably good survey, perhaps 70% of the chosen sample responds.

This practical fact imposes a heavy burden on the analysis of the survey data. One response that might be made is to take the sample as representative only of those who would have responded had they been asked. While this has the attraction of objectivistic frequentist ideological purity, it has costs. One is that the sampling frame is of unknown size. The second, and more important, is that usually the scientific or practical question being asked pertains not to the hypothetical population of persons who would have responded had they been asked, but rather to the whole original sample frame, whether responders or not. Thus to take this route risks making the conclusions of the analysis irrelevant to the main effort. This is a very high price to pay.

A second position on the question of non-response is to ignore it. This is commonly done in reports of surveys in social psychology. Typically the non-response is reported, and then inferences are made from the proportion of those answering the questions who answer it in particular ways. Standard errors are computed as if the population answering were the population asked. One way to justify this neglect is to cite conditions on the likelihood given by Rubin (1976) and Little and Rubin (1987) such that non-response may be ignored.

The judgments called for are precise, and hard to justify in an applied setting. The other line of argument that might justify neglect of non-response is that there doesn't seem to be much else that can be done. This may be true in the context of objectivistic frequentist statistics, but is not the case for Bayesians. The material presented below is an example of how a Bayesian analysis of survey data with non-response might be conducted.

4.2   Background and Analysis

The death penalty is and has been a controversial aspect of American law for some time. Continual appeals of death penalty convictions have resulted in both reforms of the procedure and in a very long average time between conviction and execution.

As matters now stand, a trial for a capital offense must be conducted in two parts. In the first, the question of guilt or innocence must be decided. In the second, the jury or judge must consider aggravating and mitigating circumstances in deciding on the penalty. The defendant has the right to a jury trial, although that right is not always exercised. If a jury hears the case, the same jurors hear both parts of the case.

Naturally it matters a great deal what jurors hear the case. Any juror who says he/she cannot hear the case fairly and impartially is excluded. But, additionally, jurors who say they can decide guilt or innocence fairly and impartially, but who could never impose the death penalty for conscientious reasons (or who would always impose it) are excluded from the jury. The question is whether this biases the jury in the guilt or innocence phase by excluding potential jurors likely to be more sympathetic to the defense than those eligible to serve. A line of research (Bronson (1970); Cowan et al. (1984); Fitzgerald and Ellsworth (1984); Goldberg (Girsch) (1970); Gross (1984); Jurow (1970); Kadane (1983); Luginbuhl and Middendorf (1988); Luginbuhl and Powers (1991); Moran and Comfort (1986); Oberer (1961); Powers and Luginbuhl (1983); Zeisel (1968) supports this hypothesis. The courts have not been very open to this argument, however. In Hovey (1980), the California Supreme Court declined to require different juries for the two phases of a capital trial because the analysis presented to it compared death-eligible jurors only to those who would never impose the death penalty, not to those who would never or always impose it. Later the US

Table 4.1: First ballot votes categorized by death penalty attitudes (numbers of jurors)

	Includable	Excludable	Unfair	Unknown	Total
Guilty	167.5	19.0	19.89	268.99	475.38
Not guilty	75.5	11.0	5.11	117.01	208.62
Total	243.0	30.0	25.00	386.00	684.00

Supreme Court in Lockhart (1986) ruled that the evidence was too fragmentary and, besides, that it found social science on this issue irrelevant legally.

The principal way of understanding the results has been a continuum suggested by Packer (1968) and emphasized by Fitzgerald and Ellsworth (1984), that some citizens stress crime control as an objective of the legal system, while others stress due process. Thus, citizens who would favor the death penalty might be thought of on the 'crime control' end of the continuum while those who would never impose it might be more toward the 'due process' end. The purpose of the current study is to examine these ideas empirically using real jurors.

Jurors in 57 trials of common (non-capital) matters in Wake County, North Carolina were asked to fill out a brief verdict questionnaire in the jury lounge, and were asked for their telephone numbers for a further interview. For the purposes of this paper, the important matters asked about in the questionnaire were what the charges were, how they have voted in the first ballot, and the distribution of votes on the first ballot. (The first ballot is used, and has been used in jury studies since Kalven and Zeisel (1966), to indicate a juror's tendency on a case with the least contamination by discussion with other jurors.) Of the 684 jurors in these 57 trials, 478 answered the verdict questionnaire.

Of these, 298 telephone interviews were conducted to determine the jurors' attitudes toward the death penalty. These answers were categorized into three groups: those includable (I) in a death-penalty jury, those excludable because of the need to have the same jury decide both guilt/innocence and penalty (E), and those who say they could not judge the issue of guilt and innocence fairly (U). Although potential respondents failed to reveal their death-penalty attitudes because they failed to clear one of several steps (no verdict questionnaire, no telephone number on verdict questionnaire, unreachable by telephone, refused to answer questions on telephone), their first ballot vote was discernible from the totals given on verdict questionnaires of others on their jury. Consequently the data may be regarded as revealing the first ballot vote of all 684 jurors, and the death-penalty attitude of 298, less than half.

The basic data used in the analyses below are given in Table 4.1. In some cases it was not clear what the vote of a given juror had been, usually because of discrepancies in the total first ballot reports for the jury given by various jurors. Primary weight was given to jurors' self-reports of their votes; and otherwise I credited each juror's report of the overall vote equally. This resulted in some non-integer best estimates and accounts for the non-integer sums reported in Table 4.1. With a very high probability, however, how each juror voted on the first ballot is known.

In order to examine the issue of whether those excluded by the death-qualification process are more likely to convict than those included, a good measure of the relationship between death-penalty attitude and first ballot vote must be found. To establish some notation, recall that I, E and U stand respectively for includable, excludable and unfair jurors (those who could not fairly decide on guilt or innocence), and let G and N stand respectively for a first ballot vote of guilty or not guilty. Then $P_{G,I}$ is the probability that a prospective juror would be includable and would vote guilty. The odds that the includable juror would vote guilty are $P_{G,I}/P_{N,I}$. Similarly the odds that an excludable juror would vote guilty are $P_{G,E}/P_{N,E}$. The odds ratio is then $(P_{G,I}/P_{N,I})/(P_{G,E}/P_{N,E}) = (P_{G,I}P_{N,E})/(P_{N,I}P_{G,E})$. A final convenient and standard transformation (see, for example, Bishop et al. (1975)) takes the logarithm of the odds ratio,

$$\phi = log[(P_{G,I}P_{N,E})/(P_{N,I}P_{G,E})]. \tag{4.1}$$

If ϕ is positive, then $P_{G,I}/P_{N,I} \geq P_{G,E}/P_{N,E}$. That is, the odds of voting guilty are greater among those included than among those excluded, which is the hypothesis. Conversely, if ϕ is negative, then the odds of voting guilty are greater among those excluded than among those included. It is important to notice that the magnitude of ϕ is of interest, since it indicates the extent to which includable jurors are harsher or more lenient than excludable jurors. The greater the absolute magnitude of ϕ, the greater the difference in tendency to vote guilty between includable and excludable jurors.

Having decided that the goal of the analysis is to determine the magnitude of ϕ, the next task is to create a statistical model relating the data in Table 4.1 to the P's. Let $m_{G,I}$ be the number of jurors who are includable and vote guilty, etc. A natural model for the first three columns of Table 4.1 is

$$\prod_{k\epsilon K, j\epsilon J} P_{k,j}^{m_{k,j}} \tag{4.2}$$

where $K = \{G, N\}$ and $J = \{I, E, U\}, P_{kj} \geq 0$, and $\sum_{k\epsilon K, j\epsilon J} P_{k,j} = 1$. Thus every juror falls into only one KJ category (e.g., an excludable juror who votes not guilty, etc.), which is reasonable and necessary. What is not reasonable is that the vote from juror to juror is assumed to be independent. This pretends as if each juror were hearing a different case, which is not true. Groups of twelve heard the same evidence, and this should lead those jurors to have somewhat similar views. This complexity will not be considered here.

The next question is how to model the missing data, that is, jurors for whom the death-penalty attitude is not available. As can be seen from Table 4.1, this is a substantial number of jurors, and consequently demands careful thought. If it were the case that among the jurors who vote guilty, the probability of non-response (i.e. no information from that juror regarding his/her attitude toward the death penalty) is the same whether they were truly includable, excludable, or unfair, then each such juror would contribute a factor $P_{G,I} + P_{G,E} + P_{G,U}$ to the likelihood. Now suppose that the probability of the juror of type k, j responding is $\alpha_{k,j}$. Then the full likelihood is proportional to

$$\prod (\alpha_{kj}P_{kj})^{m_{kj}} (\bar{\alpha}_{G,I}P_{G,I} + \bar{\alpha}_{G,E}P_{G,E} + \bar{\alpha}_{G,U}P_{G,U})^{m_G} \tag{4.3}$$
$$(\bar{\alpha}_{N,I}P_{N,I} + \bar{\alpha}_{N,E}P_{N,E} + \bar{\alpha}_{N,U}P_{N,U})^{m_N}$$

where m_G and m_N are the number of jurors for whom the death penalty attitude is missing that vote guilty and not guilty respectively and $\bar{\alpha}_{ij} = 1 - \alpha_{ij}$.

Some simplification of (4.3) is fortunately possible. First consider the probability of non-response relative to those of the largest group, those who would be included in a death penalty case. Hence define $\gamma_{G,E} = \bar{\alpha}_{G,E}/\bar{\alpha}_{G,I}$, $\gamma_{G,U} = \bar{\alpha}_{G,U}/\bar{\alpha}_{G,I}$ $\gamma_{N,E} = \bar{\alpha}_{N,E}/\bar{\alpha}_{N,I}$ and $\gamma_{N,U} = \bar{\alpha}_{N,U}/\bar{\alpha}_{N,I}$. In terms of the γ's (4.3) can be rewritten as

$$\left(\{\prod \alpha_{kj}^{m_{kj}}\}\bar{\alpha}_{G,I}^{m_G}\bar{\alpha}_{N,I}^{m_N}\right)\prod P_{kj}^{m_{kj}}\{P_{G,I} + \gamma_{G,E}P_{G,E} + \gamma_{G,U}P_{G,U}\}^{m_G} \tag{4.4}$$
$$\{P_{N,I} + \gamma_{N,E}P_{N,E} + \gamma_{N,U}P_{N,U}\}^{m_N}$$

The terms in round brackets in this product do not depend on the P's, and can hence be eliminated from the likelihood. The remainder, however, depends on the P's and on the α's through the γ's. Hence, (4.4) is considered to be the likelihood of the P's for various assumed values of γ's.

What attitude should one take toward the γ's? Recall that $\gamma_{G,E}$, for example, is defined to be $\bar{\alpha}_{G,E}/\bar{\alpha}_{G,I} = (1-\alpha_{G,E})/(1-\alpha_{G,I})$. Thus, $\gamma_{G,E}$ is the ratio of the probability that a juror voting guilty who is excludable has not provided data as to his/her death-penalty beliefs, to the probability that a juror voting guilty who is includable has not provided such data. If one believes that death-penalty attitudes (among jurors voting guilty) are not related to the probability of responding, then $\gamma_{G,E} = 1.0$. The supposition $\gamma_{G,E} = \gamma_{G,U} = \gamma_{N,E} = \gamma_{N,U} = 1.0$ will be the base case in the analysis to follow, but variations in γ's from .5 to 2 will also be studied to see how sensitive the distribution of ϕ, the quantity of interest, is to such variations in the γ's. That is, an exploration will be conducted of some fairly extreme hypothesized variations in the relationship between death penalty beliefs and tendency to convict with regard to failing to provide information regarding death penalty beliefs, to note the extent to which such variations would call the conclusions into question. It might be noted at this point that a non-Bayesian maximum-likelihood analysis can be conducted on equation (4.4), with various values of the γ's assumed. This amounts to a subjectivistic frequentistic position; subjectivistic in that one is prepared to use judgments and frequentistic in that the maximum-likelihood estimate would presumably be evaluated with a standard error calculated from a sampling distribution. This possibility will not be pursued further here.

The next issue to consider is the choice of a prior distribution over the six-dimensional simplex spanned by the P's. A convenient family of prior distributions to consider is the Dirichlet family, with density proportional to

$$\prod P_{kj}^{b_{kj}-1} \tag{4.5}$$

for various choices of the numbers b_{kj}. One possibility is the Jeffreys (1961) prior $b_{kj} = \frac{1}{2}$, which is intended to reflect 'ignorance' in a certain sense. A second prior reflects Savage (1962) personalistic position that the prior should represent a subjectivity reasonable view of the previous data. In this case, there are previous data (Kadane, 1983) on the proportion of jurors found in the national surveys to be includable (80%), excludable (12%), and unfair (8%). Additionally, there are data indicating that roughly 80% of the defendants in criminal trials are found guilty (Kalven and Zeisel, 1966). If there were independence between juror vote and death-penalty attitude these data would suggest the combination found in Table 4.2a.

Now the assumption of independence between death-penalty attitude and the first ballot vote is not reasonable. The Cowan et al. (1984) data, as reanalyzed by Kadane (1983), found an estimated odds ratio of 1.652, which corresponds to a log odds of about 0.5. Adjusting the numbers in Table 4.2a so that the log odds is of this order, while maintaining the marginals, yields Table 4.2b.

Finally, there is the question of how much weight to give the prior. Weights can range from almost zero (which gives virtually no weight to the prior information) to infinity (which gives no credence to the data from the study). Thus, the judgment of how much weight to give the prior is essentially a question of how much one believes the prior as against how much one believes the data.

Table 4.2

	Includable	Excludable	Unfair	Total
(a) Prior proportions supposing independence between juror vote and death-penalty attitudes, using previously known data				
Guilty	0.64	0.10	0.06	0.8
Not guilty	0.16	0.02	0.02	0.2
Total	0.80	0.12	0.08	1.0
(b) Prior proportions, not supposing independence				
Guilty	0.65	0.09	0.06	0.8
Not guilty	0.15	0.03	0.02	0.2
Total	0.80	0.12	0.08	1.0
(c) Informative prior hyper-parameters				
Guilty	9.75	1.35	0.90	12.0
Not guilty	2.25	0.45	0.30	3.0
Total	12.00	1.80	1.20	15.0

In this instance, the data that justify the marginals of Table 4.2 are essentially national, except for the Cowan *et al.* paper which is limited to Santa Clara County, California. While it is reasonable to have such national numbers as an expectation for jurors in Wake County, North Carolina, it is also reasonable to have greater uncertainty about them than about the national averages. As a rough guide, a weight of 15 is assigned here to the prior proportions, as if we had a flat prior informed by a survey of 15 Wake County jurors with proportions from Table 4.2b. The result is Table 4.2c, which records the prior hyperparameters used for the informative prior in this study.

Using integration methods described in Tierney et al. (1987), Figure 4.1 gives the posterior distribution of ϕ, taking the informative prior and all γ's equal to one. Recall that setting $\gamma_{k,j} = 1$ assumes that the probability of providing information about death-penalty attitudes is the same for the missing jurors, regardless of their actual death-penalty attitudes and regardless of what their vote would have been. There are several important things to notice in Figure 4.1. First is its general unimodal and normal shape. This allows the great simplification of reporting just means and standard deviations of ϕ under various assumptions, obviating the need for a plot each time. Second, the mean, at .23, is not very far from zero, when measured in units of standard deviation, here .41. Though the mean of .23 suggests some slight confirmation of the hypothesis, the extent of confirmation is meager. Using the normal approximation, $Pr\{\phi > 0\} = \Phi(.23/.41) = \Phi(.56) = .71$ where Φ is the normal cumulative distribution function (cdf). Thus, this calculation does not strongly support the main hypothesis that fair excludable jurors are more lenient than fair non-excludable jurors (i.e. $\phi > 0$). A second calculation, with the Jeffreys prior, indicates a mean of .25 and a standard deviation of .42. Thus in this instance which prior is used is not of substantive concern. The plot is visually nearly identical to that of Figure 4.1.

Before leaving the subject, I wish to explore the sensitivity of ϕ to the missing data parameters. Consider first the parameter $\gamma_{G,U} = \bar{\alpha}_{G,U}/\bar{\alpha}_{G,I} = (1 - \alpha_{G,U})/(1 - \alpha_{G,I})$, the ratio of the probability that the juror who would not decide a capital case fairly and impartially, and who votes guilty in the case actually heard, would fail to furnish death-penalty attitude information, to the probability that a juror who is includable in a capital jury case and who votes guilty in the case actually heard, would fail to do so. Similarly, consider $\gamma_{N,U} = \bar{\alpha}_{N,U}/\bar{\alpha}_{N,I} = (1 - \alpha_{N,U})/(1 - \alpha_{N,I})$. Since there are few unfair jurors, it is reasonable to expect that ϕ will be

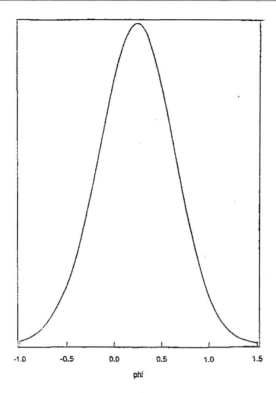

Figure 4.1: Posterior distribution of θ, with all γ's $= 1$, informative prior, full data set. The mean is 0.23, and the standard deviation is 0.41

Table 4.3

(a) Sensitivity of ϕ to changes in $\delta_{G,U}$ and $\delta_{N,U}$, holding $\delta_{G,E} = \delta_{N,E} = 1$							
	$\delta_{G,U}$					$\delta_{G,U}$	
	0.5	1	2		0.5	1	2
0.5	0.23	0.23	0.23	0.5	0.43	0.39	0.40
$\delta_{N,U}$ 1	0.23	0.23	0.23	$\delta_{N,U}$ 1	0.42	0.41	0.40
2	0.23	0.23	0.23	2	0.40	.037	0.40
	mean of ϕ				standard deviation of ϕ		

(b) Sensitivity of ϕ to changes in $\delta_{G,E}$ and $\delta_{N,E}$, holding $\delta_{\theta,U} = \delta_{N,U} = 1$							
	$\gamma_{G,E}$					$\gamma_{G,E}$	
	0.5	1	2		0.5	1	2
0.5	0.22	-0.28	-1.67	0.5	0.40	0.42	0.35
$\delta_{N,E}$ 1	0.74	0.23	-1.15	$\delta_{N,E}$ 1	0.42	0.41	0.36
2	2.01	1.50	0.11	2	0.34	0.33	0.27
	mean of ϕ				standard deviation of ϕ		

insensitive to variations in $\gamma_{G,U}$ and $\gamma_{N,U}$. To check this supposition, I calculate the mean and standard deviation of ϕ when these γ's are halved and doubled, as reported in Table 4.3a. Indeed, Table 4.3a indicates that ϕ is quite insensitive to these variations in $\gamma_{G,U}$ and $\gamma_{N,U}$. These calculations were done holding $\gamma_{G,E} = \gamma_{N,E} = 1.0$.

Next, consider the parameters $\gamma_{G,E}$ and $\gamma_{N,E}$. Both because there are more ex-

Table 4.4: Number of first ballot votes categorized by death penalty attitude and type of trial

	Includable	Excludable	Unfair	Unknown	Total
(a) Non-DWI trials					
G	86.5	8	7.89	150.27	252.66
NG	48.5	11	5.11	90.73	155.34
Total	135.0	19	13.0	241.00	408.00
(b) DWI Trials					
G	81	11	12	118.72	222.72
NG	27	0	0	26.28	53.28
Total	108	11	12	145.0	276.0

cludable jurors than unfair jurors, and because excludable jurors enter directly into ϕ, it is reasonable to expect greater sensitivity to these parameters than to $\gamma_{G,U}$ and $\gamma_{N,U}$. Holding the latter fixed at one, I compute the mean and standard deviation of ϕ, halving and doubling $\gamma_{G,E}$ and $\gamma_{N,E}$. Table 4.3b indicates very considerable sensitivity of posterior distribution of ϕ, principally the mean of the distribution, to changes in $\gamma_{N,E}$ and $\gamma_{G,E}$. Not surprisingly, down the diagonal from upper left to lower right of the matrix, where $\gamma_{N,E} = \gamma_{G,E}$, the effects are not so strong. But when $\gamma_{G,E}$ is halved and $\gamma_{N,E}$ is doubled, the estimated mean log odds is -1.67, suggesting that those included by the process of death qualification are substantially more lenient than those excluded. Conversely, when $\gamma_{G,E}$ is doubled and $\gamma_{N,E}$ is halved, the estimate mean-odds is 2.01, suggesting that they are substantially more harsh. Consequently, the following is concluded for the data set:

1. The choice between the Jeffreys prior and the informative prior does not matter much.
2. The choice of values of $\gamma_{G,U}$ and $\gamma_{N,U}$ does not matter much.
3. The choice of values of $\gamma_{G,E}$ and $\gamma_{N,E}$ matters quite a bit

Because the main case (γ's $= 1$) gives a small mean estimate (.23) with standard deviation of .41, and because it is so sensitive to $\gamma_{G,E}$ and $\gamma_{N,E}$, I conclude that, for the overall data set there is probably not a great distinction between those includable and those excludable in their degree of severity in judging cases. In other words, the hypothesis that jurors who would be excluded from a capital trial because of their death-penalty beliefs will be less likely to convict than death qualified jurors is not strongly supported.

Recall, however, that jurors listed the charges against the defendant on the verdict questionnaire. An examination of various charges revealed that 23 (approximately 40%) of the defendants had been charged with drunk driving. (The next most common crime, with which seven defendants were charged was assault with a deadly weapon.) Since drunk-driving trials accounted for such a substantial percentage of the trials studied, and also as a way of more fully exploring the relationship between attitudes toward the death-penalty and conviction proneness, the data were reanalyzed separately for drunk-driving (DWI) vs non-drunk-driving (non-DWI) trials.

Splitting the data into these two groups, DWI and non-DWI, gives the raw counts in Table 4.4. The totals are the numbers reported in Table 4.1 as they should be.

Within each group, the same likelihood [equation (4.4)], and the same log-odds target quantity, ϕ, is used in equation (4.1). Missing data can be handled as above, but the prior requires some attention. The Jeffreys prior would be unchanged. Con-

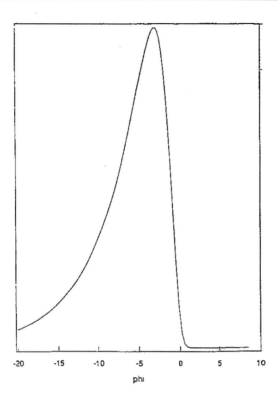

Figure 4.2: Posterior distribution of θ, with all γ's $= 1$, informative prior, DWI trials only. The mean is -5.77, and the standard deviation is 4.74

sidering that 40% of the trials were DWI, it is reasonable to take as the informative prior Table 4.4 with weight of 6 for the DWI trials, and with a weight of 9 for the non-DWI trials. Additionally, I take the informative priors over DWI and non-DWI trials as independent. Since the distinction between DWI and non-DWI trials was not anticipated when the data were collected and analyzed, the posteriors calculated are best understood in the sense of 'Had our prior been this one, our posterior, after seeing the data, would be the following'. This is consistent with much modern Bayesian thinking (see Dickey (1973); Poirier (1988); Hill (1990); Leamer (1978)).

Figures 4.2 and 4.3 give posterior distributions under the informative prior, for DWI and non-DWI trials respectively. All calculations were done with all γ's equal to 1. The results show that excluded jurors are substantially harsher than included jurors on DWI trials, and the reverse for non-DWI trials. In non-DWI trials, there are enough data to be relatively sure that the Jeffreys prior gives the same results. This is the case; the mean shifts from .88 to .90, while the standard deviation remains at .49. However, for the DWI trials, the data are sparse, so the effect of changing prior might be greater. Figure 4.4 displays the results. While the posterior distribution of ϕ is shifted to the right (and is less spread out), it is still skewed and still has little probability above zero. Hence, the same conclusion can be stated with this prior; in DWI trials, excludable jurors seem harsher than includable jurors.

Finally, I explore the sensitivity of these conclusions to the parameters γ. With respect to $\gamma_{G,U}$ and $\gamma_{N,U}$. Table 4.5 shows that again, the log odds, ϕ, is insensitive.

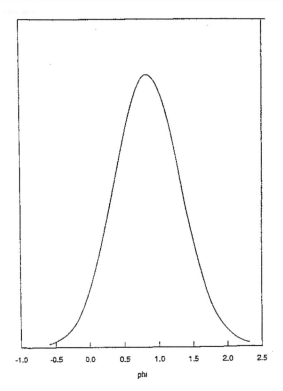

Figure 4.3: Posterior distribution of θ, with all γ's $= 1$, informative prior, non-DWI trials only. The mean is 0.88, and the standard deviation is 0.49

However, once again, with respect to $\gamma_{G,E}$ and $\gamma_{N,E}$, ϕ is more sensitive, as shown in Table 4.6.

Even though the mean of ϕ is sensitive to changes in $\gamma_{G,E}$ and $\gamma_{N,E}$, the difference between the mean of ϕ for DWI and non-DWI cases is huge. This indicates that whatever may be the most comfortable assumption about the γ's, there is a substantial difference between ϕ's, depending on the type of case heard. It should also be noted that the effects of differing γ's become strong only when quite unlikely assumptions are made, e.g. that an excludable juror who votes guilty is much more likely to have provided information about his/her death-penalty attitudes than is an includable juror who votes guilty.

Of interest is whether this difference in conviction proneness for drunk-driving vs. non-drunk-driving trials is accounted for by altered voting patterns of the excludables, the death-qualified jurors, or both. Returning to Table 4.4, note that the percentage of includables who vote guilty is similar for DWI (75%) and for non-DWI (64%) trials. However, the percentage of excludables who vote guilty in DWI trials (100%) is much greater than for non-DWI trials (42%). Thus, the pattern of results is primarily accounted for by the excludables, who convicted at a much lower rate in non-DWI trials but at a much higher rate in DWI trials than did the includable jurors.

4.3   Conclusions

That excludable and includable jurors behave so differently in DWI trials compared to non-DWI trials is unanticipated by the crime-control vs due-process continuum

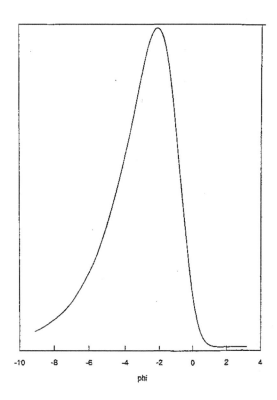

Figure 4.4: Posterior distribution of θ, with all γ's $= 1$, Jeffreys prior, DWI trials. The mean is -2.99, and the standard deviation is 2.04

Table 4.5: Sensitivity of ϕ to changes in $\gamma_{G,U}$ and $\gamma_{N,U}$, DWI Data and Non-DWI data. All Calculations with $\gamma_{G,\epsilon} = \gamma_{N,\epsilon} = 1$

		$\gamma_{G,U}$					$\gamma_{G,U}$		
		0.5	1.00	2.00			0.5	1.00	2.00
	0.5	-5.77	-5.77	-5.77		0.5	4.32	4.69	4.35
$\gamma_{N,U}$	1.00	-5.77	-5.78	-5.78	$\gamma_{N,U}$	1.00	4.47	4.78	4.50
	2.00	-5.77	-5.78	-5.77		2.00	5.01	4.63	4.53
		Mean of ϕ				Standard deviation of ϕ			

DWI data (spanning top)

Non-DWI data

		$\gamma_{G,U}$					$\gamma_{G,U}$		
		0.5	1.00	2.00		7 0.5	1.00	2.00	
	0.5	0.88	0.88	0.88		0.5	0.49	0.50	0.49
$\gamma_{N,U}$	1.00	0.88	0.88	0.88	$\gamma_{N,U}$	1.00	0.49	0.50	0.49
	2.00	0.88	0.88	0.88		2.0	0.50	0.50	0.50
		Mean of ϕ				Standard deviation of ϕ			

Table 4.6: Sensitivity of ϕ to changes in $\gamma_{G,E}$ and $\gamma_{N,E}$, DWI Data and Non-DWI data. All calculations with $\gamma_{G,U} = \gamma_{N,U} = 1$

			DWI data					
		$\gamma_{G,E}$					$\gamma_{G,E}$	
		0.5	1.00	2.00		0.5	1.00	2.00
	0.5	-5.70	-5.31	-3.53	0.5	4.51	4.25	4.95
$\gamma_{N,E}$	1.00	6.16	-5.78	-4.00	$\gamma_{N,U}$ 1.00	3.89	4.78	4.12
	2.0	-7.34	-6.96	-5.18	2.0	4.18	4.658	4.53
		Mean of ϕ				Standard deviation of ϕ		
			Non-DWI data					
		$\gamma_{G,E}$					$\gamma_{G,E}$	
		0.5	1.00	2.00		0.5	1.00	2.00
	0.5	0.85	1.43	2.64	0.5	0.48	0.50	0.44
$\gamma_{N,E}$	1.00	0.30	0.88	2.09	$\gamma_{N,E}$ 1.00	0.50	0.50	0.44
	2.00	-1.32	-0.74	0.47	2.0	0.42	0.41	0.36
		Mean of ϕ				Standard deviation of ϕ		

proposed by Packer and used by Fitzgerald and Ellsworth. While one may speculate about possible explanations, clearly further investigation is needed.

From a methodological standpoint, the subjective Bayesian approach succeeded in allowing exploration of alternative beliefs about the missing data. While opinions may legitimately differ about what values of the γ's to choose, this potential for disagreement is inherent to the situation of missing data. The necessary subjectivity is present not because agreement or objectivity is undesirable, but because it is unobtainable. In haste to obtain an 'objective' analysis, an objectivistic analysis typically sweeps the problem of missing data away and pretends that it was never there. But in doing so, it can vastly overstate the certainty with which the conclusions should be regarded.

Acknowledgements

The author thanks James Luginbuhl for supplying the data. The project was supported in part by the National Science Foundation and the National Institutes of Justice, US Department of Justice (Grant No. SES-8411106). Its completion was supported in part by NSF Grants DMS-9005858, DMS-8705646, DMS-8701770, SES-8900025 and ONR contract N00014-89-J-1851.

REFERENCES

Bishop, Y., Fienberg, S., and Holland, P. (1975). *Discrete Multivariate Analysis*. Cambridge: MIT Press. 76

Bronson, E. (1970). "On the conviction proneness and representativeness of the death-qualified jury: An empirical study of Colorado veniremen." *University of Colorado Law Review*, 42, 1–32. 74

Cowan, C., Thompson, W., and Ellsworth, P. (1984). "The effects of death qualification on jurors' predisposition to convect and on the quality of deliberation." *Law and Human Behavior*, 8, 53–80. 74, 77

Dickey, J. (1973). "Scientific reporting and personal probabilities: Student's hypothesis." *Journal of the Royal Statistical Society Series B*, 35, 285–305. 81

Fitzgerald, R. and Ellsworth, P. (1984). "Due process vs crime control: Death qualification and jury attitudes." *Law and Human Behavior*, 8, 31–52. 74, 75

Goldberg (Girsch), F. (1970). "Toward expansion of Witherspoon: Captial scruples, jury bias, and the use of psychological data to raise presumptions in the law." *Harvard Civil Rights – Civil Liberties Law Review*, 5, 53–69. 74

Gross, S. (1984). "Determining the neutrality of death-qualified juries: Judicial appraisal of empirical data." *Law and Human Behavior*, 8, 7–30. 74

Hill, B. (1990). "A theory of Bayesian data analysis." In *Bayesian and Likelihood Methods in Statistics and Econometrics: Essays in Honor of George Barnard*, eds. S. Geisser, S. P. J. Hodges, and A. Zellner. Amsterdam: North Holland. 81

Jeffreys, H. (1961). *Theory of Probability*. 3rd ed. Oxford, U.K.: Oxford University Press. 77

Jurow, G. (1970). "New data on the effect of a 'death-qualified' jury in the guilt determination process." *Harvard Law Review*, 84, 567–611. 74

Kadane, J. (1983). "Juries hearing death penalty cases: Statistical analysis of a legal procedure." *Journal of the American Statistical Association*, 78, 544–552. 74, 77

Kalven, H. and Zeisel, H. (1966). *The American Jury*. Boston: Little Brown. 75, 77

Leamer, E. (1978). *Specification Searches: Ad Hoc Inference with Nonexperimental Data*. New York: Wiley. 81

Little, R. and Rubin, D. (1987). *Statistical analysis with missing data*. New York: Wiley. 74

Luginbuhl, J. and Middendorf, K. (1988). "Death penalty beliefs and jurors' responses to aggravating and mitigating circumstances in capital trials." *Law and Human Behavior*, 12, 263–281. 74

Luginbuhl, J. and Powers, T. (1991). "Death scrupled jurors: They are (generally) less likely to convict than death qualified jurors." Unpublished manuscript. 74

Moran, G. and Comfort, J. (1986). "Neither 'tentative' nor 'fragmentary': Verdict preference of impaneled felony jurors as a function of attitude toward capital punishment." *Journal of Applied Psychology*, 71, 146–155. 74

Oberer, E. (1961). "Does disqualification of jurors for scruples against capital punishment constitute denial of fair trial on the issue of guilt?" *University of Texas Law Review*, 39, 545–567. 74

Packer, H. (1968). *The Limits of the Criminal Sanction*. Stanford: Stanford University Press. 75

Poirier, D. (1988). "Frequentist and subjectivist perspectives on the problems of model building in economics." *Journal of Economic Perspectives*, 3, 121–170. (with discussion). 81

Powers, T. and Luginbuhl, J. (1983). "Effects of death qualification in capital trials." *Social Action and the Law*, 9, 12–15. 74

Rubin, D. (1976). "Inference and missing data." *Biometrika*, 63, 581–592. 74

Savage, L. (1962). *The Foundations of Statistical Inference*. London: Methuen Monographs. 77

Tierney, L., Kass, R., and Kadane, J. (1987). "Interactive Bayesian analysis using accurate asymptotic approximations." In *Computer Science and Statistics: Proceedings of the 19th Symposium on the Interface*, ed. R. Heiberger, 15–21. Alexandria, VA: American Statistical Association. 78

Zeisel, H. (1968). *Some Data on Juror Attitudes toward Captial Punishment*. Monograph.

Center for Studies in Criminal Justice. University of Chicago Law School. 74

Cases

Hovey vs Superior Court of Alameda County 28 Cal. 3d 1, 616 P 2nd 1301, 168 Cal Rptr. 128 (1980).

Lockhart vs McCree, 476 US 162, 106 Sct. 1758, 90 LEd 2nd 137 (1986).

Epilogue

What is the scientific issue addressed?

Are jurors who are includable in death penalty cases (I) more likely to vote for conviction in ordinary (non-capital) cases than jurors who are excludable (E)?

Is justification given

a) the use of the data?

The data were collected in a survey permitted by the court. The difficult issue is that while the first ballot vote of each of the 684 jurors, data on their death-penalty attitudes were available for only 298.

b) the use of the likelihood and prior?

The likelihood is multinomial. Its principal fault is that it does not model the dependence arising from the fact that twelve jurors hear the same evidence. The priors on the main effects are based on previous studies, mainly national.

What robustness studies were conducted?

There is an extensive study of the effect of different assumptions about the relationship between missing data on death penalty attitudes and conviction proneness.

How was the computing done?

Uses the Laplace approximation.

If I were doing the problem today, how would I change the approach?

I was most concerned about the assumption of within jury independence. This was addressed in a follow-up paper.

Stasny, E., Kadane, J.B., and Frisch, K.S. (1998). "On the fairness of Death-Penalty Juries: A Comparison of Bayesian Models with Different Levels of Hierarchy and Various Mechanisms," *Journal of the American Statistical Association*, 93, 464–477.

What do I see as the contributions of this paper?

1. It addresses the scientific question, and finds that there is not a particularly strong relationship between death penalty attitudes and conviction proneness. It unexpectedly finds quite a strong relationship between death penalty attitudes and willingness to convict for drunk driving.

2. Philosophically, it shows how Bayesian analysis can be used to illuminate uncertainty occasioned by missing data in a survey, and specifically how to use an investigation of robustness to illuminate the modeling uncertainties.

Was Bayesian analysis useful here?

I claim "yes."

TEACHING SUGGESTIONS

References for theoretical ideas:

1. Multinomial distribution: *Principles* Section 2.9

2. Dirichlet-multinomial conjugate: *Principles* Section 8.9

3. Missing data as parameters: *Principles* Section 9.2

Exercises

1. What are the assumptions that go into the likelihood in equation 4.3? Which do you regard as the most questionable of those assumptions? What are the arguments for and against the most questionable assumption(s)?

2. What are the assumptions behind the three prior distributions displayed in Table 4.2? Which do you regard as closest to your own prior, and why?

3. Do you agree with the conclusion that there is not much difference in severity of judgment between the jurors who are excludable from death penalty cases and those who are not? Why or why not?

4. The distinction between DWI cases was not anticipated when the study was begun. To what extent do you think it is legitimate to conclude that excludable jurors are more harsh on DWI cases and less harsh on other cases than includable jurors? Does it matter whether the distinction between DWI cases and other cases was thought about in advance?

Chapter 5

Missing Data in the Forensic Context (1997)

Foreword

I had worked with the Public Defender's office in Gloucester County, New Jersey, previously on a challenge about whether the juries there are chosen from a pool that adequately represented the community. So I had a good working relationship with the lawyers when they called me to work on this case. I managed to interest Norma Terrin, then a member of our department at Carnegie Mellon, to work with me on it.

The case was about whether blacks were being stopped at disproportionately high rates on the southern end of the New Jersey Turnpike, between exits 1 and 3. To see whether this was so, we had to ascertain the proportion of cars driven by Blacks, and the proportion of stops of cars that were driven by blacks. The former was found from two studies. In the first, 21 randomly selected 2.5 hour sessions at four stationary sites found 13.5% had a black occupant. In the second, an observer set his cruise control for 60 (the speed limit was 55), and found that over 98% of the observed cars passed him (i.e., nearly everyone speeds), and of those, 15% had a black occupant. So we took 15% as a reasonable estimate of the proportion of blacks driving.

Ascertaining the proportion of stops of cars driven by blacks was more difficult. On 35 randomly selected days, there were 892 stops, of which 127 were of blacks, 148 of whites (actually everyone not black), and 617 of people whose race was unknown. There were two reasons for the missing data: some because the police had a policy of destroying records after a fixed period of time, and some because the officer stopping a car failed to radio the race of the driver, contrary to police standard procedure.

Ignoring the missing data, the paper shows that

$$\theta = \frac{P(\text{stop}|\text{black})}{P(\text{stop}|\text{white})} = 4.86$$

indicating that blacks are more likely to be stopped than whites. However, because of the large amount of missing data, we parameterized the odds of having a stopped driver's race reported if black to that if white. Then we showed that even if this were as large as three, the posterior on θ still put over 99% probability on blacks being more likely to be stopped than whites.

The hearing on this case extended for more than six months. In the end, much to the dismay of the Attorney General's Office and the New Jersey State Police, the court found that the police were illegally stopping blacks disproportionately. The Attorney General announced that this was a terrible insult to the State Police, and that he would appeal. A year and a half later, a week before the appeal was to be heard, the Governor and Attorney General held a press conference in which they announced that the state had done its own study, which corroborated our findings, and that they were withdrawing their appeal. Later New Jersey entered a consent decree with the Civil Rights Division of the Department of Justice, and promised to clean up its act.

Later research (Kadane and Lamberth, 2009) shows some improvement, but continuing evidence of racial disparity in stops on the New Jersey Turnpike.

While this paper addressed an important social problem, namely one aspect of racism in one state, it is also important philosophically. Paper 3 reports a Bayesian analysis that was ready to go to court, but did not because the case was settled. Paper 4 addresses an issue that was of interest in social psychology, but the Supreme Court had already ruled was of no interest to it legally. By contrast, the material in this Bayesian paper was presented in court, and survived cross-examination, It is thus an answer to the question sometimes raised of whether Bayesian work could be effective in court.

Where is she now? Norma Terrin is Director of Biostatistics, Epidemiology and Research Design Center in the Institute for Clinical Research and Health Policy Studies at Tufts Medical Center, and Professor at Tufts University School of Medicine and the Sackler School of Graduate Biomedical Sciences.

This paper was originally published in the *Journal of the Royal Statistical Society, Series A,* **160**, pp. 351–357. Permission to republish not required.

References:

Collum, J. (2010). *The Black Dragon: Racial Profiling Exposed.* Sun River, Montana: Jigsaw Press.

Kadane, J. and Lamberth, J. (2009). "Are Blacks egregious speeding violators at extraordinary rates in New Jersey?" *Law, Probability and Risk,* 8, 139–152.

Terrin, N. and Kadane, J. (1998). "Counting cars in a legal case involving differential enforcement." *Chance,* 11, 3, 25–27.

Published Paper

J.B. Kadane and Norma Terrin

Abstract

Missing survey data is difficult to present in court. This paper reflects testimony prepared and given by the authors in a case alleging that the New Jersey State Police were differentially stopping and arresting blacks at the southern end of the New Jersey Turnpike. A Bayesian technique with informative priors is used to examine the sensitivity of the inference to the missing data.

Keywords: Bayesian analysis, identification problem, racially biased traffic stopping

5.1 Introduction

Data collection efforts, whether by survey, administrative records, or other methods, often suffer from missing data (Rubin, 1987; Little and Rubin, 1987). Two classical methods to deal with such missing data are extreme: either

(a) ignore the fact that some data are missing, or

(b) declare the data set uninterpretable because of the missing data problem.

Neither of these reactions is likely to be faithful to the uncertainty introduced by missing data: it adds some uncertainty, but there is usually some inferential content to the survey even with some data missing.

These extreme reactions are likely to lead to unenlightening courtroom battles among statisticians. Whichever side wishes to use the data will choose (a) above, while the other side will find an equal and opposite statistician to argue for (b). This in turn may lead to a search for 'statistical rules', saying what proportion of the data must be missing to shift the appropriate treatment from (a) to (b).

Rather than presuming complete knowledge of the missing data, as in (a), or no knowledge at all, as in (b), one may consider various alternatives for the distribution of the missing observations, eliminating only the implausible ones.

This paper discusses the presentation in court of a Bayesian analysis of this type. The next section describes the case, the analysis offered in court, and the response of the court. Some general conclusions are given in the third section.

5.2 The New Jersey Turnpike Case

In the case, (Re: State *versus* Pedro Soto, *et al.*) the New Jersey Public Defender's Office moved to suppress evidence against seventeen black defendants (principally on charges of transporting illegal drugs) on the grounds of selective enforcement, i.e. that blacks were more likely to be stopped by the police than were others, on the southern end of the New Jersey Turnpike.

US law on discrimination is most active in the areas of jury participation and employment issues. In both these areas, the law distinguishes between discriminatory *intent* and discriminatory *impact*.

Discriminatory intent is concerned with an expressed intention to discriminate. If a state had a law forbidding blacks to serve on juries, or if an employer had a policy (expressed orally or in writing) stating that it did not hire blacks, nothing further would be required before the law would respond. The analog here would be if there were written or oral instructions to the state police to target law enforcement against blacks. The main evidence in this case is not of this nature.

The other main way of showing discrimination is by showing discriminatory impact. In such a case, what is to be shown is that persons similarly situated have a different probability of gaining something good (jury service or employment), or avoiding something bad (traffic stop and/or arrest), and that those probabilities differ systematically by race. However, 'similarly situated' requires explication.

In employment discrimination cases, a substantial paper trail is generated in the usual processes of hiring and promotion. Generally people apply in writing for jobs, and their applications state various facts about them, including their qualifications. In promotion cases, the employer generally has records relating to the employee's performance on the job. These written materials mean that substantial evidence can be brought to bear on issues of "similar situation" in employment cases. In traffic cases, the analog to an application is the appearance of an automobile and its behavior, how it is driven. The "applicants" for stopping and/or arrest do not leave a paper trail; in particular, it is very difficult to compare the 'qualifications' of 'successful applicants' (those stopped and/or arrested) with those of 'unsuccessful' applicants (those not stopped and not arrested).

Two studies were undertaken by the defense: one designed to estimate the proportion of cars on the southern end of the New Jersey turnpike carrying black occupants, and the other to estimate the fraction of traffic law violators who were black or carrying black passengers. The traffic study involved 21 randomly selected $2\frac{1}{2}$-hour sessions at four sites on the turnpike in daylight hours of June, 1993. Some 42000 vehicles were observed, of which 13.5% had a black occupant.

In the violator study, an observer drove at 60 miles per hour (the speed limit is 55 miles per hour) and observed how many cars passed him and how many he passed. Of all these 2096 cars, 2062 passed him (98.1%), and of these 15% had a black occupant. Because all these 2062 represent cars that can be stopped, we took 15% as a reasonable number for the proportion of cars containing blacks to be expected in randomly chosen stopped cars. Since virtually everyone on the turnpike was driving faster than the speed limit, the New Jersey State Police could legally stop virtually anyone they chose. The broad racial consistency between the two data sets (13.5%, 15%) lent credibility to both, in our opinion.

Finally, data collected on stops by the state police were analyzed for 35 randomly selected days between April 1988 and May 1991. Limited to the area between exits 1 and 3 on the turnpike (which is where the traffic study and violator study were done), this showed 892 stops being made, of which 127 were of blacks, 148 of whites and others, and 617 of persons of unknown race.

Concentrating first on just the racially identified stops, 46.2% were of blacks. To appreciate this number, a simple application of Bayes theorem yields

$$\Theta = \frac{P(\text{stop} \mid \text{black})}{P(\text{stop} \mid \text{white})} = \frac{P(\text{black} \mid \text{stop})P(\text{stop})/P(\text{black})}{P(\text{white} \mid \text{stop})P(\text{stop})/P(\text{white})}$$

$$= \frac{.462/(.15)}{.538/(.85)} = 4.86. \tag{5.1}$$

For brevity, the term 'white' refers to anyone who would not be identified as 'black' by the state police.

Thus, by this calculation, a black driver was 4.86 times as likely to be stopped on the New Jersey turnpike, strongly suggesting a racially non-neutral policy. The difficulty with this result is that 0.462 in equation (5.1) is actually P(black|stop and race identified), not P(black|stop).

We need to be concerned about whether the large amount of missing data (69.1%) might disturb the analysis. That such a large portion of the data is missing is due to the routine destruction of the radio logs for 10 of the 35 days, and to the failure of the state police on the other days to follow its own rules to radio the race of occupants of any car stopped. None-the-less, such a large amount of missing data, in the absence of further analysis, might create a legitimate doubt about the conclusion.

To advise the court about the likely impact of the missing data, we created the following model. The key question is the possible bias in race reporting. Let

$$
\begin{aligned}
r_1 &= P(\text{race reported} \mid \text{black and stopped}) \\
r_2 &= P(\text{race reported} \mid \text{white and stopped}) \\
t &= P(\text{black} \mid \text{stopped}) \\
1 - t &= P(\text{white} \mid \text{stopped}) \\
n_1 &= \text{number of blacks reported as stopped} \\
n_2 &= \text{number of whites reported as stopped} \\
n_3 &= \text{number of persons stopped whose race is not reported}
\end{aligned}
$$

Three events may occur with a stop: the person stopped is black and the race is reported, the person stopped is white and the race is reported, or the person who is stopped does not have their race reported. These events have respective probabilities $r_1 t$, $r_2(1 - t)$ and $(1 - r_1)t + (1 - r_2)(1 - t)$. Since, given these parameters, the stops are regarded as independent and identically distributed, the likelihood function is trinomial:

$$
(r_1 t)^{n_1} \{r_2(1 - t)\}^{n_2} \{(1 - r_1)t + (1 - r_2)(1 - t)\}^{n_3}. \tag{5.2}
$$

Treating the parameters as t, r_1 and r_2, the goal is a distribution for Θ, as in equation (5.1), which in this notation is

$$
\Theta = \frac{t/0.15}{(1 - t)/.85} = \frac{0.85t}{0.15(1 - t)}. \tag{5.3}
$$

It turns out that $\log \Theta$ is more convenient, as the posterior distributions for it are closer to symmetric.

Observe that the trinomial distribution has two dimensions of information, whereas the parameter space has three: r_1, r_2 and t. This consequence of incomplete information can be viewed as a problem of lack of identifiability. However, lack of identifiability is not a great difficulty for subjective Bayesians (Kadane, 1975).

Finally, it is necessary to choose the prior distribution for the parameters r_1, r_2 and t. What is reasonable to assume about them?

Using the violator study as an anchor, we center our prior for t at 0.15. This is an estimate of the proportion of cars violating the speed limit on the New Jersey turnpike that contain blacks, which is larger than the proportion of violating cars driven by blacks. Hence, using 0.15 as an estimate of the proportion of violating cars driven by blacks tends to exonerate the police. The beta family of distributions with mean 0.15 is a logical choice, as the distributions are concentrated on (0,1). The parameter in this beta family is a scale parameter, which can be discussed in terms of the standard deviation.

We present two rather different choices for the standard deviation of t. In court, we presented an analysis based on a standard deviation of 0.064, which corresponds to a beta (4.5, 25.5) distribution. We later explored a much larger standard deviation,

0.30, which corresponds to a beta (0.06,0.35). This latter choice can be criticized on the grounds that it forces most of the probability for t to be close to 0 or 1. These specifications are referred to below as 'small' and 'large' standard errors respectively. The analysis to come shows that the results of these two priors are indistinguishable.

Among the possible relationships between r_1 and r_2, which are plausible? Perhaps those whose race was reported are representative of all those stopped. In that case, $r_1 = r_2$, or equivalently,

$$\text{odds } (r_1) = \frac{r_1}{1 - r_1} = \frac{r_2}{1 - r_2} = \text{ odds } (r_2).$$

Equivalently, this assumption means that being black and having one's race recorded are independent, given that one is stopped. It is possible, however, that the race of the occupants of a stopped car affects the probability that the officer will report race. We do not presume to know in which direction the probability would be altered, if at all. Giving the benefit of the doubt to the prosecution, we explored the consequence of blacks having twice, and even three times, the odds of whites for having their race reported. Let r be the ratio of the odds of having a stopped driver's race reported if black to that if white, i.e.

$$r = \frac{r_1 / (1 - r_1)}{r_2 / (1 - r_2)}.$$

To complete the model, a uniform distribution is taken on r_2 (other beta distributions for r_2 could be used; again the results are robust to this choice as long as var(r_2) is appreciable).

Once the likelihood and prior are specified, the joint posterior distribution of the parameters r_1, r_2 and t is proportional to their product.

The calculations were conducted for the three cases mentioned above: odds of race reporting of a stop given black as one, two, or three times that of whites, i.e. $r = 1, 2$, and 3. The upshot is that, even with odds of race reporting for blacks at 3 times that for whites, the probability of blacks being stopped more often than whites (i.e. $P(\log \Theta > 0)$) is over 0.99. The posterior distribution of $\log \Theta$ for each case is shown in Figs 5.1 and 5.2. A comparison of these figures shows that the results are virtually identical for the two standard error cases.

We used the Laplace approximation (Kass et al., 1988) as implemented in X-LISP-STAT (Tierney, 1990) to calculate the posterior marginal distribution of $\log \Theta$; Fig 5.1 was produced from S-PLUS (Spector, 1994).

There are several things to notice from Figs 5.1 and 5.2. When $r = 1$, so that the odds of having one's race reported if stopped does not depend on race, there is a distribution for $\log \Theta$. This is a result of the fact that data are missing, which introduces uncertainty. As r increases, the curve of $\log \Theta$ shifts to the left. This is because, as r increases, it becomes increasingly more likely that each person stopped whose race is not reported was white; hence increasingly more of the races of missing persons are imputed to be white. Only if all the stopped drivers with missing race data are assumed to be white does the proportion of blacks stopped, 14.2%, approximate the 15% found in the violator study. But this corresponds to $r = \infty$, which is not plausible.

A referee suggested the following alternative formulation: since $L = \log \Theta$ is a function of t, attention can be focused on the posterior distribution of t:

$$p(t \mid n_1, n_2, n_3) = \sum_m p(t \mid n_1, n_2, n_3, m) p(m \mid n_1, n_2, n_3),$$

where m is the number of blacks stopped but not recorded. The first factor is binomial

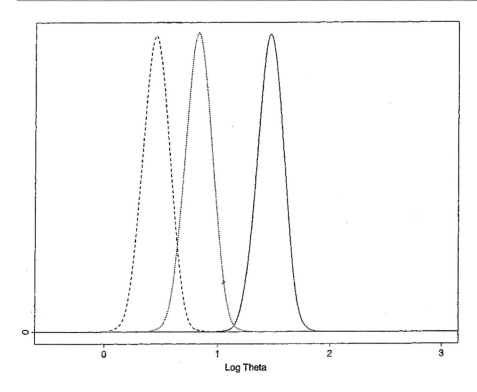

Figure 5.1: Posterior distribution of $L = \log \Theta$ as a function of r, the ratio of odds of race reporting if stopped and black to that of whites, when the prior standard deviation of t is small: ———, $r = 1$; ..., $r = 2$; ---- , $r = 3$.

with parameters t and $n_1 + n_2 + n_3$, with $n_1 + m$ 'successes' and $n_2 + n_3 - m$ 'failures'. Then attention focuses on the second factor. Although we did not use this method of decomposing the problem, we agree that it may well prove to be a useful alternative.

Judge Robert E. Francis of the Superior Court of New Jersey, in an unpublished opinion, accepted our argument and found for the defense. The case is on appeal.

5.3 Presentation to Court of Surveys with Missing Data

What has Bayesian analysis contributed in this context?

It has brought to light more of the real uncertainty engendered by the missing data. For example, taking classical solution (a) (i.e. ignoring the fact that some data are missing) yields an estimate for Θ of 4.86 (or $\log \Theta = 1.58$) as shown in equation (5.1). By contrast, if Θ is viewed as a random variable, the posterior distribution for $\log \Theta$ shown in Fig 5.1 for the case of equal odds of non-reporting for the two racial groups, has substantial variance.

Presenting the evidence this way, rather than as an estimator with a standard error, makes it more accessible to the court. Even those without statistical training can understand the conclusion of our analysis, that it is almost certain that blacks are more likely to be stopped than whites, and that we arrive at this conclusion even when our initial assumptions favor the prosecution. By contrast, a detailed explanation of a confidence interval would be much more difficult, i.e. an interval with stochastic end points having the property that before the data are observed 95% of the times that

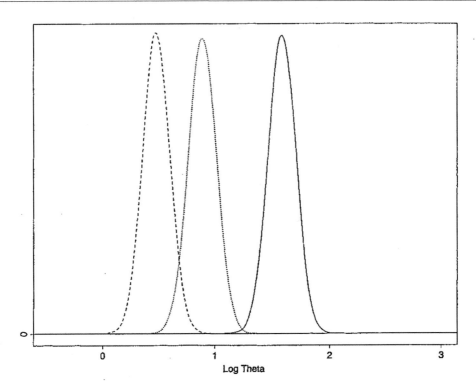

Figure 5.2: Posterior distribution of $L = \log \Theta$ as a function of r, the ratio of odds of race reporting if stopped and black to that of whites, when the prior standard deviation of t is large: _____, $r = 1$; ..., $r = 2$; ....., $r = 3$.

such an interval is used it will contain the true parameter value, the interval being evaluated after the data have been observed.

The Bayesian method by itself will not cure the problem of equal and opposing statisticians. Each side could propose its own models (likelihoods and priors), which might lead to opposite conclusions. Then the matter could come down to rhetoric, of persuading the trier of fact that one's assumptions and conclusions are the most reasonable.

Acknowledgments

We thank the New Jersey Public Defender's Office in Gloucester County, New Jersey, for involving us in the case: Jeffrey Wintner, Fred Last, and Justin Louchry. We also thank Professor John Lamberth of Temple University for his advice and help and Dr. C. Aitken of Edinburgh University for very useful comments.

REFERENCES

Kadane, J. (1975). "The Role of Identification in Bayesian Theory." In *L.J. Savage Memorial Volume Studies in Bayesian Statistics and Econometrics*, eds. S. Fienberg and A. Zellner, 175–191. Amsterdam: North Holland. 93

Kass, R., Tierney, L., and Kadane, J. (1988). "Asymptotics in Bayesian computation." In *Bayesian Statistics 3*, eds. J. Bernardo, M. DeGroot, D. Lindley, and A. Smith, 261–278. Oxford: Oxford University Press. 94

Little, R. and Rubin, D. (1987). *Statistical analysis with missing data*. New York: Wiley. 91

Rubin, D. (1987). *Multiple Imputation for Nonresponse in Surveys*. New York: Wiley. 91

Spector, P. (1994). *An Introduction to S and S-Plus*. Belmont: Duxbury. 94

Tierney, L. (1990). *Lisp-Stat: an Object-oriented Environment for Statistical Computing and Dynamic Graphics*. New York: Wiley. 94

Epilogue

What is the scientific issue addressed?

Whether the New Jersey State Police were stopping cars driven by blacks (African-Americans) at disproportional rates at the southern end of the New Jersey Turnpike.

Is justification given for

a) the use of the data?

There are three data sources used in this paper. The first two aimed at ascertaining the proportion of cars on the southern end of the New Jersey Turnpike driven by blacks. A stationary survey found 13.5%; a rolling survey found 15%. That these numbers are close gave us confidence that they were roughly correct. The third data source was records of the State Police concerning the race of those stopped. This data had recorded 892 stops, with race not recorded for 617 of them.

b) the use of the likelihood and prior?

The likelihood is trinomial, treating each stop as independent with three possible outcomes: black, white (which here means not black), and unknown. The prior for the proportion of blacks stopped is centered at the empirical proportion of black drivers, 15%. The priors for the parameters governing missingness are subject to a robustness study.

What robustness studies were performed?

The prior specifications were varied rather substantially, but the substantive conclusions were essentially unchanged.

What computational methods were used?

The Laplace approximation.

If I were doing this problem today, how would I change the approach?

I would not.

What do I see as the major contributions of this paper?

1. It answered the scientific question. It found that the New Jersey State Police were disproportionately stopping blacks on the southern end of the New Jersey Turnpike. This finding had major legal implications.

2. Philosophically, the experience showed that Bayesian analysis could withstand cross-examination in court in a high-stakes legal matter.

Was Bayesian analysis useful in this problem?

My answer is "yes."

TEACHING SUGGESTIONS

References for theoretical ideas:

1. Multinomial distribution (here trinomial): *Principles* Section 2.9

2. Laplace approximation: *Principles* Section 8.11

3. Missing data as parameters: *Principles* Section 9.2

4. Identification: *Principles* Section 8.3

5. Beta distribution: *Principles* Section 8.9

Exercises

1. Write an R program to calculate the posterior distributions in Figure 5.1, using a grid method.

2. Use the referee suggestion at the bottom of page 90 to redo the calculations. How amenable to analysis is the second factor?

3. Bayesian methods are presented, both in this volume and in *Principles* as a reflection of the opinions of the writer. Are there special issues involved in presenting such analyses in court, in your opinion? What are they?

4. In specific, with respect to this case, do you think that the court was presented with a fair and responsible analysis of the data?

5. If you were working as a statistician for the State of New Jersey on this case, how would you attack the analysis in this paper?

Chapter 6

Bayesian Demography: Projecting the Iraqi Kurdish Population, 1977–1990 (1997)

Foreword

This paper is a good example of a project that produced something that none of us could have done alone.

Beth Osborne Daponte is a demographer who had been working at the Census Bureau before she came to Carnegie Mellon. At the Census Bureau, she had the job of producing population estimates for Iraq. Since this was just after the First Gulf War, this entailed estimating the civilian and military casualties of that war. Her estimates were higher than those of the Defense Department and enraged Dick Chaney, then President George H.W. Bush's Secretary of Defense. After an acrimonious fight involving human rights organizations, lawyers and various levels of the federal bureaucracy, she came to CMU.

She was concerned that the traditional approach in demography assumed values for such key variables as the starting population (disaggregated by age and sex), fertility rates, age-specific mortality rates, and immigration and emigration. Then projecting the population is a simple matter of arithmetic. But this is not very useful to others, who need to know what is reasonable to assume about each of those quantities, and how much uncertainty there might be about them.

What was reasonable to assume was often discussed privately between professors and their graduate students, but not made public or published. Naturally, I thought that Bayesian methods could be used to model the uncertainty in the inputs, and therefore could show the consequent uncertainty in the outputs. To get beyond this general idea, we need a specific example to address.

Beth was aware of the Anfal, a particularly brutal campaign of the government of Saddam Hussein against the Kurdish people of Iraq in 1988. If we could project what the Kurdish population would have been in 1990 had the Anfal not taken place, we would have a gauge of the number of Kurds killed in the Anfal. It was possible that this information would have been used in a genocide trial of Saddam Hussein, although of course history took a different turn.

One of the requirements of our Ph.D. program in statistics is to do a year-long Advanced Data Analysis (ADA) project on data that has not been analyzed before, with a client outside the department and a statistical advisor. One of the goals of the ADA is to introduce students to the issues that attend to real data, including missing data, recording errors, modeling and computation.

To help us turn our vision of a study into reality, we recruited Lara Wolfson, then a Ph.D. student in statistics, to do her ADA project with us on this topic. It turned out that there were many sources of uncertainty, as the paper elaborates. What is important about it is that each of the modeling choices is made explicit and is justified. Of course, another demographer knowledgeable about Iraq might make different choices. Then at least it would be clear what the disagreement would be about. Furthermore, the consequences of both sets of assumptions could be compared. (I have not seen any reanalysis of this problem yet, however.) More generally, it is an example of going into detail about what assumptions are reasonable, and how much uncertainty there is about the inputs of a demographic study.

Where are they now? Beth Osborne Daponte is owner of a consulting firm, Social Science Consultants. Lara Wolfson works for Merck in its Outcomes Research group, focusing on pediatric vaccines.

This paper was originally published in the *Journal of the American Statistical Association*, **92**, pp. 1256–1267. Permission to republish granted by the American Statistical Association.

Published Paper

B.O. Daponte, J.B. Kadane and L.J. Wolfson

Abstract

Projecting populations that have sparse or unreliable data, such as those of many developing countries, presents a challenge to demographers. The assumptions that they make to project data-poor populations frequently fall into the realm of "educated guesses," and the resulting projections, often regarded as forecasts, are valid only to the extent that the assumptions on which they are based reasonably represent the past or future, as the case may be. These traditional projection techniques do not incorporate a demographer's assessment of uncertainty in the assumptions. Addressing the challenges of forecasting a data-poor population, we project the Iraqi Kurdish population using a Bayesian approach. This approach incorporates a demographer's uncertainty about past and future characteristics of the population in the form of elicited prior distributions.

Keywords: Census Data, Cohort-component projections, Elicitation, Forecasting, Population, Population projections, Subjective opinion, Vital rates.

6.1 Introduction

The problem of forecasting populations haunts demographers. To assure readers that they cannot forecast, demographers instead "project" populations, meaning that given a set of assumptions, demographers perform the arithmetic for the users of their figures. However, "a demographer makes a projection, and his reader uses it as a forecast; does the demographer's intention or the reader's use determine whether projection or forecasting has occurred?" (Keyfitz, 1972, p. 353) We, like others before us (Keyfitz, 1972; Hoem, 1973; Stoto, 1983) regard the class of population projections that use the most likely scenario as forecasts. Other classes of projections performed to demonstrate the result of hypothetical or unlikely circumstances should not be considered forecasts, but merely arithmetic exercises.

Population forecasts are used for two purposes: to suggest what a population will look like in the future, and to suggest what the population has looked like in the past when data of reasonable quality for the period are not available. Given that in fact demographers often forecast populations, this paper presents a method to create forecasts that model a demographer's uncertainty about the forecast.

In this article we expand on the work of Pflaumer (1988) and take Land (1986) up

Beth Osborne Daponte is with the University of Pittsburgh, Joseph B. Kadane is Professor at the Department of Statistics, Carnegie Mellon University and Lara J. Wolfson is Assistant Professor at the Department of Statistics and Actuarial Science, University of Waterloo. We thank Peter Johnson of the U.S. Census Bureau for helpful conversations and for sharing with us the computer software projection package, RUP. Joost Hiltermann, Shorsh Resool, and Middle East Watch shared with us their knowledge and materials on the Iraqi Kurdish population. We thank Heidi Rhodes Sestrich for her patient secretarial support. We thank Sam Preston, Noreen Goldman, and the referees for their helpful comments on previous versions of this paper. This research was supported in part by NSF Grants DMS-9303557 and SES-9123370 and by Office of Naval Research Contract N00014-89-J-1851.

on his suggestion to integrate statistical and demographic methodologies in performing population projections. Land wrote that "statisticians and demographers need to take a much more statistical perspective on population forecasting. A full statistical forecast of an uncertain future population quantity even if based entirely on informed expert judgments would be a probability density for it....This suggests, for instance, that it would be instructive to examine the implicit Bayesian decision theoretic basis that lies beneath the production of projection intervals..." (p. 899). We also show how current methods used by demographers can be adapted to integrate a Bayesian approach.

The Bayesian approach expresses uncertainty in terms of probability distributions. These distributions generally reflect the views of the analyst, although in some cases they can model the views that others do or might hold. Because they represent personal opinion, they are referred to as "personalistic" or "subjective" in the Bayesian literature (Savage (1954, p. 27)).

Conducting Bayesian demographic analysis promises three important advantages. First, utilizing this approach would enhance communication among demographers. Making one's beliefs explicit using probability distributions allows other demographers to observe exactly how one views the sources of uncertainty in the phenomenon. Others can then know on what they agree or disagree. The reasons given for particular probability distributions can be an important source of insight. The second important advantage of Bayesian demographic analysis pertains to the user. The consequence of the explicitly probabilistic inputs is explicitly probabilistic output. Population "projections" become forecasts with explicit probability distributions. These can be used in whatever inference or decision the users face, if the input probabilities are acceptable.

A third advantage of a Bayesian analysis is its greater flexibility in reflecting demographic beliefs. Classical models either include or exclude a parameter about which no prior is expressed, which is often equivalent to expressing certainty about its value. Using probability distributions permits one to express states of knowledge in between these two alternatives.

Hyppölä, Tunkelo and Törnqvist (1949) (see also Tornquist's appendix in Hoem (1973)) preceded us in developing a subjective approach to population forecasting. To forecast the population of Finland to the year 2000, they used the 20th, 50th, and 80th percentiles of their (subjective) fertility distributions, together with what they took to be pessimistic, most likely, and optimistic assumptions about mortality, to produce what they took to be the 10th, 50th, and 90th percentiles in the resulting population, but they had no firm basis for this claim. We think that Hyppölä et al. were years ahead of their time in what they wanted to do and had they had access to adequate computing power, they might have performed a forecast similar to the one we present herein.

This article offers a case study in projecting the Iraqi Kurdish population under a certain hypothetical scenario explained later. We first discuss current practices in performing population forecasts. Then, we consider ways that others have proposed to integrate uncertainty into the forecasts. We conduct a forecast of the Kurdish population of Iraq from 1977–1990 that integrates Bayesian and demographic analysis. To conclude, we present summary results for the projection. We project the Iraqi Kurdish population only to 1990 so one can consider what the Iraqi Kurdish population would have looked like prior to the 1991 Persian Gulf War had the repression of the Kurds since 1977– and particularly the Anfal (a state-sponsored campaign of violence against the Iraqi Kurds described later) not occurred. This projection is part of a larger project that has the goal of estimating the detrimental demographic effects attributable to the Anfal and other oppression of the Kurds. The specific effects estimated (e.g., excess mortality and diminished fertility) depend on the form of data on the post-Anfal Kurdish population. For example, the population projection reveals the number of Iraqi

Kurds that would have died had "normal" mortality levels prevailed. If and when data on actual mortality among Iraqi Kurds during this time period become available, the magnitude of excess mortality can be calculated. Thus the population that we project is hypothetical.

The Iraqi Kurdish population lacks high quality data, making it similar to the populations of many developing countries. Demographers studying the populations of developing countries are often confronted with fragmentary or incomplete information on the population. This is the case in the Lesotho highlands water project, which successfully applied this methodology (Daponte and Wolfson, 1995).

6.2   Current Practices

In any population projection, a demographer makes a number of decisions with respect to the population processes involved. These decisions are subjective guesses of what is most likely to occur based on what already has occurred in the population and on professional opinion.

The first decision a demographer makes when projecting a population is which type of projection to perform. Although mathematical functions are sometimes used (Smith and Sincich, 1990), in general the cohort-component method is the preferred procedure (Arriaga, 1993, p. 309). The U.S. Census Bureau, United Nations, and World Bank all perform cohort-component projections. We focus our discussion on this class of projections.

Projecting a population using the cohort-component method involves a number of steps, each of which utilizes the demographer's expert opinion. First, "a component projection requires a population properly distributed by sex and age to serve as the base population for the starting date of the projection" (Arriaga, 1993, p. 314). This population is usually based on the most recent census, "moved" from the census date to midyear (July 1) and adjusted for underenumeration and overenumeration and for age misreporting. The raw census data are evaluated in light of recent fertility and mortality surveys. The demographer relies on scientific knowledge and experience to judge the quality of the raw data and makes proper adjustments subjectively. Where one demographer may adjust the data in a certain way to meet his or her interpretation of "proper," another may adjust the data differently.

Second, the demographer makes assumptions regarding the levels and patterns of fertility that will (or have) prevail(ed) since the census date. Often, the level of fertility (total fertility rate) is projected and then a pattern of fertility (age-specific fertility rates) is assumed. A similar process is used to project mortality, where the demographer projects the general level of mortality (expectation of life at birth) by sex and then assumes age-specific mortality rates (Arriaga, 1993). Finally, levels and patterns of net migration are assumed. The projected levels and patterns of the components of population change are applied to the base population to yield the projected population for a given year.

Uncertainty is introduced into the forecast in a number of ways. At all stages in the process, a demographer uses judgment based on professional experience to arrive at the most "reasonable" set of future demographic indices. Projecting a population becomes an art influenced by scientific techniques. Opinions, judgments, experience, and outlook are all used at various stages of the projection process. Further, the quality of the data on which the projection is based may be dubious, or data that do exist may not be available (e.g., the Iraq 1989 Subcensus of Population), leading to additional uncertainty in the projection. Also, the model may be misspecified. Hoem (1973) provided a detailed discussion of sources of uncertainty.

How is uncertainty about various elements of the projections integrated into the results? Current methods used to forecast populations generally do not allow the demographer to state explicitly his or her probability of demographic events occurring. Instead, demographers generally forecast a population using different sets of assumptions and allow the user to choose the projection that will best fit the user's needs. The range of results of projections based on various sets of assumptions is assumed to reflect "uncertainty."

> No one admits to making an arbitrary choice of assumptions for population projections; each author selects a set corresponding to the relations that he sees as persisting into the future. Since what will persist is uncertain at the time the projection is being made, he is well advised to try more than one set of assumptions and work out future numbers from each. In due course censuses will be taken in what was the future at the time the projection was made. The hope is that the several future numbers will turn out to straddle each subsequent census, but official agencies, unwilling to present their projections as predictions, do not assign any probability that they will straddle. (Keyfitz, 1972, p. 353).

Current practices vary. The United Nations allows a user to choose among four scenarios: high-, medium-, low-, and constant-fertility variants, which differ primarily in the assumed future trends in fertility (United Nations, 1993). The World Bank presents only one series of projections per country but rather explicitly presents the assumed changes in vital rates (World Bank, 1992).

The U.S. Census Bureau projects populations two ways. The Center for International Research performs projections for every country in the world. For all countries except the very smallest, the center uses the cohort-component method. Rather than perform a number of projections under various assumptions, the center makes only one projection for each country. Users and producers of the data generally accept the projection as the most likely scenario. The center evaluates and, when it seems necessary, adjusts raw census data, even of developed countries.

The Population Division, which projects the population of the United States, produces 10 series of projections (U.S. Bureau of the Census, 1992, p. xxiv). "Although the middle series is presented in great detail, there are nine other alternative projection series" (U.S. Bureau of the Census, 1992, p. xxiv). These projections begin with an unadjusted population. "This method does not correct for the net undercount in the 1990 census....The inflation-deflation variant yields a population distribution in each projected year which is similar to that which would result if a census with the 1990 pattern of undercount (as estimated by Demographic Analysis) were conducted in that year" (U.S. Bureau of the Census, 1992, p. x). Therefore, rather than forecast the future expected population, the Population Division instead forecasts the enumerated population and assumes that the Census Bureau's techniques of enumerating the population will not improve or deteriorate. Among the 10 projections are three named "high," "medium," and "low."

> The logic of this approach is that the demographer presents a few main possibilities in respect of the components of population growth, shows what population will result in twenty or more years later, and leaves the selection to the user. It is up to the user to study the assumptions on which the components were projected forward, choose the set of assumptions that seems right to him, and then accept only the demographers' arithmetic to read out the resulting future population.... (Keyfitz, 1987, p. 17-3).

This practice is analogous to a physician giving many alternatives for treating a disease without guiding the patient toward what the physician considers advisable. Demographers could be more useful to their readers if they more fully report their opinions, which reporting probabilities encourages and requires.

Presenting many projections does not substitute for stating the amount of uncertainty in the "medium" projection for three reasons. First, the demographer instead performs many projections, only one of which he or she thinks is most likely to occur. The other projections are generally seen as implausible or unlikely. Second, although the high and low projections take into account different future scenarios, they generally do not take into account the uncertainty in the baseline data. The projections generally start with the same data and apply different assumptions. Alho and Spencer (1985) have made some strides in this area by taking into account some, but not all, sources of error for the "jump-off" population. They assume that although there is uncertainty in the nonwhite population, the white population is perfectly known. Third, the demographer generally does not give his or her opinion of the likelihood of the other projections occurring. Are the "high" and "low" scenarios analogous to 95% confidence intervals? Stoto (1983, p. 19) found and Alho (1992) assumed that the high and low scenarios represent roughly 66% confidence intervals. Lee and Tuljapurkar (1994, p. 1176) assumed that US high and low projection scenarios provide "perhaps a 98% confidence interval" (p. 1176). Alho and Spencer (1985) write that the Census Bureau's "high-low forecast variants are too narrow to be interpreted as .67-level prediction intervals" (p. 313). It is unclear how the high-medium-low approach reflects uncertainty. Hoem (1973, p. 10) wrote that "several authors have insisted that forecasters should bring the [custom of presenting several alternative forecasting series to reflect uncertainty] to an end and that they should change over to specifying probability distributions for future population numbers. Much more precise statements about forecasting uncertainty would then be possible. In principle, this type of approach evidently is a goal towards which forecasters should strive and to which one may possibly find a reasonably accurate and operational solution some time in the future."

Some demographers Lee (1992); Lee and Carter (1992) have put confidence intervals around future estimates of components of population change by using time series methods. For example, Lee and Carter forecast mortality with confidence intervals around future mortality extrapolations. "Their projections capture the implications of a continuation of past exponential trends in age-specific mortality rates, uncomplicated by expert opinion or assumptions about medical advances, delay of deaths by cause, or ultimate levels of life expectancy" (McKnown, 1992, p. 671).

Another methodology–stochastic projection, (Alho, 1990, 1992; Lee, 1992, 1994; Lee and Tuljapurkar, 1994)–shares some of our orientation but differs from it in other respects. Lee and Tuljapurkar (1994) join us in believing that a fully stochastic analysis is preferable to the traditional high, medium and low forecasts. However, the so-called confidence intervals they calculated take some estimated quantities as known, ignoring standard errors of the estimates–although Lee (1994) noted that this matters only sometimes. Lee (1992) and Lee and Tuljapurkar (1994) begin their projections with a point-estimated base population, whereas our technique accounts for uncertainty in the base population. Lee and Tuljapurkar's data situation differs from ours–whereas they dealt with the relatively data-rich projection of the U.S. population, we deal with a data-poor population.

Pflaumer (1988) also shares with us the goal of stochastically projecting a population. Whereas he stated "we prefer subjective specifications of demographic distributions" (p. 137), he actually uses a piece-wise uniform distribution "with no a priori information about the distribution being available" (p. 137). In his empirical example of projecting the U.S. population for nearly 100 years, he remarks "the assumptions of the Census Bureau shall here only serve as examples to demonstrate the simulation procedure rather than to provide reliable estimates" (p. 139). Thus Pflaumer does not take scientific responsibility for the distributions that he uses.

This article represents another step toward the Tornquist-Hoem goal of stochastic projection. We advance beyond Pflaumer in that the model we propose and the inputs that we use are subjectively determined to represent seriously considered opinion. Before applying our approach to the Iraqi Kurdish population, we provide some background.

6.3   The Iraqi Kurdish Population

The Iraqi Kurds[1] are an Indo-European people living in the northern reaches of Iraq. Urban Kurds live in the fertile plains, an area rich in oil and mineral resources, while rural Kurds live further north in the mountainous zones bordering Turkey and Iran. The Kurds, desiring a greater measure of self-government, have at times negotiated with and at other times fought with the Iraqi central government over the nature of their relationship.

In 1975 the Iraqi government embarked on a campaign to "arabize" Kurdish areas. The "arabization" involved relocating Arabs from southern to northern Iraq to live near and work in oil fields. The relocated Arabs, overwhelmingly males of working age, were given land and jobs. In the late 1970s, the Ba'thist regime in Baghdad, facing little opposition from the Kurdish parties, was able to create a "cordon sanitaire" in the area of its northern borders, destroying all Kurdish villages in a band approximately 15-20 km wide. After receiving symbolic compensation for their lost property, the population was moved to housing complexes in valleys closer to urban centers.

During the 1980s, the Kurds became increasingly exposed to official state violence in the wake of the Iraqi invasion of Iran and the start of the Iran-Iraq war. During this war, fought between 1980 and 1988, the Iraqi regime witnessed rural Kurdish areas slipping from its control. The *peshmergas*, guerrillas belonging to the outlawed Kurdish political parties, took advantage of this power vacuum and reasserted claims to Kurdish self-government.

In April 1987 the Iraqi regime responded by bombarding the areas over which it had lost control and systematically destroying many Kurdish villages that remained under its control. The government relocated rural Kurds to newly built housing complexes, again offering them symbolic compensation.

In the spring of 1988, as the war with Iran came to an end, the Iraqi regime launched a major military campaign against the Kurdish insurgency. The campaign, called the Anfal Operation, covered most of the Kurdish countryside. It was conducted in eight separate stages divided over a period of $6\frac{1}{2}$ months, starting in February 1988 and ending with a general amnesty decree on September 6, 1988. Stages of the Anfal Operation generally shared the following features:

- Chemical attacks on selected targets (some military and others strictly civilian).

- A massive military assault by land and by air.

- Detention of all those found in the area, including civilians, and their transfer to holding centers and from there to unknown destinations. Evidence suggests that most of those detained either were killed or died from hunger and disease while in captivity. Many women, children, and elderly who survived detention were released under the September amnesty.

---

[1]The information in this section is primarily based on Middle East Watch (1993) and S. Resool (personal communication).

- Complete destruction of villages in the area.

Following the Anfal, the rural areas remained off-limits to people, at penalty of summary execution. Those who survived the Anfal and benefited from the September amnesty typically spent the first several months without shelter until they obtained the resources to build a house, often in large housing complexes. Not until after the popular uprising of March 1991 (following the 1991 Persian Gulf War) and the subsequent Iraqi military withdrawal from most of the Kurdish areas 8 months later did some rural Kurds return to the sites of their villages of origin and begin rebuilding their homes.

The 1987 census played a unique role in the Anfal. Before conducting the census in October, in August 1987 the Iraqi government ordered that "steps should be taken to hold public seminars and administrative meetings to discuss the importance of the general population census scheduled to be held on October 17, 1987, and to stress clearly that anyone who fails to take part in the process without a valid excuse shall lose his Iraqi nationality. He shall also be regarded as an army deserter...." (Middle East Watch, 1993, pp. 86). In January 1988 a decree was issued stating that "capital punishment shall be imposed.. on any deserter..." (Middle East Watch, 1993, pp. 86–87). Describing the instructions for the 1987 census, Middle East Watch noted:

> The instructions were quite different from those of the five previous censuses. Those who were not included in the census would no longer be considered Iraqi nationals...; they would cease to be eligible for government services and food rations. And people could be counted only if they made themselves accessible to census-takers. For anyone living in a prohibited area, this meant abandoning one's home (Middle East Watch, 1993, p. 87).

As a form of civil protest, many Kurds did not register for the 1987 census, making any estimates of the Kurdish population based on the 1987 census inaccurate. Therefore, for our projection we rely on the previous census conducted in 1977.

The Kurdish population has certain peculiarities that make estimation especially challenging. There has never been an Iraqi census that has collected data on whether a person is a Kurd. However, the Iraqi Kurdish population is geographically concentrated and lives primarily in four Iraqi governorates: Arbil, Dahuk, Tamim, and Sulamaniya. To arrive at a base population of Iraqi Kurds, we first start with the unadjusted 1977 census population of these four governorates. The adjusted base population that we estimate approximates the actual 1977 Iraqi Kurdish population.

Four possible problems with the census counts of 1977 arose:

- Arabization. The "arabization" of these areas which began in the mid-1970s implies that some people living in these areas were not Kurds but instead Arabs. Rural Arabs migrated from Southern Iraq to Kurdistan because of economic incentives and generally lived near oil fields located in urban areas (Resool, 1994). So, there existed the problem of removing enumerated Arabs from the population of the four governorates.

- The draft. At the time of the 1977 census, the Iraqi government drafted all males aged 18 years. To avoid military service, many Kurdish males 18 years of age would not report themselves as such. This implies that there would be disproportionately high numbers of males both younger and older than 18, but a dearth of males aged 18.

- Underreporting of females. In many developing areas where females' status is low (compared to males'), females are underenumerated. We suspect this to be the case in the four Kurdish governorates in question.

- General age misreporting. This is a problem common to the censuses of developing countries, and there is no reason to think that the Iraqi census data would be exceptional.

All four of these potential problems add to the uncertainty in our projection of the Iraqi Kurdish population. Further, there is a dearth of fertility and mortality data on Iraqi Kurds, forcing one to base estimates for the population on data for the entire Iraqi population. In the absence of data distinguishing these demographic phenomena of the Kurds from those of the Iraqi population as a whole, this approach is reasonable. The projection is performed to see what the population of Iraqi Kurds would have been in 1990 in the absence of state-sponsored violence in the 1980s.

6.4   Overview of Projection Procedure

A Bayesian demographic projection combines expert opinion (see, e.g., Kadane et al. (1980) and Wolfson (1995)) with traditional demographic projection techniques (i.e., those used by the U.S. Census Bureau's Center for International Research). The projection period lasts from a base year to an end year. The cohort-component approach requires a midyear population for the base year by age and sex and for the projection period levels and patterns of migration and vital rates (fertility and mortality). Rather than have point estimates for the base population, migration, and vital rates, the Bayesian approach instead explicitly models the uncertainty inherent in these estimates by specifying distributions for them.

Rather than forecast into the future, the forecast goes from one past date to another. We have available some information on the vital rates during the forecast period. The availability of information during the projection period might make one more certain of one's estimates than one would have been without such information at hand.

We project the rural and urban populations separately to allow for differences in their demographic events. Because we do not know the form that data on the post-Anfal Iraqi Kurdish population might take, for the purpose of later evaluating the demographic effects of the Anfal (which might have had differential effects on the urban and rural populations), we choose to project the rural and urban populations separately. However, the projection program that we modified allows us to aggregate these populations, if we so choose.

The projection procedure presented computational challenges. Our procedure adapted publicly available demographic software. Specifically, source code from the U.S. Census Bureau's Rural-Urban Projection Package (RUP) and the United Nations' MORTPAK were obtained to create a Fortran program that could project a population multiple times.

6.5   Projecting the Iraqi Kurdish Population

We project the vital rates of the population, consider migration, and then arrive at a base population. The projection of fertility is addressed first.

6.5.1   Fertility

There is one comforting thought to offer before starting our analysis of fertility. Our analysis of the Kurdish population of Iraq is from 1977–1990, a span of 13 years. Because this represents less than one generation, fertility has only a linear relationship to our projections, not the polynomial or exponential relationship that results from projections over several to many generations. For this reason, the projections that we offer are less sensitive to assumptions about fertility than would be the case for a longer projection. Therefore, we can model fertility in a somewhat crude way and still have reasonable projections.

The fundamental quantity for understanding fertility is the age-specific fertility rate for age x at year t (ASFR_x^t), the proportion of women of age x at year t who have a child in that year. The total fertility rate in year t (TFR_t) is the sum of the age-specific fertility rates in that year; that is

$$\text{TFR}^t \equiv \sum_x \text{ASFR}_x^t.$$

It is a traditional and useful summary of over-all fertility at a particular point in time.

Because no data are available on the fertility of the Kurdish population, we consider data available on Iraqi fertility. For Iraq as a whole, we use two sources of information about total fertility. (For a discussion of various fertility estimates of Iraq, see Daponte (1993).) A 1974 survey (United Nations Economic Commission for Western Asia, 1980) shows a 1974 total fertility rate (TFR) of 7.1 and the United Nations Socio-Economic Data Sheets (United Nations Economic and Social Commission for Western Asia, 1989) give a 1988 rate of 6.1.

Because we examine the Iraqi Kurdish population from 1977–1990, the first task is to estimate fertility rates for the starting and endpoints of the projection. It is likely that fertility in Iraq was decreasing, hence the 1977 rate is somewhat less than the 1974 rate of 7.1 and the 1990 rate is somewhat less than the 1988 rate of 6.1. In areas where fertility is declining and the time period is short, a logistic function should provide reasonable estimates of fertility (Arriaga, 1993, p. VIII 20). Here the extrapolation of 1977 and 1990 rates was done with a logistic curve with total fertility rates asymptotes of 8 (long ago) and 2 (long into the future). Doing so yields TFR's of 7.0 for 1977 and 6.0 for 1990. We take these as the means of our fertility distributions for the start and end year of the projections. In considering sources of uncertainty of fertility in the start and end years of the projection, one should include uncertainty in how well Iraqi fertility reflects Kurdish fertility and mismeasurement error.

Next we consider urban-rural differences in fertility. The 1974 fertility survey found rural fertility to be 20% higher than urban fertility. During the projection period, we take this differential to be stochastic, with a mean of 20% (constant over time) and with a standard deviation expressing uncertainty about it. These weights are applied to the TFR for the entire country to get rural and urban TFRs.

There exists uncertainty in the TFRs obtained for the rural and urban areas – mean TFRs in 1977 of 7.6 in rural and 6.4 in urban and in 1990 of 6.5 in rural and 5.5 in urban. We model this uncertainty as a standard deviation; sources of uncertainty include doubts as to whether the 20% rural-urban differential remained constant over time, concerns over the initial measurement of fertility, and concerns over whether the logistic interpolation yields correct TFRs. In considering the mismeasurement issue, (Daponte, 1992) evaluated Iraqi fertility using several demographic techniques applied to the relevant data sources. Based on her evaluation of Iraqi fertility and the sources of uncertainty mentioned earlier, we set our 95% credible intervals of the TFR 6.0 - 6.8 in 1977 and 5.15 - 5.85 in 1990 for urban areas, and 7.1 - 8.1 in 1977 and 6.1 - 6.9 in for rural areas, with normal distributions assumed for convenience and because they reasonably represent our beliefs.

Hence, our evaluation of the marginal densities of urban and rural fertility in 1977 and 1990 fertility is presented in Figure 6.1.

To specify a joint normal distribution with marginal densities shown in Figure 6.1, it is necessary to specify correlations. We assume that the TFR's, both urban and rural, are uncorrelated in the base and end years. Further, we take the correlation between rural and urban TFR's in both the base and end years to be 1, because the

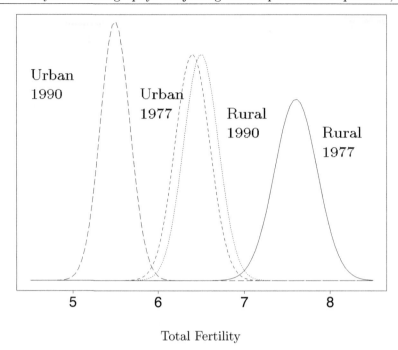

Total Fertility

Figure 6.1: Probability Density Function of Elicited Total Fertility Rates, 1977 and 1990, for Urban and Rural Areas. From left to right, pdf's are for urban areas, 1990 (large dash) ($N(5.5, (0.175)^2)$), urban areas, 1977 (small dash) ($N(6.4, (0.2)^2)$), rural areas, 1990 (dotted) ($N(5.6, (0.2)^2)$), and rural areas, 1977 (solid) ($N(7.6, (0.25)^2)$)

major source of our uncertainty about the TFR's is measurement error, which would apply equally to both urban and rural areas in both 1974 and 1988.

Thus the vector (TFR_{77}^U, TFR_{77}^R, TFR_{90}^U, TFR_{90}^R) (with superscripts indicating urban and rural), is taken to be jointly normal, with margins specified in Figure 6.1 and correlation matrix

$$\begin{bmatrix} 1 & 1 & 0 & 0 \\ 1 & 1 & 0 & 0 \\ 0 & 0 & 1 & 1 \\ 0 & 0 & 1 & 1 \end{bmatrix}$$

This completely specifies their joint distribution.

Having drawn values of the base and end year urban and rural TFR's from this distribution, we extrapolated them for the intervening years using the logistic function in RUP, which uses an upper asymptote of $1 + \max(6, TFR_{77}, TFR_{90})$, and a lower asymptote of 2. Thus we obtain a (stochastic) series of urban and rural TFR's from 1977 to 1990.

The next step in the analysis is to distribute the TFR by age. The 1974 fertility survey (UN ECWA 1980) is unique, in our view, among data sources in giving reasonable fertility patterns by age for Iraq. Dividing the 1974 ASFR's by the TFR_{74} yields the proportion of the TFR contributed by women of each age. Those proportions are reported in Table 6.1 separately for urban and rural Iraq.

Alternatively, one could model the age pattern of fertility as uncertain. We do not

Table 6.1: Proportional Fertility rates per year

Age	Urban	Rural
15 - 19	.0172	.0199
20 - 24	.0447	.0440
25 - 29	.0479	.0459
30 - 34	.0407	.0392
35 - 39	.0306	.0301
40 - 44	.0140	.0157
45 - 49	.0048	.0052

NOTE: Rates by age and location for Iraq (From United Nations Economic Commission for Western Asia 1980). *Source: Calculated from age-specific fertility.*

do so here because the level of fertility did not change drastically since 1974, and introducing uncertainty about the age pattern of fertility would have little effect on the results.

Assuming that the fertility pattern reflected in Table 6.1 is constant for the 13 years in question, multiplying the weights for age x in Table 6.1 by TFR_t yields an estimate for ASFR_x^t. Finally, multiplying ASFR_x^t by N_x, the number of women of age x, yields an estimate of the number of births in year t to women of age x. Summed over mothers' ages x, this gives an estimate of the number of births in year t.

6.5.2 Mortality

The existing mortality data for the Kurdish population is also limited. Thus indirect estimation techniques must be used to obtain estimates of mortality between 1977 and 1990. Because far more is known about the Iraqi population's infant and child mortality levels than about adult mortality, indirect estimates of age-specific mortality rates over the life cycle are based on infant and child mortality.

The best estimates of Iraqi infant mortality for the latter half of the twentieth century have been provided by Jones (1992), who reviewed mortality estimates for Iraq. Jones provided a series of infant mortality rates for both sexes combined based on reconciling mortality estimates from various survey and census data. He gives an infant mortality rate (IMR) of 39 per 1,000 live births in 1990, which we use as the mean of our distribution for IMR in 1990. He also gave IMRs of 75 for 1975 and 63 for 1980. We slightly prefer the estimate of 70.4 for 1977 given by a logistic fit (using FITL-GSTC, Version 100 of the U.S. Bureau of the Census) to the estimate of 70.2 for the same year that comes from a linear extrapolation. Sources of uncertainty in the IMR include measurement error, questions about the appropriateness of using Iraqi IMRs for the Kurdish population, and basic uncertainty in Jones' evaluation of mortality. Figure 6.2 illustrates the densities, means and standard deviations of the IMRs for both sexes combined for the base and end years of the projection. Again normality is assumed, both for simplicity and as a reasonable representation of belief. Also, 1977 and 1990 IMR's are taken to be independent.

Next, the sex differential in infant mortality is considered. In 1989, the United Nations (United Nations Economic and Social Commission for Western Asia, 1989, p. 55) reported that the IMR in Iraq in 1988 was 62.5–63.4 for males and 61.6 for females. The level of the IMR was based on the UN's analysis of children ever born/children surviving information from the 1974 fertility survey, a 1980 survey, and the 1987 cen-

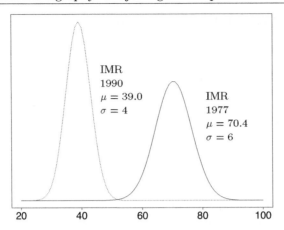

Figure 6.2: Probability Density Function of Elicited Joint Infant Mortality Rates (IMR). (Dotted), the pdf of the 1990 IMR ($\mu = 39$; $\sigma = 4$); (solid), the 1977 IMR ($\mu = 70 : 4$; $\sigma = 6$).

Table 6.2: Elicited Quantiles of Δ_{MF} Conditional on IMR

	Quantiles of Δ_{MF}		
IMR	50th	75th	97.5
90	0	4	12
70	-2	1	7
50	-4	-2	2
30	-6	-5	-3

sus. This level is substantially higher than that reported by Jones (1992) because the UN had not yet incorporated data from more recent surveys on child health conducted in 1989 and 1990 (Republic of Iraq, Ministry of Health, 1990; UNICEF, 1990). The UN bases its sex differential in infant mortality on 1987 census data on infant mortality. We rely on the survey data for the level of infant and child mortality and the UN's estimates for the sex differential in mortality.

Based on these fragmentary data, one can model the sex differential $\Delta_{MF} = IMR_F - IMR_M$, the difference between male and female infant mortality rates. As mortality decreases, the tendency for excess female mortality also decreases (Hill and Brown, 1994; Langford and Storey, 1993). Considering Δ_{MF} at four distinct points of the IMR–90, 70, 50, and 30–we modeled Δ_{MF}'s uncertainty as follows.

Here we express the belief that the uncertainty decreases as the IMR decreases. These values indicate that both the mean and standard deviation of the resulting normal distribution are linear in IMR, so the conditional distribution of Δ_{MF}, given IMR, is a normal distribution with mean and standard deviation:

$$\widehat{\mu}(\Delta_{MF}) = .1 \times \text{IMR} - 0.9;$$

and

$$\widehat{\sigma}(\Delta_{MF}) = 0.059 \times IMR. \tag{6.1}$$

That ((6.1)) fits the elicitations reported in Table 6.2 exactly is convenient but not necessary.

After sampling the IMR from the normal distribution defined in Figure 6.2, a conditional value of Δ_{MF} is sampled from ((6.1)). From this, the IMRs for each sex are obtained using a sex ratio at birth of 1.05 as:

$$\text{IMR}_F = IMR - \left(\frac{1.05}{1+1.05}\right) \Delta_{MF} \tag{6.2}$$

and

$$\text{IMR}_M = IMR + \left(\frac{1}{1+1.05}\right) \Delta_{MF}. \tag{6.3}$$

Because we project the rural and urban populations separately, we next consider the differential in mortality between the urban and rural populations. A 1974 survey (United Nations Economic Commission for Western Asia, 1980) showed no difference between mortality rates in rural and urban areas. However, our analysis of recent data collected by the International Study Team (1992) indicates that between July 1985 and July 1990, children in urban areas had a substantial survival advantage over their rural counterparts – IMRs of $\approx$33 and 44. This difference seemed too large to be believed, so we examined the urban-rural mortality differential in Jordan, a country socio-economically similar to Iraqi Kurdistan. The 1990 Jordan Population and Family Health Survey (Zou'bi, 1992) showed that infants in urban areas had an approximate 10% survival advantage over rural infants, a level that seemed more credible. Because this seems more reasonable, we assume that when compared to Kurdish rural infants, the IMR among urban Kurds will be approximately 10% lower, although we are uncertain about this assumption.

The difference between rural and urban infant mortality rates is

$$\Delta_{\text{RU}} = \frac{\text{IMR}_{\text{RURAL}} - \text{IMR}_{\text{URBAN}}}{\text{IMR}_{\text{URBAN}}} \tag{6.4}$$

This difference we model as normally distributed with a mean and standard deviation as follows:

$$\widehat{\mu}(\Delta_{RU}) = .1; \widehat{\sigma}(\Delta_{RU}) = 0.05 \tag{6.5}$$

To establish some additional notation, let R be the rural population, U the urban population, $r = R/(R+U)$ be the rural proportion, and $u = U/(R+U)$ be the urban proportion. Because the IMR for an entire area is a weighted average of the IMR$_{\text{RURAL}}$ and the IMR$_{\text{URBAN}}$, for a given sex the rural and urban infant mortality rates are computed as

$$\text{IMR}_{J,RURAL} = \frac{1+\Delta_{RU}}{r(1+\Delta_{RU})+u}\text{IMR}_J \tag{6.6}$$

$$\text{IMR}_{J,URBAN} = \frac{1}{r(1+\Delta_{RU})+u}\text{IMR}_J, \tag{6.7}$$

where J=F, M.

The proportion of the population living in rural areas in 1977 is .51 and this proportion is kept constant throughout this projection. A more precise approach would have this proportion vary based on the midyear geographic distribution of the population for each of the projection years. Considering that our point estimate projection showed 51% of the population in rural areas in 1990, in our view correcting this extremely minor source of error would not have produced results much different from the ones we present.

Once rural and urban infant mortality rates by sex have been determined, one needs to estimate mortality at other ages in the life cycle. Although Kohli (1976) provided life tables for Iraq, an evaluation of these life tables showed them to be implausible, especially with respect to the mortality estimates of rural females. His life tables were essentially based on a newly developed incomplete vital registration system, and Kohli himself wrote that the table should be interpreted with caution (p. 16). We do not use these life tables or any information contained in his article for our analysis. The existence of contradictory mortality estimates demonstrates the extent of uncertainty in the estimates.

The South model of life tables assumes "high mortality under age 5, low mortality from about ages 40–60, and high mortality over age 65" (Coale and Demeny, 1966, p. 14), which describes the situation in Iraq in the 1970s quite well. Thus we used these tables for 1977.

The West model is the model most commonly used and assumes a level of child mortality relatively lower than the South's. During the 1980s, Iraq made a concerted and successful effort to reduce its infant and child mortality. The reduction of mortality among the young makes the West model life tables appropriate in 1990; thus we use the West tables for 1990. For the 1978–1989 period, age-specific mortality rates are linearly interpolated between the two levels and patterns. We used the UN's MORTPAK computer software package to generate model life tables for each sex.

6.5.3   Migration

Two types of migration–interregional (international) and rural-urban–should be addressed. Considering the former type, we assume that except for the arabization of the region, Iraqi Kurdistan was neither a net sending nor receiving area. Other countries were not willing to accept Iraqi Kurds on a permanent basis, and Kurdistan, being a remote area, was not receiving immigrants. Since 1977, the Iraqi government used forced migration against rural Kurds three times, in the late 1970's, in 1987, and in 1988. Because our purpose is to find a distribution for the population had the Anfal and other forced migration not occurred and because natural migration was trivial, it is appropriate for this purpose not to include interregional migration in our projections.

For the period of interest, normal rural-urban migration is probably negligible. Our analysis of 1977 and 1987 Iraqi census data shows very low rates of rural-urban migration (less than 1% of the rural population per year). One cannot necessarily assume, however, that rural-urban migration rates observed for all of Iraq apply to Iraqi Kurdistan.

Even though we do not model rural-urban migration, because they have different growth rates, it is still useful to project the rural and urban populations separately, Treating the population as a whole would ignore the differences in the vital rates to which both populations were exposed, and hence result in a less accurate projection.

6.5.4   Obtaining a Base Population

When conducting a cohort-component projection, one starts with a base population as of July 1 categorized by 5-year age groups and sex, typically based on census data. To obtain a base population, we first take the raw data from the 1977 census and distribute persons of unknown ages according to the age distribution of persons of known ages. Next, examining the observed sex ratios

$$\text{SR} = \frac{\text{No. of males}}{\text{No. of females}}, \tag{6.8}$$

we observe (Figure 6.3) that the sex ratios between contiguous age groups vary considerably, and that for most age groups the ratio of males to females in the population

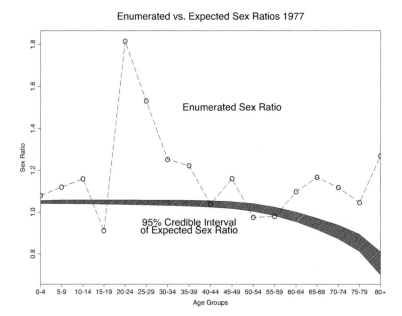

Figure 6.3: 1977 Sex Ratios by Age. The circles plot the enumerated sex ratios from the unadjusted 1977 Iraqi census. The solid area gives the 95% credible interval of the expected sex ratios.

is too high, considering that neither female emigration nor excess female mortality occurred.

To resolve the variation in sex ratios between age groups, a moving average technique smoothed the ratios of the rural and urban areas separately. The sex ratios are smoothed for all ages except for the age groups 80+, 0-4, and 5-9. Although this helps the situation somewhat, the overall sex ratio was 1.19, reflecting a population that in the absence of male in-migration, would appear disproportionately male. Whereas in rural areas the sex ratio is 1.10, in urban areas it is 1.28. In the absence of urban migration by males, one would expect rural sex ratios to exceed urban sex ratios because of rural-urban migration of females (Davis, 1995, p. 159). The urban population particularly showed inflated sex ratios in young adult (age 15-49), typical migration ages, and we assume that these excess males are probably Arabs. The problem that presents itself, then, is how to remove Arabs living in Kurdish areas from the 1977 population.

Expected sex ratios reveal what the sex ratios of a population would be given a set of age-specific mortality rates. We calculate expected sex ratios separately for rural and urban areas for each age group by taking the ratio of the male to the female stationary populations obtained from model life tables using the IMR estimates described earlier and multiplying this ratio by the sex ratio at birth (Shryock et al., 1971, p. 221). Although we calculated expected sex ratios based on both the West model and the South model, the West model showed sex ratios that seemed too high and that reached unity too late in life. The South-expected sex ratios appeared more reasonable. Therefore, the expected sex ratios for each age group used to estimate the base population were based on the South model life tables.

When comparing the 95% credible intervals of the expected sex ratios with the enumerated sex ratios, one sees (Figure 6.3) discrepancies which may be accounted for by the following: in the rural population, an undercounting of females; in the urban areas, the inclusion of Arab men who migrated to Kurdish areas to work in the oil fields; and in both areas at draft ages, an underenumeration and age misreporting of males. All three of these factors would mask the actual Kurdish population.

To obtain an estimate of the Kurdish population in 1977 and account for these three factors, it is necessary to stochastically adjust the rural and urban populations separately using expected sex ratios. For the rural population, we generally start with the male enumerated population and adjust the figures for females based on the expected sex ratios to correct for possible underenumeration. This is done for all age groups except for those surrounding the 15-19 age group because of the draft issue and implies a 9.5%–12.5% undercount among females. For the age groups 10-14, 15-19, and 20-24, we start with the female population, adjust it upwards based on the implied undercount, and then adjust the male population based on expected sex ratios.

In urban areas, for the population younger than 20, we accept the male population and adjust the female population. For the population group 20-49, we accept the female population and adjust the male population. This results in removing many men from the population, assumed to be Arab migrants. For the ages 50+, we accept the male population, and adjust the female population. Because of a lack of data, no adjustment is made that might remove the presumably very small number of Arab women who might have accompanied Arab men. However, no undercount adjustment was made to women 20-49 and, hopefully, these two factors balance. These adjustments yield a stochastically adjusted October 1977 population.

6.6   Results

For the population projection to reflect the uncertainty in the baseline data and fore-casted demographic phenomena, the projection is a Monte Carlo simulation run 10,000 times using the demographic distributions specified earlier. Considering the mortality component of the projection, the process of generating the four infant mortality rates (rural by sex and urban by sex) is repeated 10,000 times, each time taking an independent random sample from the densities specified in Figure 6.2 and equations (6.1) and (6.4). The respective IMRs are then used as input to MORTPAK to obtain model life tables that contain mortality rates for the rest of the life cycle. The male and female life tables for the rural and urban areas in 1977 are used to calculate expected sex ratios for each of the areas, and then the census population (with the unknowns proportionally distributed) is adjusted based on these expected sex ratios.

Similarly, a TFR is randomly selected from the density specified in Figure 6.1. Although urban and rural fertility are assumed to be correlated, no correlation between fertility and mortality is assumed. If fertility rates were assumed to drop from a very high to a very low level (e.g., 7 to 2), then perhaps the assumption of independence should be reconsidered. Alho (1990, 1992) noted that zero correlation is appropriate in most cases. Age patterns of fertility, based on urban and rural age-specific fertility rates reported in the 1974 survey, are proportionally adjusted to the selected TFR.

Finally, the population is "moved" from the census date of October 17, 1977 to midyear by adding in the deaths that occurred during this 3.5 month period by age and sex and subtracting births from the population under age 1. Because both the mortality and fertility rates are uncertain quantities, the adjusted October 1977 and the midyear base or populations are stochastically adjusted quantities.

Figures 6.6a and 6.6b display the population pyramids for the 1977 enumerated population and the coefficient of variation of the 1977 stochastically adjusted midyear base population. Figure 6.6a clearly shows the anomalies in the Kurdish population for which we adjusted. Figure 6.6b shows that uncertainty in the base data affects some age and sex categories more than others. Given the base data, the manifestation of uncertainty for most of the age-sex categories seems quite small.

The population pyramid for the projected 1990 population (Figure 6.6c) shows that all age-sex categories are affected by the uncertainty inherent in the projected vital rates. Among age groups older than the projection period (in this case those older than 13) the uncertainty in the projected population is minimal, except for the small group of elderly, where baseline 1977 uncertainty and mortality uncertainty affects the coefficients of variation. Compared with those older than the projection period and middle-aged, the younger age groups have considerably greater associated uncertainty. Our simulations give a probability distribution for the population in each age and sex category, of which the figures are a summary.

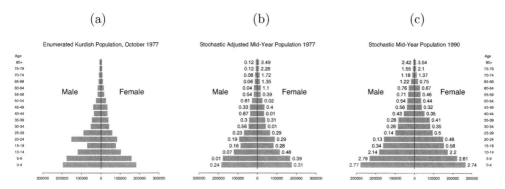

Figure 6.4: Population pyramids. Solid bars on left of each pyramid represent the male population, shaded bars on right display the female population. (a) Estimated Kurdish population based on Iraqi census data, October 1977. (b) Stochastically adjusted 1977 mid-year population. (c) Stochastic 1990 mid-year population. In graphs (b) and (c), the median population of the age group is given by the bar's length; the coefficient of variation is shown numerically.

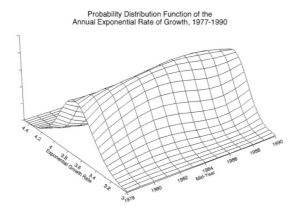

Figure 6.5: Probability Density Function of the Annual Exponential Rate of Growth, 1977–1990.

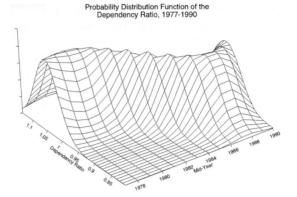

Figure 6.6: Probability Density Function of the 1977–1990 Dependency Ratio, the Population not Age 15–64 divided by the Population Age 15–64.

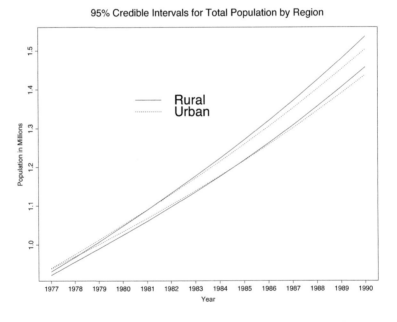

Figure 6.7: 95% Credible Intervals for Total Population by Region and Year. 95% Credible Intervals for the Rural (solid) and Urban (dotted) Populations.

Figure 6.5 displays the probability density function (pdf) of the annual exponential rate of growth over time. Due to our assumptions that as fertility and mortality decrease, the range of possible vital rates also decreases, the exponential rate of growth over time becomes more certain, as is manifested in this graph as a narrowing of the pdf.

A Bayesian approach has ramifications for the dependency ratio (defined here as the population not age 15-64 divided by the population 15–64). Figure 6.6 shows that the pdf of the dependency ratio flattens over time. The age distribution of the uncertainty affects this particular indicator. The pdf expands because more uncertainty is

Table 6.3: Expected Deaths, 1988; 95% Credible Interval

Age	Males			Females		
	Lower Limit	Upper Limit	Mean	Lower Limit	Upper Limit	Mean
0-4	2,096	4,355	3,169	2,007	4,049	2,991
5-9	110	300	197	113	264	186
10-14	64	169	111	65	145	104
15-19	114	291	198	136	276	207
20-24	118	291	203	140	288	214
25-29	96	226	160	95	202	149
30-34	125	275	199	113	238	175
35-39	131	264	197	117	238	178
40-44	120	211	166	111	207	161
45-49	158	244	203	158	259	213
50-54	208	301	258	225	335	286
55-59	324	440	387	382	516	458
60-64	384	503	449	63	592	538
65-69	377	462	424	451	542	504
70-74	522	603	568	613	703	664
75-79	568	628	601	656	733	698
80+	1,052	1,179	1,112	1,255	1,467	1,364

attached to the youngest age groups and, over time, these age groups in the projection period compose more of the group of people not age 15–64. Because the pdf changes considerably from year to year, the pdf over time appears wavy. The assumptions in the projection and the changing age structure yield a slight rise in the pdf between 1989 and 1990.

To investigate the effect of the Anfal in particular on the mortality of Iraqi Kurds, one might first consider the expected number of deaths in 1988 in the absence of state-sponsored violence. Table 6.3 shows the range of the 95% credible interval of expected deaths by age and sex. If a tally of deaths during this period ever becomes available, then the expected range could be compared with the actual tally to estimate the number of excess deaths (see Daponte (1993)).

Finally, Figure 6.7 exhibits the 95% credible intervals for the total rural and urban populations. The assumptions of the projection yield a somewhat narrower range of the total urban population than the total rural population. The credible interval widens over time because here the uncertainty in the estimate at one date is a function of the uncertainty in the estimate at a previous date and uncertainty in the vital rates between two dates. Information relevant to assessing the demographic impact of the Anfal on Iraqi Kurds may come in a form somewhat different than the summary measures presented here. The computer program design allows one to retrieve nearly any demographic measure and to aggregate the urban and rural populations to the total population.

The approach that we take to project a population yields a number of summary indicators. The amount of uncertainty across indicators varies, depending upon which age-sex categories the indicator addresses and the length of time projected.

6.7   Discussion

This article integrates a Bayesian approach with traditional demographic methods. Although we have demonstrated this approach using the population of a developing country, in the future we intend to apply this technique on a population of an industrialized country that has an abundance of reliable demographic data (including migration). We expect the projection of such a population to yield relatively narrow credible intervals.

Overall, the approach advocates that demographers consider for each component of the projection sources and magnitudes of uncertainty. We describe the decisions we made for this population, at the same time acknowledging that others may have put different weights on factors and may have made different decisions. Demographers should consider and try to model uncertainty in fertility, mortality, base population, and perhaps migration. At times, the mean and standard deviation might be based on nothing more than the demographer's educated guess, whereas at other times, the demographer might have data available that enables modeling of uncertainty.

Rather than dismiss what is known about populations and the evaluation of data sources, Bayesian demography instead forces the demographer to confront uncertainty in the demographic phenomena and baseline data. The projection is guided by the traditional approach that demographers use to create a point estimate of the population at a future date. We believe that by encouraging demographers to state their uncertainties explicitly, the Bayesian approach offers a more precise way for demographers to communicate among themselves, and a more useful product for decision makers who use demographic projections.

REFERENCES

Alho, J. (1990). "Stochastic methods in population forecasting." *International Journal of Forecasting*, 6, 521–530. 105, 116

— (1992). "The magnitude of error due to different vital processes in population forecasts." *International Journal of Forecasting*, 8, 301–314. 105, 116

Alho, J. and Spencer, B. (1985). "Uncertain Population Forecasting." *Journal of the American Statistical Association*, 80, 390, 306–314. 105

Arriaga, E. (1993). "Population analysis with microcomputers." U.S. Bureau of the Census, Center for International Research. 103, 109

Coale, A. and Demeny, P. (1966). *Regional model life tables and stable populations*. Princeton, New Jersey: Princeton University Press. 114

Daponte, B. O. (1992). "Iraqi casualties from the Persian Gulf War and its aftermath: Technical Documentation." Unpublished Manuscript, H. John Heinz School of Public Policy and Management, Carnegie Mellon University. 109

— (1993). "A case study in estimating casualties from war and its aftermath: The Persian Gulf War." *PSR Quarterly*, 3, 2, 57–66. 109, 119

Daponte, B. O. and Wolfson, L. (1995). "Report on projecting the population of Lesotho." Unpublished report. 103

Davis, K. (1995). "The effect of outmigration on regions of origin." In *Internal Migration: An internal perspective*, eds. Brown and Neuberger, 147–166. Academic Press. 115

Hill, K. and Brown, L. (1994). "Gender differences in child health: Evidence from the demographic and health surveys." Paper presented at the Annual Meetings of the Population Association of America. Miami, Florida. 112

Hoem, J. (1973). "Levels of error in population forecast with an appendix by Leo Thornquist." *Artikler fra Statistic Sentralbyrja*, 61, Central Bureau of Statistics, Oslo. 101, 102, 103, 105

International Study Team (1992). "Infant and child mortality and nutritional status of Iraqi children after the Gulf conflict: Results of a community-based survey." Not published. 113

Jones, G. (1992). "Note for the Record. Iraq: Estimation of U5MR and IMR." Not published. 111, 112

Kadane, J., Dickey, J., Winkler, R., Smith, W., and Peters, S. (1980). "Interactive elicitation of opinion for a normal linear model." *Journal of the American Statistical Association*, 75, 845–854. 108

Keyfitz, N. (1972). "On future population." *Journal of the American Statistical Association*, 67, 338, 347–363. 101, 104

— (1987). "The social and political context of population forecasting." In *Readings in Population Research Methodology*, eds. D. Bogue, E. Arriaga, and D. Anderton, vol. 5, chap. 17. Chicago: Social Development Center. 104

Kohli, K. (1976). "Current life tables for Iraq and its rural urban areas, 1973–1974." *The Egyptian Population and Family Planning Review*, 9, 1, 15–23. 113

Land, K. (1986). "Methods for National population forecasts: A review." *Journal of the American Statistical Association*, 81, 396, 888–901. 101

Langford, C. and Storey, P. (1993). "Sex differentials in mortality early in the twentieth century: Sri Lanka and Iinda compared." *Population and Development Review*, 19, 2, 263–282. 112

Lee, R. (1992). "Stochastic demographic forecasting." *International Journal of Forecasting*, 8, 315–327. 105

— (1994). "Private Communication." 105

Lee, R. and Carter, L. (1992). "Modeling and forecasting the time series of U.S. mortality." *Journal of the American Statistical Association*, 87, 659–671. 105

Lee, R. and Tuljapurkar, S. (1994). "Stochastic population forecasts for the United States: Beyond high, medium and low." *Journal of the American Statistical Association*, 89, 1175–1189. 105

McKnown, R. (1992). "Comment." *Journal of the American Statistical Association*, 87, 419, 671–672. 105

Middle East Watch (1993). *The Scourge of the Fire: A narrative account of the 1988 Heroic Anfal Campaign against the Iraqi Kurds*, vol. 1 of *Final Draft*. New York: Middle East Watch. 107

Pflaumer, P. (1988). "Confidence intervals for population projections based on Monte Carlo methods." *International Journal of Forecasting*, 4, 135–142. 101, 105

Republic of Iraq, Ministry of Health (1990). "National Child Health Survey 1989: Preliminary Report." Not published. 112

Resool, S. (1994). "Personal Communication." 107

Savage, L. (1954). *The Foundations of Statistics*. New York: J. Wiley & Sons. 102

Shryock, H., Siegel, J., and Associates (1971). "The methods and materials of demography: Volume I." *US Department of Commerce, Bureau of the Census, US Government Printing*

Office. 115

Smith, S. and Sincich, T. (1990). "The relationship between the length of the base period and population forecast errors." *Journal of the American Statistical Association*, 85, 410, 367–375. 103

Stoto, M. (1983). "The accuracy of population projections." *Journal of the American Statistical Association*, 78, 381, 13–20. 101, 105

The International Bank for Reconstruction and Development/The World Bank (1992). "World Population Projections 1992-93 Edition." Baltimore: The Johns Hopkins University Press. 104

UNICEF (1990). "Iraq immunization diarrheal disease, Maternal and childhood mortality survey, 1990." UNICEF, Regional Office for the Middle East and North Africa. 112

United Nations (1993). "The sex and age distribution of the world populations: The 1992 Revision." United Nations Publication, New York. 104

United Nations Economic and Social Commission for Western Asia (1989). "Demographic and related socio-economic data sheets for countries of the economic and social commission for Western Asia as assessed in 1988." No. 6. 109, 111

United Nations Economic Commission for Western Asia (1980). "The population situation in the ECWA region: Iraq." UN ECWA. 109, 113

U.S. Bureau of the Census (1992). "Current population reports P25-1092, Population projections of the United States by Age, sex, race and hispanic origin: 1992 to 2050." U.S. Government Printing Office, Washington, DC. 104

Wolfson, L. (1995). "Elicitation of priors and utilities for Bayesian analysis." Ph.D. thesis, Department of Statistics, Carnegie Mellon University. 108

Zou'bi, A. (1992). "Jordan Population and Family Health Survey, 1990. Amman, Jordan: Department of Statistics, Ministry of Health." IRD/Macro International, Columbia, MD. 113

Epilogue

What is the scientific issue addressed?

Whether the Bayesian approach offers a more explicit method for demographers to explain their assumptions. The particular example chosen is a counterfactual - to estimate the Kurdish population of Iraq had the Anfal not occurred. There is no prior to posterior use of Bayes Theorem in the paper.

Is justification given for the likelihood and prior?

The likelihood is essentially the cohort-component method, which is the dominant way demographers think about projections and/or forecasts. The age-specific birth and death rates are discussed in detail, giving judgements on which data sources are trusted, and why.

What robustness checks were conducted?

The only sense of robustness here is the replacement of the hypothesized constants with probability distributions.

How was the computing done?

By simulating the results of the model and prior chosen.

If I were doing this problem today, how would I change the approach?

I would not.

What do I see as the contributions of this paper?

1. It shows by example that Bayesian analysis can make demographic assumptions explicit, contributing to more accurate communication.

2. It illuminates the demography of an important segment of the Iraqi population.

Was Bayesian analysis useful in this problem?

I would say "yes."

TEACHING SUGGESTIONS

References for theoretical ideas:

1. Subjectivity of probabilities: *Principles* Section 1.1.2
2. Multivariate normal distribution: *Principles* Section 6.10

Exercises

1. Are you persuaded that demographers would produce more useful products if they gave probabilistic forecasts reflecting their opinions, rather than deterministic projections that are arithmetic consequences of their assumptions? Why or why not?

2. In *Principles*, (p. 6, top), it says "An author using probabilities to express uncertainty must accept the burden of explaining to potential readers the considerations and reasons leading to the particular choices made." To what extent have the authors of this paper explained their reasons? In your opinion, which of the choices made is the most questionable, and why?

3. Are the results presented here technically prior distributions or posterior distributions? Explain your answer.

Chapter 7

An Allegation of Examination Copying (1999)

Foreword

We think of the legal system in terms of a court, lawyers, and perhaps a jury. But there are many other settings in which institutionally neutral parties are called upon to settle or adjudicate disputes, including administrative hearings, mediation and arbitration. Every university and college has developed its own legal system as well, to deal with issues involving students and/or faculty. One matter that university legal systems deal with routinely is allegations of breaches of academic integrity by students. The stakes in such matters are very high. For the student, a conviction can result in punishments up to expulsion from the university, and being excluded from many professions that require integrity, such as law, accounting and medicine. For the university, too lax a view of academic integrity can lead to an atmosphere in which the honest students feel disadvantaged, and the educational mission of the university is regarded with disdain.

In this case, a student at another university was accused of copying examination answers from adjacent students in a series of multiple choice examinations. I was hired by the family of the student to look into the data. The university provided me with the answers each student gave to each of 11 examinations, with the answers of the accused student and the alleged copyees identified. Additionally, I was given the answer keys (some questions had more than one correct answer!). Finally, I had data on the accused student's erasures, including some questions in which more than one answer was erased. However, they did not have seating charts for the examinations.

How should I address the data? First, it is obvious that I could not address whether the accused student had copied a single answer from one other person on a single exam. All I could hope to detect is whether there was a broad pattern of copying, which was the allegation. Second, there was no hope for a formal Bayesian analysis that would specify a probability for the data set had there been no pattern of copying, and had there been a pattern of copying. Instead I decided to use five indicia which I judged would be different if there were a pattern of copying. These were:

(i) There were two highly proctored examinations given after the accusations surfaced. Did the accused student do as well in those examinations as he or she did in the previous examinations?

(ii) Did the accused student do as well in the examinations in which no copying was alleged as in the examinations in which copying was alleged?

(iii) Did the accused student score better, generally, than the students from whom he or she was alleged to have copied from?

(iv) Compared to the similarity of all pairs of student answers in the examinations in which copying was alleged, were the similarity of the alleged copier's and alleged copyee's answers typical?

(v) Were the erasures that correct wrong answers to right answers as common in the tests in which copying was not alleged as in the tests in which it was alleged?

The answers to each of these questions were "yes," from which I concluded that there was not a general pattern of copying.

The alleged copier was found guilty at an initial hearing, but was exonerated on appeal. My report was available to both courts, but I was not invited to testify. I do not know whether or how much my report was influential in those decisions.

This paper was originally published in *Chance*, **12**, pp. 32–36. Republication by permission of the American Statistical Association.

Published Paper

J.B. Kadane

The maintenance of a fair environment for students who are competing in the classroom is an essential function of a modern university. When a breach of academic integrity is alleged, the consequences are very important, to both the academic community and to the persons involved. For the accused, expulsion from the university and inability to enter a profession that requires character checks – law, medicine, the military – can result. For the academic community, a perceived inability to provide an atmosphere free of cheating is debilitating.

In the case reported here, I was asked to assess whether the data support an accusation by classmates of copying multiple-choice examination answers from neighbors on several occasions in a professional program.

7.1 Data and Formal Analysis

Let us call the accused student S. I was retained by S's family and was given the answers by each student on each of 11 examinations taken that semester. S's answers were identified, as were the answers of each student S was alleged to have copied from on each exam on which copying was claimed. I also had the answer sheets giving the correct answers, sometimes more than one for a single question. In addition, I was given erasure data indicating which of S's answers had been erased (sometimes more than one on a single question) and what the final answer had been. Finally, two of the examinations occurred after the accusations had been made, and were taken under special and extra-secure proctoring arrangements, at S's request. I did not have seating charts from the exams, nor did I have, other than for S, cross-examination identification of students.

Methodologically, my first impulse given such a question is to think about a likelihood for the problem. There were about 5 answers per problem, and perhaps 60 questions per exam. Hence, there are about 5^{60} (more than 8×10^{41}) possible exam answers by a particular student to a particular exam. Something over 90 students took each exam, so for each exam the number of possible answers by all students is 90 raised to the 5^{60} power...an enormous number. Finally, there are 11 examinations, so the number of possible datasets is bigger still. Moreover, this calculation does not include any information about erasures or alleged sources of copying. The difficulty of modeling in this space in a way that would be convincing seemed daunting, especially since it would be necessary to develop a model in this big space conditional on copying having taken place and conditional on copying not having taken place.

Even though a formal model seems hopeless, I find it useful to think in Bayesian terms (see sidebar) about what I would expect to find in the data if copying took place as alleged, and if it did not. Only by finding aspects of the data that are differently probable under these two hypotheses can the data be informative. This less formal analysis is set out in the next section.

7.2   Priors: What to Look For

The use of Bayesian ideas in an informal manner requires that I state the kinds of indications of copying I looked for and the alternative explanations I could imagine. In each case, I intend to make use of the fact that copying is alleged in only some of the examinations.

I first comment on what one might expect to see on S's examinations compared to those of others. If S were copying, one would expect that S's scores on the examinations would be low and in particular would be lower than those of classmates S is alleged to have copied from. Furthermore, one would expect S's performance to be better on those examinations in which copying is alleged as compared to the others. Finally, one would expect that, if S had copied as alleged, S would have had lower performance on the last two examinations. On the other hand, because those two examinations were taken after S had been informed of the allegations, it is also possible that S's performance would suffer in the last two examinations if the allegations were false simply because of the psychological pressure of the situation.

All of these statements have to do with how S performs compared to other students in the class. Thus my concern is not with S's score but rather S's rank in class on an examination. I define this to be 1 plus the number of students who did better than S plus one-half of those who did as well on a given examination. This is the measure of performance I used to compare S to other students. A rank of 1 would indicate that S outperformed every other student on the examination. If 95 students took the examination, a rank of 95 would indicate that every other student did better.

If there were copying, I would expect to see a greater proportion of wrong answers changed to right answers in the examinations in which copying is alleged than in the other examinations. Conversely, if copying did not take place, I would expect the proportion of correction of wrong answers to be about the same in the two sets of examinations.

Finally, I can compute an index of how similar two papers are. For the moment, suppose I have a satisfactory such index. Without any copying, there are many reasons why papers would be similar. First, students may independently know the correct answers. (As teachers we hope for this). The students were exposed to the same texts and lecturers. Students study together, or otherwise discuss the course materials. Hence, they would be expected to think similarly about the material. Moreover, some wrong answers are "closer" to the correct ones–are better distractors–than others. Thus, there are several innocent reasons why student papers would be expected to show similarities without copying. One would expect that, if there were copying as alleged, the pairs of examinations of S and the student(s) S is alleged to have copied from would be more similar than those of other pairs of students.

7.3   An Index

It remains to specify a measure of similarity between two examinations. To do this, it is important to think about the possible explanations for various patterns of answers that might occur. In conducting this analysis, one feature of the data – the existence of more than one correct answer to certain problems – is important to keep in mind. I distinguish four different configurations:

1. Different answers. I believe this to be evidence against copying, whether both answers are correct, one is correct and another incorrect, or both are incorrect. Moreover, if they are different because one is blank and the other not, this is equally evidence against copying. Score each such case as 0.

2. A shared blank. This I would take to be ambiguous. It is hard for me to imagine why a student would want to copy a blank from another. These are omitted from scoring.

3. A shared correct answer. Shared correct answers might be evidence of cheating but could equally well be evidence that two students independently know the answer. (As teachers, we hope for this sort of thing). I treat this as an ambiguous circumstance. These are also omitted from scoring.

4. A shared incorrect answer. This I take to be evidence for copying, stronger if the shared incorrect answer is unusual, and weaker conversely. Suppose that the relative frequency of the shared incorrect answer is p_i among other students. I would score each such question by $1 - p_i$.

The index I propose is then the average score among scored questions. The lower the score, the weaker the evidence of copying, and conversely.

There are several reasons why two students' indices might be high. One, of course, is that one may have copied from the other. There are other reasons, however. The students are in the same class, studied from the same materials, and heard the same lectures. Some of them may have studied together. All of these reasons can cause them to have high similarities without having copied. The same considerations, however, apply to every pair of students in the class. I would suspect a pair of students of having been involved in copying not on the basis of a high index *per se* but a high index compared to other students in their class. In the case in question, copying was alleged from one to five other students, depending on the examination. If those one to five pairs do not exhibit very high indices compared to the other pairs of students in the class, I would take this as evidence against copying. Conversely, if one or more of these pairs is extraordinarily high given the distribution of indexes in the class, I would take this as evidence in favor of copying.

To complete the definition, I must say what index to give a pair of students with no scored questions–that is, all their questions are of type 2 and 3. In this case, I would give them the average score for pairs from the class.

Finally, I use the rank of the similarity index for pairs of students to indicate how high the index is compared to the index of other members of the class. Thus, if a particular pair is ranked 1, that means that their examinations' similarity is higher than the similarity of the examinations of every other pair of students in the class. If 95 students take an examination, there are $95 \times 94 \div 2 = 4{,}465$ pairs of students. Thus, a pair of students whose similarity is ranked 4,465 would have examinations less similar than any other pair of students in the class.

7.4 Results

The results concerning scores and similarities are given in Table 7.1 and Figure 7.1. To take the columns in Table 7.1 from left to right, examinations 8 and 11 are those that took place after allegations of copying were made. S's rank was 7 and 11 in those examinations, out of 90+ students. So there is no evidence that S did poorly in a more highly supervised situation. This is contrary to what one would have expected had copying occurred.

In each of the other examinations, as Figure 7.1 shows, S scores well into the top quarter of the class and sometimes extremely well. S does not do particularly better on examinations in which examination copying is alleged, again contrary to the hypothesis of examination copying.

Comparing the ranks of alleged copiees to those of S, in each case but one S does better on the examination in question than does the alleged copiee. This again is contrary to what one would expect were there examination copying. Generally one

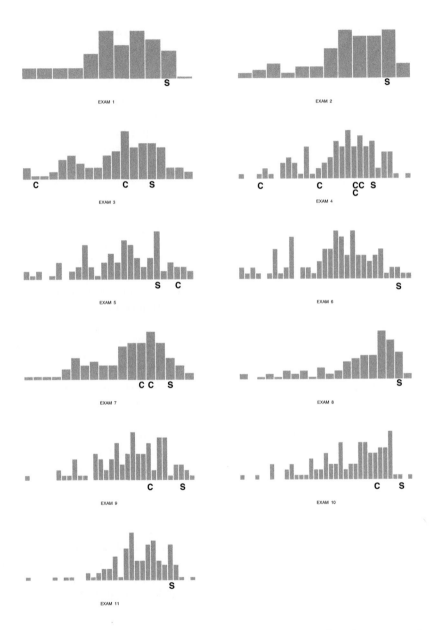

Figure 7.1: Histograms of examination results for each of the eleven examinations. "S" represents S's score, "C" represents the score of alleged copiees.

Table 7.1: Summary of examination results: scores and similarities

Rank by score on the exam of accused copier, S	Rank by score on the exam of alleged copiee	Rank of similarity between alleged copiee and S's answers	Number of students taking exam	Number of questions
1*	6			96	56
2*	13.5			95	39
3	21	48.5	1090	95	51
		92	925.5		
4	18	38.5	90.5	95	88
		31.5	191		
		71.5	1741.5		
		38.5	767.5		
		94	2664.5		
5	20	7	3596.5	96	63
6*	3			94	79
7	9.5	40.5	3256	94	65
		29	3256		
8*	7			93	69
9	5	32	337	95	92
10	2	27	1605	95	94
11*	11			95	86

*There were no allegations of copying on these exams.

thinks of a weaker student copying from a stronger one. Indeed it requires far-fetched reasoning to imagine why a stronger student would copy from a weaker one.

To appreciate the similarity column, recall that higher similarities reflect greater agreement between the examinations. The similarities are ranked in the same way as were the examinations, so lower ranks indicate higher agreement. As an illustration, the number 1,090 indicates that the pair of S and the first alleged copiee in examination 3 had a similarity with 1,043 pairs higher and 92 pairs the same, for a rank of $1,043 + 1 + 92/2 = 1,092$. These numbers are very high, indicating that the similarity between S's examination answers and those of the alleged copiees are not extraordinarily high. Again this is contrary to what one would have expected had examination copying occurred.

The results on erasures are given in Table 7.2. In the examinations in which there is not an allegation of examination copying, out of 16 questions with changed answers, $13/16 = 81.25\%$ were changing wrong answers to correct ones. In the examinations in which copying is alleged, there were two questions on each of which S erased two answers. In both cases, the final answer given was correct. It is ambiguous how to count the change in examination 4 from a right answer to another right answer. Depending on how one chooses to treat these two circumstances, the proportion of wrong answers changed to correct ones is $30/39 = 76.92\%$, $30/38 = 78.95\%$, $32/40 = 80.0\%$, or $32/41 = 78.05\%$. A case might be made for any one of them. For the purposes of this analysis, however, they are numerically similar. In all four cases, the proportion of wrong answers corrected is slightly less among the examinations in which copying is alleged than among examinations in which copying is not alleged. Thus, the erasure

Table 7.2: Erasures of answers by S

| | Examinations in which copying is not alleged | | | | |
| | Numbers of questions with answers changed | | | | |
Exam	wrong → right	wrong → wrong	right → wrong	right → right	total erasures
1	0	0	0	0	0
2	2	1	0	0	3
6	7	0	2	0	9
8	2	0	0	0	2
11	2	0	0	0	2
Total	13	1	2	0	16
	Examinations in which copying is alleged				
	Numbers of questions with answers changed				
Exams	wrong → right	wrong → wrong	right → wrong	right → right	total erasures
3	2	0	0	0	2
4	6	3	0	1	10
5	4	0	0	0	4
7	1	1	0	0	2
9	9	0	2	0	11
	(10 answers)				(12 answers)
10	8	1	1	0	10
	(9 answers)				(11 answers)
Total	30	5	3	1	39
	(32 answers)				(41 answers)

evidence fails to support the hypothesis of examination copying and, in fact, supports the contrary hypothesis that no examination copying took place.

7.5 Conclusion

There are five ways in which the data are examined to see if they are consistent with the hypothesis of examination copying. These are as follows:

- S did well in the two highly proctored examinations, contrary to the hypothesis.
- S is a very strong student and did as well in tests in which copying is not alleged as in those in which it is, again contrary to the hypothesis.
- S did better than each of the alleged copiees except one, again contrary to the hypothesis of copying.
- The similarity between S's examination and the alleged copiees indicates lack of extraordinary similarity compared to other pairs of students in the class. Again this is contrary to the hypothesis of examination copying.
- The proportion of erasures that correct wrong answers is slightly less among the examinations in which copying is alleged than among the examinations in which copying is not alleged. This, too, is contrary to the hypothesis of examination copying.

On the basis of these tests I conclude that the examination data do not support the hypothesis of examination copying. Rather the reverse, they support the conclusion that S was wrongly accused.

What would I have done if some of my indicators had suggested that copying had taken place and others had indicated that it had not? I would have had to think much harder about the degree to which each part of the evidence pointed in each direction, and my conclusions would have had to be much more equivocal.

Finally, a reader might be interested in knowing what actually happened. There was an initial hearing before an honor court, in which most of the evidence of cheating was about body language during the examinations in question. My report was presented to this court, and I was available by telephone for questions, had there been any. S was found guilty, and the matter was appealed within the university's structure. At the appeals level, the attorney presenting the case for the prosecution was asked by a member of the appeals court what her view was of the statistical evidence, and said she thought it was inconsequential. "Oh, I disagree" said the appeals court member. S was exonerated. Other than that remark, I have no idea what role my report may have played in that decision.

7.6 Other Purposes, Other Indices

There are kinds of cheating on multiple choice examinations other than examination copying–for example, impersonation and theft of the answer key. Each kind of possible cheating and each circumstance requires its own investigation and analysis.

The statistical perspective that underlies many of the articles in this literature is that of significance testing. For example, Angoff (1974) reported that the Education and Testing Service uses one of several indexes and investigates further only if at least one of them departs from the mean by 3.72 standard deviations or more. (Apparently no account is taken of the fact that several tests are being used simultaneously). If an examinee's test fails this screen, a retest is invited and no further consequence ensues.

Frary et al. (1977) proposed an index of examination copying that depends on both the number of common wrong answers and the number of common correct answers. Like Angoff, they looked for a significance test computed on the basis of no copying and used high departures from the expected as evidence of copying. For reasons given previously, I am not comfortable with the idea of using common correct answers as evidence of cheating. (Thus, two students who write perfect examinations might be prime suspects to Frary et al. but not to me).

A general review of the performance of the indexes was conducted in a technical report from the national testing organization ACT, and it found that the theoretical significance levels of the indexes of various authors did not coincide well with the false-positive rates of their benchmark data. The reasons for this appears to be that innocent behavior can lead to high indexes under certain circumstances. The adherents of the significance-level approach are thus left in the position of knowing that their analysis exaggerates the weight of evidence on the guilt of the suspected copier without being able to say by how much it does so. By contrast, this article does not use significance testing but instead, (implicitly), Bayes' theorem as its fundamental analytic tool. This permits, and in fact requires, consideration of innocent explanations of the phenomena studied. I have not, however, refined the approach quantitatively to the point that I can give a plausible likelihood ratio for examination copying. Much remains to be done, both in the analysis of specific cases and in generalizing from them.

[I thank Dan Cork, Jonathan Forster and Robert Frary for helpful discussions in the preparation of this article.]

Sidebar
Bayesian Statistics

Bayesian statisticians use Bayes' theorem, a result in standard probability theory, to measure the extent to which data change a current, or prior, opinion to a new, or posterior opinion. The distinguishing feature of Bayesian inference is the use of probability distributions on the parameter space to describe and convey uncertainty.

Elementary expositions of Bayesian ideas can be found in the following references:

Berry, D. (1996), *Statistics, A Bayesian Perspective*, Belmont: Duxbury Press.
Lindley, D.V. (1985), *Making Decisions*, London: Wiley.

REFERENCES

Angoff, W. (1974). "The development of statistical indices for detecting cheaters." *Journal of the American Statistical Association*, 69, 44–49. 133

Frary, R., Tideman, T., and Watts, T. (1977). "Indices of cheating on multiple-choice tests." *Journal of Educational Statistics*, 2, 235–256. 133

Hansen, B., Harris, D., and Brennan, R. (1987). "A comparison of several statistical methods for examining allegations of copying." Research Rep. Series No. 87-15, Iowa City: American College Testing Program. 133

Epilogue

What is the scientific issue addressed?
   Whether the data support an allegation of examination copying against a particular student.
Is justification given for
   a) the use of the data?
   The data were provided by the university where the incidents in question occurred.
   b) the use of the likelihood and prior?
   There is no likelihood in this paper, and there are "indicia" instead of priors.
What robustness checks were conducted?
   Only checks that small variations in the data would not change the overall picture.
How was the computing done?
   They are basically counts and some simple graphs.
If I were doing this problem today, how would I change the approach?
   I would not.
What do I see as the contributions of this paper?
   It addressed (after a fashion) the scientific question.
Was Bayesian analysis useful in this problem?
   No. I argue that Bayesian thinking was useful, but the connection could be regarded as tenuous.

TEACHING SUGGESTIONS

References for theoretical ideas:

1. Significance testing: *Principles* Section 12.2

Exercises

1. In what sense is the analysis in the paper "informal Bayes?" Is there such a method of analysis?

2. Do you agree with the indicators suggested in Section 7.2? Why or why not? If you were going to improve one of them in some way, which would it be and how would you propose to improve it? In what way would your suggestion be an improvement?

3. Should shared correct answers be regarded as evidence of copying? Make the best case you can for and against.

4. Suppose you were a member of an honor court hearing this case. There is some evidence concerning body language against student S, and there is this statistical report. What weight would you give to the statistical report, and why?

Chapter 8

Vote Tampering in a District Justice Election in Beaver County, PA (2001)

Foreword

This is the story of an engagement as an expert witness that started out in a mis-understanding of the legal situation, but nonetheless led to a scientifically successful project.

At the time, Beaver County used paper ballots, which were counted by running them through the same sort of machine used to grade multiple choice tests in very large classes. In the election of November 1993, as originally counted, Zupsic defeated Laughlin by 36 votes. In January 1994, in a recount requested by Laughlin, she appeared to have won by 46 votes. Zupsic challenged this result, alleging vote tampering.

How might vote tampering been physically possible? The ballot boxes were locked, but every ballot box could be opened by the same key, which was widely available. The boxes were stored in a locked room, but many keys to that room were available. Finally, each box was sealed with a special seal, but a county detective, claiming he wanted them for an art project, got a supply from the company that makes them. Thus, it was plausible that vote tampering might have taken place.

A three judge panel of the Beaver County Court of Common Pleas heard this suit, found that there had been vote tampering, and ordered a new election. The evidence included five voters who are able to identify their ballots and who testified that their ballots had been altered. [How could they identify their ballots, you might ask? The reason is that they had written in, for a race that did not matter, a peculiar name, such as Bugs Bunny, or Mickey Mouse. And why would they do that? This is how a political boss could see that they had voted as they had been instructed. Apparently the political culture of Beaver County at the time tolerated a certain amount of corruption.]

Both candidates appealed. The Pennsylvania Supreme Court overruled the Court of Common Pleas. It sent the case back with instructions to specify which specific ballots it found had been altered, and to award those votes to the candidate the court found had been the voter's intention to vote for.

It was at this point that I was hired by attorneys for Beaver County to do a statistical analysis of the ballots. I learned about overcounts (votes for both candidates), undercounts (votes for neither candidate), and overrides (a vote for all candidates of a given party, overridden by a specific vote for a candidate of another party). To analyze the data, I created an index of vulnerability of a precinct, equal to the increase in overvote minus the decrease in the undervote. The results, shown in Table 8.1, indicate 5 precincts in which it was plausible that vote tampering had taken place. This was the heart of the testimony I was prepared to give.

However, the court declined to hear my testimony, for the good reason that my testimony would not help them with the task they had been given by the Supreme Court: to identify specific ballots they believed had been altered, explain why they believed those ballots had been altered, and award the votes as they believed the voters intended.

So I was left with a very interesting data set. I was able to persuade Ilaria DiMatteo, then a graduate student, to work with me on it. We had the November and January tabulations of the votes in all races, by precinct, but did not have data on individual ballots. Our basic model is a Markov Chain in which most ballots are counted the same way in the two tabulations, with parameters for whether tampering had occurred in that precinct's ballot box, and, if it had, the extent of overcount and undercount alteration.

The Court of Common Pleas found 45 ballots it believed had been altered, and found that Zupsic had won the race by 8 votes. This decision was upheld on appeal, and Zupsic took office. The precincts in which ballots found by the court to have been altered were broadly similar to those found in my initial analysis to have been most vulnerable. And they coincided well with what DiMatteo and I found from our Bayesian model.

This paper was originally published in the *Journal of the American Statistical Association*, **96**, pp. 510–518. Republication by permission of the American Statistical Association.

Where are they now? Ilaria DiMatteo is a statistician working at the United Nations.

Published Paper

Ilaria DiMatteo and Joseph B. Kadane[1]

Abstract

This article examines the evidence of vote tampering in a District Justice election in Beaver County, Pennsylvania. An informal exploratory data analysis and a legal history are followed by a formal Bayesian model of the data from the vote count on election night and the recount completed 2 months later. The evidence suggests that persons unknown could have gained access to the boxes containing the paper ballots, and surprising patterns of changes in the counts support the inference that certain boxes were tampered with. Three methods are compared not only with respect to the overall matter of whether tampering occurred, but also with respect to which precincts were likely to have been tampered with, and to what extent. The results are generally consistent across methods. The Bayesian model is validated by using it on the data for a race (for Superior Court) in the same election in which vote tampering is not suspected. The results show that the model gives a predictive distribution of a few votes uncertainty for the Superior Court race but of around 60 votes in the District Justice race, enough to swing the election. Technically, the computations involve a Markov chain Monte Carlo. Because it is not possible to observe how each individual ballot was counted each time, data augmentation is required to fill in a Markov matrix given both margins. The fact that both margins are given restricts the kinds of proposals that the chain considers.

Keywords: Ballots, Data augmentation, Markov chain Monte Carlo

8.1 Introduction

On November 2, 1993 in a general election, Joseph Zupsic apparently defeated Delores Laughlin for the office of District Justice in Beaver County, Pennsylvania by a vote of 3,783 to 3,747, a 36-vote margin. Laughlin requested a recount, which on January 5, 1994, showed her the victor by 3,793 to 3,747. This article addresses whether the data support the conclusion that sometime in the intervening period, the ballots (which were paper) were tampered with, to Laughlin's benefit.

A District Justice is the only judge most citizens ever appear before. This court handles civil cases with a value less than $7000, and screens out inappropriate arrests. Elections for this office are often hotly contested, especially when a vacancy occurs.

The ballot boxes were locked and sealed with special, numbered seals. The boxes were stored in a locked room. However, every ballot box in the county could be unlocked with the same key, copies of which were widely distributed, and there were several keys to the locked storage room. The Board of Elections failed to record the

[1]Ilaria DiMatteo is Associate Statistician at the United Nations, New York, New York (email: ilaria@un.com). She completed this work while a Ph.D. student at Carnegie Mellon. Joseph B. Kadane is Leonard J. Savage University Professor, Department of Statistics, Carnegie Mellon University, Pittsburgh, PA 15213 (email: kadane@stat.cmu.edu). Kadane was a consultant to the Beaver County government in the matter of this election. The subsequent research was supported by the National Science Foundation, under Grant DMS-9801401.

numbers on the seals until after the recount. Finally, a county detective testified that he had obtained seals from the manufacturer by claiming that he needed them for an art project. Thus it is plausible that access to the ballot boxes might have been gained between the election night and January 5th, 1994, when the recount was complete. The evidence about whether this occurred then rests on a physical examination of the ballots, on which the courts relied, and on a comparison of the two vote counts, that of November 2 and of January 5, which were conducted by vote-tabulating machines.

A vote is recorded for a candidate if either a box is marked for all candidates of the candidate's party, or if a box is marked specifically for that candidate. For example, if a ballot were marked for the candidates of the Democratic Party, then Zupsic, the Democratic Party nominee, would receive a vote, unless the ballot were marked specifically for Laughlin, in which case she would get the vote. If neither party's box were marked, and neither candidate's box were marked, an "undervote" would occur, and neither candidate would get a vote. If neither party's box were marked and both candidates' boxes were marked, then an "overvote" would occur, and again neither candidate would get a vote. The tabulation of votes records the number of votes for each candidate, and the numbers of undervotes and overvotes, but not the number of votes gained by each candidate by party designation.

How would an additional ballot mark made by an intruder for a candidate, say candidate A, affect the vote totals? This would depend on how the ballot had been marked by the voter. If the ballot had been marked for candidate A's party, no change would result. If it had been marked for candidate B's party, candidate B would lose a vote and candidate A would gain one, a shift of two. If the ballot had been marked for candidate B, then candidate B would lose a vote, and the overvote would increase by one. Finally, if the ballot had been unmarked, then candidate A would gain a vote and the undervote would decrease by one.

For these reasons, it is reasonable to use as an index of precinct vulnerability the increase in overvote plus the decrease in undervote between the two ballot countings. High values of this index indicate precincts where ballot boxes may have been tampered with. Under the hypothesis that no tampering occurred, we would expect the shift in votes to be centered at zero, not favoring either candidate particularly. A shift favoring one of the candidates only, particularly in highly vulnerable precincts, would, under this argument, favor the hypothesis of vote tampering. Table 8.1 gives the results for all precincts.

Table 8.1 suggests that the precincts 56, 114, 115, 138 and 149 are most vulnerable. Examining the last column in Table 8.1, which indicates the vote shift by precinct between the two counts, shows a very large shift favorable to Laughlin occurring in exactly the suspect precincts. This supports the hypothesis of vote tampering.

The total vote counts were not exactly the same in each precinct in the original count and in the recount. As noted earlier, the total count, as recorded in the court decisions, increased from $3,783 + 3,747 = 7,530$ to $3,793 + 3,747 = 7,540$. This explains why there are precincts with no change in overvote or undervote, yet the shift in vote is not divisible by two. We thank an attentive referee for pointing this out.

Moreover, it is necessary to address the question of whether index numbers and vote shifts of the size reported in Table 8.1 are unusual. The correlation between the index and the vote shift is .844. We drew 10,000 random permutations of the index; in no case was the absolute correlation with the vote shift greater than .844. Fortunately, other data at hand allows us to examine this issue more precisely. Other races were to be decided in this election in the five suspect precincts, and all of these were counted on November 2 and then recounted on January 5. Concentrating only on the single-office races, 202 other vote counts involving the same precincts were decided at the same time. Among these, the largest index was 3, which occurred once. Thus we conclude

Table 8.1: Changes in Vote Count by Precinct, November 2, 1993–January 5, 1994.

Precincts voting for District Justice	Increase in Overvote	Decrease in Undervote	Index	Votes Shift Z to L
49	-1	1		2
50		2	2	-3
51		1	1	-2
52				-1
53		-3	-3	2
54				1
55				-1
56	5	8	13	25
82				
84				1
93				
114	3	5	8	20
115	3	5	8	24
116		1	1	4
117				-3
118				2
119				-2
138	5	4	9	10
140		3	3	-1
141				
149		7	7	4

NOTE: Blanks indicate 0's

that indices of the sizes reported in Table 8.1 for the suspect precincts are highly unusual. We also calculated the vote shifts between November 2 and January 5 for these 202 precinct races. The largest shifts were two of size 6, followed by two of size 4. Hence, of the vote shifts among the suspect precincts reported in Table 8.1, only the shift for precinct 149 is within range of the 202 others.

Thus the evidence suggests vote tampering, but the foregoing informal analysis does not indicate the strength of the evidence. To measure this is our task. The article is organized as follows. Section 8.2 gives the history of the litigation surrounding this matter, Section 8.3 describes our model, and Section 8.4 gives the results.

8.2   Legal History

During the recount process between November 2 and January 5, a total of 87 ballots were challenged, 69 by Zupsic and 18 by Laughlin. On January 10, 1994, Zupsic filed a lawsuit seeking to overturn the Recount Board's awarding of the election to Laughlin.

After three hearings, a three-judge panel of the Court of Common Pleas's in Beaver County issued an opinion on April 8, 1994, finding that vote tampering had occurred, that "in all probability, a sufficient number of ballots were altered...so as to change the outcome of the election," and that striking the altered ballots would unfairly disenfranchise voters. On this basis it set aside the election and ordered a new one.

In a further elaboration of its ruling issued on May 5, 1994, the Court of Common Pleas panel noted that there were five voters who, because of idiosyncratic write-in votes, were able to identify their ballots specifically and testified that their ballots had been altered to include a mark for Laughlin. A total of 45 of the 87 contested ballots had marks for Laughlin inconsistent with the other marks on those ballots.

This decision was appealed by both candidates. The appeal was heard by the Supreme Court of Pennsylvania on September 19, 1994; the opinion was announced

Table 8.2: Common Pleas Court Findings of Vote Tampering, By District, from the July 12, 1996 Decision.

District Number	Voter Testimony	Agreed by Parties	Court Finding	Total
49			1	1
56	1	4	5	10
114			6	6
115	1	4	9	14
116			2	2
138	3	2	1	6
149			6	6
Total	5	10	30	45

on January 22, 1996. The Supreme Court (543 Pa. 216; 670 A.2d 629 (Pa. 1996)) found the Court of Common Pleas's decision was insufficiently precise in that it did not specify which ballots that it found to have been altered and why it thought so. It also ruled that if the Court of Common Pleas found that ballots had been altered, it should award the votes in question to the candidate for whom the voter had intended to vote. With these instructions, the Supreme Court reversed the decision of the Court of Common Pleas to set aside the election, and remanded the case back to the Court of Common Pleas.

On July 12, 1996 the same three-judge panel of the Court of Common Pleas issued an opinion in which it specified 45 of the 87 challenged ballots as having been tampered with: 5 from direct testimony referred to earlier, 10 by agreement between the attorneys for Zupsic and Laughlin, and 30 more by similarity to the previous 15. The distribution of these challenged ballots by district is given in Table 8.2.

As a result of these changes, Zupsic got 45 more votes and Laughlin 21 fewer votes. From other challenged votes, Laughlin got 5 more votes and Zupsic 1 more vote. The final result was 3,786 for Zupsic, and 3,778 for Laughlin. On this basis, the Court declared Zupsic the winner.

Laughlin appealed this decision to the Commonwealth Court of Pennsylvania, an intermediate appellate court. A three-judge panel heard this case and upheld the new decision of the Court of Common Pleas on June 4, 1997 (695 A.2d 476). Finally, the Supreme Court declined to rehear the case on October 14, 1998. On November 17, Zupsic was sworn in as District Justice. He was re-elected, unopposed, in November, 1999.

8.3 Model

To assess whether the ballots were altered between the two counts in the race for District Justice, we can examine the conditional classification probabilities of each vote in the second count given its first count classification. If there was no "human intervention" between the two counts, with few exceptions each vote should be classified the same on the second count as on the first. Because the exceptions would occur from machine errors in counting, it is reasonable to believe that when there is a change in that classification, that vote is equally likely to fall in any one of the other categories. On the other hand, if vote tampering occurred, then a clear structure in the transition probabilities, as specified in Section 8.3.3, would be expected.

To estimate the normal counting error, represented by the transition probabilities, we use the data from the other races. We assume that no vote tampering has occurred in those races and thus they provide information on the likelihood of each vote being classified after the second count in the same category as in the first count, absent vote tampering.

The next three sections present the Bayesian hierarchical model used to analyze the data. Section 8.3.2 specifies the structure of the data; as stated earlier, the interest is in estimating the transition probabilities for a single ballot, but the observed data represent the aggregate behavior of the ballots (i.e., we observe only the total number of ballots in a voting precinct classified in each category in the two counts). We therefore augment the data (Tanner and Wong, 1987) by introducing a variable representing single ballot behavior. Section 8.3.3 presents the details of the hierarchical model.

8.3.1 Data Structuring

Consider a generic race r with m candidates and a precinct g. The data are tabulated as follows: for each category i (namely candidate 1 ..., candidate m, undervote, overvote, and scattered vote) the total number of votes is recorded after the first count, $y_{i\cdot}^{rg}$, and after the second count, $y_{\cdot i}^{rg}$. Table 8.3 shows the data format for race r and precinct g, where as before we classify as undervote the ballots with no mark for either candidate or candidate's party, as overvote the ballots with more than one mark, and as scattered the ballots with a preference different from the candidates listed on the ballot.

Table 8.3: Data for a Race r with m Candidates and Precinct g

States	1st count	2nd count
Candidate 1	$y_{1\cdot}^{rg}$	$y_{\cdot 1}^{rg}$
$\vdots$	$\vdots$	$\vdots$
Candidate m	$y_{m\cdot}^{rg}$	$y_{\cdot m}^{rg}$
Undervote	$y_{m+1\cdot}^{rg}$	$y_{\cdot m+1}^{rg}$
Overvote	$y_{m+2\cdot}^{rg}$	$y_{\cdot m+2}^{rg}$
Scattered Vote	$y_{m+3\cdot}^{rg}$	$y_{\cdot m+3}^{rg}$

We can imagine the data in Table 8.3 in the following way: The totals resulting from first count and the second count are the row and column marginals of a $k \times k$ ($k = m + 3$) contingency table whose elements z_{ij}^{rg} represent the number of ballots that were classified in category i in the first count and in category j in the second count. Table 8.4 shows the matrix representation of the data for a race r and precinct g.

The data are therefore augmented by introducing the interior elements Z^{rg} of the contingency table for each race r and precinct g in order to estimate the transition probabilities of a single ballot.

8.3.2 Model Specification

In this section we present the four stages in the model. First, we introduce some notation used throughout this section. We let $\mathbf{y}_1^{rg} = (y_{1\cdot}^{rg}, \ldots, y_{k\cdot}^{rg})^T$ and $\mathbf{y}_2^{rg} = (y_{\cdot 1}^{rg}, \ldots, y_{\cdot k}^{rg})^T$ denote the vector of counts in the first and second count in race r with m candidates and precinct g. (Note that $k = m + 3$ and that in general the

Table 8.4: Data for a Race r With m Candidates and Precinct g

				1st count
				$y_{1 \cdot}^{rg}$
	(not observed)			$\vdots$
	$Z^{rg} = \{z_{ij}^{rg}\}$	$\cdots$		$y_{i \cdot}^{rg}$
	$\vdots$			$\vdots$
				$y_{k \cdot}^{rg}$
2nd count	$y_{\cdot 1}^{rg}$	$\cdots$	$y_{\cdot j}^{rg}$	$\cdots$ $\quad y_{\cdot k}^{rg}$

number of candidates depends on the race, but for simplicity of notation we write k instead of k^r).

Also let $Y_1 = \{\mathbf{y}_1^{rg}, \forall g, r\}$, $Y_2 = \{\mathbf{y}_2^{rg}, \forall g, r\}$ and $Z = \{Z^{rg}, \forall r, g\}$ be the collection of the results of the first count, the second count, and the collection of the augmented data Z^{rg}.

Likelihood. We specify in this stage the conditional distribution of the results of the second count given the results of the first count and the augmented data. It is obvious that

$$Pr(\mathbf{y}_2^{rg}|\mathbf{y}_1^{rg}, Z^{rg}) = I_{\{JZ^{rg}=\mathbf{y}_1^{rg}, JZ^{rg^T}=\mathbf{y}_2^{rg}\}}(\mathbf{y}_2^{rg}) \qquad \forall g, r$$

where $J \in \mathbb{R}^k$ is a vector containing all 1's, and $I_{\{A\}}(x) = 1$ if $x \in A$ and 0 otherwise. The foregoing model simply states that the conditional probability of the column marginal given the row marginal and the interior elements of the table is 1 if the column marginals satisfy the constraints, and 0 otherwise.

Furthermore we assume that given the latent variable and the results of the first count, the results of the second count are independent across races and precincts:

$$L(Z|Y_2, Y_1) = \prod_{rg} I_{\{JZ^{rg}=\mathbf{y}_1^{rg}, JZ^{rg^T}=\mathbf{y}_2^{rg}\}}(\mathbf{y}_2^{rg})$$

In particular, let r' denote the race District Justice, then the likelihood can be written as

$$L(Z|Y_2, Y_1) = \prod_g I_{\{JZ^{r'g}=\mathbf{y}_1^{r'g}, JZ^{r'g^T}=\mathbf{y}_2^{r'g}\}}(\mathbf{y}_2^{r'g})$$

$$\prod_{r \neq r', g} I_{\{JZ^{rg}=\mathbf{y}_1^{rg}, JZ^{rg^T}=\mathbf{y}_2^{rg}\}}(\mathbf{y}_2^{rg}) \qquad (8.1)$$

Latent variables. In this stage we specify a probability model for the latent variables. We assume that for each race r and precinct g, there is a transition probability matrix Q^{rg} that characterizes the shift of each ballot from one category to another between the two counts. Each element q_{ij}^{rg} of this transition probability matrix represents the conditional probability of a ballot classified in category i in the first count shifting to category j in the second count. Obviously it must be that for every i, $\sum_j q_{ij}^{rg} = 1$ for all r and g.

For a race r and a precinct g, given the transition matrix Q^{rg} and the row margins, we assume that the interior elements follow a product of multinomial sampling scheme,

$$Pr(Z^{rg}|\mathbf{y}_1^{rg}, Q^{rg}) = \prod_{i=1}^{k} \frac{y_{i\cdot}^{rg}!}{\prod_{i=j}^{k} z_{ij}^{rg}!} \prod_{j=1}^{k} q_{ij}^{z_{ij}^{rg}} I_{\{JZ^{rg}=\mathbf{y}_1^{rg}\}}(Z^{rg}) \qquad (8.2)$$

where q_{ij} is the ijth element of Q^{rg}. Models of this type were discussed in Lee et al. (1970).

We now describe the structure of the transition probability matrix in the cases of no-cheating, cheating in favor of candidate 1, and cheating in favor of candidate 2. Consider first the case of no vote tampering in race r and precinct g. We assume that $Q^{rg} = P$, where

$$P = \begin{bmatrix} p & \frac{1-p}{k-1} & \cdots & \frac{1-p}{k-1} \\ \frac{1-p}{k-1} & p & \frac{1-p}{k-1} & \vdots \\ \vdots & \frac{1-p}{k-1} & \ddots & \frac{1-p}{k-1} \\ \frac{1-p}{k-1} & \cdots & \frac{1-p}{k-1} & p \end{bmatrix} \qquad (8.3)$$

Note that P depends on the race through the number of categories k (its dimensions change with k), but the parameter p characterizing P does not depend on the race or the precinct.

This form of the transition matrix P relies on the assumption that if there is no vote tampering, then the transition probabilities are concentrated on the main diagonal and are uniformly spread on the off-diagonal elements, representing the normal misclassification error. As mentioned before, we assume that no vote tampering has occurred in any of the other races (i.e., all but the District Justice race). This assumption corresponds to setting $Q^{rg} = P$ for all races $r \neq r'$ and all precincts g. In addition we assume that p is close to 1.

In the District Justice race, (i.e. $r = r'$), we assume that the transition probability matrix $Q^{r'g}$ takes the form

$$Q^{r'g} = P + X_g C_\eta(\gamma_1, \gamma_2, \delta) \qquad (8.4)$$

where X_g is an indicator variable which is 1 if vote tampering occurred in precinct g and 0 otherwise (in which case the transition probability matrix is just P). If $X_g = 1$, then the transition probability matrix changes according to the parameter η, which denotes the candidate for whom the vote tampering is in favor. If the shift in votes is in favor of candidate Zupsic, then $\eta = 1$, in which case

$C_1(\gamma_1, \gamma_2, \delta) =$

	Zupsic	Laughlin	Undervote	Overvote	Scattered Vote
Zupsic	0	0	0	0	0
Laughlin	$+\gamma_1$	$-(\gamma_1 + \gamma_2)$	0	$+\gamma_2$	0
Undervote	$+\delta$	0	$-\delta$	0	0
Overvote	0	0	0	0	0
Scattered Vote	0	0	0	0	0

If the shift in votes is in favor of candidate Laughlin, then $\eta = 2$, in which case

$C_1(\gamma_2, \gamma_2, \delta) =$

	Zupsic	Laughlin	Undervote	Overvote	Scattered Vote
Zupsic	$-(\gamma_1 + \gamma_2)$	$+\gamma_1$	0	$+\gamma_2$	0
Laughlin	0	0	0	0	0
Undervote	0	$+\delta$	$-\delta$	0	0
Overvote	0	0	0	0	0
Scattered Vote	0	0	0	0	0

These two matrices represent the expected increments in the transition probabilities when vote tampering has occurred in a particular precinct. They correspond to the ways in which ballots could be altered to increase the number of votes for one candidate and decrease the number of votes for the other candidate. Suppose, for example, that cheating is in favor of Laughlin (i.e., $\eta = 2$); then a ballot can be altered in the three ways:

- an undervote ballot becomes a vote for Laughlin by simply marking that blank ballot in favor of Laughlin. This leads to an increase of the number of votes for this candidate and therefore an increase of the probability of going from undervote to Laughlin. This increment in the transition probability is represented by the parameter δ.

- a ballot in favor of Zupsic becomes an overvote by adding marks on that ballot. This leads to an increase of the transition probability of a ballot to shift from Zupsic to overvote, which is represented by the parameter γ_2. This also leads to a decrease in the number of votes for Zupsic.

- a party vote for Zupsic becomes a vote for Laughlin by marking that ballot in favor of Laughlin. This shift increases the corresponding transition probability by an amount γ_1. The consequence of this shift is that the number of votes for Laughlin increases and the number of votes for Zupsic decreases.

Thus the parameters γ_1, γ_2 and δ represent therefore the possible increases in the transition probabilities from the case of vote tampering. These parameters are constrained as follows to guarantee that the elements q_{ij} are nonnegative and less than 1:

$$\gamma_1, \gamma_2 \in \Gamma = \{(\gamma_1, \gamma_2) \in I\!\!R^2 : \gamma_1 \geq 0, \gamma_2 \geq 0, \gamma_1 + \gamma_2 \leq p\}$$

and

$$\delta \in [0, p].$$

Modeling the "cheating" Parameters. In this stage we model the parameters that indicate whether cheating has occurred and, if so, its strength. We start modeling the variables X_g, which indicate for each precinct g whether cheating has occurred in that precinct. Recall that the ballots from a precinct were stored together in a box, and the boxes for the 21 precincts were gathered together in the same room. To alter the result of the election, someone would have had to enter the room, pick a box of ballots, open it and examine the ballots to alter them. We assume that each box, and thus each precinct, has the same probability θ of being opened and altered,

$$\theta = Pr(X_g = 1) \qquad \forall g$$

and that the indicator variables $(X_1, \cdots, X_{21})^T$ are exchangeable,

$$P\left(\sum_g X_g = x | \theta\right) = \binom{21}{x}\theta^x(1-\theta)^{21-x} \qquad x = 0, \ldots, 21.$$

If vote tampering has occurred, then its direction of it is given by the parameter η. If $\eta = 1$, then cheating is in favor of Zupsic; if $\eta = 2$, then cheating is in favor of Laughlin. By assuming that η does not depend on the precinct g, we force the precincts to have the same direction of cheating. We assume a priori that η is a Bernoulli random variable with probability τ,

$$\pi_\eta(\eta) = \begin{cases} \tau & \text{if } \eta = 1 \\ 1 - \tau & \text{if } \eta = 2 \end{cases}$$

where τ is known (we have used $\tau = 0.5$ in estimation).

The parameters γ_1, γ_2 and δ in (8.4) give a measure of the strength of cheating; they measure how much the transition probabilities in case of vote tampering differ from the "normal" transition probabilities. They are assumed to be the same for all of the precincts in which cheating has occurred. A priori we assume uniform distributions over the space Γ for γ_1 and γ_2 and a uniform distribution in $[0, p]$ for δ. We also assume a beta(θ_1, θ_2) prior for θ.

Modeling the "normal" Transition Probability. In the last stage of the hierarchical model we specify a distribution on the transition probability p in (8.3). We note that p represents the probability that each ballot is classified in the same category in the two counts; if there were no errors in the counting mechanism, we would expect p to be exactly 1. In the real world there are errors, but we still expect this probability to be close to 1 with a very small variance. These considerations help us to elicit a prior for p, which in general is a beta distribution,

$$\pi_p(p) = \text{Beta}(\alpha, \beta)$$

with α and β known.

8.3.3 Estimation with Markov Chain Monte Carlo

The stages of the hierarchical model are summarized as follow:

$$\begin{cases} Pr(Y_2|Z, Y_1) = \prod_{rg} I_{\{JZ^{rg} = \mathbf{y}_1^{rg}, JZ^{rgT} = \mathbf{y}_2^{rg}\}}(\mathbf{y}_2^{rg}) \\ Pr(Z|Y_1, X_1, \cdots, X_{21}, \eta, \gamma_1, \gamma_2, \delta, p) = \prod_{r \neq r'} \prod_g Pr(Z^{rg}|\mathbf{y}_1^{rg}, p) \\ \qquad\qquad \prod_g Pr(Z^{r'g}|\mathbf{y}_1^{r'g}, X_1, \ldots, X_{21}, \eta, \gamma_1, \gamma_2, \delta, p) \\ Pr\left(\sum_g X_g = x|\theta\right) = \binom{21}{x}\theta^x(1-\theta)^{21-x} \\ \pi(\gamma_1, \gamma_2, \delta, \eta|p) = \pi_{\gamma_1, \gamma_2}(\gamma_1, \gamma_2|p)\pi_\delta(\delta|p)\pi_\eta(\eta) \\ \pi_p(p) \sim \text{Beta}(\alpha, \beta) \\ \pi(\theta) \sim \text{Beta}(\theta_1, \theta_2) \end{cases} \qquad (8.5)$$

Simulations from the posterior distributions of the parameters in model (8.5) are obtained using the Metropolis-Hastings algorithm within Gibbs sampling. Although sampling from the conditional posteriors of the parameters p, γ_1, γ_2, δ and η is straightforward, updating the latent variables Z^{rg} and the indicator variables of precinct subject to tampering, X_g, requires some explanation, as we describe in the Appendix.

After simulating the joint posterior distribution of the parameters, we can estimate the posterior probability of vote tampering. The event "no vote tampering" in the election is formally represented in our model by $\left(x = \sum_{g=1}^{21} X_g = 0\right)$. In computing the posterior probability of "no vote tampering," we use the marginal posterior distribution of x.

8.4 Results

In this section we report the MCMC estimate of the parameters in (8.5), which are based on 50,000 iterations and a burn-in of 10,000 iterations. In each run, plots of the results suggest good mixing. To check convergence we used standard convergence diagnostics from the Bayesian output analysis (BOA) program. These tests include the Geweke convergence test, the Raftery–Lewis test, and the Heidelberg–Welch stationarity and interval halfwidth tests. (More information on BOA is available at `http://www.public-health.uiowa.edu/boa/`).

We assumed a beta$(50, 3)$ distribution for the transition probability p, which corresponds to assuming a priori that p has mean .94 and variance .001. Thus we are assuming that around 94% of the votes are counted the second time in the same way that they were the first time, which seems to us a minimal assumption in this context. It turns out (see Figure 8.1 below) that the data indicate a higher rate than 94%. Sensitivity analyses to the different prior distributions for p suggest that the estimates of the parameters remains unchanged. Figure 8.1 depicts the posterior distribution of the parameters in the model.

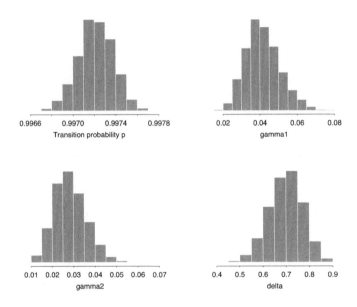

Figure 8.1: Posterior Distribution of (a) p, (b) γ_1, (c) γ_2, and (d) δ.

Table 8.5 gives the posterior means of the parameters together with the 95% credible intervals. The estimates of the parameters in Table 8.5 are insensitive also to the choices of the prior distribution of θ; we obtain the same estimates of the parameters when we assume very different priors for θ and therefore for the number of cheating precincts, $\sum_g X_g$. Figure 8.2 displays the prior and posterior distributions on $\sum_g X_g$ corresponding to a beta$(2,6)$ for θ in the (a) row, and corresponding to a beta$(2,20)$ in the (b) row. Note that the posterior distributions, shown in (a2) and (b), are very similar, although the prior distributions, in (a1) and (b1), are not.

We can summarize the findings as follows: Vote tampering has occurred in the District Justice race with probability 1. Furthermore, because $Pr(\eta = 2|data) = 1$, we can also assess with probability 1 that vote tampering occurred in favor of candidate 2, namely Laughlin, as shown in Table 8.5.

Table 8.5: MCMC Results for the District Justice Race Assuming Priors $p \sim$ beta(50,3) and $\theta \sim$ beta(2, 6)

	Posterior Median	95% Credible Interval
p	0.997	(.997, .998)
γ_1	0.041	(.025, .062)
γ_2	0.028	(.015, .045)
δ	0.697	(.547, .824)
η	2.000	
θ	0.243	(.111, .423)

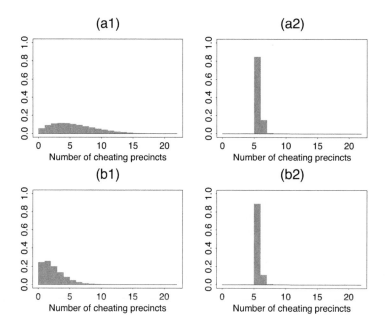

Figure 8.2: Prior (1) and Posterior (2) Distributions on the Number of Precincts in Which Cheating Occurred for (a) a $\theta \sim \beta(2, 6)$ Prior and (b) a $\theta \sim \beta(2, 20)$ Prior.

There is a significant increment of the probability of reclassifying as an overvote a ballot initially classified in favor of Zupsic; the estimate of the parameter γ_2 representing this increment in probability is .029 and has a 95% credible interval $(0.015, 0.045)$. The transition probability γ_1 of a ballot to shift from Zupsic to Laughlin also increases significantly, by .041 (.025, .062). Finally there is a significant increment of the transition probability of a ballot to shift from undervote to Laughlin; the estimate of δ is .697 with 95% credible interval (.547, .824).

These results should be considered jointly. If tampering were associated with very small values of γ_1, γ_2 and δ, then one might find a high probability of tampering, but to such a low degree that it would be in name only. That in the districts found to have been tampered with, roughly 3% of Zupsic's votes were transformed into overvotes, and 4% of Zupsic's votes were transformed into Laughlin's votes is suspicious, but that 70% of the undervotes become Laughlin's votes is an extremely large shift. We consider this strong evidence of real vote-tampering.

To determine the precincts in which vote tampering occurred, we look at the posterior probability $Pr(X_g = 1)$ for each precinct $g = 1, \cdots, 21$. Table 8.6 presents comparisons between the precincts in which the Court found physical evidence of altered ballots and the precincts in which our model detected alterations in transition probabilities. The Court's findings were based almost entirely on the physical evidence presented by challenged ballots, whereas our model uses the comparison between the counts of November 2 and January 5.

Table 8.6: Comparison of the Court Findings of Vote Tampering and Our Estimates of the Probability of Vote Tampering by District.

District Number	Number of altered ballots found by the Court	Posterior Probability of cheating	Expected Number of altered ballots
49	1	0.00	0
56	10	1.00	22
114	6	1.00	11
115	14	1.00	16
116	2	0.07	1
138	6	1.00	9
149	6	1.00	7
Total	45		66

Note that our estimates of tampered precincts agree with the Court's decision: Our model found with probability 1 all of the precincts in which the Court found at least six altered ballots. Precinct 116 has a very low posterior probability of vote tampering, and this agrees with the fact that the Court found only two altered ballots–insufficient evidence considering that the total number of ballots in that precinct is 305. Similarly in District 49 the posterior probability of vote tampering is zero, but the Court found one altered ballot out of 331 total ballots.

The posterior probability of vote tampering for all the other precincts are zero except for districts 82 and 93 which have probability .08 and .09. A possible explanation for this might rely on the small number of ballots in these districts: 69 and 52, compared to more than 300 in most of the other districts.

8.4.1 Model Validation

In this section we investigate how our model performs on election data in which no vote tampering is suspected. As the race that might be contested, we choose the Beaver County vote in the (statewide) Pennsylvania Superior Court, taking the role of the District Justice election between Mr. Zupsic and Laughlin. For this calculation, we assume that only the Supreme Court and School District Director races were without tampering, and do not use the data from the other races.

Although the estimates of the model are robust to the prior distributions of p, γ_1, γ_2 and δ, they are not to the prior on θ. Note that the number of races used here as comparison data is much smaller than that in the analysis of the District Justice race. We used three prior distributions on θ, representing very different beliefs on the number of cheating precincts.

Table 8.7 shows the effects of the different prior distributions on the estimates of the parameters. Assuming a beta(2,6) distribution for θ, which corresponds to a prior knowledge on $\sum_g X_g$ represented in Figure 8.2, the posterior probability of no vote tampering in the Superior Court race is .01. However, the estimates of the cheating parameters are negligible. Thus this prior leads to high probability of a trivial amount of tampering. On the other hand, assuming for a beta(2,50) for θ distribution leads to a posterior probability of no vote tampering in the race for Superior Court of .81 and higher cheating parameters. So in this case, the results suggest a low probability of substantial tampering.

Table 8.7: Posterior Medians of the Parameters in the Superior Court Race Together With Their 95% Credible Intervals Obtained Under Different Prior Distributions on θ

	$\theta \sim$ beta(2,6)	$\theta \sim$ beta(2,20)	$\theta \sim$ beta(2,50)
γ_1	.0065 (0.0017, .0164)	.0074 (.0010 .0242)	0.0083 (0.0008, 0.0723)
γ_2	.0007 (1.6e-05, .0040)	.0010 (2.7e-05 .0157)	.0032 (7.4e-05, .0575)
δ	.0037 (.0001, .0268)	.0062 (.0002, .1946)	.0487 (.0007, .4192)
p	.9967 (.9961, .9972)	.9967 (.9961, .9972)	.9967 (.9962, .9972)
Pr(no cheating)	.01	.32	.81

Figure 8.3 gives the posterior distributions for the number of altered ballots in favor of candidate 2 for both Superior Court and District Justice race under different priors for θ. The histograms relative to the Superior Court clearly show that in all three cases the number of altered ballots is small in magnitude and its posterior distribution is not affected by the prior choice. In the District Justice race the number of altered ballots in favor of candidate 2 is much higher.

8.5   Discussion

We find that three different analyses of the District Justice race lead to the same conclusions. The informal data analysis of Section 1, the Court's findings based on an examination of particular ballots, and the model of this article all find that vote tampering occurred in favor of Laughlin and against Zupsic. Furthermore, these analyses generally agree on the districts involved: 56, 114, 115, 138 and 149. These results are reasonably insensitive to the priors used.

The corroborating model check used the Superior Court race. Depending on the prior used, this analysis found a low probability of a substantial amount of vote tampering or a high probability of a trivial amount of tampering. Thus we find that the model strongly distinguishes these data sets.

The model and mode of analysis that we have chosen is strongly influenced by the particulars of the dataset and the problem we address. There are, however, important statistical analyses related to other problems of determining a winner in a close election. Finkelstein (1978) and Gilliland and Meier (1986) have considered the probability that an election outcome would be reversed with the elimination of votes from ineligible voters, under the assumption that the ineligible voters are drawn from the same population as the eligible ones.

In a more recent case (Marks v. Stinson, U.S. District Court for the Eastern District of Pennsylvania, 1994 U.S. Dist. Lexis 5273), the Court, after finding evidence of fraud in the administration of absentee ballots, used various methods, including regression (Ashenfelter, 1994) to estimate what the result of the election would have been absent the fraud. This led to a reversal of the election outcome, with Marks, not Stinson, seated in the State Senate.

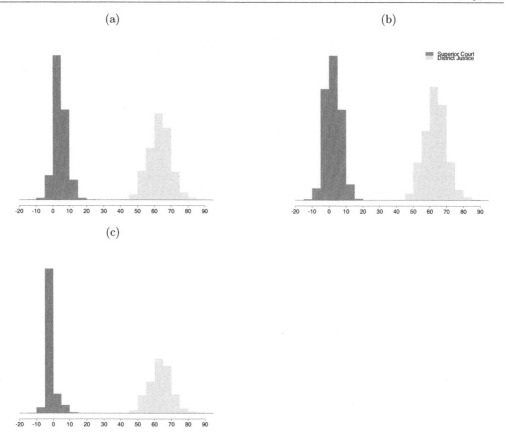

Figure 8.3: Posteriors on the Number of Altered Ballots for the Superior Court and the District Justice Races Under Different Priors for θ. (a) $\theta \sim Beta(2,6)$; (b) $\theta \sim Beta(2,20)$; (c) $\theta \sim Beta(2,50)$.

Appendix: Markov Chain Monte Carlo Estimation

Updating Z^{rg}.

Updating the augmented data Z^{rg} for each race r and district g corresponds to updating a matrix of counts with fixed row and column marginals according to a conditional posterior given by

$$Pr(Z^{rg}|\mathbf{y}_2^{rg}, \mathbf{y}_1^{rg}, \ldots) \propto Pr(Z^{rg}|\mathbf{y}_1^{rg}, \ldots) I_{\{JZ^{rg}=\mathbf{y}_1^{rg}, JZ^{rg^T}=\mathbf{y}_2^{rg}\}}(\mathbf{y}_2^{rg})$$

where $Pr(Z^{rg}|\mathbf{y}_1^{rg}, \ldots)$ is a product of multinomials as specified in (8.2). Given the current state Z^{rg}, a candidate configuration, $Z^{rg^{(c)}}$, is generated according to the following scheme: choose randomly two rows (i_1, i_2) and two columns (j_1, j_2); given the elements in those rows and columns, choose randomly a sign for the element $z_{i_1 j_1}^{rg}$. Then the candidate configuration $Z^{rg^{(c)}}$ has the elements in rows (i_1, i_2) and columns (j_1, j_2) altered by 1 depending on the sign. For example, if the sign is positive, then the candidate configuration is given by

$$
Z^{rg^{(c)}} = \begin{bmatrix}
 & \vdots & & \vdots & \\
\cdots & z_{i_1 j_1}^{rg} + 1 & \cdots & z_{i_1 j_2}^{rg} - 1 & \cdots \\
 & \vdots & & \vdots & \\
\cdots & z_{i_2 j_1}^{rg} - 1 & \cdots & z_{i_2 j_2}^{rg} + 1 & \cdots \\
 & \vdots & & \vdots &
\end{bmatrix}
$$

Clearly the margin constraints are satisfied. The proposal distribution $q(Z^{rg^{(c)}}|Z^{rg})$ is therefore defined as

$$
q(Z^{rg^{(c)}}|Z^{rg}) = Pr(i_1, i_2, j_1, j_2) \times Pr(\text{sign}|i_1, i_2, j_1, j_2)
$$

where $Pr(i_1, i_2, j_1, j_2) = Pr(i_1, i_2)Pr(j_1, j_2) = \binom{k}{2}^{-2}$, because it corresponds to independent samplings without replacement two elements out of k (with k the dimension of the matrix). To guarantee that the elements of the $Z^{rg^{(c)}}$ are nonnegative, we define

$$
Pr(+|i_1, i_2, j_1, j_2) = \begin{cases}
1/2 & \text{if} & z_{i_1 j_1} > 0, \ z_{i_2 j_2} > 0 \\
 & & z_{i_2 j_1} > 0, \ z_{i_1 j_2} > 0 \\
0 & \text{if} & z_{i_1 j_1} > 0, \ z_{i_2 j_2} > 0 \\
 & & z_{i_2 j_1} = 0 \text{ or } z_{i_1 j_2} = 0 \\
1 & \text{if} & z_{i_1 j_1} = 0 \text{ or } z_{i_2 j_2} = 0 \\
 & & z_{i_2 j_1} > 0, \ z_{i_1 j_2} > 0
\end{cases}
$$

In all of the other cases–namely, when there are two 0's in the same row or column–we do not update Z^{rg}. Once we generate a candidate configuration $Z^{rg^{(c)}}$, the acceptance probability becomes:

$$
\alpha = \min\left\{1, \frac{Pr(Z^{rg^{(c)}}|\mathbf{y}_2^{rg}, \mathbf{y}_1^{rg}, \ldots)}{Pr(Z^{rg}|\mathbf{y}_2^{rg}, \mathbf{y}_1^{rg}, \ldots)} \frac{q(Z^{rg}|Z^{rg^{(c)}})}{q(Z^{rg^{(c)}}|Z^{rg})}\right\}.
$$

This formula can be further simplified. Suppose, for example, that all elements in rows $(i_1 i_2)$ and columns $(j_1 j_2)$ are strictly positive and the sign is $+$; it can be easily shown that the acceptance probability of $Z^{rg^{(c)}}$ is given by

$$
\alpha = \min\left\{1, \frac{z_{i_1 j_2}^{rg} z_{i_2 j_1}^{rg}}{(z_{i_1 j_1}^{rg} + 1)(z_{i_2 j_2}^{rg} + 1)} \frac{q_{i_1 j_1} q_{i_2 j_2}}{q_{i_1 j_2} q_{i_2 j_1}}\right\}
$$

where q_{ij}'s are the transition probabilities corresponding to each cell above, as described in (8.4).

Updating $X_1, \ldots X_{21}$

In updating the exchangeable indicator variables X_g, we first integrate out analytically the hyperparameter θ. Specifying the prior of $\sum_g X_g$ in two stages helps us to better understand the prior assumptions. After integrating out θ, we have the following prior for $\sum_g X_g$:

$$
\pi\left(\sum_g X_g = x\right) = \binom{21}{x} \frac{B(\theta_1 + x, 21 + \theta_2 - x)}{B(\theta_1, \theta_2)}
$$

where $B(\alpha, \beta)$ denotes the beta function. Since updating $\sum_g X_g$ obviously corresponds to a change in the single variables X_g, we update $\sum_g X_g$ and the X_g's jointly. Let $\sum_g X_g = x$ be the current number of cheating precincts, then with equal probability the candidate value, $x^{(c)}$, can take values $x - 1$, x, and $x + 1$. If $x^{(c)} = x + 1$, then one precinct, j, is chosen at random from the set $C_0 = \{g : X_g = 0\}$ and set $X_j = 1$. If $x^{(c)} = x - 1$, then one precinct, j, is chosen at random from the set $C_1 = \{g : X_g = 1\}$ and set $X_j = 0$. Finally, if $x^{(c)} = x$, then two precincts, (i, j), are chosen at random from the set $C_1 = \{g : X_g = 1\}$ and $C_0 = \{g : X_g = 0\}$, and set $X_i = 0$ $X_j = 1$. In each of these cases the candidate vector $(X_1^{(c)}, \cdots, X_{21}^{(c)})$ differs from the current vector $(X_1, \cdots, X_{21})$ only in the element i and/or j, depending on the value of $x^{(c)}$. We report the acceptance probability of a candidate vector $(X_1^{(c)}, \cdots, X_{21}^{(c)})$ when $x^{(c)} = x + 1$, in which case

$$\alpha = \min\left\{1, \frac{Pr(\mathbf{y}_2^{r'j}|X_1^{(c)}, \cdots, X_{21}^{(c)}, \ldots)}{Pr(\mathbf{y}_2^{r'j}|X_1, \cdots, X_{21}, \ldots)} \frac{\pi(x^{(c)})}{\pi(x)} \frac{21 - x}{x + 1}\right\}$$

The acceptance probabilities in the other cases are obtained similarly.

To obtain convergence for the Superior Court race data Monte Carlo runs, we had to add an importance sampling component. As is evident from the third column of Table 8.7, with an informative prior on θ, there is little evidence of cheating in this race. Because the parameters γ_1, γ_2 and δ are all defined as conditional on cheating, if the chain were run using the prior of interest, then it would take a long time to assemble data on these parameters. A solution is to run the chain with a different prior that puts more probability on cheating than the prior of interest, and reweight the observations by the ratio of the prior of interest to the prior used for the runs. This permits the chain to converge, and allows the parameters to be well estimated. We used a beta(2,6) prior for θ for these runs, with 10,000 iterations burn-in, and 50,000 total iterations.

[Received February 2000. Revised January 2001.]

REFERENCES

Ashenfelter, O. (1994). "Report on Expected Absentee Ballots." Unpublished. 151

Finkelstein, M. (1978). *Quantitative Methods in Law*. New York: The Free Press. 151

Gilliland, D. and Meier, P. (1986). "The Probability of Reversal in Contested Elections." In *Statistics and the Law*, eds. M. DeGroot, S. Fienberg, and J. Kadane. John Wiley & Sons. 151

Lee, T., Judge, G., and Zellner, A. (1970). *Estimating the Parameters of the Markov Probability Model from Aggregate Time Series Data*. Amsterdam: North Holland Publishing Company. 145

Tanner, M. and Wong, W. (1987). "The calculation of posterior distribution by data augmentation." *Journal of the American Statistical Association*, 82, 528–540. 143

Epilogue

What was the scientific issue addressed?

Whether the data support the allegation of vote tampering, and, if so, whether the specific precincts in which it took place could be identified.

Is justification given for

a) the use of the data?

Yes. The data were counts, by precincts, of votes in the District Justice and other races, once close to election day, and again in a recount later.

b) the likelihood and the prior?

The likelihood is a Markov chain whose states are how an individual ballot would be recorded in the November count and in the January recount. The prior reflects the idea that the vast majority of votes would be recorded the same way.

What robustness checks were conducted?

There are several. The most important check is comparison with a race for a seat on Pennsylvania's Superior Court, in which no vote tampering was alleged. The comparison shows that very few votes shifted between the two vote counts for that race.

How was the computing done?

By Markov chain Monte Carlo.

If I were doing the problem today, how would I change the approach?

I would not.

What do I see as the contributions of this paper?

1. It finds strong evidence of vote tampering. The specific precincts in which it is found coincide broadly with those found in an informal data analysis and with those found by the court.

2. Philosophically, while this particular race happened only once, there is a sense of repetition in that other races were decided by the same voters at the same time. We took advantage of that to show that the results for the District Justice were different in ways that made vote tampering more likely.

Was Bayesian analysis useful for this problem?

Yes.

TEACHING SUGGESTIONS

References for theoretical ideas:

1. Hierarchical models: *Principles* Chapter 9

2. Unobserved data as parameters: *Principles* Section 9.2

3. Metropolis Hastings with a Gibbs sampler: *Principles* Section 10.3

4. Reweighting using importance sampling: *Principles* Section 10.5

Exercises

1. Of the assumptions made in Section 8.3, which do you find least reasonable and why? What would you replace it with?

2. Suppose you were hired by Laughlin to challenge this analysis in court. How would you criticize it?

3. Do you agree with the conclusion of Table 8.6 that the court found some, but not all, of the altered ballots? Why or why not?

Chapter 9

The Effect of Intensity of Effort to Reach Survey Respondents: A Toronto Smoking Survey (2001)

Foreword

The ideas behind this paper started to germinate some 15 years before. I recently started at Carnegie Mellon when I was asked to do some work for Mr. Rogers' Neighborhood, a very popular children's TV program. (I did not know much about Mr. Rogers; the TV program of my youth was the Howdy Doody Show.)

Mr. Rogers' Neighborhood sold magazine subscriptions to a publication they produced. They did a survey of their subscribers asking them to rate the various features in the magazine. I was hired to address the question of which features would appeal most to viewers of the show who had not yet subscribed. Thus I had no direct information about the population of interest. I did have one additional piece of information from the subscribers who answered the questionnaire: when they answered. I reasoned that the subscribers who answered quickly are likely to be the most enthusiastic Mr. Rogers supporters. Hence those who delayed their responses would be those most like the target population, the viewers less enthusiastic but still possible subscribers. So I looked at how supportive viewers were of various magazine features as a function of how long it took them to answer the questionnaire, and made my recommendations accordingly. I never did hear from Mr. Rogers' Neighborhood about how well it worked.

It took roughly two decades before a suitable dataset and an interested student, Lou Mariano, coincided to allow further exploration of this idea. Toronto had passed a new law regulating smoking in the workplace. A series of telephone surveys were conducted to ascertain people's attitudes toward smoking in the workplace as a function of their knowledge of the health effects of second-hand smoke, whether they were or had been a smoker, whether second-hand smoke bothered them, and their age and sex. This survey was conducted by telephone, with the telephone numbers chosen by random digit dialing. Of course, many telephone numbers corresponded to entities not in the sampling frame. Each number was called up to 12 times, until a person was interviewed or refused. Fortunately, the number of calls was recorded. Of course there were many numbers that had not answered, even after 12 calls.

Theoretical results of Rubin (1976) gave necessary and sufficient conditions for the missing data to be missing at random [MAR] (given the covariates), and hence ignorable. The danger is that statisticians may assume MAR without thinking deeply about whether the assumption is reasonable in the applied context. In this paper we model response with a geometric distribution (each additional call reaches a fraction of those who have not yet responded). However, borrowing from the biometrics literature, we also allow for "immunes," people who for a variety of reasons are never going to respond.

Our results show that people who did not respond (but ultimately would if calls kept being made) were twice as likely to favor unrestricted smoking in the workplace as those who did respond. This is not too surprising, since it is more socially acceptable to favor restricting workplace smoking. Thus non-response is, given our estimates, not ignorable in this survey.

Where are they now? Lou Mariano is a statistician at the RAND Corporation in Washington, DC.

This paper was originally published in *Survey Methodology*, **27**, (#2), pp. 131–142. It is in the public domain.

Published Paper

Louis T. Mariano[1] and Joseph B. Kadane[2]

Abstract

The number of calls in a telephone survey is used as an indicator of how difficult an intended respondent is to reach. This permits a probabilistic division of the non-respondents into non-susceptibles (those who will always refuse to respond), and the susceptible non-respondents (those who were not available to respond) in a model of the non-response. Further, it permits stochastic estimation of the views of the latter group and an evaluation of whether the non-response is ignorable for inference about the dependent variable. These ideas are implemented on the data from a survey in Metropolitan Toronto of attitudes toward smoking in the workplace. Using a Bayesian model, the posterior distribution of the model parameters is sampled by Markov chain Monte Carlo methods. The results reveal that the non-response is not ignorable and those who do not respond are twice as likely to favor unrestricted smoking in the workplace as are those who do.

Key Words: Call-backs, numbers of; Bayesian analysis; Markov chain Monte Carlo method; Informative non-response; Ignorable non-response.

9.1 Introduction

Given the reality of non-response in every survey, it is of interest to determine how to account for this non-response in the interpretation of the collected data. Rubin (1976) gives necessary and sufficient conditions for such an analysis to be identical from, respectively, a frequentist, likelihood, and Bayesian perspectives, to an analysis based on a model incorporating a missingness mechanism. Building on this, Little and Rubin (1987) led to an extensive literature modeling non-response in an informative, non-ignorable way.

Information about the interaction between the survey and the surveyed can sharpen the analysis of the import of missing data in a survey. The example in this paper concerns the attitudes of Toronto citizens about smoking in the workplace. Random telephone numbers were chosen; at least twelve calls were made to try to reach the intended respondents. Our data for the respondents includes only the number of calls until the survey was completed, not the timing of the unsuccessful calls. With even this attenuated data on how difficult the respondent was to reach, we find our view of the results of the survey to be importantly informed by the number of unsuccessful calls.

The use of information on the number of calls to a subject chosen to participate in a survey is not unique. Potthoff et al. (1993) present a method for correcting for survey

---

[1]Louis T. Mariano is a Ph.D. candidate, Department of Statistics, Carnegie Mellon University, Pittsburgh, PA 15213

[2]Leonard J. Savage University Professor of Statistics and Social Sciences, Department of Statistics, Carnegie Mellon University, Pittsburgh, PA 15213

bias due to non-availability by weighting based on the number of call-backs. While our analysis also focuses on the bias due to non-availability, there are major differences. Instead of assuming that refusals do not exist, we allow for and utilize their potential existence in modeling the mechanism which causes non-response. In the analysis that follows, the relationship of non-response to the response variable of interest in the survey is evaluated along with other explanatory variables, after weighting for both household size and the appropriate population demographics. In doing so we address not only whether error exists due to non-availability, but also whether stratification of the respondents by household size and the then current age/sex distribution may eliminate the necessity for accounting for the error by the introduction of a mechanism which describes the non-response. Note that here we match the groupings of Pederson et al. (1996) used in the original published analyses of the dataset; more complex cell adjustment procedures are possible (*e.g.*, Little (1996), Eltinge and Yansaneh (1997), and references cited therein).

The remainder of this article is organized as follows: Section 9.2 gives more detail on the survey; Section 9.3 introduces the methodology employed; Sections 9.4 and 9.5 respectively explore missing-at-random and non-ignorably-missing models; Section 9.6 discusses the priors distributions chosen for the main analysis, whose results are explained in Section 9.7. Finally, Section 9.8 gives our conclusions.

9.2 The Survey

A bylaw regulating smoking in the workplace in the City of Toronto took effect on March 1, 1988. From January 1988 to the present, a series of six surveys have been conducted to assess attitudes of the public toward smoking, awareness of health risks related to smoking, and the impact of the law on the residents of Metropolitan Toronto. The data being utilized in this analysis comprises the third phase of this series. Northrup (1993) provides the technical documentation for this survey. For clarity, when necessary, the data being analyzed here is referred to as the Phase III data, and information from the first two surveys is referred to as the Phase I & II data.

Northrup (1993) indicates that the data of interest, which were made available by the Institute for Social Research (ISR) at York University, were collected from 1,429 residents of the Metropolitan Toronto area in December 1992 and March 1993. A two-stage probability selection process was utilized to select survey respondents. The first stage employed random digit dialing. The second stage used the most recent birthday method to select one adult individual once an eligible residence was reached. The responses were then weighted by the number of adults in the household. In the analysis that follows, post-stratification weighting was also applied to the census age-sex distribution to adjust for the underrepresentation of some population subgroups. The number of distinct phone lines in the household was not taken into consideration during the data collection.

The number of calls it took to reach each respondent is included as a variable in the dataset, and there are no missing values for this variable. Northrup (1993) explains that the 1,429 responses came from a sample of 5,702 telephone numbers generated by the random digit dialing method. Of these numbers, 2,286 were verified to be eligible households, and 3,150 of the numbers in the sample were not eligible. The status of the remaining 266 numbers was not able to be determined. It has been assumed by ISR that the household eligibility rate of these 266 numbers was equal to the rate for the rest of the sample. This eligibility rate implies an estimated total of 2,398 households in the sample and a response rate of 60%. Thus, an estimated 969 subjects chosen to participate in the survey did not respond. Each subject received a minimum of 12 calls, including day, night, and weekend calls, before being classified as non-respondent.

The dependent variable, for the purpose of this analysis, is an individual's opinion on the regulation of smoking in the workplace, in one of three categories. Category "0" indicates smoking should be permitted in restricted areas only, category "1" indicates smoking should not be permitted at all, and category "2" indicates smoking should not be restricted at all. For each subject chosen to participate in the survey, let $Y_i \in \{0, 1, 2\}$ represent the opinion of subject i.

The data comprises of the answers to 50 survey questions as well as 18 other variables identifying characteristics of the subject. Included in these are:

- "K –risk" is an integer score from 0 to 12 which indicates knowledge of the risks and effects of second-hand smoke.

- "Smoker" indicates the smoking status of the subject: "Current smoker" (S), "Former smoker" (SQ) or, "Never smoked" (NS).

- "Bother" indicates if second-hand smoke bothers the subject: "Always bothers" (b.A), "Usually bothers" (b.USUL), or "Does not bother" (b.NO).

- "Age": (Age in years - 50)/10.

Pederson et al. (1989) created a "knowledge of health effects score" on passive smoking out of the answers to six survey questions, which measured a subject's knowledge of the effects of second-hand smoke. Pederson *et al.*'s questions were used in Phase III to create their score, here renamed "K – risk". A higher K – risk score indicates a greater knowledge of the risks of second-hand smoke. The variable "Age" was shifted and rescaled to match how age was treated by Bull (1994) in the Phase I & II analysis.

9.3 Overview of Methodology

The fundamental question of interest is: "May we ignore the unit non-response and treat the observed data as a random subsample of the population?" Mapping to the terminology of Little and Rubin (1987) and Rubin (1976): If we may treat the observed data for the dependent variable of interest as a random subsample, we call the missing data "missing completely at random" (MCAR). If we may treat the observed data for the dependent variable of interest as a random subsample, after conditioning on the explanatory variables, we call the missing data "missing at random" (MAR). Let θ represent the parameters of the data and let π represent the parameters describing the missing data process. Rubin (1976) calls the parameters π and θ distinct "if there are no *a priori* ties, via parameter space restrictions or prior distributions, between π and θ." If either the MCAR or MAR cases apply and if π and θ are distinct, the mechanism which causes the missing data is said to be "ignorable" for inference about the distribution of the variable of interest. If the missing data for the dependent variable of interest is dependent on the values of that data, then the mechanism which causes the missing data is said to be "non-ignorable" (NI). Groves and Couper (1998) note that when the likelihood of participation is a function of the desired response variable, the non-response bias can be relatively high, even with a good response rate.

Let R_i be an indicator of response. $R_i = I_{\text{respondent}}$ (subject i) and $R = (R_1, \ldots, R_n)^T$. Little and Rubin (1987) suggest that one possible method for accounting for the non-response mechanism is to include this response indicator variable in the model. We may call the mechanism which causes the missing data ignorable if π and θ are distinct and:

$$f(R|Y_{\text{obs}}, Y_{\text{mis}}, \pi) = f(R|Y_{\text{obs}}, \pi) \tag{9.1}$$

where Y_{obs} and Y_{mis} represent the observed and missing portions of the dependent variable of interest.

The terms "MAR assumption" and "NI assumption" will be used throughout this analysis. For clarity, the term "MAR assumption" is defined as the assumption that the missing data mechanism is ignorable for inference with respect to the dependent variable identified in section 9.2. That is, the observed values of that variable are a random subsample of the population, possibly within post-strata, and it is not necessary to account for the missing data mechanism. The term "NI assumption" is defined as the assumption that the missing data mechanism is non-ignorable and the data collected for the dependent variable of interest cannot be treated as a random subsample. Specifically, inference for the population must involve the missing data mechanism.

The approach to assessing the MAR assumption is comprised of three steps. The first step is the examination of what one might do under the MAR assumption. Since the dependent variable of interest has three categories and some of the explanatory variables are quantitative, polytomous logistic regression is employed. Both frequentist and Bayesian forms of the logistic regression model are examined.

In the second step, an NI model is constructed. The non-response mechanism is modeled utilizing the information available about the number of calls made to each subject. Here, the idea of a surviving fraction in the sample is examined to model whether it is actually possible to reach all the intended respondents. Then, the non-response mechanism is related to the dependent variable by including the number of calls in the logistic regression model.

In the development of the NI model, we employ a Bayesian approach to allow for an examination of the values the missing data are likely to take, given the observed data and the model parameters. This is accomplished by utilizing a data augmentation approach, where the missing data are imputed in each iteration of a Markov Chain Monte Carlo (MCMC) simulation. A possible alternative would be to utilize the expectation-maximization (EM) algorithm (Dempster et al., 1977) to compute the maximum likelihood estimates (MLE's) of the missing values.

In the third step, an evaluation of the MAR assumption is made. Non-zero coefficients for the number of calls in the logistic regression portion of the NI model will imply that the number of calls does make a difference: *i.e.*, the opinions of those who did not respond in the first 12 calls are likely to differ from those who responded in just a small number of calls. In this case, the missing data mechanism is not independent of the values of the missing data and an MAR assumption would be inappropriate. Next, the log odds of response among the three models are examined. Differences here identify the magnitude of the error that a faulty MAR assumption causes. So, in the evaluation of the MAR assumption, the questions "is there a difference?" and "how large is the difference?" are both addressed.

9.4   MAR Models

9.4.1   *Logistic Regression*

Using the data collected from the ($m = 1,429$) subjects that did respond to the survey, weighted logistic regression was employed to model the public's opinion on smoking in the workplace. The collection of candidate predictors found in the survey questions and the background information was narrowed utilizing a series of Wald tests. Then likelihood ratio tests, AIC, and BIC were used to compare the possible models. The model with the best fit was found to be the one which included additive terms for the variables "K - risk", "Smoker", "Bother", and "Age", as defined in section 9.2.

As each of the models examined in this analysis employs a logistic regression component, it is useful here to illustrate the notation being used. Category "0", "smoking allowed in restricted areas only" was chosen to be the reference category. Recall $Y_i \in \{0, 1, 2\}$. For the MAR model, we use only the observed values of the subjects opinion on workplace smoking, $Y_{\text{obs}} = (Y_1, \ldots, Y_m)$. Let $Y_{ij} = I_j(Y_i)$ be an indicator of subject i responding in category j, and let W_i represent the weight each subject received. As in the original published analyses of this dataset (Pederson et al., 1996) both household (see Northrup (1993)) and post-stratification (see Appendix A) weighting were used in the consideration of all models here.

The two categorical explanatory variables, "Smoker" and "Bother", were included in the model by utilizing indicator variables for two of the three categories, with the effect of the third category being absorbed in the intercept term. For "Smoker", "S_i" and "SQ_i" were included as indicators that subject i was either a current smoker or a smoker who had quit. For "Bother", "b.USUL$_i$" and "b.NO$_i$" were included as indicators that second hand smoke usually bothered or did not bother subject i.

Let $X_i =$ represent the vector for explanatory variables for subject i. Then,

$$X = (K - \text{risk}, S_i, SQ_i, \text{b.USUL}_i, \text{b.NO}_i, \text{Age}_i).$$

Here we use an unordered multinomial logit model to consider $p_j(x_i) = P(Y_{ij} = 1 | X_i = x_i)$, the probability that subject i responds in category $j \in \{0, 1, 2\}$, given the observed explanatory variables for subject i. This model, of course, utilizes linear equations η_{ij} describing the log odds of subject i responding in category j versus the reference category $j = 0$. So, for $j = 1, 2$ we wish to examine:

$$ln \frac{p_j(x_i)}{p_0(x_i)} = \eta_{ij} = \beta_{0j} + X_i \beta_j, \tag{9.2}$$

with $\eta_{i0} = 0$. The two resultant linear equations, η_{i1} and η_{i2}, each have seven coefficients, including an intercept term β_{0j} and those displayed below:

$$\beta_j = (\beta_{K-\text{risk}_j}, \beta_{S_j}, \beta_{SQ_j}, \beta_{\text{b.USUL}_j}, \beta_{\text{b.NO}_j}, \beta_{\text{Age}_j}).$$

The MAR logistic regression model has 14 parameters. The vector of these 14 parameters, represented by $\beta = (\beta_{01}, \beta_1, \beta_{02}, \beta_2)$ has the likelihood (or, more appropriately, pseudo-likelihood, since the weights are incorporated through the variable W_i):

$$L(\beta) \propto \prod_{i=1}^{m} \prod_{j=0}^{2} \left(\frac{e^{\eta_{ij}}}{1 + e^{\eta_{i1} + e^{\eta_{i2}}}} \right)^{y_{ij} w_i}. \tag{9.3}$$

9.4.2 Bayesian Logistic Regression

The likelihood in equation (9.3) and the data collected from the survey respondents are utilized in the Bayesian analysis. The same four explanatory variables selected in the frequentist analysis above are used as the explanatory variables here. Prior distributions, discussed in section 9.6, were assigned to the logistic regression parameters. An MCMC simulation is utilized in order to draw from the posterior distribution of the parameters.

9.5 NI Model

9.5.1 Modeling the Non-Response Mechanism

Since the missing values are not necessarily missing at random, the mechanism which caused them to be missing must be addressed. Northrup (1993) indicates that non-respondent subjects chosen to participate in the survey were called a minimum of

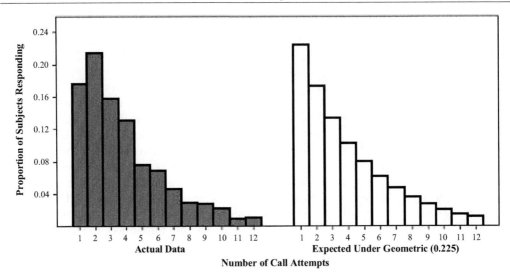

Figure 9.1: Comparison of the actual survey data for successful calls in the first 12 attempts to expected results based on a Geometric (0.225) distribution for the number of calls needed to complete the survey.

12 times, including a minimum of three day, four evening and four weekend calls. Unfortunately, other useful information regarding the number of calls was not retained. We do not know which of the non-respondents were called more than twelve times or whether an individual call was placed during the day, evening, or weekend. We also are unaware of the details of the non-response, such as whether the subject was contacted but refused to participate, whether the calls were ever answered by a machine, or whether they were answered at all. Thus, stratification of the non-respondents was not possible, and they were all treated as exchangeable in this analysis.

Each subject was called a number of times until the survey was successfully completed or they were classified as non-respondent. For the respondents, the number of calls variable (C_i) describes the number of trials until the first success for subject i. Thus, one might expect the number of calls to follow a Geometric distribution with truncated observations for the non-respondents. Specifically, let $\pi = P$ (a call is successful) then, consider $C_i \sim Geometric\ (\pi)$ and $P(C_i = c_i) = \pi(1 - \pi)^{c_i - 1}$. Note that if auxiliary information about the number of calls to the non-respondents were available (*e.g.*, Groves and Couper (1998)), we could have also considered conditional response probabilities here.

The histograms in Figure 9.1 compare the data (through the first twelve calls) to a Geometric distribution with parameter $\pi = 0.225$, which appears to match fairly well. The sample order statistics suggest $\pi \in (0.2, 0.25)$. The histogram of the actual survey data reveals that the number of subjects reached on the first call are fewer than the number reached on the second call. It is possible that more of the second calls were placed at a time which had a higher success rate.

Suppose $\pi = 0.225$; by the memoryless property of the Geometric distribution, we would expect 218 of the 969 non-respondents to reply on the 13th call. This would make the data through the first 13 calls appear as in Figure 9.2. Clearly, Figure 9.2 does not display the behavior of a Geometric random variable. Consider the following question: "If all subjects were called an unlimited amount of times, would they all have been reached?" Answering "yes" to that question for this dataset results in the problem illustrated in Figure 9.2.

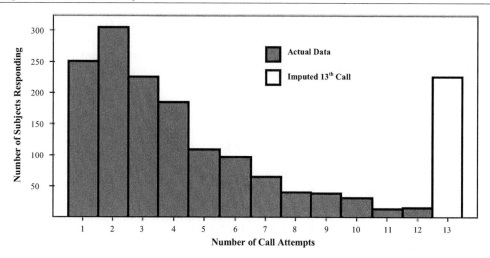

Figure 9.2: Display of the actual number of successful calls on each attempt through the first 12 and the expected number of successful calls on the 13th attempt. The expectation for the 13th call is based on a Geometric (0.225) distribution to model the number of calls until the survey is completed.

Given the information outlined above, the assertion that "not all subjects chosen for the survey are reachable" is a viable one. Maller and Zhou (1996) discuss immune subjects – individuals who are not subject to the event of interest. Following their terminology, if it is not possible to procure a response from a subject chosen for the survey given an unlimited amount of calls, that subject is categorized as immune. Subjects who are not immune are categorized as "susceptible". The set of immune (*i.e.*, non-susceptible) subjects comprise the "surviving fraction" of the sample. Mapping to more familiar terminology, the immune subjects include those who were reached and refused, those who would have refused if they had been reached, and those cases of a physical or mental inability to ever participate. Northrup (1993) indicates that those who initially refused to participate were subsequently contacted by the most senior interviewers, so, we make the assumption here that all remaining refusals would not ever participate. The susceptible group includes the respondents, those who would have responded if successfully contacted, and those who were physically or mentally unable to participate during the data collection period but were willing and able at some other time.

Let the variable $Z_i = I_{\{\text{susceptible}\}}$ (subject i) be an indicator of the susceptibility of subject i, and $\rho = P$ (subject i is susceptible), *i.e.*, $Z_i \sim$ Bernoulli (ρ). Now suppose that the number of calls to the susceptible subjects follows a Geometric distribution, *i.e.*, $C_i | Z_i = 1 \sim$ Geometric (π). Does this eliminate the problem illustrated in Figure 9.2?

Let R_i be an indicator of response of subject i. The non-response mechanism can be accounted for by including these response indicators in the model. However, the introduction of the susceptibility variable implies two distinct classes of non-response. So, it is possible to be more detailed and use both the susceptibility $Z = (Z_1, \ldots, Z_n)^T$ and the response R indicators in a mixture model describing the non-response. Updating Equation (9.1), the missing data mechanism is ignorable if and only if (π, ρ) is distinct from θ and

$$f(R, Z | Y_{\text{obs}}, Y_{\text{mis}}, \pi, \rho) = f(R, Z | Y_{\text{obs}}, \pi, \rho). \tag{9.4}$$

Let $C_{obs} = (C_1, \ldots, C_m)$ and $Z_{obs} = (Z_1, \ldots, Z_m)$ be the vectors of the number of calls and the observed susceptibility for each respondent. Also, let $R = (R_1, \ldots, R_n) =$ be the vector of response for each intended respondent. Every subject, i, may be classified by response into three mutually exclusive groups, A_{obs} –observed, A_{mis} –missing, and A_{imm} –immune, where:

$$A_{obs} = \quad \{i : i \text{ was Susceptible and Responded}\}$$
$$A_{mis} = \quad \{i : i \text{ was Susceptible but did not Respond in 12 calls}\}$$
$$A_{imm} = \quad \{i : i \text{ was not Susceptible}\}.$$

The probability that a subject is in each of these categories maybe calculated as follows:

$$
\begin{aligned}
P(i \in A_{obs}) & \quad P(Z_i = 1, R_i = 1, C_i = c_i) & = \rho\pi(1-\pi)^{c_i - 1} \\
P(i \in A_{mis}) & \quad P(Z_i = 1, R_i = 0, C_i > 12) & = \rho(1-\pi)^{12} \\
P(i \in A_{imm}) & \quad P(Z_i = 0) & = 1 - \rho.
\end{aligned}
$$

The data indicates $m = 1,429$ subjects in A_{obs} and $n - m = 969$ non-responsive subjects in $A_{mis} \cup A_{imm}$; $n = 2,398$ is the estimated total number of subjects chosen to participate in the survey. Thus, the joint density of Z_{obs}, R and C_{obs} given ρ and π is:

$$f(Z_{obs}, R, C_{obs}|\rho, \pi) \quad \propto \quad \left[\rho^m \pi^m (1-\pi)^{(\sum_{i=1}^m c_i) - m}\right] \tag{9.5}$$
$$\times \quad \left[(1-\rho) + \rho(1-\pi)^{12}\right]^{n-m}$$

The mixture model described by Equation (9.5) may be viewed as a special case of the nonresponse models discussed in Drew and Fuller (1981).

It would be useful to confirm that the above joint distribution accurately represents the response pattern of the susceptibles in the dataset. The MLE estimate for ρ is simply the proportion of respondents in the sample, which clearly underestimates ρ. Setting $U(0,1)$ prior distributions for both ρ and π and examining their joint posterior distribution by MCMC simulation, the posterior medians are found to be $\rho = 0.636$ and $\pi = 0.205$, with equal-tailed posterior credible intervals of $(0.613, 0.659)$ and $(0.191, 0.219)$ for ρ and π respectively. Figure 9.3 illustrates how the dataset might look after imputing the missing number of calls for our susceptible non-respondents based on these posterior medians. The problem previously displayed in Figure 9.2 has now been mostly eliminated.

While the Geometric distribution appears sufficient (after accounting for susceptibility), a referee questions the use of the Geometric distribution as it does not make use of possibly useful covariates. As explained above, the covariates we think would be most useful for this purpose were not collected. One alternative for modeling the response mechanism of the susceptibles is to use a discretized Gamma distribution. In cases where more complexity is necessary, the ν-Poisson [now known as the Conway-Maxwell-Poisson Distribution] (a two parameter Poisson which generalizes some well known discrete distributions, including the Geometric) of Shmueli et al. (2004) may also be considered.

9.5.2   *Relating Non-Response to the Dependent Variable - The NI Model*

Since the non-response of the susceptibles is described by the conditional Geometric distribution of the number of calls, the effect of the non-response of the susceptibles on the dependent variable may be considered by including the number of calls as an additional explanatory variable in the logistic regression likelihood. This will create

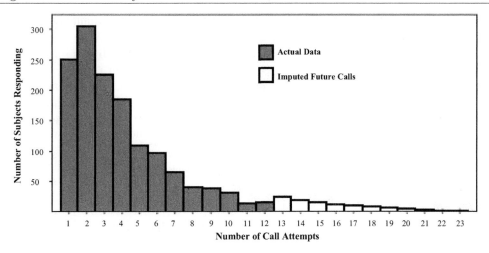

Figure 9.3: Display of the actual number of successful calls on each attempt through the first 12 and the expected number of successful calls for call attempts 13 and higher. Imputed values are based on a probability of successful call of 0.205 and a probability of susceptibility of 0.6363.

two additional parameters in the logistic regression portion of the model, which are the coefficients of the number of calls, β_{call} in each of the linear equations η_{ij} described in equation (2).

Non-zero coefficients for the number of calls, then, would indicate that the dependent variable is not independent of the non-response mechanism, and, hence the non-response mechanism is non-ignorable. If these coefficients are zero, the non-response of the susceptibles is ignorable. Conclusions made here rely upon the underlying modeling assumption that the relationship among the number of calls, the dependent variable and the other explanatory variables considered is the same for the respondents and susceptible non-respondents. Including the number of calls in the logistic regression portion of the model does not address the immune subjects, since there will never be the realization of a successful call to them.

The full pseudo-likelihood for the NI model (or, more precisely, the susceptible NI model) is the product of the non-response and logistic regression pieces:

$$
\begin{aligned}
L(\rho, \pi, \beta) \quad & \propto \quad \left[\rho^m \pi^m (1 - \pi)^{(\sum_{i=1}^{m} c_i) - m} \right] \\
& \times \quad \left[(1 - \rho) + \rho(1 - \pi)^{12} \right]^{n-m} \\
& \times \quad \left[\prod_{i=1}^{m} \prod_{j=0}^{2} \left(\frac{e^{\eta_g}}{1 + e^{\eta_{i1} + e^{\eta_{i2}}}} \right)^{y_{ij} w_i} \right].
\end{aligned}
\tag{9.6}
$$

Note that the household and post-stratification weighting variable W_i is included here in an effort to account for whether proper stratification of the respondents may eliminate the necessity for the introduction of a mechanism to describe non-response.

9.5.3 Data Augmentation

Tanner and Wong (1987) suggest an iterative method for computation of posterior distributions when faced with missing data. This method applies whenever augmenting the dataset makes it easier to analyse and the augmented items are easily generated.

Consider the following additional notation: Let S represent the total number of susceptible subjects in the sample. $S = \sum_{i=1}^{n} Z_i$, $S \sim \text{Binomial}(\rho)$. Let X be the matrix of explanatory variables (including the number of calls) for all the subjects selected to participate in the survey. Let $Y = (Y_1, \ldots, Y_n)$ be the vector of their responses. Partitions X into $\{X_{\text{obs}}, X_{\text{mis}}, X_{\text{imm}}\}$ and Y into $Y_{\text{obs}}, Y_{\text{mis}}, Y_{\text{imm}}\}$. Also, by the memoryless property of the Geometric distribution, the distribution of the additional number of calls required to reach the subjects in A_{mis} is known, and may be expressed: $\forall i \in A_{\text{mis}}$, let $V_i = C_i - 12$, which is also distributed as a Geometric random variable with parameter π.

Now suppose that the true values of S, X_{mis}, and Y_{mis} were known. The likelihood could then be considered in the form:

$$
\begin{aligned}
L(\rho, \pi, \beta| \quad & X_{\text{obs}}, Y_{\text{obs}}, Y_{\text{mis}}, S, R) \\
\propto \quad & \left[(\rho\pi)^s (1 - \pi)^{(\sum c_{sus}) - s} \right] \times \left[(1 - \rho)^{n-2} \right] \\
\times \quad & \left[\sum_{i=1}^{s} \sum_{j=0}^{2} \left(\frac{e^{\nu_{ij}}}{1 + e^{\nu_i 1} + e^{\nu_i 2}} \right)^{y_{ij} w_i} \right],
\end{aligned}
\tag{9.7}
$$

where $\sum C_{\text{sus}} = \sum C_{\text{obs}} + \sum (V_i + 12)$ is the number of calls that would have been necessary to reach all susceptibles and the summands are taken over the appropriate range of subjects.

Although the true values of S, X_{mis}, and Y_{mis} are unknown, one may utilize what is known about the behavior of these variables to impute stochastically possible values for them within the MCMC algorithm. Given ρ, a value for S may be drawn from a truncated Binomial $(2,398, \rho)$, where $1,429 \leq S \leq 2,398$. Given S, the number of subjects in A_{mis} is known. For each of these subjects in A_{mis} a value $V_i \sim \text{Geometric} (\pi)$ may be drawn, which results in an imputation for the number of calls needed to reach each susceptible but unreached subject. The relationships among the number of calls and the other explanatory variables may then be exploited to impute values for the rest of X_{mis}. Specifically, the missing values of Age and K - risk are imputed by regressing Calls on Age and K - risk respectively and predicting from the resultant linear equations. Similarly, the missing values of Smoker and Bother are imputed via logistic regression on each, using Calls as the explanatory variable. Here the model assumptions are checked using the respondents data, and an assumption is being made that these same relationships hold for the susceptible non-respondents. Note that these regression and logistic regression equations are fit in the Bayesian context (*e.g.*, Gelman et al. (1998)) and necessitate the inclusion of additional parameters, β_I, in the MCMC process which describe these relationships (see Appendix B for more detail). We chose this imputation plan in the interest of the efficiency of the full MCMC algorithm. An alternative would be to impute the missing values for a particular explanatory variable conditional on all the remaining variables (*e.g.*, Rubin (1996)). Finally, Y_{mis} may be predicted by utilizing the imputed values of X_{mis} and the relationship described in the logistic regression model. In the interest of the exchangeability of the susceptible non-respondents in the absence of subsequent stratification information, we apply a weight of 1.0 to all the imputed Y_{mis} values; an alternative here would be to impute the sex and household size of the susceptible non-respondents, in addition to their age, and apply the weighting procedure described in Appendix A to the imputed Y_{mis}.

9.5.4 Sampling from the Posterior Distribution

The full MCMC simulation consists of a Metropolis algorithm supplemented in every iteration with the data augmentation described above. An outline of the MCMC algorithm used may be found in Appendix B. Convergence was assessed utilizing the method of Hiedelberger and Welch (1983) as described in Cowles and Carlin (1996). MacEachern and Beliner (1994) assert that, under loose conditions, subsampling the MCMC simulated values to account for autocorrelation will result in poorer estimators. Following their suggestion, all simulated values, after an appropriate burn-in period, were used in the analysis that follows.

9.6   Choice of Prior Distributions

In the evaluation of possible prior distributions for the parameters of both the NI and MAR models, the goal of the comparison of the various models was taken into consideration. The choice of prior distributions for the parameters was made from the perspective of the MAR belief. Two possibilities were examined.

The first option is built around the utilization of the Phase I & II surveys. Since these surveys were similar to and were completed prior to the Phase III survey which comprises our data, information contained in these first two surveys may be utilized in the construction of priors. The same dependent variable was contained in the Phase I & II dataset, along with the variables Smoke, Age, and K - risk. A logistic regression model was compiled from the Phase I & II data to describe the relationship between the opinion on workplace smoking and these three explanatory variables. Normal priors were constructed for the coefficients of these three variables centered at their MLE's, but with increased standard error. The error terms were increased due to three factors:

i) There was a three year span between the Phase II and Phase III surveys; opinions may have changed over that time, possibly as a result of the impact of the bylaw.

ii) The MLE's were calculated under the same MAR assumption being evaluated.

iii) Prior to the collection of the Phase III data, there existed the possibility that other explanatory variables would be included in the model; in the presence of other variables, the effect of these three could be altered.

Although the variances were increased, the means were not changed, since it was unknown, *a priori*, in what direction any change might occur. Since the available Phase I & II data contained no information about the Calls or Bother variables, the coefficients of these were assigned a diffuse Normal (0,9) prior. For clarity, this option will be referred to as the "Phase I & II prior" in this analysis.

In the second option Normal (0,9) priors are assigned to each of the logistic regression coefficients. One motivation for this choice is that, for the same three reasons the error terms were increased above, the variables common to the Phase I & II and Phase III surveys are not exchangeable. Thus, construction based on the Phase I & II results would be inappropriate. This option will be referred to as the "Central Prior".

The choice to use Normal (0,9) distributions here is for convenience. Centering the prior at zero gives equal weight to either direction of the relationship. We believe the choice of a variance of nine to be adequate without being overly diffuse. The use of improper priors could lead to a Markov Chain Monte Carlo simulation that never converges, and, as Natarajan and Kass (2000) show, an overly diffuse proper prior may behave like an improper one. In section 9.7.2, we offer a sensitivity analysis to evaluate how the results are effected by the choice of prior.

The non-response parameters of the NI model, ρ and π, were treated the same under both prior options. There was no additional information available about the probability of a successful call or the probability of susceptibility. Thus, ρ and π were each assigned a $U(0,1)$ prior.

The data augmentation parameters found in each of the logistic regression equations, β_l, were independently given diffuse Normal (0,9) priors. For each linear regression equation found in the data augmentation process, the coefficients, β_r, and variance, σ^2, were set to $p(\beta_r, \sigma_r^2) \propto 1/\sigma_r^2$, the standard non-informative prior distribution (*e.g.*, Gelman et al. (1998)). Note that the closed forms of the posterior distributions of the linear regression parameters are known and may be drawn from directly.

9.7   Results

First, the validity of the MAR assumption is examined through the coefficients of the number of calls variable. Then, the NI model is evaluated with respect to sensitivity to the choice of prior. Finally, the magnitude of the impact of a faulty MAR assumption for this dataset is investigated by illustrating the change in the odds of response.

9.7.1   Coefficients for the Number of Calls

For both the Phase I & II and Central priors, Figure 9.4 displays the posterior density (solid line) and 95% credible interval estimates (dotted lines) of the coefficient of the calls variable in η_{i1} in the NI model, and compares them to the point $\beta_{\text{call}_1} = 0$ (dashed lines). The results clearly indicate this coefficient differs from zero. We also find a non-zero result in η_{i_2}, where, using the Phase I & II prior, the 95% HPD credible interval for β_{call_2} is (0.03613, 0.11595).

The non-zero coefficient of C_i demonstrates a dependence between the number of calls and the subjects' opinions on smoking in the workplace. Thus, the dependent variable and the non-response mechanism are not independent under the conditions discussed in section 9.5.2. This result implies that an assumption that the missing observations are missing at random prior to accounting for the non-response mechanism is incorrect for this dataset.

There is a hint in Figure 9.3 that the probability of a successful call decreases as the call number increases. To verify the assumption that the relationship between the number of calls and the log odds of response is linear, a second Bayesian NI model was constructed. This model split the calls variable into two, $C_i I_{\{C_i < 7\}}$ and $C_i I_{\{C_i \geq 7\}}$, based on whether the number of calls were fewer than seven. The posterior distributions of the coefficients of these two variables were then compared and evidence that they are essentially different was not found. In particular, for η_{i1} the 95% credible interval for $C_i I_{\{C_i \geq 7\}}$ contained the same interval for $C_i I_{\{C_i < 7\}}$, and for η_{i2} the 95% credible intervals strongly overlapped.

9.7.2   Sensitivity to Priors

Would different prior distributions, either on the calls coefficient or on the others, make a difference in the effect illustrated above? Table 9.1 displays 95% HPD credible intervals for the coefficient of the calls variable in the first logit equation of the NI model for six different priors. The priors include the Phase I & II and Central priors as well as four others – labeled options 3, 4, 5, and 6. Option 3 and 4 resemble the Central prior except that they change the prior distribution on the coefficient of the number of calls to Normal (1,9) and Normal (-1,9) respectively. Option 5 places Normal (0, 9) priors on β_{call_1}, β_{age_1}, and $\beta_{\text{b.USUL}_1}$, a Normal (1,9) prior on β_{01}, a Number (0.5, 9) prior on $\beta_{\text{K-risk}_1}$, a Normal (-1, 9) prior on β_{S_1} and Normal (-5, 9) priors on β_{SQ_1} and $\beta_{\text{b.NO}_1}$. Option 6 takes the Central Prior and reduces all the variances from nine to two.

Under all six priors, Table 9.1 demonstrates that the coefficient of the calls variable in the first logit equation clearly differs from zero. The finding that the missing data

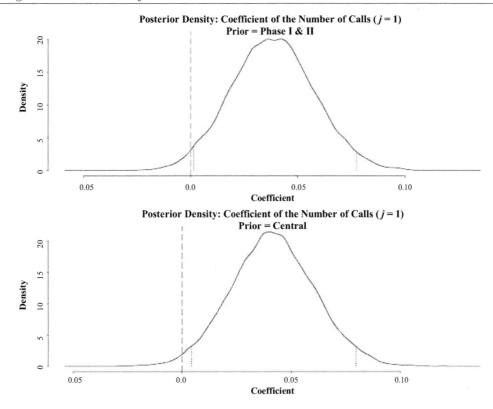

Figure 9.4: Display of β_{call}, the coefficient of the calls variable in η_{i1}: posterior density (solid line) and 95% equal tailed credible interval (dotted line), compared to $\beta_{\text{call}_1} = 0$ (dashed line).

Table 9.1: 95% HPD Credible Intervals for β_{call} Under Six Different Prior Distributions

Prior	Coefficient of the number of Calls "C_i" in η_{i1}	
	95% Intervals	
	Lower Bound	Upper Bound
Phase I & II	0.00129	0.07746
Central	0.00446	0.07980
Option 3	0.00447	0.07983
Option 4	0.00441	0.07975
Option 5	0.00440	0.07970
Option 6	0.00436	0.07944

mechanism is non-ignorable for this dataset does not appear to be effected by the choice of prior among these options.

9.7.3 Effect on Odds of Response

Given the failure of the MAR assumption shown above, it is of interest to question the relevance of the error that using the MAR assumption would create. The magnitude

Table 9.2: Comparison of the Odds of Response for 4 Typical Subjects. Posterior Medians Were Used As the Point Estimates for the Coefficients in the Bayesian Models; the Mle Was Used for the Frequentist Model

	Subject 1	Subject 2	Subject 3	Subject 4
Smoker	No	No	Former	Yes
Age	30	50	27	40
Bother	Usually	Always	No	No
K - risk	11	12		
Model	Odds $Y = 1/Y = 0$			
MAR MLE	0.674	2.105	0.457	0.396
MAR Phase I & II prior	0.703	4.487	0.209	0.116
NI Phase I & II prior: 2 calls	0.640	4.024	0.202	0.108
NI Central prior: 2 calls	0.593	4.442	0.162	0.102
Option 3: 2 calls	0.594	4.449	0.162	0.102
Option 4: 2 calls	0.592	4.435	0.162	0.101
Option 5: 2 calls	0.590	4.423	0.161	0.101
Option 6: 2 calls	0.590	4.426	0.161	0.101
NI Phase I & II prior: 13 calls	0.974	6.128	0.308	0.165
NI Central prior: 13 calls	0.936	7.013	0.256	0.160
Option 3: 13 calls	0.937	7.026	0.256	0.161
Option 4: 13 calls	0.934	7.000	0.255	0.160
Option 5: 13 calls	0.930	6.975	0.254	0.159
Option 6: 13 calls	0.931	6.980	0.254	0.160

of the error induced by a faulty MAR assumption may be illustrated by examination of its effect on the odds ratio $p_1(x_i)/p_0(x_i)$. First, we consider the effect on a typical respondent profile. The modal respondent was a non-smoker between the ages of 25 - 35 years old who was usually bothered by secondhand smoke, had a K - risk of 11 and could be reached in 2 calls. We label this modal respondent as Subject 1. Table 9.2 demonstrates the change in posterior odds for Subject 1 when called 13 times.

The subject 1 column Table 9.2 indicates a dramatic difference in the posterior odds when the nonresponse mechanism is taken into consideration. For this typical respondent profile, when the number of calls is increased from two to thirteen the posterior odds of choosing "Smoking should not be permitted at all" over "Smoking should be permitted in restricted areas only" increases by 52.18% under the Phase I & II prior and 57.84% when using the Central prior. This is dramatic evidence of the relationship between the dependent variable and the non-response mechanism.

Are the results for the modal subject above typical? Table 9.2 also displays the effects on the odds of response under the NI model for three additional test subject profiles for each of the six different priors considered above. Subject 2 is a fifty year old non-smoker who is always bothered by smoke and has a perfect "K - risk" score. Subject 3 is a 27 year old former smoker who is not bothered by smoke and has a "K - risk" score of seven. Subject 4 is a 40 year old smoker who is not bothered by smoke and has a "K - risk" score of three. On multiple subjects with multiple priors, Table 9.2 consistently shows the same result. Increasing the number of calls to greater than 12 will increase the posterior odds of choosing category "1" over category "0". For each of the test subjects and priors found in Table 9.2, the increase was between 52.18% and 58.41%.

Similar results were found when examining the odds of choosing the "Smoking should not be restricted at all" category over the "Smoking should be permitted in restricted areas only" category. Using test subjects which were a current and a former smoker (Subjects 3 and 4 above), the posterior odds increased 46.7% when the number of calls was increased from 2 to 13 under the Phase I & II prior.

9.7.4 Effect on Probability of Response

With the shift in posterior odds illustrated above comes a corresponding shift in the estimated probabilities that a subject will respond in a particular category. Among the respondents, 57.45% chose category "0", 40.64% chose category "1", and 1.91% chose category "2". The number of non-respondent susceptibles have a posterior median of 469, with a 95% credible interval of (25,944). On average, 55.88% of the simulated non-respondent susceptibles chose category "0", 40.03% chose category "1", and 4.08% chose category "2". While, for categories "0" and "1", the average values for the non-respondent susceptibles fall within the 95% confidence intervals for the proportions of the respondents in these categories, the point estimates for each category shift when the non-response mechanism is included in the model. In comparing the category "2" results, we estimate that non-respondents are twice as likely to favor no restrictions on smoking (category "2") than are respondents. While the low number of subjects found in category "2" are unlikely to provoke a change in workplace smoking law, the increase noted in the non-respondents in this category serves as an example of how the lack of proper consideration of the non-respondents could lead to flawed conclusions about the data.

9.8   Conclusion

Section 9.7 demonstrates that, for the dependent variable of interest in this dataset, an assertion that the missing observations are missing at random, prior to accounting for the missing data mechanism, is incorrect, assuming the relationship among the relevant variables is the same for all susceptible subjects. Furthermore, the use of a faulty MAR assumption in the evaluation of this dependent variable risks serious error in the calculation of the posterior odds and in any conclusion drawn from them. In order to perform a proper evaluation of the opinion on smoking in the workplace in Toronto in early 1993 via the dependent variable of interest in this survey, it is necessary to account for the non-response mechanism in the model structure.

In this analysis, only one simple piece of information, the number of calls, was utilized. A more complete treatment could have been made, had more information been available. Knowledge of the exact number of calls to the non-respondents, instead of a minimum, and the time of day of the calls could have enabled this analysis to be more precise. In addition, knowledge of the type of non-response, refusal or non-availability, and the number of times the non-respondents were actually contacted could have allowed for better classification of the non-respondents. Groves and Couper (1998) point out that statistical errors arising from non-availability and those arising from refusals are likely to differ. As they further comment, the evaluation of how efforts to seek cooperation effect measurement error is an important area of research.

The results illustrated above apply only to this one dependent variable assessing smoking in the workplace in this one dataset. Given the perception that smoking has become less socially acceptable over recent years, it would be reasonable to think that non-response error due to questions about smoking may be more severe than other topics. A comparison of non-response bias including various smoking related questions and others which do not concern smoking may be found in Biemer (2001);

this comparison lends no credence to the idea that non-response error is unique to questions relating to smoking.

Although the above results make no implications about the missing data mechanisms in other surveys, there is a clear demonstration here that blindly assuming that the respondents of a survey constitute a random subsample of the population for the variables of interest can be an unwise choice. Information, available at the time of data collection, can enable the evaluation of whether or not the mechanism which causes the non-response is ignorable. In light of this observation, then, it should be [of, added for clarity, JBK] interest to those who work with such data to make use of the available information pertaining to the non-response in the evaluation of that data and to make such information available to others who utilize the dataset. As a general matter, we believe that the collection and analysis of data on where and how respondents were found, as well as how difficult they were to find, is an important future direction for survey methodology and practice.

Acknowledgements

This research was funded by National Science Foundation Grant DMS-9801401. The authors thank Shelley Bull for her many helpful comments and suggestions and for assistance in the acquisition of the data and John Eltinge and the anonymous referees and Associate Editor for their valuable comments.

Data from the Attitudes Toward Smoking Legislation, which was funded by Health and Welfare Canada, were made available by the Institute for Social Research at York University. The data were collected by the Institute for Social Research for Dr. Linda Pederson of the University of Western Ontario, Dr. Shelley Bull of the University of Toronto and Dr. Mary Jane Ashley of the University of Toronto. The principal investigators, the Ontario Ministry of Health and the Institute for Social Research bear no responsibility for the analysis and interpretations presented here.

Appendices

A. Post-Stratification Weighting

HHW_i is the household weight of subject i as described in Northrup (1993).

- Let m = the number of respondents.
- Let r = the cumulative number of adults in the responding households.
- Let h_i = the number of adults in subject is household.
- $HHW_i h_i \cdot m/r$.

Proportions in the sample falling into the following age groups were calculated for both male and female respondents: 18–24 years, 25–44 years, 45–64 years, and over 65 years old. These proportions were then compared to the age/sex distribution in Metropolitan Toronto.

- Let p_{1i} = the proportion of adult Metropolitan Toronto residents falling into the same age/sex category as subject i, as per the 1991 Census.
- Let p_{2i} = the proportion of survey respondents with the same age and sex categories as subject i.
- $W_i = HHW_i \cdot p_{1i}/p_{2i}$, where W_i is the final post-stratification weight used in the analysis.

B. MCMC Implementation

The full MCMC simulation for the NI model consists of a Metropolis algorithm supplemented with the data augmentation described in section 9.5.3. The following is an overview of the MCMC algorithm. Variables used below are defined in section 9.5. At each iteration t,

1. Draw ρ_i for $Beta(s_{t-1} + 1.2398 - s_{t-1} + 1)$.
2. Impute s_t from $Binomial(\rho_t) \geq 1.429$.
3. Impute C_{mis_t} : draw $(s_t - 1.429)\nu_i$'s from $Geometric(\pi_{t-1})$ and $\forall c_i \in c_{\text{mis}}, c_i = \nu_i + 12$.
4. Draw π_t from $Beta(s_t + 1, \prod c_{\text{sus}}, -s_t + 1)$.
5. Impute values for the rest of X_{mis} by utilizing the relationships with the number of calls, as described in section 9.5.3.
6. Update the additional parameters used in the data augmentation of X_{mis}.
   - Update linear regression parameters, β_r and σ_r by drawing directly from the closed form of their posteriors.
   - Update logistic regression parameters, β_l using a Metropolis step on each.
7. Impute Y_{mis_t} : $\forall y_i \in y_{\text{mis}}$ draw y_i from a $Multinomial(p_0(x_i), p_1(x_i), p_2(x_i))$.
8. Update each β_{kj} using a Metropolis step on the conditional likelihood and a Normal Jump function.

REFERENCES

Biemer, P. (2001). "Nonresponse bias and measurement bias in a comparison of face to face and telephone interviewing." *Journal of Official Statistics*, 17, 2, 295–320. 173

Bull, S. (1994). *Case Studies in Biometry*, chap. 16: Analysis of attitudes toward workplace smoking restrictions, 249–270. New York: John Wiley & Sons, Inc. 161

Cowles, M. and Carlin, B. (1996). "Markov Chain Monte Carlo convergence diagnostics: A comparative review." *Journal of the American Statistical Association*, 91, 883–904. 169

Dempster, A., Laird, N., and Rubin, D. (1977). "Maximum likelihood from incomplete data via the EM algorithm (with discussion)." *Journal of the American Statistical Association*, B 39, 1–38. 162

Drew, J. and Fuller, W. (1981). "Nonresponse in complex multiphase surveys." In *Proceedings of the section on Survey Research Methods*, 623–628. American Statistical Association, Alexandria, VA. 166

Eltinge, J. and Yansaneh, I. (1997). "Diagnosis for formation of nonresponse adjustment cells, with and application to income nonresponse in the U.S. Consumer Expenditure Survey." *Survey Methodology*, 23, 33–40. 160

Gelman, A., Carlin, B., Stern, H., and Rubin, D. (1998). *Bayesian Data Analysis*. London: Chapman & Hall. 168, 170

Groves, R. and Couper, M. (1998). *Nonresponse in Household Interview Surveys*. New York: John Wiley & Sons, Inc. 161, 164, 173

Hiedelberger, P. and Welch, P. (1983). "Simulation run length control in the presence of an initial transient." *Operations Research*, 31, 1109–1144. 169

Little, R. (1996). "Survey nonresponse adjustments for estimates of means." *International Statistical Review*, 54, 139–157. 160

Little, R. and Rubin, D. (1987). *Statistical Analysis with Missing Data*. New York: Wiley. 159, 161

MacEachern, S. and Beliner, L. (1994). "Subsampling the Gibbs sampler." *The American Statistician*, 48, 188–189. 169

Maller, R. and Zhou, X. (1996). *Survival Analysis with Long Term Survivors*. Chichester, New York: John Wiley & Sons, Inc. 165

Natarajan, R. and Kass, R. (2000). "Reference Bayesian methods for generalized linear mixed models." *Journal of the American Statistical Association*, 95, 227–237. 169

Northrup, D. (1993). "Attitudes towards workplace smoking legislation: A survey of residents of metropolitan Toronto, Phase III, 1992/93 Technical Documentation." Tech. Rep. Institute for Social Research, York University, unpublished. 160, 163, 165, 174

Pederson, L., Bull, S., and Ashley, M. (1996). "Smoking in the workplace: Do smoking patterns and attitudes reflect the legislative environment?" *Tobacco Control*, 5, 39–45. 160, 163

Pederson, L., Bull, S., Ashley, M., and Lefcoe, N. (1989). "A population survey on legislative measures to restrict smoking in Ontario: 3. Variables related to attitudes of smokers and nonsmokers." *American Journal of Preventive Medicine*, 5, 313–322. 161

Potthoff, R., Manton, K., and Woodbury, M. (1993). "Correcting for nonavailability bias in surveys by weighting based on number of callbacks." *Journal of the American Statistical Association*, 88, 1197–1207. 159

Rubin, D. (1976). "Inference and missing data." *Biometrika*, 63, 581–592. 157, 159, 161

— (1996). "Multiple imputation after 18+ years." *Journal of the American Statistical Association*, 91, 473–489. 168

Shmueli, G., Minka, T., Kadane, J., Borle, S., and Boatwright, P. (2004). "A Useful Distribution for Fitting Discrete Data: Revival of the COM-Poisson." *Journal of the Royal Statistical Association C*, 54, 127–142. 166

Tanner, M. and Wong, W. (1987). "The calculation of posterior distribution by data augmentation." *Journal of the American Statistical Association*, 82, 528–540. 167

Epilogue

What is the scientific issue addressed?

Is the number of times a telephone survey tried to reach a respondent informative for the respondent's attitude about smoking in the workplace?

Is justification given for

a) the use of the data?

The data are from a survey of Toronto citizens about their attitude about smoking in the workplace. In addition to the usual demographic information, the data also, crucially, gives the number of times the surveyors tried to reach the respondent before they succeeded in doing so.

b) the likelihood and priors?

There are many formulations compared. They are justified as different possible beliefs about the data, and specifically about the non-response mechanism.

What robustness checks were performed?

There are many, especially comparing the models for non-response.

How was the computing done?

Markov chain Monte Carlo.

If I were doing this problem today, how would I change the approach?

I would not.

What do I see as the contributions of the paper?

1. The number of calls, here modelled as a fraction of immunes who will not

respond no matter how many calls are made to them, and a geometric distribution for the rest, matters. Those who did not answer were estimated to object to smoking in the workplace substantially less than those who did answer.

2. Surveys, in principle, look like experimental data. But when, inevitably, non-response occurs, the analysis of the data draws on methods for observational studies. The paper suggests ways in which a richer data set could be collected by recording more detail on what was done to obtain response.

Was Bayesian analysis useful in this problem?

I argue for "yes."

TEACHING SUGGESTIONS

References for theoretical ideas:

1. Missing data: *Principles* Section 9.2

2. Markov chain Monte Carlo: *Principles* Section 10.3

3. Geometric distribution: *Principles* Section 3.7

4. Hierarchical model: *Principles* Chapter 9

Exercises

1. Why does missing data matter? Can't you just ignore it, and analyze the results of a survey pretending that those who responded are typical of those who did not?

2. Explain in your own words, "MCAR," "MAR," "NI" and "distinct."

3. Given that the persons who did not respond have yielded no information about their attitudes about smoking (or anything else about themselves), how is it possible to say anything useful about their attitudes about smoking?

4. What is a "surviving fraction?" In this application, what did they survive?

5. For future surveys on this subject, what additional information would you suggest should be gathered?

Chapter 10

Comparing Harm Done by Mobility and Class Absence: Missing Students and Missing Data (2003)

Foreword

I first met Michelle Dunn when she was an incoming statistics masters student and was assigned to be my Teaching Assistant. She agreed to do the work under one condition: that I would promise to take issues of academic integrity seriously. (She was appalled at how lax her undergraduate college had been.) I agreed, and she did an excellent job.

After finishing her master's degree, she left to fulfill an obligation to work for the federal government. We kept in touch, and four years later she returned to CMU to pursue a Ph.D. Michelle wanted to work in secondary education, feeling that this was, and is, a critical issue for our country. This paper is the result of her ADA project.

Through friends at the University of Pittsburgh's Learning and Development Center, we met administrators at the Pittsburgh Public Schools. Through them, we gained access to the School Board's database. After discussions, the issue we focused on had to do with whether schooling matters. In particular, what are the impacts of absences and changing schools on student performance in standardized tests.

We found that both absences and changing schools matter, and both degrade student performance. Roughly, we found that changing schools at least once in the three years preceding eleventh grade had the same (negative) effect on student scores as would missing 14 days of school in the year of the examinations, or 32 days of school in the previous year.

The models used in the study are principally normal linear models. The priors involve some elicitation from our client, Jack Garrow, who was a data analyst for the Pittsburgh Public Schools. One issue that required special care was what it meant when a student chose not to take a mathematics course, or what it meant when a student chose to be absent from school when the standardized exam was administered.

This paper was originally published in the *Journal of Educational and Behavioral Statistics*, **28**, (#3), pp. 268–288. Republished with the permission of SAGE Publications.

Where are they now? Michelle Dunn works as an administrator at the National Cancer Institute. I have lost track of Jack Garrow.

Published Paper

Joseph B. Kadane, Michelle Dunn and John R. Garrow

Abstract

This article addresses the relationship between academic achievement and the student characteristics of absence and mobility. Mobility is a measure of how often a student changes schools. Absence is how often a student misses class. Standardized test scores are used as proxies for academic achievement. A model for the full joint distribution of the parameters and the data, both missing and observed, is postulated. After priors are elicited, a Metropolis-Hastings algorithm within a Gibbs sampler is used to evaluate the posterior distributions of the model parameters for the Pittsburgh Public Schools. Results are given in two stages. First, mobility and absence are shown to have, with high probability, negative relationships with academic achievement. Second, the posterior for mobility is viewed in terms of the equivalent harm done by absence: changing schools at least once in the three year period, 1998-2000, has an impact on standardized tests administered in the spring of 2000 equivalent to being absent about 14 days in 1999-2000 or 32 days in 1998-1999.

Keywords: data augmentation, Markov Chain Monte Carlo, missing data

10.1 Introduction

Absence and mobility are critical problems for the Pittsburgh Public Schools (PPS). They are among a student's lifestyle factors that could affect his or her learning environment. The focus of this study is on factors that students and parents have relative influence on rather than the factors that they cannot control. This article compares the detriments of absence and mobility both in absolute terms and relative to one another.

Mobility is a measure of how often a student changes schools. Absence is how often a student misses class. By modeling standardized test scores (proxies for students' academic achievements) in terms of mobility, absence and other covariates, a comparison is made by considering the ratios of the mobility and absence model coefficients.

This study is premised on two ideas. The first is that students learn more about academic subjects while in school than out of school. The second is that students learn better when exposed to a cohesive course of study that reinforces and builds upon previously learned concepts.

The purpose of this study is two-fold. The first goal is to affirm that in-school instruction and an uninterrupted curriculum have a positive (or non-negative) relationship with a student's academic achievement. Equivalently, the goal is to affirm that mobility and absence have negative relationships with academic achievement. The second goal is to compare the harm of an interruption of curriculum to that of

The authors thank Dr. Shula Nedley and Professor Lauren Resnick, for their support and expert advice. They also thank Howard Wainer and the anonymous referees for their many helpful comments and suggestions.

missing school: in other words, to view mobility in terms of the equivalent harm done by absence.

The variables under study, absence (number of days of class missed) and mobility (the number of times a student changed schools), do not reveal whether a student paid attention to the teacher while in school or whether the curricula at the two schools between which a student transferred are synchronized. However, absence and mobility can act as substitutes for the effects of in-school instruction and an uninterrupted curriculum.

How the quantity of instruction or learning time relates to achievement has long been of concern (Carver, 1970). Also of concern is how patterns of absence, both of an individual student and of the classroom,[1] relate to achievement (Monk and Ibrahim, 1984). The data in this study allow consideration only of the quantity of absence.

The use of standardized test scores as a proxy for academic achievement is not unusual (Hanson and Schutz, 1986). However, educational evaluation experts disagree whether they should be used. Opponents of standardized tests argue that they are not general enough to adequately measure how schools are meeting their overall goals, especially their noncognitive goals such as improving self-confidence and motivation. In addition, they argue that standardized tests are not specific and sensitive enough to evaluate educational programs (Madaus et al., 1980). Since the purpose of this study is to relate mobility and absence to general academic achievement, rather than to evaluate a particular basic skills program or measure noncognitive achievement, the use of achievement tests is acceptable.

If complete data were available, standardized test scores could be predicted from mobility, absences, and other covariates using linear regression. What make this problem hard are missing data. After specifying a model and eliciting prior distribution parameters, Bayesian methods are used to explore the posterior distribution of the model parameters.

This article is organized as follows. Data from the PPS, both observed and missing, are discussed in Section 10.2. A model for the full joint distribution of the parameters, the missing data, and the observed data is proposed in Section 10.3. Prior distributions of the parameters are also presented in Section 10.3. Section 10.4 describes how the model is fit using Bayesian methods. Section 10.5 presents the relationships of mobility and absence to the 2000 standardized test as well as to each other in the form of a ratio of coefficients. Conclusions are drawn in Section 10.6.

10.2   Data

The data consist of assessment, course, and demographic information for the years 1998-2000[2] for the PPS cohort of students in the 11th grade in 2000. The data fields are described in Section 10.2.1. The missing data are described in Section 10.2.2.

10.2.1 *Data Description*

A student record consists of an ordered list of 17 data fields. Demographic information and mobility comprise the first five fields. The next 12 fields consist of absences, grades (math and English), and standardized test scores for 1998, 1999, and 2000. Demographic information and mobility for each student are summarized in Table 10.1.

---

[1]For individual students, the authors of the cited work hypothesize that absence has varying effects, depending on the time of year that it occurs. The authors also hypothesize that absence when a large proportion of the class is absent is not as harmful as other absence since a teacher may decide to postpone a major lesson.

[2]A school year is referred to by the year in which it ends.

Table 10.1: Demographic Information and Mobility

Variable	Zero corresponds to	One corresponds to
Gender	Female	Male
Race	Non-black	Black
Guardian	Two parental figures	Other
Subsidized lunch status	Regular	Free
Mobility	Did not transfer	Transferred

Small categorizations of race, guardian, and lunch status are collapsed to form two categories for each variable. Guardian is defined to be the authority figure(s) with whom the student resides. Subsidized lunch status is used as a proxy for socio-economic status.

Mobility is a count of the number of times that a student changed schools[3] in 1998-2000. For students who transfer into the PPS, the number of moves prior to arriving in the PPS is not known. Thus, for many students who transferred at least once, the count of transfers in this data is a minimum number of transfers. For this reason and because only 57 out of 1888 students are known to have transferred more than once in the three years, mobility is collapsed into two categories. It is 0 if the student has not transferred in the three-year period and 1 if the student transferred at least once. A total of 362 of the 1888 students in the cohort under study transferred at least once in the three-year period.

Absence is measured by the sum over semesters of the median number of days per semester that a student is absent from class, where the median is taken over all classes. This is done because formal attendance is not taken in some classes, but instead students are arbitrarily marked all present or all absent for that class. The average numbers of days absent for the students in this cohort are 15.6, 20.4, and 26.6 days respectively for 1998, 1999, and 2000.

Alphabetical English and math grades for each semester are translated to a numerical scale ($0 = F, \ldots, 4 = A$) and the two semesters of each academic year are summed. If a student takes more than one math class in a semester,[4] the median math grade for that semester is taken; taking multiple English classes in one semester is handled similarly.[5] Only English and math grades are considered because most students have these and no other classes in common.

Various "brands" of standardized tests are given every year to students in the PPS, each with unique styles and objectives.[6] The cohort of students in this study took the Iowa Test of Basic Skills (ITBS) in 1998, the New Standards Reference Exam (NSRE) in 1999, and the Pennsylvania System of School Assessments (PSSA) in 2000.[7] In 1999, only Geometry students took the math section of the New Standards exam. For this reason, only the English sections of the three tests are used in the model. Scores for the PSSA and the ITBS tests are given in percentiles, while scores for the NSRE are integers from 1 to 5 for each of four reading tests; the four tests are summed and rescaled to range from 0 to 100.

---

[3]Taking vocational classes at a school other than the student's primary school does not count as transferring, and moving from one school to another and back counts as two moves.

[4]Ten percent of the students take two math classes and 1% take three.

[5]Thirteen percent take two English classes and 1% take three.

[6]Only one cohort of students is used in this study because the different brands of tests are not directly comparable.

[7]The Iowa test is a national multiple choice exam. The New Standards exam asks open-ended questions to which students give a written answer. The Pennsylvania test contains both types of questions.

Table 10.2: Percentage of Data Missing

Variable	2000	1999	1998
Standardized test	12%	22%	9%
Absences	3%	18%	9%
English grades	11%	23%	10%
Math grades	16%	26%	11%
Gender		0%	
Race		0%	
Guardian		2%	
Subsidized lunch status		2%	
Mobility		0%	

Students in special schools or in certain types of special education (learning disabled, mentally retarded, severely emotionally disturbed, brain injured, developmentally delayed, and having multiple handicaps) are excluded from this study. Excluding these students, there are a total of 1,888 students in the cohort of students in the 11th grade in 2000.

10.2.2   Missing Data

Test scores, grades, absences, and some demographic information are missing. The amount of missing data varies with the category of the information and the year. Table 10.2 summarizes how much data are missing for each of the variables.[8]

There are a variety of reasons why the data are missing. Any of the fields may be missing due to incorrectly entered student identification numbers or a lack of reporting by a school to the central administration. In addition, grades and test scores may also be missing if the student did not take the particular class or test.

Three reasons for a student not to take a test are

1. The student is sick on the test day and all makeup days.

2. The student moves into the PPS after the test was administered.

3. The student chooses not to come to school on test and makeup days.

This study ignores the unlikely event of the first reason. The second reason is addressed by the mobility coefficient. The third reason to miss a test is by the student's choice, which is addressed in Section 3 via the construction of a choice indicator. Three reasons (other than due to lack of reporting) that math grades might be missing are

1. The student has exhausted all available math classes.

2. The student moves into the PPS.

3. The student chooses not to take math.

Because the students are (at oldest) in the 11th grade, the first reason is unlikely to happen and so is ignored. As in the treatment of the missing tests, the second reason is addressed by the mobility coefficient, and the third is addressed via a choice indicator. All students in the cohort are required to take an English class. The mobility coefficient addresses the only reason for English grades to be missing other than due to lack of reporting.

A choice indicator is an indicator variable that differentiates students who choose

---

[8]The most missing data occur in 1999, possibly due to a conversion between two data management systems.

not to take a test or class from those who choose to take it. A missing math grade in the presence of English grades indicates the choice by the student not to take math. Similarly, the absence of test scores in the presence of absence information indicates a choice not to take the standardized test. There are six choice indicators, one math and one test indicator for each year.

10.3 Model Specification

Inference is based on the posterior distribution of the parameters and the missing values given the observed data. Since the posterior is proportional to the full joint distribution of the data and the parameters, it is sufficient to specify the full joint distribution. The full joint distribution is specified by the prior distribution of the parameters, which is discussed in Subsection 10.3.4, and the likelihood of the data, described in Subsections 10.3.2 and 10.3.3. Subsection 10.3.2 describes the model as if no data were missing. Subsection 10.3.3 incorporates the choice indicators into the model in order to account for the missing data. Subsection 10.3.1 describes the notation.

10.3.1 Notation

Let (T_{00}, T_{99}, T_{98}) be the English standardized test scores from 2000, 1999 and 1998 respectively. Likewise, let math grades, English grades, and absences be defined respectively

$$
\begin{aligned}
M &= (M_{00}, M_{99}, M_{98}) \\
E &= (E_{00}, E_{99}, E_{98}) \\
A &= (A_{00}, A_{99}, A_{98})
\end{aligned}
$$

The five discrete variables (sex, race, guardian, lunch, mobility) are collectively referred to as D and individually by name.

The six choice indicators are defined to be 1 if the corresponding variable is missing due to choice and 0 otherwise. The choice indicators share the same symbol as the variable they correspond to, but are superscripted with an open ball: $T_{00}^{o}, T_{99}^{o}, T_{98}^{o}, M_{00}^{o}, M_{99}^{o}, M_{98}^{o}$.

10.3.2 Likelihood without Choice Indicators

Ignoring the choice indicators, the likelihood of the data is determined by sequentially specifying the conditional distribution of a group of variables, conditional on the ones previously specified. The distribution of the discrete variables (D) is specified first, followed by the conditional distributions of English grades (E) and absences (A), and then followed by the math grades (M) and standardized test variables.

10.3.2.1 Discrete Variables

The five discrete variables, with two levels each, define a $2 \times 2 \times 2 \times 2 \times 2$ contingency table with 32 "cells". These cells are interchangeably indexed by one index taking values from 0 to 31 or by five indices $\{srglm\}$ where s varies over the two values of sex, r varies over race, g varies over guardian, l varies over subsidized lunch status, and m varies over mobility. Let $g(D)$ be a mapping from a set of discrete variable realizations to $\{0, \ldots, 31\}$.

A count of the number of students in each cell is considered to be a draw from a multinomial distribution of $N = 1888$ students with cell probabilities π_{srglm}. Let

$G(D)$ be a representation of the contingency table as a 32-long vector of counts

$$G(D)|\{\lambda\} \sim \text{Multinomial}(N, \{\pi_{srglm}\}),\qquad(10.1)$$

where λ is a vector of parameters defined in the next equation. In order to reduce the number of parameters, a loglinear model is used for the expected number of students in each cell

$$
\begin{aligned}
\log(N\pi_{srglm}) \;=\;\; &\lambda^{mean} + \lambda_s^{sex} + \lambda_r^{race} + \lambda_g^{guardian} + \lambda_l^{lunch} + \lambda_m^{mobility} + \lambda_{rg}^{race,guardian}\\
&+\lambda_{rl}^{race,lunch} + \lambda_{rm}^{race,mobility} + \lambda_{gl}^{guardian,lunch} + \lambda_{gm}^{guardian,mobility}\\
&+\lambda_{lm}^{lunch,mobility}
\end{aligned}
$$

The loglinear model makes the usual assumption that all the expected cell means are greater than zero. By using a restricted set of two-way interactions, the model incorporates the assumption that sex is independent of the other discrete variables.

10.3.2.2   English Grades and Absences

English grades and absences are modeled jointly as a multivariate normal, conditional on the discrete variables. Let $\mu = (\mu_0, \ldots, \mu_{31})$ be a 6×32 matrix of means where each column corresponds to a cell and each row within a column corresponds to one of the English or absence variables. Let $C = (E_{00}, E_{99}, E_{98}, A_{00}, A_{99}, A_{98})$, so μ_i is the mean vector of the variables in C for a particular cell. Let Σ be the 6×6 matrix of covariances of the English and absence variables; the same Σ is used for each cell. Then

$$C|(D, \mu, \Sigma) \sim \text{MultiN}_6\{\mu_{g(D)}, \Sigma\},\qquad(10.2)$$

where the $\mu_{g(D)}$s are hierarchically modeled by

$$\mu_{g(D)} = \rho_0 + \rho_1\text{sex} + \rho_2\text{race} + \rho_3\text{guardian} + \rho_4\text{lunch} + \rho_5\text{mobility}.$$

in order that cells with small numbers of observations may draw strength from cells with larger numbers of observations. Each ρ_i for $i = 0, \ldots, 5$ is a 6-long vector.

English grades and absences are modeled jointly for two reasons. First, for each student, absences and grades from one year to the next are related because students' study habits and abilities change gradually. Second, within a year, absences and grades are related directly because students who are absent miss the benefit of in-class explanation. In addition, the teacher's perception of the student's abilities may be affected by the students lack of attendance.

10.3.2.3   Standardized Tests and Math Grades

The distributions of the standardized tests and math grades are specified conditional on English grades, absences, and the discrete variables. Because analysts at the Pittsburgh Board of Education are familiar with interpreting linear regressions, a linear model with normal errors is used. Tests and math grades are modeled sequentially rather than jointly in order to allow freedom in the placement of the choice indicator, as described in Subsection 10.3.3. The linear model describing the 2000 standardized test is

$$
\begin{aligned}
T_{00} \;=\;\; &\beta_0^{T_{00}} + \beta_1^{T_{00}} T_{99} + \beta_2^{T_{00}} T_{98} + \beta_3^{T_{00}} M_{00} + \beta_4^{T_{00}} M_{99} + \beta_5^{T_{00}} M_{98} + \beta_6^{T_{00}} E_{00}\\
&+\; \beta_7^{T_{00}} E_{99} + \beta_8^{T_{00}} E_{98} + \beta_9^{T_{00}} A_{00} + \beta_{10}^{T_{00}} A_{99} + \beta_{11}^{T_{00}} A_{98} + \beta_{12}^{T_{00}}\text{sex}\\
&+\; \beta_{13}^{T_{00}}\text{race} + \beta_{14}^{T_{00}}\text{guardian} + \beta_{15}^{T_{00}}\text{lunch} + \beta_{16}^{T_{00}}\text{mobility} + \epsilon^{T_{00}}
\end{aligned}\qquad(10.3)
$$

where the errors $\epsilon^{T_{00}} \sim N(0, \sigma^{2T_{00}})$ are independent between students. Equation 10.3 is summarized by

$$T_{00}|(T_{99}, T_{98}, M, E, A, D, \theta) \sim N[(1, T_{99}, T_{98}, M, E, A, D) \cdot \beta^{T_{00}}, \sigma^{2T_{00}}], \qquad (10.4)$$

where θ represents all of the parameters used in the entire model, $a \cdot b$ denotes the dot product of a and b, and $\beta^{T_{00}} = (\beta_0^{T_{00}}, \beta_1^{T_{00}}, \ldots, \beta_{16}^{T_{00}})$.

Similarly, the distributions for remaining standardized tests and math grades are expressed compactly as

$$
\begin{aligned}
T_{99}|(T_{98}, M, E, A, D, \theta) &\sim N[(1, T_{98}, M, E, A, D) \cdot \beta^{T_{99}}, \sigma^{2T_{99}}], &(10.5)\\
T_{98}|(M, E, A, D, \theta) &\sim N[(1, M, E, A, D) \cdot \beta^{T_{98}}, \sigma^{2T_{98}}], &(10.6)\\
M_{00}|(M_{99}, M_{98}, E, A, D, \theta) &\sim N[(1, M_{99}, M_{98}, E, A, D) \cdot \beta^{M_{00}}, \sigma^{2M_{00}}], &(10.7)\\
M_{99}|(M_{98}, E, A, D, \theta) &\sim N[(1, M_{98}, E, A, D) \cdot \beta^{M_{99}}, \sigma^{2M_{99}}], &(10.8)\\
M_{98}|(E, A, D, \theta) &\sim N[(I, E, A, D) \cdot \beta^{M_{98}}, \sigma^{2M_{98}}], &(10.9)
\end{aligned}
$$

where the regression coefficient vectors $\beta^{T_{99}}, \beta^{T_{98}}, \beta^{M_{00}}, \beta^{M_{99}}$, and $\beta^{M_{98}}$ are of decreasing sizes, from 16 to 12-dimensional.

Distributions 1-2, and 4-9 relate the 2000 standardized test to previous standardized tests, grades, absences, mobility and demographic information. There are many other factors for which we do not have data that could be related to performance on the 2000 standardized test, such as teacher absences, teacher qualifications and recent student attentiveness and effort. Since there are factors relating to the 2000 standardized test that are not included in the model or controlled in an experiment, the coefficients in Equation (10.3) cannot be interpreted as the effect of a variable. In other words, the relationship is not necessarily causal, but rather associational.

10.3.3 Likelihood with Choice Indicators

The likelihood in the previous section must be modified due to the selection bias caused by students choosing not to take an exam or math class. The distributions of the discrete variables, English grades and absences do not change from the previous section; only the distributions of the test and math variables change.

To take selection bias into account, choice indicators are included in the model. Six choice indicators, one for each test and math class, are incorporated into Equation (10.3) and the similar equations corresponding to Distributions 4 through 9 as another term in the linear model. With the choice indicator, Equation (10.3) becomes

$$
\begin{aligned}
T_{00} = {}& \beta_0^{T_{00}} + \beta_1^{T_{00}} T_{99} + \beta_2^{T_{00}} T_{98} + \beta_3^{T_{00}} M_{00} + \beta_4^{T_{00}} M_{99} + \beta_5^{T_{00}} M_{98} + \beta_6^{T_{00}} E_{00} \\
& + \beta_7^{T_{00}} E_{99} + \beta_8^{T_{00}} E_{98} + \beta_9^{T_{00}} A_{00} + \beta_{10}^{T_{00}} A_{99} + \beta_{11}^{T_{00}} A_{98} + \beta_{12}^{T_{00}} \text{sex} + \beta_{13}^{T_{00}} \text{race} \\
& + \beta_{14}^{T_{00}} \text{guardian} + \beta_{15}^{T_{00}} \text{lunch} + \beta_{16}^{T_{00}} \text{mobility} + \beta_{17}^{T_{00}} T_{00}^o + \epsilon^{T_{00}}, \qquad (10.10)
\end{aligned}
$$

where $\beta^{T_{00}}$ is now 18-dimensional. The errors $\epsilon^{T_{00}}$ are independent and normal as before. Only one of the six choice indicators is included in each linear model. The distributions of all of the test and math variables can be compactly described by

$$
\begin{aligned}
T_{00}|(T_{00}^o, T_{99}, T_{98}, M, E, A, D, \theta) &\sim N[(1, T_{99}, T_{98}, M, E.A, D, T_{00}^o) \cdot \beta^{T_{00}}, \sigma^{2T_{00}}], &(10.11)\\
T_{99}|(T_{99}^o, T_{98}, M, E, A, D, \theta) &\sim N[(1, T_{98}, M, E, A, D, T_{99}^o) \cdot \beta^{T_{99}}, \sigma^{2T_{99}}], &(10.12)\\
T_{98}|(T_{98}^o, M, E, A, D, \theta) &\sim N[(1, M, E, A, D, T_{98}^o) \cdot \beta^{T_{98}}, \sigma^{2T_{98}}], &(10.13)\\
M_{00}|(M_{00}^o|M_{00}^o, M_{99}, M_{98}, E, A, D, \theta) &\sim N[(1, M_{99}, M_{98}, E, A, D, M_{00}^o) \cdot \beta^{M_{00}}, \sigma^{2M_{00}}] &(10.14)\\
M_{99}|(M_{99}^o, M_{98}, E, A, D, \theta) &\sim N[(1, M_{98}, E, A, D, M_{99}^o) \cdot \beta^{M_{99}}, \sigma^{2M_{99}}] &(10.15)\\
M_{98}|(M_{98}^o, E, A, D, \theta) &\sim N[(1, E, A, D, M_{98}^o) \cdot \beta^{M_{98}}, \sigma^{2M_{98}}], &(10.16)
\end{aligned}
$$

where the regression coefficient vectors $\beta^{T_{00}}, \beta^{T_{99}}, \beta^{T_{98}}, \beta^{M_{00}}, \beta^{M_{99}}$, and $\beta^{M_{98}}$ are of decreasing sizes, now from 18 to 13-dimensional.

A negative choice indicator coefficient means that a student who chooses not to take an exam or class tends to have a lower 2000 standardized test score than a similar student who does take the exam or class.

The choice indicators are modeled to depend on the test and math variables through the fitted value of the linear models, excluding the choice indicator terms. For example, let $\tilde{T}_{00}$ denote the fitted value of the linear model describing T_{00}, excluding the choice indicator term

$$
\begin{aligned}
\tilde{T}_{00} \ = \ & \beta_0^{T_{00}} + \beta_1^{T_{00}} T_{99} + \beta_2^{T_{00}} T_{98} + \beta_3^{T_{00}} M_{00} + \beta_4^{T_{00}} M_{99} + \beta_5^{T_{00}} M_{98} + \beta_6^{T_{00}} E_{00} \\
+ \ & \beta_7^{T_{00}} E_{99} + \beta_8^{T_{00}} E_{98} + \beta_9^{T_{00}} A_{00} + \beta_{10}^{T_{00}} A_{99} + \beta_{11}^{T_{00}} A_{98} + \beta_{12}^{T_{00}} \text{sex} \\
+ \ & \beta_{13}^{T_{00}} \text{race} + \beta_{14}^{T_{00}} \text{guardian} + \beta_{15}^{T_{00}} \text{lunch} + \beta_{16}^{T_{00}} \text{mobility}
\end{aligned}
$$

and similarly define $\tilde{T}_{99}, \tilde{T}_{98}, \tilde{M}_{00}, \tilde{M}_{99}$, and $\tilde{M}_{98}$. Then for each $X \in \{T_{00}, T_{99}, T_{98}, M_{00}, M_{99}, M_{98}\}$

$$X^o \mid (\tilde{X}, \delta_X) \sim Bernoulli(p_X), \tag{10.17}$$

where

$$\text{logit}(p_x) = \delta_X^0 + \delta_X^1 \tilde{X},$$

and where $p_X = Pr(X^o = 1)$ and $\delta_X = (\delta_X^0, \delta_X^1)$ is a 2-dimensional parameter. The choice indicator is modeled by a Bernoulli distribution with the probability of success described by a generalized linear model with a logit link function.

Test and math grade variables are modeled separately (as opposed to fitting a covariance matrix to the six variables) in order to allow the test and math variables to depend on the choice indicators and to allow the choice indicators to depend on the previous years test and math variables. Because the choice indicators and the test and math grade variables are intertwined, a single multivariate normal distribution cannot be used to describe the test and math grade variables.

10.3.4   Prior Distributions

Multiplying the densities associated with Distributions 10.1, 10.2, and 10.11 through 10.17 gives a function proportional to the likelihood of the data. Multiplying this by the prior distributions of the parameters yields a function proportional to the full joint distribution of the parameters and the data.

The parametric families of the prior distributions are chosen for convenience and the parameters of the prior distributions are elicited when feasible. In particular, the means of the linear model coefficients are elicited directly. Elicitation of the spreads of the linear model coefficients is described below. The linear model coefficients are all modeled as having normal distributions. The other variables have a less intuitive interpretation and thus diffuse but proper priors are used. The opinions elicited are those of one of the authors (John Garrow), who is an expert in the educational assessment of Pittsburgh students.

Spreads of the linear model coefficients are elicited at one of three levels: the expert is "very sure," "sure," or "not sure" of the mean estimate. "Sure" and "very sure" are interpreted as being confident of the sign of the estimate. Being "very sure" of a mean estimate corresponds to placing 95% of the mass of the prior distribution within $\pm 25\%$ of the mean estimate. Being "sure" of the mean estimate corresponds to 95% of the mass being within 100% of the mean estimate - in other words, being fairly certain of the sign of the estimate. "Not sure" is interpreted as having 95% of the mass of the prior distribution within ±300% of the mean estimate.[9]

Table 10.3 summarizes the parametric family, parameter sizes and values of the diffuse prior distributions. Tables 10.4 and 10.5 present the elicited priors for both the standardized tests and math grades.

10.4 Methodology for Sampling from the Posterior Distribution

Samples are obtained by running a Metropolis-Hastings algorithm within a Gibbs sampler (see Gelfand and Smith (1990); Gilks et al. (1996); Gelman et al. (1995)) twice, for 50,000 iterations each; the first half of each run is considered a burn-in period and is discarded.

A Gibbs sampler is applied to the current problem by treating the missing data and the model parameters as two random vectors. This technique is known as data augmentation, developed by Tanner and Wong (1987). An iteration consists of first drawing values for the parameters assuming a full data set and then drawing values for the missing data assuming the parameter values are known. Because the distribution of the parameters given all of the data is not easy to sample from directly, a Metropolis-Hastings is used for groups of parameters. For all parameters but Σ and σ_i^2, the candidate value is drawn from a normal proposal distribution centered at the current value. The proposal distributions for Σ and σ_i^2 are Wishart and truncated normal, respectively. Samples drawn in this way are proven to converge to the target distribution of the chain in Tierney (1994). The Gelman-Rubin convergence diagnostic, discussed in the Appendix, is used to assess convergence.

10.5 Results

The first question of interest, how mobility and absences relate to student performance, can be answered by the marginal posterior distribution of the mobility and absence variables. The second question of interest, how mobility and absences relate to one another, can be answered by examining the distribution of the ratio of the mobility to absence coefficients. Both questions can be addressed with samples from the joint distribution of the parameters and the missing data, conditional on the observed data. Although there are mobility and absence variables throughout the model, those in $\beta^{T_{00}}$ are of particular interest because they relate mobility and absence to the standardized test in the year in which the students were selected.

Figure 10.1 shows the marginal prior and posterior distribution of the mobility component of $\beta^{T_{00}}$ based on 50,000 post-burn-in samples. Figure 10.1 also contains the same information for the three absence coefficients. The solid line on the figures is the prior distribution, and the histogram is made from samples from the posterior, scaled to integrate to 1.

The posterior median of the mobility coefficient is -2.5, with a 90% credible interval of (-4.5, -.63). A coefficient of -2.5 means that a student who moved at least once in the three year period has a score of 2.5 percentile points lower than a similar student who did not move, according to this model. Because the posterior distribution of the mobility coefficient has 99.9% of its mass below 0, mobility almost certainly hurts a student's academic performance, as measured by the 2000 English given to 11th graders in the PPS.

---

[9]The expert states that "sure" corresponds to ±100%, but feels that "not sure" and "very sure" could just as reasonably correspond to 75% and 125% as the values given. These prior spread values produced no noticeable difference in the posteriors from those specified in the text and figures.

Table 10.3: Summary of Unelicited Prior Distributions

Model parameter	Dimension	Prior family	Mean vector	Covariance matrix
$\delta_{T_{00}}$	2	Normal	(0,0)	$100I_2$
$\vdots$	$\vdots$	$\vdots$	$\vdots$	$\vdots$
$\delta_{M_{98}}$	2	Normal	(0,0)	$100I_2$
λ^{mean}	1	Normal	-1.5	100
λ^{gender}	1	Normal	0	100
$\vdots$	$\vdots$	$\vdots$	$\vdots$	$\vdots$
$\lambda^{lunch,mobility}$	1	Normal	0	100
ρ_0	6	Normal	(4,4,4,15,15,15)	$100I_6$
ρ_1	6	Normal	(0,0,0,0,0,0)	$100I_6$
$\vdots$	$\vdots$	$\vdots$	$\vdots$	$\vdots$
ρ_5	6	Normal	(0,0,0,0,0,0)	$100I_6$

Model parameter	Dimension	Prior family	Parameters
$\sigma^2_{T_{00}}$	1	Scaled Inv - χ^2	100, 14.7
$\vdots$	$\vdots$	$\vdots$	$\vdots$
$\sigma^2_{M_{98}}$	1	Scaled Inv - χ^2	100, 14.7
Σ	6 by 6	Inv-Wishart	10

Note 1: I_2 is a $k \times k$ identity matrix.
Note 2: The two parameters of the scaled inverse χ^2 distribution are called the degrees of freedom and scale parameters, respectively.

Table 10.4: Means and Spreads of Elicited Standardized Test Linear Model Coefficient Distributions

Variable	$\beta^{T_{00}}$		$\beta^{T_{99}}$		$\beta^{T_{98}}$	
Math grade	2.75	(2)	3	(2)	2.5	(2)
English grade	4.5	(2)	5	(2)	4	(2)
Absence	-0.113	(2)	-0.125	(3)	-0.1	(1)
Gender	-3.5	(2)	-3	(1)	-4	(3)
Race	-3.5	(2)	-3	(1)	-4	(3)
Guardian	-17	(2)	-15	(2)	-19	(3)
Lunch	-22.5	(3)	-20	(3)	-25	(3)
Mobility	-3.5	(2)	-3	(2)	-4	(3)
1999 test	0.4	(1)	N/A		N/A	
1998 test	0.4	(1)	0.6	(1)	N/A	
Missing value	-10	(2)	-10	(2)	-10	(2)

Table 10.5: Means and Spreads of Elicited Math Linear Model Coefficient Distributions

Variable	$\beta^{T_{00}}$		$\beta^{T_{99}}$		$\beta^{T_{98}}$	
English grade	0.5	(2)	0.5	(2)	0.5	(2)
Absence	-0.05	(3)	-0.05	(3)	-0.05	(3)
Gender	-0.01	(1)	-0.01	(1)	-0.01	(1)
Race	-1	(1)	-1	(1)	-1	(1)
Guardian	-0.25	(2)	-0.25	(2)	-0.25	(2)
Lunch	-1	(3)	-1	(3)	-1	(3)
Mobility	-0.3	(2)	-0.3	(2)	-0.3	(2)
1999 math grade	0.4	(2)	N/A		N/A	
1998 math grade	0.4	(2)	0.6	(2)	N/A	
Missing value	-1	(2)	-1	(2)	-1	(2)

Note. Numbers in parentheses are the spread estimates: 3 = "very sure,"
2 = "sure," 1 = "not sure."

The three absence coefficients in Figure 10.1 relate absence in 1998, 1999 and 2000 to the 2000 English PSSA. The relationship of absence and student achievement is generally negative. The posterior medians of the 2000, 1999 and 1998 absence coefficients are -0.18, -0.07 and -0.02 respectively. 90% credible intervals for the 2000, 1999, and 1998 absence coefficients are (-0.23, -0.13), (-0.14, -0.02) and (-0.08, 0.06) respectively. Absences in 2000 have a stronger relationship to performance on the 2000 standardized test than absences in 1999, as 97% of the sampled 2000 absence coefficients are smaller than the 1999 absence coefficients. Since 78% of the sampled 1999 absence coefficients are smaller than the 1998 absence coefficients, absences in 1999 have a stronger relationship to the 2000 standardized test than absences in 1998. The direction of the relationship between absences in 1998 and the 2000 standardized test is not clear when absences in more recent years are taken into account. In general, an absence coefficient of -0.2 means that being absent an extra day in the particular year is associated with a decrease in a student's 2000 achievement test by two-tenths of a percentile point.

To summarize the coefficients in Equation 10.10, Table 10.6 gives 90% credible intervals for the linear model coefficients. Thirteen of the seventeen credible intervals do not contain zero. In general, better grades and previous test scores are associated with better 2000 standardized test scores. Mobility and more absence are associated with lower 2000 standardized test scores.

Because absence in 2000, absence in 1999, and mobility are related to student performance in a clearly negative way, mobility can be expressed in terms of the equivalent number of absences using the ratio of mobility to absence in a particular year. The second question of interest is answered with the posterior distributions of the ratio of the mobility coefficient to the 2000 and 1999 absence coefficients, shown in Figure 10.2. The solid lines in Figure 10.2 represent the prior distributions. Both of the distributions in Figure 10.2 have heavy right tails, with very little mass below zero. The histograms show that on average (as measured by the median), being absent about 14 days in 2000 or 32 days in 1999 is equivalent to having moved at least once, in terms of the relationship of each to a student's 2000 standardized test score. Because the mass of the distribution of the mobility to 1999 absence is much greater than mobility to 2000, absences in 2000 are more closely related to a student's performance on the 2000 standardized test than absences in 1999. This is plausible since prior to

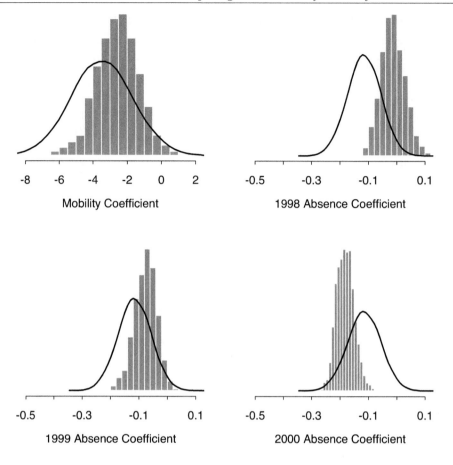

Figure 10.1: Marginal prior and posterior for mobility and absence coefficients.

taking the 2000 standardized test, a student has more opportunities to learn material missed on a particular day in 1999 than material missed in 2000.

10.6   Conclusions

The results of this study indicate that absence and mobility are negatively correlated to a student's standardized test scores and hence to academic achievement. An observational study such as this one does not provide evidence that these relationships are causal, as opposed to merely associative. However, if even part of the association is causal, then the results of this study could guide policymakers when presented with a choice between paying for programs to decrease mobility[10] or programs to encourage students to attend school more regularly. Even if none of the association is causal, the results of this study provide a warning to policymakers that students who move or are chronically absent need special attention.

While the results of this study may be relevant to a choice between decreasing mobility or decreasing absence, there are other factors to consider. On one hand, even if the relationship between moving and standardized test scores is purely causal (an

---

[10]For example, buses could be used to keep students in the same school despite within PPS moves. Alternatively, curriculum content and order could be unified across the district to lessen the academic disruption of a move.

Table 10.6: 2000 Standardized Test Linear Model Coefficient Posteriors

2000 Standardized Test Linear Model Coefficient Posteriors		
Variable	90% Credible Interval	
Test 1999	(0.4, 0.5)	(*)
Test 1998	(0.3, 0.6)	(*)
Math 2000	(0.3, 1.0)	(*)
Math 1999	(0.1, 1.0)	(*)
Math 1998	(0.4, 1.1)	(*)
English 2000	(0.9, 1.7)	(*)
English 1999	(-0.4, 0.6)	
English 1998	(-0.9, -0.04)	(*)
Gender	(-1.0, 1.7)	
Absence 2000	(-0.2, -0.1)	(*)
Absence 1999	(-0.1, -0.02)	(*)
Absence 1998	(-0.08, 0.06)	
Race	(-4.2, -0.8)	(*)
Guardian	(-0.5, 2.5)	
Lunch	(-4.3, -1.5)	(*)
Mobility	(-4.5, -0.6)	(*)
Choice indicator	(-18.5, -1.7)	(*)

Note. (*) indicates that the credible interval does not contain zero.

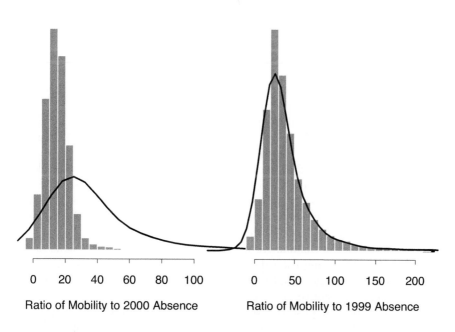

Figure 10.2: Prior and posterior for the number of days of absence equivalent to changing schools.

unlikely scenario), the effect of moving cannot be eliminated for two reasons. First, only students who move within the district would benefit from a busing program or a curriculum unification program. Second, in addition to a disruption in curriculum, moving creates a disruption in a student's social support network, which may affect academic performance. On the other hand, all students with less than perfect attendance would benefit from a program that increases attendance. Good overall classroom attendance would allow a teacher to assume more common background and allow him or her to spend time taking a subject further in depth rather than repeating basics for students who were absent. In conclusion, the data used in this study support the view that mobility and absence have a negative relationship with student academic achievement, as measured by the PSSA in 2000. The harm associated with mobility is, on average, equivalent to being absent 14 days in 2000 or 32 days in 1999.

10.7   Discussion

The data used in this study are not ideal due to the limited geographic area and diversity of one district and limited types of data collected about that district. Because the data are drawn from databases meant to track student performance, desirable but not available are data about schools, such as a measure of the academic strength of each school, and data about teachers, such as the number of days that a teacher is absent. Absence of the teacher may lead to a lack of in-class instruction if the teacher has not prepared a suitable lecture or activity for the substitute teacher. Although a lack of in-class instruction for the entire class due to teacher absence may not be as harmful as student absences, teacher absences would be useful to include in the model if the data were available.

Ideally, in order to draw conclusions about the nation's school population, a national data set, such as the National Assessment of Education Progress (NAEP), would be used. The authors leave this as future work.

Appendix

The Metropolis-Hastings Algorithm within a Gibbs sampler converges to the full joint distribution of the data and the parameters, but whether convergence has been reached at any given time is always a concern. By running two overly dispersed chains for the initial runs described above and the sensitivity runs described below, convergence is tested by comparing the two chains. The Gelman-Rubin Convergence diagnostic is used as implemented in BOA (Bayesian Output Analysis), an Splus software plug-in.

Details of the Gelman-Rubin convergence diagnostic are found in (Gilks et al., 1996). The diagnostic is based on a comparison of within chain variance and between chain variance. If these two are different enough, convergence has not been reached and the chains should be run longer. Neither this convergence diagnostic nor any other guarantee that convergence has been reached.

In this application, the Gelman-Rubin diagnostics are run on the second half of the 50,000-long chains. Following the rule of thumb suggested by Gelman in Gilks et al. (1996) (i.e., declare convergence if the statistic is less than 1.2), the chains do not need to be run any longer for convergence reasons.

Because the prior and posterior distributions of the mobility coefficient in Figure 10.1 are so similar, the sensitivity of the model to this prior distribution is addressed by considering two alternative priors. Markov Chains are run using prior means of -5 and -2 (the original prior is centered at -3.5) and prior standard deviations of 2.5. The results are shown in Figure 10.3. Compared to the original elicited prior, the posterior mean of the prior centered at -5 is slightly more negative and has increased

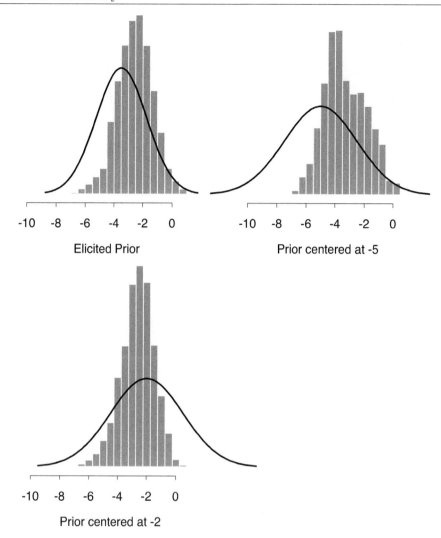

Figure 10.3: Marginal prior and posterior for mobility coefficients elicited prior and two alternate priors.

uncertainty. The posterior distribution based on the prior centered at -2 did not change much compared to the original prior distribution. Therefore, mobility appears to be slightly sensitive to negative changes in the prior but not positive ones.

In addition to evaluating the sensitivity of the results to the prior, the sensitivity of the results to the model for missing data should be considered. The definition of p_X following Equation (10.17) has the form of a generalized linear model with a logit link function. Figure 10.4 shows the same information as Figure 10.1 but corresponding to a probit rather than a logit link function. While the mobility and 1999 absence coefficients are virtually identical to the corresponding ones for the logit link function, there are noticeable differences in the posterior distributions of 2000 and 1998 absence. The probit model leads to increased uncertainty and more negative values in both absence coefficients.

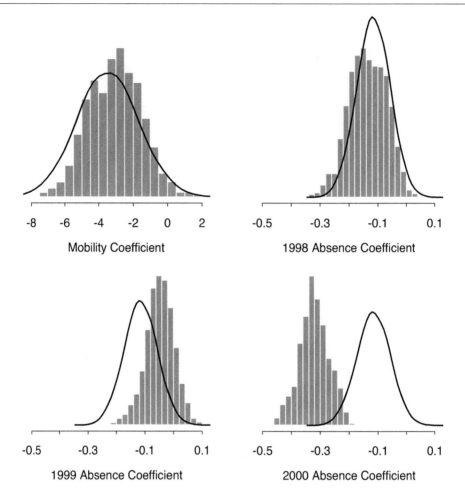

Figure 10.4: Marginal prior and posterior for mobility and absence coefficients (probit missing data model).

REFERENCES

Carver, R. (1970). "A test of an hypothesized relationship between learning time and amount learned in school learning." *The Journal of Educational Research*, 64, 2, 57–58. 182

Gelfand, A. and Smith, A. (1990). "Sampling based approaches to calculating marginal densities." *Journal of the American Statistical Association*, 85, 398–409. 189

Gelman, A., Carlin, J., Stern, H., and Rubin, D. (1995). *Bayesian data analysis*. New York: Chapman & Hall. 189

Gilks, W., Richardson, S., and Spiegelhalter, J. (1996). *MCMC in Practice*. New York: Chapman & Hall. 189, 194

Hanson, R. and Schutz, R. (1986). "A comparison of methods for measuring achievement in basic skills program evaluation." *Educational Evaluation and Policy Analysis*, 8, 1, 101–113. 182

Madaus, G., Airasian, P., and Kellaghan, T. (1980). *School effectiveness, a reassessment of the evidence*. New York: McGraw Hill. 182

Monk, D. and Ibrahim, M. (1984). "Patterns of absence and pupil achievement." *American Educational Research Journal*, 21, 2, 295–310. 182

Tanner, M. and Wong, W. (1987). "The calculation of posterior distribution by data augmentation." *Journal of the American Statistical Association*, 82, 528–540. 189

Tierney, L. (1994). "Markov chains for exploring posterior distributions (with discussion)." *Annals of Statistics*, 22, 1701–1762.

Authors

MICHELLE C. DUNN is a graduate student in the Department of Statistics, Carnegie Mellon University, Pittsburgh, PA 15213; mcdunn@stat.cmu.edu. Her areas of specialization are applied statistics and Bayesian inference.

JOSEPH B. KADANE is Leonard J. Savage University Professor of Statistics and Social Sciences, Department of Statistics, Carnegie Mellon University, Pittsburgh, PA 15213; kadane@stat.cmu.edu. His areas of specialization are Bayesian theory and applications.

JOHN R. GARROW is Data Analyst, Pittsburgh Board of Education, Office of Assessment, Evaluation and Research, 341 South Bellefield Avenue, Room 225, Pittsburgh, PA, 15213; jgarrow1@pghboe.net. His areas of specialization are design and applied educational research.

Editor's Foreword

Howard Wainer
National Board of Medical Examiners

Historically it has been sufficient for statisticians to be involved on the periphery of educational research. We could sit and listen in on the methodological problems that researchers were having, go back to our offices, do some algebra, and then publish the solution complete with a toy example. Researchers could then follow the procedures laid out and, voila they would have an answer! R. A. Fisher's Statistical Methods for Research Workers is the prime example of this model. The fact that it has been reprinted 14 times attests to the value of this approach.

But as problems became more complex, or at least as our understanding of them grew more sophisticated, the methods that were required to solve them grew more complex as well. We could not merely write down a solution of the relevant likelihood equation and think that was enough. If we wanted the method to be used we had to prepare and distribute computer programs that could do it. BILOG and BUGS are two examples and there are many others. However, for complex specialized problems just preparing software and letting researchers run with it turned out to be insufficient. Special instruction in the use of the software and the models underlying it were required, and traveling road shows proliferated (Karl Jreskog and LISREL, Jeremy Finn and MULTIVARIANCE, David Thissen and MULTILOG, are only the tip of the iceberg).

The following article by Michelle Dunn, Joseph Kadane, and John Garrow (DK&G) provides a dramatic example of the next step in this trend in educational research. The powerful methods that are now available are not likely to be effectively used by amateurs. Any research team using these methods needs a statistician onboard who will work on the project from inception to write-up.

DK&G is a model for collaborative research. It demonstrates how difficult it is to get answers to important, but in the end, simple questions within the practical constraints imposed by the real world. Questions of missing data dominate any discussion. Which data are ignorable? Which are not? How are missing data modeled? How are priors to be chosen? What are the conclusions that we can safely make? Are there any other, perhaps more speculative, conclusions worthy of follow-up?

DK&G is not only a model for modern educational research, but also a model for researchers who would like to publish in this journal-they have an important substantive question, a dataset with the capacity to answer it within a nontrivial environment, an analysis model of interest and generality, and clear prose describing it. As editor, I hope that prospective authors will take note.

REFERENCES

Fisher, R.A. (1925). Statistical methods for research workers. Edinburgh, Scotland: Oliver & Boyd.

HOWARD WAINER is the Editor in Chief of the Journal of Educational and Behavioral Statistics. He can be reached at `Hwainer@NBME.org`.

Comment

Eric T. Bradlow
The Wharton School, University of Pennsylvania

Real practical applications of Bayesian methods that are "serious empirical research" are hard to come by. This article, by Dunn, Kadane, and Garrow (hereafter DKG) is serious empirical research. How can you tell? There are many signs in this research that I would like to touch on. Why? Because I hope in some way that this article serves as a model for future applications of Bayesian methods into important educational research problems. And, I believe, that few would dispute that the impact of student absences and movement between schools on educational attainment is an important problem. On the other hand, utilizing models for applied problems involves making choices, and with those choices come tradeoffs. I hope to provide insight, or at least my opinion, on the choices that were made in this research.

To start, an author of the article, John Garrow, is a data analyst with the Pittsburgh Public Schools. This suggests that not only is the article more likely to be tied to the science of the problem, and that the models will also be "understandable" to the ultimate users, but that the policy implications of the article may reach their intended target. Of course, before one could assess the societal costs of absences and school movement, one would need to study the relationship between educational attainment and social welfare, and the potential ability one would have to impact these measures.

Second, rather than just having the "practitioner" on the article provide background (as is common in some "not-so-real" applications), DKG utilize Garrow's expertise to construct informative priors that, in this case, play an integral role in the analysis. While the mapping between the three point scale of very sure, sure, and not sure (of the prior means for the model coefficients) for establishing prior variances is somewhat arbitrary, it does reflect some combination of data knowledge and subjective beliefs that should play a role. It was pleasing to see that DKG assessed the sensitivity of posterior inferences to the variance of the prior, as noted in footnote 10.

Third, rather than simply report parameter estimates and standard errors, the authors do something quite important in practical problems, that is tie their parameter estimates back to the underlying scale of interest, in this case percentile scores. As many decisions (admissions, financial aid, etc . . .) are based upon percentiles, it ties each absence or movement directly to the scale of interest.

Fourth, and I think the authors do not give themselves enough credit for this, rather than treating the "non-taking" of tests as ignorably missing (which is highly suspect), the authors posit a model for the link between predicted test score (without the absence variable), and the probability that the individual would be absent for the exam. Since the predicted test score is a function of the model parameters, this is a non-ignorable missing data process and may significantly impact the model results. In this regard, I laud the authors, but ask for two additional things. First, what would the model results have been without this non-ignorable process, i.e. $\delta_x^1 = 0$, and secondly, how sensitive is the choice indicator effect to the functional form of the model, i.e. would a probit model have led to the same conclusion.

Finally, many modeling choices the authors made in the paper were either justified by practical considerations, interpretation ease, and/or modeling "experience"; a stable of real practical problems. For instance, consider DKG's use of EDA techniques leading to the inclusion of interaction terms in Equation 1, but not in Equation 2-not a formal test procedure; the use of a multivariate normal distribution for C-English scores and absences are in fact integer valued and significant mass may be at 0; and the use of a common covariance matrix for each cell of the discrete background variable contingency table-an empirical issue. While from a formal procedure point of view, such choices may seem concerning, in the context of the problem here, they seem inconsequential to the rigor that was utilized.

In summary, DKG should be lauded for their use of Bayesian methods which allowed them to not only make average association statements between absences, mobility, and achievement, but also valid statements of uncertainty through Bayesian p values. Furthermore, this is one of the few published articles utilizing a non-ignorable missing data process, and I hope is not the last. As the authors demonstrate, these models are now estimable and provide insights beyond the model for test scores themselves.

ERIC T. BRADLOW is Associate Professor of Marketing and Statistics, The Wharton School of the University of Pennsylvania, 3730 Walnut Street, 761 JMHH, Philadelphia, PA 19104, ebradlow@wharton.upenn.edu. He is also the Senior Associate Editor of the Journal of Educational and Behavioral Statistics.

Epilogue

What is the scientific issue addressed?

How many days of missing school is as damaging to a student's performance on standardized tests as changing schools?

Is justification given for

a) the use of the data?

The data were provided by the Pittsburgh School Board. A first task was to understand the structure and limitations of the data, to find a subset that could address the issues of interest.

b) the likelihood and prior?

The likelihood is a sequence of normal linear models. The priors were elicited, in a crude form, from the educational specialist on the team, John R. Garrow.

What robustness checks were performed?

We checked robustness of a key prior (See Figure 10.3).

How were the computations conducted?

Markov chain Monte Carlo.

If I were doing the problem again, how would I change the approach?

With the same data, this is the best I can think of. With more extensive data, a more general finding is possible.

What do I see as the contributions of the paper?

It answers the scientific question posed.

Was Bayesian analysis useful in this problem?

Yes, particularly in addressing the choice variables concerning what courses a student took, and whether the student took the standardized exams.

TEACHING SUGGESTIONS

References for theoretical ideas:

1. MCMC: *Principles* Section 10.3

2. Hierarchical models: *Principles* Chapter 9

3. Missing data: *Principles* Section 9.2

4. Multinomial distribution: *Principles* Section 2.9

5. Multivariate normal distribution: *Principles* Section 6.10

6. Normal/normal conjugate analysis: *Principles* Chapter 8

Exercises

1. The data in the study were drawn from administrative records routinely gathered by the Pittsburgh Public Schools. Suppose it were possible to design the data gathering. What additional data would you suggest collecting, and why? In which equations in the paper would your additional data be inserted?

2. The use of standardized tests to measure academic performance has been criticized because it omits other desirable features of student maturation and growth. Do you think this criticism is pertinent to the use of standardized tests in this paper? Why or why not?

3. Why are the choice indicators important? What do the results show about them?

Chapter 11

Hierarchical Models for Employment Decisions (2004)

Foreword

I met George Woodworth in 1966, as he was coming to the Statistics Department at Stanford as an incoming Assistant Professor, and I was leaving to take my first job as Assistant Professor at Yale. Because he, like me, had a taste and respect for doing statistics, I passed to him my consulting contacts at Stanford's Political Science Department.

Years later, George was a regular visitor at CMU because his daughter was a CMU undergraduate. When George spent a sabbatical at CMU, we had time to get reacquainted. It turned out that we both had experience testifying as expert witnesses, and in fact we had worked on similar cases involving employers disadvantaging older workers. Additionally, we agreed on the strength of Bayesian analyses in general, and in particular in legal settings. The work I had done in Kadane (1990) [paper #3 in this volume] was satisfying as far as it went. It was premised on firing events at four discrete time points. In the cases that George and I had to confront more recently, firings did not happen in discrete lumps, but rather gradually over a period of years. At first George proposed dividing time into quarters of a year, but agreed that such a division was arbitrary and unsatisfying. We wanted to think of time as a continuous variable, although of course the events of interest occurred at particular discrete moments.

Thinking of time continuously leads to the following issue. Suppose the log odds ratio is the fundamental quantity of interest. Imagine that one day there is only one person fired, and this person is over forty. On the next day, again only one person is fired, and this person is under forty. Then the empirical log odds ratio will have swung from $+\infty$ on the first day to $-\infty$ on the second. We would not want to over-smooth either, (for example, by assuming a constant log odds ratio over the entire period). Clearly informative priors are needed to smooth the data.

Using a Cox proportional hazards model and a Gaussian process prior on the time-varying, log-relative hazard $\beta(t)$, the question comes down to what to assume about the smoothness parameter τ. To find a reasonable prior, we reverted to thinking about how much change in $\beta(t)$ would we expect in a quarter of a year. We decided that low probability of more than 15% change in a quarter was reasonable, and this led to a gamma prior on τ with mean .005 and shape 1.

The computation of the posterior distribution was an issue because the Markov Chain Monte Carlo did not mix well. This was overcome by using only the largest principal components of the underlying integrated Weiner process.

The results showed that in case K, the plaintiff was very likely disproportionately disadvantaged because of age, and this result is robust to changes in the mean of the smoothness parameter τ. However, for case W, involving two plaintiffs and a change in the top management of the company, the results were less clearcut.

Where is he now? George Woodworth is enjoying a well-deserved retirement.

This paper was originally published in the *Journal of Business and Economic Statistics*, **22**, (#2), pp 182–193. Republication by permission of the American Statistical Association.

Published Paper

Joseph B. Kadane and George G. Woodworth

Abstract

Federal law prohibits discrimination in employment decisions against persons in certain protected categories. The common method for measuring discrimination involves a comparison of some aggregate statistic for protected and non-protected individuals. This approach is open to question when employment decisions are made over an extended time period. We show how to use hierarchical proportional hazards models (Cox regression models) to analyze such data.

Key words: Age discrimination; Bayesian analysis; Hierarchical model; Proportional hazards model; Smoothness prior.

11.1   Introduction

Federal law forbids discrimination against employees or applicants because of an employee's race, sex, religion, national origin, age (40 or older), or handicap. General discrimination law–say discrimination by race or sex–offers two somewhat distinct legal theories. A disparate treatment case involves policies that on their face treat individuals differently depending on their (protected) group membership, such as a rule prohibiting women from being firefighters.

A disparate impact case, however, permits evidence that a facially neutral policy –say a height requirement for firefighters –has the effect of making it relatively more difficult for women than men to obtain such employment. If the data show a pattern of unfavorable actions (firing, failure to hire, failure to promote, low raises, etc.) disproportionately against the protected group, this can establish or help to establish a prima facie case against the defendant. A prima facie case does not establish the defendant's liability. Instead it shifts the burden of producing evidence to the defendant to explain the business necessity of the disproportionately adverse actions taken against the protected group. In such a case the employer would have to justify the requirement in terms of the needs of the job, and the fact finder (judge or jury) would have to determine whether the justification is a pretext for discrimination or not (Gastwirth, 1992; Kadane and Mitchell, 1998).

Race and sex discrimination cases fall under Title VII of the Civil Rights Act of 1964, whose provisions permit a prima facie case to be made by statistical evidence that members of the protected class are more likely to experience the adverse outcome of an employment decision. However, age discrimination cases are heard under the Age Discrimination in Employment Act of 1967, whose provisions allow differential

Joseph B. Kadane is Leonard J. Savage Professor of Statistics and Social Sciences, Department of Statistics, Carnegie Mellon University, Pittsburgh, PA 15213. George G. Woodworth is Professor, Department of Statistics and Actuarial Science and Department of Preventive Medicine, University of Iowa, Iowa City, IA 52242.

treatment of employees based on "reasonable factors other than age," which could be interpreted as barring a disparate impact age discrimination case. The Supreme Court in *Hazen Paper v. Biggins*, 123 L.Ed. 2d 338, 113 S.Ct. 1701 (1993), explicitly declined to decide this matter. Various courts and judges have discussed it [Judge Greenberg in *DiBiase v. Smith Kline Beecham Corp.* 48 F. 3rd 719 (1995), Judge Posner in *Finnegan et al. v. Transworld Airlines*, 967 F. 2nd 1161 (7th Cir., 1992), and the references cited there].

However this legal debate is resolved, we expect that statistical evidence of how an employer's policies affect older workers will continue to be relevant, in the legal sense, for the following reason. Federal Rule of Evidence 401 defines relevant evidence as evidence that has "any tendency to make the existence of any fact that is of consequence to the determination of the action more probable or less probable that it would be without the evidence." The issue in disparate treatment cases is establishing the intent of the employer. If an analysis shows that the facially neutral policy of the employer did differentially harm older workers, that reasonably makes it more probable that the employer intended the harm. Thus, we expect our analyses to continue to be relevant, regardless of the fate of the doctrine of disparate impact in age discrimination cases.

In this article we advocate the use of Bayesian analysis of employment decisions, which raises a second legal issue concerning the admissibility of such analysis to age discrimination cases. The rules on what constitutes admissible expert testimony in U.S. courts have changed. Under the Frye rule [*Frye v. United States*, 54 App.D.C. 46, 47, 293 F. 1013, 1014 (1923)], expert opinion based on a scientific technique is inadmissible unless the technique is "generally accepted" as reliable in the scientific community. Congress adopted new Federal Rules of Evidence in 1975. Rule 702 provides "[i]f scientific, technical or other specialized knowledge will assist the trier of fact to understand the evidence or to determine a fact in issue, a witness qualified as an expert by knowledge, skill, experience, training or education, may testify thereto in the form of an opinion or otherwise." In the case of *Daubert, et ux. etc. et al. v. Merrell Dow Pharmaceuticals, Inc.* 509 U.S. 579; 113 S.Ct. 2786 (1993), the Supreme Court unanimously held that Federal Rule 702 superseded the Frye test.

The *Daubert* decision, continuing with dicta (of lesser standing than holdings), of seven Supreme Court justices, goes on to define "scientific knowledge." "The adjective 'scientific' implies a grounding in the methods and procedures of science. Similarly, the word 'knowledge' connotes more than subjective belief or unsupported speculation." Thus the *Daubert* decision might be read as casting doubt on the admissibility of Bayesian analyses in Federal court, because the priors (and likelihoods) are intended to express subjective belief. We think that this reading of *Daubert* is occasioned by a misinterpretation of what Bayesian statisticians mean by subjectivity. The alternative, that is, claims of objectivity in the sense that anyone who disagrees is either a fool or a knave, is without basis, and appears to be an attempt at proof by verbal intimidation. To hold as we do, that every model (including frequentist models) reflects and expresses subjective opinions, is not to hold that every such opinion has an equal claim on the attention of a reader or a court. For an analysis to be most useful, it should be persuasive to a fact finder that an analysis done with his or her own model–likelihood and prior–would result in similar conclusions. This can be done with a combination of arguments based on reasons for the chosen likelihood and prior (other data, scientific theory, etc.) and robustness (the conclusions would be similar with other models "not too far" from the one analyzed). Thus, our view is that an analysis ought neither to be admissible nor inadmissible because it uses a subjective Bayesian approach. Instead its admissibility ought to depend on its persuasiveness in explaining, with a combination of specific arguments and robustness, why the conclusions of a trier of facts might be similar to, and hence influenced by, the analysis offered.

An alternative interpretation of the same activity is that the statistician is providing the fact finder with "scientific methodology" for combining information, including subjective information. The unavailability of the fact finder for elicitation means that the statistician has to present results in the form of "If you believe this, then the results of the data analysis would be these." We believe that under either interpretation a properly grounded and explained Bayesian model, of the kind proposed here, is both admissible and relevant in age discrimination cases. We confine our discussion to binary employment decisions such as hiring, job assignment, promotion, layoff, or termination. The outcome of such a decision is either favorable or unfavorable to the employee, who may or may not be in a legally protected class. We use age discrimination in termination decisions to illustrate our ideas because age discrimination cases dominate our experience. Age discrimination over a short period of time, for example, when an employer makes a large reduction in the workforce over a matter of a few days or weeks as the result of a single policy decision, is comparatively easy to analyze (Kadane, 1990) mainly because it is reasonable to assume that the odds ratio is constant; however, age discrimination over an extended time period is more difficult to model, both because the same individual can over time move from the unprotected to the protected class and because, unlike gender or race, age is a continuous characteristic and consequently the hazard rate may vary within the protected class. Following Finkelstein and Levin (1994), we find that proportional hazards (Cox regression) models provide the flexibility to deal with these issues.

11.2   Proportional Hazards Models

Suppose that we wish to analyze the employment decisions (e.g., involuntary terminations) of a firm over a given period of observation. The kind of analysis we propose requires data sufficient to determine for each day during the period of observation, the status (protected or unprotected) of each employee and the number of involuntary terminations (if that is the decision to be analyzed) of protected and unprotected employees. Perhaps it is most convenient to obtain this information in the form of flow data for each individual who was employed at any time during the period of observation.

Flow data consists of beginning and ending dates of each employee's period of employment, that employee's birth date, and the reason for separation from employment (if it occurred). We have seen no examples in which employees were rehired for nonoverlapping terms, but such cases could easily be handled by entering one data record for each distinct period of employment. Table 11.1 is a fragment of a dataset gathered in a hypothetical age discrimination case. Data were obtained on all persons employed by the firm any time between 01/01/94 and 01/31/96. Entry Date is the later of 01/03/1994, or the date of hire. The first record is right censored; that is, that employee was still in the work force as of 1/31/96, and we are consequently unable to determine the time or cause of his or her eventual separation from the firm (involuntary termination, death, retirement, etc.).

The plaintiff obtains such data from the employer in the pre-trial discovery phase. It is generally necessary for the plaintiff's attorney to justify the need for obtaining data over a particular time period–for example, it might be the period from the imposition of a particular policy to the end of the plaintiff's employment. Frequently the defendant can convince the court to narrow the scope of the data provided, arguing, for example, that retrieving records more than 5 years old or linking records involving employee transfers between divisions would be burdensome.

In many litigated cases the observation period is short and corresponds to one large-scale reduction in force (RIF) in which a substantial number of employees were

Table 11.1: Flow data for the period January 1, 1994 to December 31, 1996

Employee ID	Birth date	Entry date	Separation date	Reason
01	05/23/48	07/27/94		
02	12/17/31	01/03/94	11/20/94	Involuntary termination
03	03/14/48	06/29/94	07/27/94	Involuntary termination
04	02/26/40	10/05/94	06/07/95	Resigned
...	...	...	...	...

terminated in a comparatively short period. Kadane (1990) discussed such a case involving four massive firing waves. Data of this sort can be treated as an analysis of the odds ratios (odds on termination of protected versus unprotected employees) in a small number of two-by-two contingency tables. Kadane considered two models for the prior distribution of the odds ratios. In the homogeneous, common odds ratio model, he gave the log odds ratio, β, a normal distribution with zero mean and fixed precision. He computed the posterior probability of adverse impact ($\beta > 0$) of the employer's policy on the protected class for various values of the prior precision. For the inhomogeneous odds ratio model, he assumed independent distributions for the log odds ratios for the four waves of terminations and computed the probability of adverse impact separately for each wave.

This article is an attempt to tackle the analysis of terminations occurring at a comparatively low rate, perhaps one or two employees at a time, over a long time period. The problem with this sort of situation is that the disaggregated data consist of numerous two-by-two tables, each involving a small number of terminations but any aggregation of the data (quarterly, semiannually, etc.) into more substantial two-by-two tables is arbitrary and somewhat distorts the numbers at risk because some employees will not have been in the workforce for the entire period represented by a given aggregated table. A second, and more important issue is how to deal with the possibility of inhomogeneous odds ratios.

Finkelstein and Levin (1994) suggested that proportional hazards (Cox regression) models could be used to deal with disaggregated employment decisions; however, they assumed a constant log odds ratio over the observation period. We like their idea and in this article show how to allow for the possibility that the relative risk of termination varies over the observation period.

Cox (1972) considered a group of individuals at risk for a particular type of failure (involuntary termination) for all or part of an observation period. The jth person enters the risk set at time h_j (either the date of hire or the beginning of the observation period) and leaves the risk set at time T_j either by failure (involuntary termination) or for other reasons (death, voluntary resignation, reassignment, retirement, or the end of the observation period). The survival function $S_j(t) = P(T_j > t)$ is the probability that the jth employee is involuntarily terminated sometime after time t. The hazard function, $\lambda_j(t)$, is the conditional probability that person j is terminated at time t given survival to time t, that is,

$$\lambda_j(t) = \frac{-s_j(t)}{S_j(t)} = -\frac{d}{dt}\log(S_j(t)). \tag{11.1}$$

where s_j is the derivative of S_j. Integrating (11.1) produces

$$S_j(t) = \exp\left(-\int_{h_j}^{t}\lambda_j(t)dt\right). \tag{11.2}$$

The Cox proportional hazards model is

$$\lambda_j(t) = \lambda(t) \exp(\beta(t) z_j(t)).$$

where $\lambda(t)$ is the (unobserved) base hazard rate; $z_j(t)$ is an observable, time-varying characteristic of the j_{th} person; and $\beta(t)$ is the unobserved, continuous, time-varying log relative hazard. In our application, $z_j(t) = 1(0)$ if person j is (is not) protected, that is, is (is not) aged 40 or older at time t, and $\beta(t)$ is the logarithm of the odds ratio at time t. The parameter $\beta(t)$ is the instantaneous log odds ratio:

$$\beta(t) = \lim_{dt \to 0} \ln \left(\left[\frac{P(t \leq T_j < t + dt | z_j(t) = 1)}{P(t + dt \leq T_j | z_j(t) = 1)} \right] \right.$$
$$\left. \times \left[\frac{P(t \leq Tj < t + dt | z_j(t) = 0)}{P(t + dt \leq T_j | z_j(t) = 0)} \right]^{-1} \right). \quad (11.3)$$

The observed data are (h_j, T_j, c_j, z_j), $1 \leq j \leq M$, where M is the number of individuals who were in the workforce at any time during the observation period, and $c_j = 0$ if the jth employee was terminated at time T_j and $c_j = 1$ if the employee left the workforce for some other reason. The likelihood function is

$$\ell(\lambda, \beta | \text{Data}) = \prod_{j=1}^{M} (\lambda_j(T_j))^{(1-c_j)} S_j(T_j)$$
$$= \prod_{c_j=0} \lambda(T_j) e^{\beta(T_j) z_j(T_j)} \quad (11.4)$$
$$\times \exp \left(- \sum_{j=1}^{M} \int_{h_j}^{T_j} e^{\beta(t) z_j(t)} \lambda(t) dt \right).$$

In practice, times are not recorded continuously, so let us rescale the observation period to the interval $[0,1]$ and assume that time is measured on a finite grid, $0 = t_0 < t_1 < \ldots < t_p = 1$. A sufficiently fine grid is defined by the times at which something happened (someone was hired, or left the workforce, or reached age 40). The data are reduced to N_i and n_i, the numbers of employees and protected employees at time t_{i-1}, and k_i and x_i, the numbers of employees and protected employees involuntarily terminated in the interval $(t_{i-1}, t_i]$. For data recorded at this resolution, the likelihood is

$$\ell(\lambda, \beta) = \sum_{i=1}^{p} e^{\beta_i \cdot x_i} \Lambda_i^{k_i} \exp(\Lambda_i(n_i e^{\beta_i} + (N_i - n_i))), \quad (11.5)$$

where $\beta_i = \beta(t_i)$ and $\Lambda_i = \Lambda(t_i) - \Lambda(t_{i-1}) = \int_{t_{i-1}}^{t_i} \lambda(t) dt$. The function $\Lambda(t) = \int_0^t \lambda(t) dt$ is called the cumulative base rate. The likelihood depends on the log odds ratio function and the cumulative base rate function only through a finite number of values, $\boldsymbol{\beta} = (\beta_1, \ldots, \beta_p)'$ and $\boldsymbol{\Lambda} = (\Lambda_1, \ldots, \Lambda_p)'$.

11.2.1 Hierarchical Priors for Time Varying Coefficients

Sargent (1997) provided an excellent review of penalized likelihood approaches to modeling time-varying coefficients in proportional hazards models. He argued that these are equivalent to Bayes methods with improper prior distributions on $\beta(\cdot)$ and proposed a "flexible" model with independent first differences $\beta(t_{i+1}) = \beta(t_i) + u_{i+1}$, where the innovations u_{i+1} are mutually independent, normal random variables with mean 0 and precision τ/dt_{i+1} and $dt_{i+1} = t_{i+1} - t_i$. Under this model $\beta(t)$ is nowhere smooth–policy, in effect, changes abruptly at every instant. However, in the employment context, we expect changes to be gradual and smooth in the absence of identifiable causes such as a change in top management. For that reason we propose a smoothness prior for the log odds ratio, $\beta(t)$. The smooth model that we describe later is an integrated Wiener process with linear drift. Lin and Zhang (1998) used this prior for their generalized additive mixed models; however, their quasi-likelihood approach based on the Laplace approximation appears to fail for employment decision analyses when, for one or more time bins, all or none of the involuntary terminations are in the protected class.

11.2.2 Smoothness Priors

Let $\beta(t)$ be a Gaussian process, let $\beta_i = \beta(t_i), 0 \le t_i \le 1, \le i \le M$, and define $\boldsymbol{\beta} = (\beta_1, \ldots, \beta_M)$. Specifying a "smoothness" prior requires that we have an opinion about the second derivative of $\beta(t)$ (see Gersch (1982) and the references cited there). To this end we use the integrated Wiener process representation (Wahba, 1978):

$$\beta(t) = \beta_0 + \beta_0' t + \sqrt{1/\tau} \int_0^t W(t) dt, \tag{11.6}$$

where $W(\cdot)$ is a standard Wiener process on the unit interval, τ (the precision or "smoothness" parameter) has a proper prior distribution, and the initial state (β_0, β_0') has a proper prior distribution independent of $W(\cdot)$ and τ. Integrating by parts, we obtain the equivalent representation:

$$\beta(t) = \beta_0 + \beta_0'(t - t_0) + \frac{1}{\sqrt{\tau}} \int_0^t (t - s) dW(s). \tag{11.7}$$

Because $dW(s)$ is Gaussian white noise, the conditional covariance function of $\beta(\cdot)$ is

$$\text{cov}(\beta(t), \beta(t + d) | \beta_0, \beta_0', \tau)$$
$$= \frac{1}{\tau} E \left(\int_0^t \int_0^{t+d} (t + d - u)(t - v) dW(u) dW(v) \right)$$
$$= \frac{1}{\tau} \int_0^t (t + d - u)(t - u) du$$
$$= \frac{t^3}{3\tau} + \frac{dt^2}{2\tau}. \tag{11.8}$$

11.2.3 Forming an Opinion about Smoothness

The remaining task in specifying the prior distribution of the log odds ratio is to specify prior distributions for the initial state (β_0, β_0') and for the smoothness parameter, τ. We have found that the posterior distribution of $\beta(\cdot)$ is not sensitive to the prior distribution of the initial state, so we give the initial state a diffuse but proper bivariate normal distribution. However, the smoothness parameter τ requires more care.

As $\tau \to \infty$, the Wiener process part of (1.7) disappears, so this would express certainty that $\beta(\cdot)$ is exactly linear in time. As $\tau \to 0$, the variance of the $\beta(\cdot)$ around the linear-in-time mean goes to ∞, so a good point estimate of $\beta(\cdot)$ would go through each of the sample points exactly, which offers no smoothness at all. It should come as no surprise, then, that what is essential about a prior on τ is not to allow too much probability close to 0. In the employment discrimination context, in the examples we have studied the data do not carry much information about smoothness and it is necessary to have an informative opinion about this parameter. In eliciting opinions about how fast an odds ratio might change, we find it easiest to think about what might happen during a business quarter. We will use as a reference the prior distribution of a person who thinks that, absent any change in business conditions or management turnover, there is a small probability that the odds of terminating a protected employee relative to an unprotected employee would change more than 15% in a single quarter. For example, if at the beginning of a quarter a protected employee is 5% more likely to be terminated than an unprotected employee, it would be surprising to see a 20% disparity at the beginning of the next quarter. Our purpose here is to demonstrate a way to develop a reference prior distribution consistent with easily stated assumptions. When such analyses are used in litigation, it will be important for the expert to be able to state that his or her conclusions are robust over a wide range of prior opinions, which is true in the first case (Case K) that we present but is not in the second case (Case W).

To see what the "no more than 15% change per quarter" assumption implies about the prior distribution of the smoothness parameter, consider the central second difference $\Delta'' = \beta(t+d) - 2\beta(t) + \beta(t-d)$, where d represents a half-quarter expressed in rescaled time (i.e., as a fraction of the total observation interval). From the covariance function 11.8 (1.8), it is easy to compute, variance $(\Delta'') = 2d^3/3\tau$. It is easy to see that if β changes by at most .15 over the interval $(t-d, t+d)$, then $|\Delta''| \leq .30$. Because we regard values larger than this to be improbable a priori, we can treat .30 as roughly two standard deviations of Δ''. Thus, the prior distribution of τ should place high probability on the event, $2d^3/3\tau < .15^2$, that is, $30d^3 < \tau$. Thus, for example, if the observation period is about 16 quarters, then a rescaled half quarter is $d = 1/32$. So the prior distribution should place high probability on the event, $\tau > 30/32^3 \approx .0005$. A gamma distribution with mean .005 and shape 1 places about 90% of its mass above .0005.

The important thing about a prior on τ is where it puts most of its weight. We believe that other choices of the underlying density would not change the conclusions much. However, shifts in the mean are important, because such shifts control how much smoothing is done. Hence, we study sensitivity mainly by varying the mean, holding the rest of the distributional specification unchanged.

11.2.4 Posterior Distribution

Employers have an absolute right to terminate employees; what they do not have is the right to discriminate on the basis of age without a legitimate business reason unrelated to age. Thus, the base rate is irrelevant to litigation, and we believe that a neutral analyst should give it a flexible, diffuse but proper prior distribution. For convenience, we have chosen to use a gamma process prior with shape parameter α and scale parameter $\alpha\gamma$. In other words, disjoint increments $\Lambda_i = \Lambda(t_i) - \Lambda(t_{i-1}) = \int_{t_{i-1}}^{t_i} \lambda(t)dt$, are independent and have gamma distributions with shape parameter $\alpha(t_i - t_{i-1}) = \alpha dt_i$, and scale parameter $\alpha\gamma$. The hyperparameters α and γ have diffuse but proper log-normal distributions. Consequently, the posterior distribution is proportional to

$$\ell(\beta, \Lambda)p(\beta|\beta_0, \beta_0', \tau)p(\beta_0, \beta_0')p(\tau)p(\Lambda|\alpha, \gamma). \tag{11.9}$$

The goal is compute the posterior marginal distributions of the log odds ratios β_i, $1 \leq i \leq p$, in particular, to compute the probability that the employer's policy discriminated against members of the protected class at time t_i; that is, $P(\beta_i > 0|\text{Data})$,

$$P(\beta_i > 0|\text{Data}) = \frac{\int_{\beta_i > 0} d\text{P}(\boldsymbol{\beta}, \Lambda, \tau, \beta_0, \beta_0', \alpha, \gamma|\text{Data})}{\int d\text{P}(\boldsymbol{\beta}, \Lambda, \tau, \beta_0, \beta_0', \alpha, \gamma|\text{Data})}. \tag{11.10}$$

Closed form integration in (11.10) is not feasible. Owing to the high dimensionality of the parameter space, numerical quadrature is out of the question and the Laplace approximation (Kass et al., 1988) would require the maximization of a function over hundreds of arguments. For these reasons we chose to approximate moments and tail areas of the posterior distribution by Markov chain Monte Carlo (MCMC) methods (Tierney, 1994; Gelman et al., 1995).

MCMC works by generating a vector-valued Markov chain that has the posterior distribution of the parameter vector as its stationary distribution. An algorithm that generates such a Markov chain is colloquially called a *sampler*. Let $\boldsymbol{\theta}$ denote the parameter vector, let $f(\boldsymbol{\theta}|\text{data})$ denote the posterior distribution, and let $\theta_1, \ldots, \theta_M$ be successive realizations of $\boldsymbol{\theta}$ generated by the sampler. The ergodic theorem (a weak law of large numbers for Markov chains) implies that

$$\frac{1}{M} \sum_{i=1}^{M} h(\theta_i) \xrightarrow{P} \int h(\boldsymbol{\theta}) f(\boldsymbol{\theta}|\text{data})$$

for any integrable function $h(\cdot)$. In particular, if we select $h(\cdot)$ to be the indicator function of an event such as $\beta_{15} > 0$, then the ergodic theorem states that the relative frequency of that event in the sequence $\theta_1, \ldots, \theta_M$ is a consistent estimate of the posterior probability of that event. However, if the successive realizations generated by the sampler are highly correlated, then the relative frequency may approach the limit very slowly; in this situation the Markov chain is said to "mix" slowly.

In our initial attempts to apply MCMC, we found that the Markov chain did mix very slowly, probably because of the highly collinear covariance matrix of the $\boldsymbol{\beta}$ vector. We were able to reduce the collinearity, with a resulting improvement in the rate of convergence of the Markov chain, by re-expressing $\boldsymbol{\beta}$ as a linear combination of the initial state vector and the dominant principal components of the integrated Wiener process.

11.2.5   *Reexpressing β*

The conditional prior distribution of $\boldsymbol{\beta}$ is

$$p(\boldsymbol{\beta}|\beta_0, \beta_0', \tau) = N_p \left(\boldsymbol{L} \begin{bmatrix} \beta_0 \\ \beta_0' \end{bmatrix}, \frac{1}{\tau} \boldsymbol{V} \right) = N_p \left(\boldsymbol{\mu_\beta}, \frac{1}{\tau} \boldsymbol{V} \right), \tag{11.11}$$

where matrix $\boldsymbol{V}$ depends only on the observation times,

$$v_{i,j} = \frac{\tau_i^3}{3} + \frac{(t_j - t_i)t_i^2}{2}, \quad i \leq j$$

[see (11.8)[1]]. The spectral decomposition is $\boldsymbol{V} = \boldsymbol{U}\text{diag}(\boldsymbol{w})\boldsymbol{U}'$, where $\boldsymbol{U}$ is the orthonormal eigenvector matrix and $\boldsymbol{w}$ is the vector of eigenvalues. Suppose that the first r eigenvalues account for, say, $1 - \epsilon^2$ of the total variance and let $\boldsymbol{T} = \boldsymbol{U}_r\text{diag}(\sqrt{\boldsymbol{w_r}})$ and $\boldsymbol{z} = \text{diag}(\boldsymbol{w_r^{-.5}})\boldsymbol{U}_r'(\boldsymbol{\beta} - \boldsymbol{\mu_\beta})\sqrt{\tau}$, where $\boldsymbol{U}_r$ is the first r columns of $\boldsymbol{U}$ and $\boldsymbol{w_r}$ is the first r components of $\boldsymbol{w}$. Clearly, the components of z are iid standard normal and

$$E\left[||\tau(\boldsymbol{\beta} - \boldsymbol{\mu_\beta}) - \boldsymbol{T}\boldsymbol{z}||^2 \right] = \epsilon^2 E\left[||\tau(\boldsymbol{\beta} - \boldsymbol{\mu_\beta})||^2 \right].$$

---

[1]This corrects a typographical error in the published paper

Consequently,

$$\beta \approx \mu_\beta + \frac{1}{\sqrt{\tau}} T z \approx L \begin{bmatrix} \beta_0 \\ \beta_0' \end{bmatrix} + \frac{1}{\sqrt{\tau}} T z. \tag{11.12}$$

11.3 Examples

The data in two of these examples come from cases we were involved in–we'll call them Case K and Case W. In each case one or more plaintiffs were suing a former employer for age discrimination in his or her dismissal. Data for these cases are available in StatLib (Kadane and Woodworth, 2001). The third example is a reanalysis of a class action against the U.S. Postal Service (USPS) reported in Freidlin and Gastwirth (2000). All three cases were analyzed via WinBUGS 1.3 (Spiegelhalter et al., 2000). For Cases K and W we used the principal component representation (11.12).

11.3.1 Case K

In this case flow data for all individuals employed by the defendant at any time during a 1,557-day period (about 17 quarters) were available to the statistical expert. During that period 96 employees were involuntarily terminated, 79 of whom were age 40 or above at the time of termination. The data were aggregated into 288 time intervals, or bins, bounded by times at which one or more employees entered the workforce, left the workforce, or reached a 40th birthday. The median bin width was 4 days, the mean was about 5 days, and the maximum was 24 days. Based on the discussion in Section 11.2.3, we prefer that the prior distribution for the smoothness parameter place most of its mass above .0007, so we selected a gamma prior with shape parameter 1 and mean .007; the other parameters were given diffuse but proper priors. Table 11.2 shows the data, mean, standard deviation, and positive tail area of the log odds ratios for bins with one or more involuntary terminations.

In Figure 11.1 we show how the smooth model fits the unsmoothed underlying data. To do this, we grouped cases by quarters and computed 95% equal-tail posterior-density credible intervals for the log odds assuming a normal prior with mean 0 and standard deviation 8. We like a standard deviation of 8 for this sort of descriptive display because it is fairly diffuse (there is, for example, 16% prior probability that the odds ratio exceeds 3,000) yet prevents infinite credible intervals when one category or the other has no terminations. Because this prior pulls the posterior distribution toward 0, it would be difficult for the respondent (the firm) to argue that it is biased in favor of the plaintiff.

Sensitivity to the prior mean of the smoothness parameter is explored in Figure 11.2 and sensitivity to the shape of the prior distribution of the smoothness parameter is explored in Figure 11.3. Between days 528 and 1,322 the probability of discrimination $P(\beta(t) > 0|data)$ exceeds .99 and is insensitive to the prior distribution of the smoothness parameter. The plaintiff in Case K had been dismissed within that interval at day 766. It is not surprising that greater sensitivity to the smoothness parameter is shown at the start and the end of the period. Thus, if the date of termination of the plaintiff is near the start or the end of the observation period, the conclusions will be more sensitive to how much smoothing is assumed. This suggests the desirability of designing data collection so that it includes a period of time surrounding the event or events in question.

In addition, we analyzed Case K with Sargent's (1997) first-difference prior. The first-difference prior models the log odds ratio as a linear function plus a Wiener process with precision τ. Thus, the log odds ratio is continuous but not smooth. To scale the prior distribution of the precision of the log odds ratio, we again argue

Table 11.2: Data and Posterior Marginal Distributions of the Log Odds Ratio for Case K

Day	N	n	k	x	Posterior distribution Mean	SD	$P(\beta > 0)$
3	190	102	1	1	-1.5	1.3	0.111
175	208	110	1	0	-0.95	0.82	0.110
406	273	150	1	1	0.25	0.51	0.702
444	273	151	1	1	0.50	0.47	0.858
507	283	159	1	0	0.91	0.41	0.985
528	283	159	2	1	1.05	0.39	0.994
535	284	161	1	1	1.10	0.39	0.997
555	286	164	1	0	1.23	0.38	0.999
567	289	167	1	0	1.30	0.37	1.000
582	287	167	1	1	1.40	0.36	1.000
605	293	170	10	9	1.53	0.36	1.000
661	290	165	1	1	1.82	0.35	1.000
668	290	165	1	1	1.85	0.35	1.000
696	287	163	9	8	1.96	0.35	1.000
703	278	155	4	3	1.98	0.35	1.000
710	276	152	1	1	2.00	0.35	1.000
731	272	150	1	1	2.07	0.35	1.000
752	270	147	2	2	2.12	0.35	1.000
766	269	143	1	1	2.15	0.35	1.000
784	269	141	1	1	2.18	0.35	1.000
797	266	138	2	2	2.20	0.35	1.000
846	264	136	1	1	2.25	0.35	1.000
847	263	135	2	2	2.25	0.35	1.000
850	261	133	3	3	2.25	0.35	1.000
857	258	130	4	4	2.25	0.35	1.000
863	245	120	1	1	2.25	0.35	1.000
864	244	119	1	0	2.26	0.35	1.000
927	247	121	1	0	2.25	0.35	1.000
955	245	120	1	1	2.24	0.35	1.000
980	242	118	4	4	2.23	0.35	1.000
1,008	236	113	3	3	2.20	0.35	1.000
1,017	234	111	1	0	2.19	0.35	1.000
1,018	233	111	5	5	2.19	0.35	1.000
1,025	227	105	1	1	2.18	0.35	1.000
1,037	227	105	1	1	2.16	0.35	1.000
1,095	230	105	1	1	2.05	0.36	1.000
1,102	226	101	2	1	2.04	0.36	1.000
1,106	224	101	1	1	2.03	0.36	1.000
1,113	223	100	3	2	2.01	0.36	1.000
1,116	220	98	1	0	2.00	0.36	1.000
1,141	220	97	1	1	1.94	0.36	1.000
1,200	217	93	1	1	1.77	0.38	1.000
1,214	216	91	1	1	1.72	0.38	1.000
1,224	215	90	2	2	1.69	0.39	1.000
1,225	213	88	1	1	1.69	0.39	1.000
1,253	215	89	1	1	1.58	0.40	1.000
1,256	214	88	1	1	1.56	0.40	1.000
1,284	213	89	1	1	1.44	0.41	1.000
1,319	210	89	1	1	1.27	0.44	0.998
1,322	207	88	1	0	1.27	0.44	0.997
1,361	207	89	1	0	1.06	0.48	0.982
1,375	204	89	1	1	0.99	0.50	0.972
1,557	205	90	2	1	0.09	0.93	0.568

NOTE: Data and posterior distributions for bins with one or more involuntary terminations. N workforce; n, protected; k, involuntary terminations; x, involuntary terminations of protected employees. The smoothness parameter, τ, had a Gamma(1) prior distribution with mean .007, as described in the text. Two chains were run with 50,000 replications each, discarding the first 4,000. The Gelman-Rubin statistic indicated that the chains had converged.

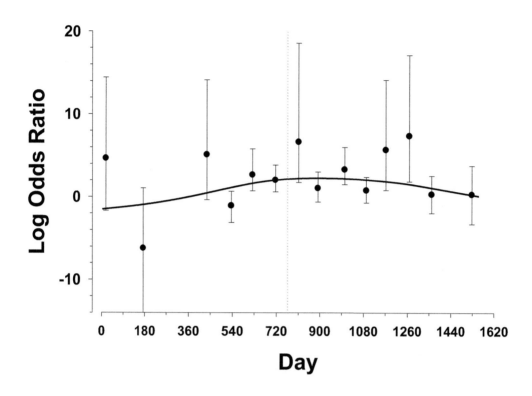

Figure 11.1: Case K: Posterior Mean and Probability of Discrimination for Our Preferred Prior Distribution of the Smoothness Parameter. Vertical bars are 95% posterior highest density regions for quarterly aggregates with iid $N(0, 64)$ priors. Vertical dotted line indicates date of plaintiff's dismissal.

from our prior opinion that the log odds ratio is unlikely to change more than 15% within a quarter. We interpret this as two standard deviations of the first difference, $\beta(t + d) - \beta(t)$. The variance of a one-quarter first difference is d/τ, where $d \approx 1/19$ is one quarter expressed as a fraction of the total observation period. Thus, $2\sqrt{d/\tau} \leq .15$, which implies that the prior should place most of its mass on $\tau \geq 9.4$. A gamma prior with mean 100 and shape 1 places about 90% of its mass above 9.5. Figure 11.4 compares the posterior mean log odds ratio for the Sargent's smooth model and our continuous model. We found that the posterior distribution for Sargent's model was not sensitive to the prior means of τ between 1 and 100.

We conducted what we believe would be an acceptable frequentist analysis via proportional hazards regression to model the time to involuntary termination. The initial model included design variables for membership in the protected group and for the linear interaction of this variable with time. The linear interaction was insignificant, so we presume that a frequentist would opt for a constant odds model. The maximum likelihood estimate (and asymptotic standard error) of the log odds ratio is 1.51 (.27), which approximates the posterior mean and standard deviation of this parameter for large values of the smoothness parameter (see Table 11.3).

Although the frequentist and Bayesian analyses reach the same conclusion regard-

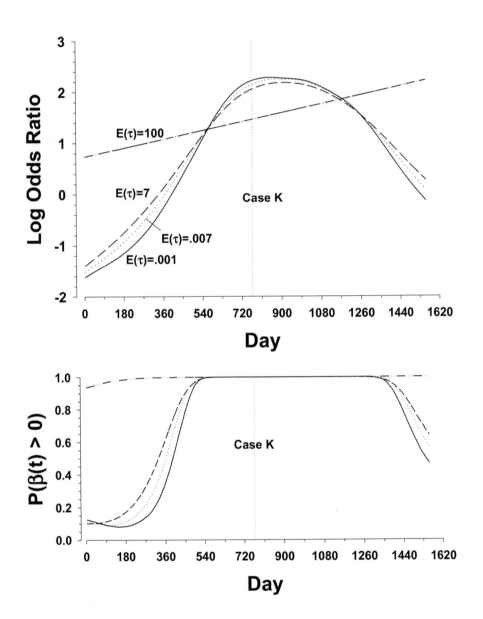

Figure 11.2: Case K: Effect of Varying the Prior Mean of the Smoothness Parameter (all distributions are Gamma with shape parameter 1).

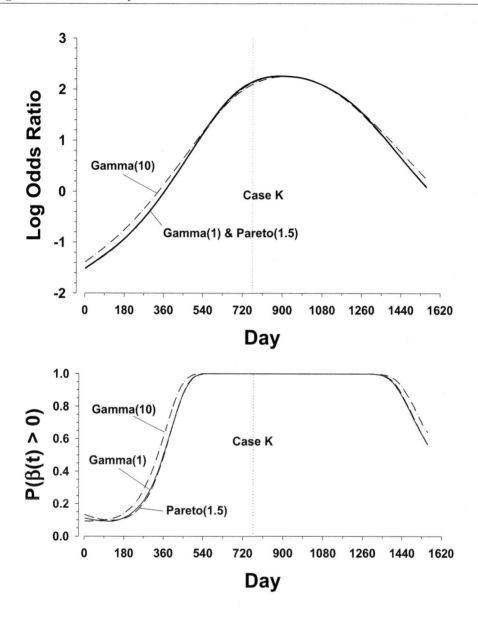

Figure 11.3: Case K: Effect of Varying the Shape of the Prior Distribution of the Smoothness Parameter (all distributions have mean .007 and the indicated shape parameters).

ing the presence of discrimination in Case K, we believe that the frequentist analysis does not produce probability statements relevant to the particular case in litigation and in no way constitutes a gold standard for our analysis. On the bases of these analyses, a statistical expert would be able to report that there is strong, robust evidence that discrimination against employees aged 40 and above was present in terminations between days 528 and 1,322, and, in particular, on the day of the plaintiff's termination.

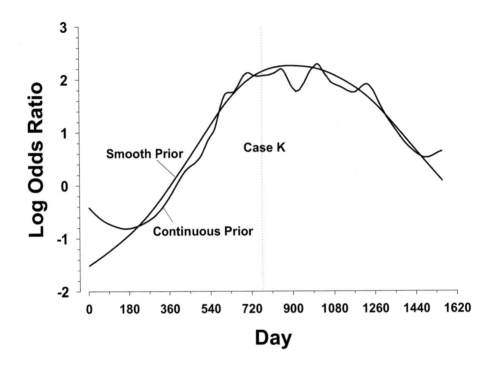

Figure 11.4: Case K: Posterior mean for continuous (Wiener process, prior mean smoothness, 100) and smooth (integrated Wiener process, prior mean smoothness, .007) Distributions of the Log Odds Ratio.

Table 11.3: Sensitivity Analysis[a] for Case K

		Posterior distribution for Case K		
Model	Prior[b]	Mean	SD	$P(\beta > 0/\text{Data})$
Smooth	$E(\tau) = .001$	2.22	.37	1.0000
	$E(\tau) = .007$			
	Gamma(1)	2.15	0.35	1.0000
	Gamma(10)	2.10	0.33	1.0000
	Pareto(1.5)	2.13	0.35	1.0000
	$E(\tau) = .07$	2.06	0.37	1.0000
	$E(\tau) = 100$	1.46	0.28	1.0000
Continuous	$E(\tau) = 100$[c]	2.11	0.49	1.0000
Maximum likelihood[d]	Linear log odds ratio	1.44	0.28	n/a
	Constant log odds ratio	1.51	0.27	n/a

[a] $P(\beta > 0)$ for Case K (day 766) is robust to specification of the prior distribution of the log odds ratio.

[b] Where not indicated otherwise, the smoothness parameter, τ, had a Gamma(1) prior with the indicated mean.

[c] The shape parameter was 1 except for the smooth prior with mean 100, which had shape parameter 5.

[d] Maximum likelihood estimates were computed by proportional hazards regression; asymptotic approximations to the one-sided p values are less than .0005.

11.3.2   Case W

Two plaintiffs, terminated about a year apart, brought separate age discrimination suits against the employer. The plaintiffs' attorneys requested data on all individuals who were in the defendant's workforce at any time during an approximately 4.5-year observation period containing the termination dates of the plaintiffs. Dates of hire and separation and reason for separation were provided by the employer as well as age in years at entry into the dataset (the first day of the observation period or the date of hire) and at separation. The data request was made before the expert statistician was retained and it failed to ask for dates of birth; however, from the ages at entry and exit, it was possible to determine a range of possible birth dates for each employee. Thus, at any given time during the observation period, there is some uncertainty about whether the handful of nonterminated employees near the protected age (40 and older) were or were not in the protected class. We did not attempt to incorporate that uncertainty into this analysis and resolved ambiguities by assuming the birth date was at the center of the interval of dates consistent with the reported ages.

Over an observation period of about 1,600 days, the workforce was reduced by about two-thirds; 103 employees were involuntarily terminated in the process. A new CEO took over at day 862, near the middle of the observation period. The plaintiffs asserted that employees aged 50 (or 60) and above were targeted for termination under the influence of the new CEO. So in our reanalysis we have divided the protected class into two subclasses: ages 40–49 and ages 50–64 and estimated separate log odds ratios for each of the protected subclasses relative to the unprotected class. Here we present a fully Bayesian analysis of two models, one with smoothly time varying odds ratios for each protected subclass and one with smoothly time varying odds ratios in two phases–before and after the arrival of the new CEO.

The personnel data were aggregated by status (involuntarily terminated, other) into 171 time bins as described in Case K and three age categories (< 40, 40-49, 50-64). Aggregated data along with posterior means, standard deviations, and probabilities of discrimination for the two protected subclasses for bins containing at least one termination are reported in Table 11.4. Table 11.4 also reports posterior means, standard deviations, and probabilities of discrimination for our preferred choice of the prior distribution of the smoothness parameters–gamma with shape parameter 1 and mean .007. Figure 11.5 shows posterior means and probabilities of discrimination for different choices of the prior mean of the smoothness parameter. Figure 11.6 contrasts two-phase and non-interrupted models for employees aged 50–64.

The figures make it clear that the log odds ratios for either protected subclass were close to 0 before the new CEO arrived. After his arrival it appears that terminations of employees aged 40–49 declined and terminations of employees aged 50–64 increased. This is clearest in the interrupted model, but present to some extent in all models for all smoothness parameter values.

Two plaintiffs, indicated by vertical dotted lines in Figures 11.5 and 11.6, brought age discrimination suits against the employer. Plaintiff W1, who was between 50 and 59 years of age, was one of 12 employees involuntarily terminated on day 1,092. His theory of the case was that the new CEO had targeted employees aged 50 and above for termination. Under the two-phase model, which corresponds to the plaintiff's theory of the case, the probability of discrimination at the time of this plaintiffs termination was close to 1.00. However, the posterior probability of discrimination in this case is somewhat sensitive to the choice of model and smoothness parameter (Figure 11.6).

In the original case the plaintiff's statistical expert tabulated involuntary termination rates for each calendar quarter and each age decade. He reported that, "[involuntary] separation rates for the [period beginning at day 481] averaged a little above

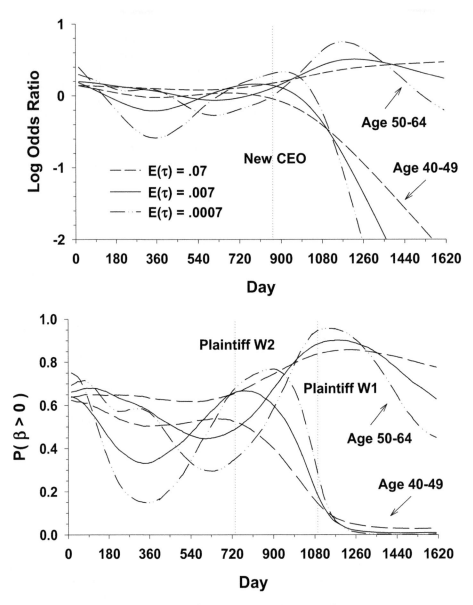

Figure 11.5: Case W: Sensitivity to the smoothness parameter.

three percent of the workforce per quarter for ages 20–49, but jumped to six and a half percent for ages 50–59. The 50-59 year age group differed significantly from the 20-39 year age group (signed-rank test, $p = 0.033$, one sided)." Our reanalysis is consistent with that conclusion (Figure 11.6, two-phase model). The plaintiff alleged and the defendant denied that the new CEO had vowed to weed out older employees. The case was settled before trial.

The case of plaintiff W2 went to trial. This 60-year-old plaintiff was one of 18 employees involuntarily terminated on day 733. On that day three of eight employees (37.5%) aged 60 and up were terminated compared to 15 of 136 (11.0%) employees terminated out of all other age groups (one-sided hypergeometric $p = .0530$). Although

| | Workforce | | | Terminated | | | Posterior distributions of Log Odds Ratios | | | | | |
| | | | | | | | Age 40-49 vs. unprotected | | | Age 50-64 vs. unprotected | | |
Day	< 40	40-49	50-64	< 40	40-49	50-64	Mean	StdDev	$P(\beta > 0)$	Mean	StdDev	$P(\beta > 0)$
13	77	58	58	0	1	0	.18	.52	.642	.20	.49	.662
35	77	57	58	1	1	1	.15	.48	.632	.19	.46	.667
38	76	56	57	2	0	0	.15	.47	.631	.19	.45	.668
39	74	56	57	1	0	0	.15	.47	.630	.19	.45	.668
42	73	56	57	1	1	0	.14	.42	.628	.19	.45	.669
75	70	55	58	0	1	0	.10	.42	.601	.18	.40	.678
80	70	54	58	3	3	6	.09	.41	.594	.18	.40	.680
81	67	51	52	0	0	1	.09	.41	.593	.18	.40	.680
84	67	51	51	0	0	0	.08	.39	.589	.18	.40	.679
115	68	51	50	1	0	0	.04	.38	.548	.17	.37	.679
161	67	52	50	1	1	0	-.03	.38	.478	.14	.35	.666
164	66	51	50	0	0	0	-.04	.38	.474	.14	.35	.666
175	66	51	50	1	1	0	-.05	.39	.457	.14	.35	.661
209	65	50	49	0	0	0	-.10	.41	.411	.12	.35	.643
252	61	53	49	0	1	1	-.15	.41	.372	.11	.35	.623
259	61	53	48	2	0	0	-.16	.42	.367	.11	.35	.620
263	59	53	48	1	0	0	-.17	.42	.363	.10	.36	.619
266	58	53	48	1	0	0	-.17	.45	.361	.10	.36	.619
353	56	52	49	0	0	4	-.21	.45	.332	.07	.37	.579
357	56	51	45	0	1	1	-.21	.43	.334	.07	.37	.576
490	50	54	44	1	1	1	-.11	.40	.419	-.02	.39	.487
571	47	54	44	0	1	0	.00	.40	.507	-.06	.39	.451
573	47	54	44	0	1	0	.00	.37	.511	-.06	.39	.450
658	51	56	44	0	1	0	.10	.37	.601	-.05	.38	.455
665	51	55	44	1	0	0	.10	.36	.610	-.05	.37	.457
733	47	54	50	6	6	6	.15	.36	.661	-.02	.36	.489
735	41	48	43	0	1	0	.15	.37	.662	-.01	.36	.491
773	40	48	40	1	0	0	.16	.37	.668	.01	.36	.523
838	40	46	39	3	1	1	.16	.39	.653	.06	.36	.590
				New CEO arrives								
901	35	43	37	0	1	0	.11	.41	.599	.16	.36	.681
907	35	42	35	0	1	1	.11	.41	.592	.17	.36	.688
924	34	42	34	0	0	1	.08	.42	.570	.20	.36	.711
948	35	41	34	0	1	0	.05	.43	.537	.23	.36	.746
1,017	34	36	33	1	0	0	-.13	.45	.389	.34	.36	.830
1,029	34	36	34	3	0	0	-.17	.45	.358	.36	.36	.842
1,092	30	36	34	0	3	6	-.42	.48	.185	.44	.37	.885
1,113	27	32	27	0	0	1	-.52	.49	.139	.46	.37	.893
1,121	27	31	26	1	0	1	-.56	.50	.124	.47	.37	.896
1,148	27	31	25	0	0	0	-.70	.54	.082	.49	.38	.901
1,162	25	31	25	0	0	1	-.78	.56	.066	.50	.39	.901
1,173	25	31	23	0	0	1	-.84	.58	.058	.50	.39	.904
1,239	23	30	22	0	0	1	-1.23	.74	.024	.51	.41	.895
1,390	24	28	22	0	0	1	-2.21	1.29	.009	.43	.49	.816
1,397	24	28	20	0	0	1	-2.25	1.32	.009	.43	.50	.809
1,438	23	28	19	0	0	0	-2.53	1.50	.008	.39	.54	.773
1,579	20	30	19	1	0	0	-3.48	2.21	.009	.27	.77	.655
1,612	19	30	19	0	0	1	-3.71	2.40	.010	.24	.85	.628

The smoothness parameter had a Gamma(1) prior with mean .007. Computations were via WinBUGS 1.3. There were 25,000 replications of two chains discarding the first 4,000.

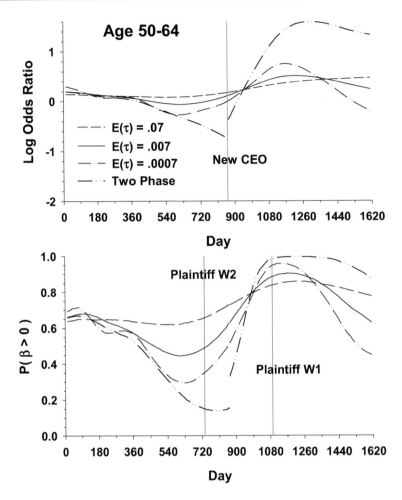

Figure 11.6: Comparison of Noninterrupted and Two-Phase Odds Ratio Models. For the two-phase model the prior distributions of the four smoothness parameters were gamma with shape 1 and mean .007.

the plaintiff had been terminated in the quarter prior to the arrival of the new CEO, the plaintiff's theory was that the new CEO had been seen on site before he assumed office and had influenced personnel policy decisions prior to his official arrival date.

The defense statistician presented several analyses of the quarterly aggregated data involving different subsets of the observation period and different subgroups of protected and unprotected employees. Based on two-sided p values, he reported no significant differences between any subgroups; however, one-sided p values are more appropriate in age discrimination cases and several of these are "significant" or nearly so. According to his analysis, for the period after the new CEO was hired, employees aged 50-59 were terminated at a significantly higher rate than employees aged 20-39 ($p = .053$, one sided) and employees aged 40-49 ($p = .050$, one sided); for the period beginning with the new CEO's second quarter in office the one-sided p values were .039 and .038, respectively. The defense expert did not analyze the interval beginning one quarter prior to the arrival of the new CEO–the quarter in which plaintiff W2 was terminated. Thus, the defense expert's analysis generally agrees with the reanalysis presented in this article (Figure 11.6). The defense expert also reported several discriminant analyses meant to demonstrate that the mean age of involuntarily terminated employees was not different from the mean age of the workforce.

In response to the latter analysis, the plaintiff's statistician argued that this was accounted for by a high rate of termination of employees in their first year of service ("short term employees"), and presented the results of a proportional hazards regression analysis with constant odds ratios over the entire observation period. The model involved design variables for employees in the first year of service and for employees aged 50 and above (thus, the reference category was long-term employees under the age of 50). Employees in their first year of service were terminated at a significantly higher rate relative to the reference category (odds ratio $= 2$, $p = .01$, two sided) as were employees aged 50 and older (odds ratio $= 1.58$, $p = .03$, two sided).

The plaintiff's theory of the case, as we understand it, had three components, (1) that the new CEO had been seen on site on several occasions in the quarter before he assumed office and was presumably an active participant in personnel policy decisions prior to his official arrival date, (2) that the CEO had stated his intent to weed out older employees, and (3) that this had an adverse impact on employees aged 60 and above. The preceding proportional hazards analysis, and the analysis of the 18 terminations on day 733 (37% of 60-year-olds terminated versus 11% of all other employees) support the disparate impact theory.

The plaintiff had refused the defendant's offer of a different job at lower pay. The judge instructed the jury that the plaintiff had a duty under the law to exercise reasonable diligence to minimize his damages and if they found that he had not done so, then they should reduce his damages by the amount he reasonably could have avoided if he had sought out or taken advantage of such an opportunity. The jury found that the plaintiff had proven that age was a determining factor for his discharge but that he had failed to mitigate his damages. Therefore, the award was the difference between what he would have earned at his original salary prior to discharge minus the amount he would have earned had he accepted the lower salaried job. The defendant appealed the case, but settled prior to trial of the appeal.

Our reanalysis, with time-varying odds ratios, does not support a theory of adverse impact against employees aged 50-64 prior to the arrival of the new CEO; however, the plaintiff's specific claim was discrimination against employees aged 60 and older and there does seem to be evidence of this at the time of the plaintiff's termination (one-sided hypergeometric $p = .053$).

One-sided or Two-sided? Bayesians compute probabilities of relevant events; that is, $P(\beta(t) > 0|\text{data})$, the conditional probability of discrimination at time t given the data. Frequentists favor two-sided p values (roughly speaking, the conditional probability, given the assumption of no discrimination, of getting the data we got plus the probability of getting even more deviant hypothetical data). As Bayesians, we think such probabilities are legally irrelevant. Even within the frequentist paradigm, however, we think that the use of two-sided p values is wrong in age discrimination cases. We say this because frequentist inference claims to control "Type I error," that is, to control the conditional probability that an "innocent" employer will be found to discriminate. In age discrimination cases the Type I errors can occur on one side only because only protected employees have the right to sue under the age discrimination act. Type I errors in the "other tail" would be produced by evidence of discrimination against the unprotected class but the unprotected class has no legal right to relief.

11.3.3   *Valentino v. United States Postal Service*

Freidlin and Gastwirth (2000) discussed a case in which the plaintiff filed a charge of sex discrimination in promotion at the U.S. Postal Service after she was denied a promotion in mid-1976. The judge certified the women employed at grade 17 and higher as a class. The underlying data, raw log odds ratios, and posterior distributions of the log odds ratios for three different specifications of the prior are shown in Table 11.5.

Using frequentist methods, Freidlin and Gastwirth (2000) reported that the p value for discrimination against women was .0006 in period 06/74-03/75, .020 in 03/75-01/76, and greater than .5 in subsequent periods. The authors advocate using CUSUM methods "...to determine the time period when the pattern [of discrimination] remained the same. If the original complaint was filed during a period of statistically significant [discrimination] before the change to fair [employment practices] occurred, then the data are consistent with the plaintiffs claim." They reported that their CUSUM tests showed a significant change in discrimination over time and that this effect was concentrated in grades 17-19 and 23-25. Apparently they argued from the significant CUSUM and the pattern of p values for individual time periods that there was discrimination in 1974-75 and 1975-76 but not later. However, no formal test or estimate of the location of the changepoint was offered, instead, "...the graph of [the CUSUM test statistic against time] helps to identify the time of the change if one exists..." Thus, what we appear to be offered is a test of inhomogeneity of the odds ratio over time combined with inspecting a CUSUM graph and a list of p values for individual time periods.

We have reanalyzed the data using three specifications of the joint prior distribution of promotion probabilities for each period, grade, and gender. In the completely independent model, each probability has a prior beta(0.1,0.1) distribution. In the random effects model, the log odds ratio (female versus male) for each year and grade consists of a year effect, a grade effect, and an interaction. In the exchangeable model, each class of effects (time, grade, interaction) has an exchangeable multivariate normal prior distribution. In the $AR(1) \times AR(1)$ model, time and grade effects have multivariate normal priors with AR(1) covariance structure and the interactions are exchangeable.

Table 11.5 shows the posterior mean and standard deviation of the log odds ratio and the probability of discrimination (negative log odds ratio) for each year and grade. We agree with Freidlin and Gastwirth that there is strong evidence of discrimination against women in grades 17-19 in periods 1974-75 and 1975-76 and against women in grades 23-25 in year 1974-75 and not much evidence of discrimination elsewhere. However, we do not see the relevance of a formal changepoint test. If there is inhomogeneity, then it should be incorporated into the model. Our analysis does this and it shows that not all members of the certified class have equal claims for relief. We believe that a neutral statistician analyzing these data would report that the evidence of discrimination is not uniform over grades or time periods, but is concentrated in grades 17-19 and 23-25 in year 1974-1975 and in grades 17-19 in year 75-76. We believe that this is precisely the information that the court needs to determine how the award (if any) should be distributed among members of the certified class.

11.4   Discussion

A standard criticism of Bayesian analyses is that the prior assumptions are arbitrary. One response is, "Compared to what?" Bayesian analysis can be explained to a jury in less convoluted ways than frequentist analyses and makes explicit the necessity to think about sensitive assumptions, rather than covering them with a mantle of false objectivity. The assumption of constant odds ratios in particular and the functional form of a model in general are examples of unexamined subjectivity. The Bayesian approach to model specification involves specifying a prior distribution over a more

Table 11.5: Aggregated data and Posterior Distributions for Valentino v. USPS
Posterior Moments and Tail Areas

Time	Grade	Males N[a]	Males x	Females N	Females x	lor	Independent[b] μ	σ	P(−)[c]	Exchangeable μ	σ	P(−)	AR(1) × AR(1) μ	σ	P(−)
06/74-03/75	17-19	229	67	73	5	-1.73	-1.80	0.50	1.000	-1.55	0.44	1.000	-1.51	0.43	1.000
	20-22	360	74	48	9	-0.11	-0.14	0.40	0.631	-0.17	0.38	0.661	-0.16	0.38	0.655
	23-25	703	132	33	2	-1.28	-1.47	0.81	0.986	-1.00	0.60	0.966	-0.94	0.59	0.961
	26-28	236	28	7	1	0.21	-0.13	1.30	0.491	-0.21	0.87	0.580	-0.14	0.84	0.553
	29-31	82	8	1	0	∞	-7.75	10.17	0.800	-0.55	1.21	0.675	-0.45	1.22	0.636
03/75-01/76	17-19	205	40	89	6	-1.21	-1.27	0.47	0.999	-1.12	0.43	0.998	-1.10	0.42	0.998
	20-22	373	39	43	5	0.12	0.05	0.52	0.439	-0.04	0.49	0.514	-0.03	0.48	0.513
	23-25	716	41	36	1	-0.75	-1.16	1.22	0.845	-0.58	0.75	0.776	-0.53	0.73	0.759
	26-28	277	85	9	1	-1.26	-1.64	1.26	0.938	-0.89	0.76	0.888	-0.83	0.74	0.877
	29-31	85	7	1	0	∞	-7.55	10.18	0.785	-0.50	1.21	0.661	-0.43	1.23	0.632
01/76-01/77	17-19	233	31	101	10	-0.33	-0.36	0.39	0.820	-0.34	0.37	0.820	-0.33	0.36	0.818
	20-22	396	32	52	4	-0.05	-0.13	0.58	0.571	-0.12	0.51	0.582	-0.11	0.50	0.574
	23-25	721	54	36	5	0.69	0.63	0.52	0.116	0.54	0.48	0.133	0.55	0.48	0.126
	26-28	271	28	9	2	0.91	0.77	0.89	0.180	0.45	0.74	0.263	0.46	0.72	0.252
	29-31	85	5	2	0	∞	-8.08	10.15	0.823	-0.28	1.15	0.584	-0.21	1.17	0.554
01/77-01/78	17-19	200	43	86	18	-0.03	-0.04	0.32	0.548	-0.03	0.31	0.531	-0.03	0.31	0.534
	20-22	377	80	52	9	-0.25	-0.28	0.39	0.548	-0.03	0.31	0.531	-0.03	0.31	0.534
	23-25	680	57	35	6	0.82	0.77	0.48	0.062	0.66	0.45	0.077	0.66	0.45	0.076
	26-28	262	18	8	1	0.66	0.32	1.28	0.350	0.16	0.86	0.408	0.18	0.85	0.397
	29-31	89	14	3	0	∞	-9.65	1006	0.933	-0.53	1.06	0.681	-0.48	1.11	0.653
01/78-01/79	17-19	196	29	90	8	-0.58	-0.61	0.43	0.928	-0.48	0.40	0.889	-0.43	0.40	0.861
	20-22	325	45	50	7	0.01	-0.03	0.45	0.511	0.04	0.42	0.444	0.09	0.41	0.396
	23-25	685	3	35	14	5.02	5.15	0.71	0.000	3.49	0.51	0.000	3.51	0.51	0.000
	26-28	252	14	9	1	0.75	0.41	1.28	0.32	0.40	0.86	0.304	0.57	0.84	0.234
	29-31	78	6	3	1	1.79	1.64	1.49	0.127	0.72	1.00	0.227	0.91	1.02	0.176

[a] N is the number of employees, x is the number promoted. [b] Prior models are: independent log odds ratios, exchangeable main effects of time and grade, exchangeable interactions, and AR(1) main effects of time and grade and exchangeable interactions. [c] $P(-)$ is the posterior probability that the log odds ratio is negative i.e. women are less likely to be promoted.

general class of time-varying odds ratio models. The subjective component of model specification resides in the prior distribution of the smoothness parameter. To some the need to think carefully about the prior distribution of the smoothness parameter may seem fatally to open the analysis to attack by opposing counsel on the grounds of arbitrariness. To that we respond that the assumption of constant or (piecewise) linear odds ratio is not only arbitrary but implausible on its face and that a more realistic analysis has a better chance of prevailing.

Acknowledgments

The research of Joseph B. Kadane was partially supported by NSF Grant DMS-9303557. We thank Michael Finkelstein, Joseph Gastwirth, Christopher Genovese, Bruce Levin, John Rolph, and Ashish Sanil for their helpful comments on an earlier draft. We also thank Kate Cowles for a key insight in specifying the prior distribution of the smoothness parameter. Finally, we thank Caroline Mitchell for her help with the legal aspects of the problem.

[Received December 2001. Revised January 2003.]

REFERENCES

Cox, D. (1972). "Regression Models and Life-Tables." *Journal of the Royal Statistical Society Series B*, 34, 187–220. 206

Finkelstein, M. and Levin, B. (1994). "Proportional Hazard Models for Age Discrimination Cases." *Jurimetrics Journal*, 34, 153–171. 205, 206

Freidlin, B. and Gastwirth, J. (2000). "Changepoint Tests Designed for the Analysis of Hiring Data Arising in Employment Discrimination Cases." *Journal of Business & Economic Statistics*, 18, 315–322. 211, 221, 222

Gastwirth, J. (1992). "Employment Discrimination: A Statistician's Look at Analysis of Disparate Impact Claims." *Law and Inequality: A Journal of Theory and Practice*, 11, 1, 151–179. 203

Gelman, A., Carlin, J., Stern, H., and Rubin, D. (1995). *Bayesian Data Analysis*. London: Chapman & Hall. 210

Gersch, W. (1982). "Smoothness Priors." In *Encyclopedia of Statistical Sciences*, eds. S. Kotz, N. L. Johnson, and C. B. Read, vol. 8, 518–526. John Wiley & Sons. 208

Kadane, J. (1990). "A Statistical Analysis of Adverse Impact of Employer Decisions." *Journal of the American Statistical Association*, 85, 925–933. 201, 205, 206

Kadane, J. and Mitchell, C. (1998). "Statistics in Proof of Employment Discrimination Cases." In *Controversies in Civil Rights: The Civil Rights Act of 1964 in Perspective*, ed. B. Grofman. University of Virginia Press. 203

Kadane, J. and Woodworth, G. (2001). "Employment Discrimination Data." Available at http://lib.stat.cmu.edu/datasets/caseK.tex and caseW.txt. 211

Kass, R., Tierney, L., and Kadane, J. (1988). "Asymptotics in Bayesian computation." In *Bayesian Statistics 3*, eds. J. Bernardo, M. DeGroot, D. Lindley, and A. Smith, 261–278. Oxford: Oxford University Press. 210

Lin, X. and Zhang, D. (1998). "Semiparametric Stochastic Mixed Models for Longitudinal Data." *Journal of the American Statistical Association*, 93, 710–719. 208

Sargent, D. (1997). "A Flexible Approach to Time-Varying Coefficients in the Cox Regression Setting." *Lifetime Data Analysis*, 3, 13–25. 207

Spiegelhalter, D., Thomas, A., and Best, N. (2000). *WinBUGS Version 1.3 User Manual.* MRC Biostatistics Unit, London. 211

Tierney, L. (1994). "Markov Chains for Exploring Posterior Distributions (with discussion)." *Annals of Statistics*, 22, 1701–1762. 210

Wahba, G. (1978). "Improper Priors, Spline Smoothing and the Problem of Guarding Against Model Errors in Regression." *Journal of the Royal Statistical Society Series B*, 40, 364–372. 208

Epilogue

What is the scientific issue?

How can time be treated continuously in the context of a disparate treatment employment lawsuit.

Is justification given for

a) the use of the data?

The data were from lawsuits each of us had been hired to address. They both involved firings of workers over a period of time.

b) the likelihood and the prior?

We used a Cox regression for the likelihood. The prior is a Weiner process in which the key parameter τ expresses smoothness. We explain why we chose a particular gamma distribution as the prior for τ.

What robustness checks were performed?

A variety of different priors for τ are examined. It turned out that the results for case K were quite insensitive, but those for case W were more sensitive.

How were the computations done?

Markov chain Monte Carlo, after restricting the space to the eigenspace containing 95% of the variance.

If I were doing the problem again, how would I change the approach?

I would not.

What do I see as the contribution of the paper?

To demonstrate a method for smoothing log-odds ratios in a disciplined manner.

Was Bayesian analysis useful in this problem?

Yes, Bayesian methods, particularly the hierarchical structure, were important to the solution.

TEACHING SUGGESTIONS

References for theoretical ideas:

1. Weiner process: Kleinbaum, D.G. and Klein, M. (2005). Survival Analysis: A Self-Learning Text, (2nd ed.) Springer, NY, Chapter 3

2. Cox proportional hazard model: Billingsley, P. (1995). Probability and Measure (3rd edition) J. Wiley & Sons, Section 27

3. Markov chain Monte Carlo: *Principles* Chapter 10

4. Principal components decomposition: *Principles* Section 5.8, Theorem 5.8.2

5. Gamma distribution: *Principles* Section 8.4

Exercises

1. Is it useful to think of time in these problems as continuous rather than discrete? Why or why not?

2. Using the data in Table 11.2, plot x/k against time, and draw a smooth curve through the points using your favorite method. How well does the curve represent the points?

3. In Table 11.2, the last column shows that the probability that β is positive drops at both the start and at the end of the period. Why does this occur?

4. In Figure 11.4, which do you prefer: the smooth prior or the continuous prior, and why?

5. Suppose you had been on a jury that heard the case of plaintiff W2, and had been presented with the evidence in this paper. Would you have found in favor of W2? Why or why not?

Chapter 12

Age- and Time-Varying Proportional Hazards Models for Employment Discrimination (2010)

Foreword

It turned out that George and I were not done with this topic yet. The impetus was partly legal. In our previous work (papers #3 and 11 in this volume), we had categorized employees as being either over 40 or under 40. But legally, that is not the whole story. Suppose an employer replaces employees in their 60s with others in their 40s. Both are in the protected class. Hence on the basis of our previous work, the 60s have a valid claim, because they are over 40 and they were replaced, in this hypothetical, because of their age. Thus, to be most helpful to the court, age, as well as time, should be treated as a continuous variable.

The results of such analysis are shown in Figures 12.11 and 12.2 in the paper. Figure 12.1 plots the median log odds relative to under 40 employees, with stripes marked for the day that employee W1 in case W was fired, and W1's age at that time. Because the point of intersection is above the grey surface, this is evidence that employee W1 was disproportionately disadvantaged by age. How sure can we be of this conclusion? That's addressed in Figure 12.2, which shows that the posterior probability of disproportionate disadvantage is about 70%.

Technically we use a thin-plate spline as a bivariate smoothness prior, generalizing our prior in paper #11. We used the same intuition as in paper #11 to find a prior for the smoothness parameter. However, there is a new parameter introduced because we are dealing with smoothing in two dimensions, namely an anisotropy parameter ρ, which governs the relative amount of smoothing by age and time.

The anisotropy parameter turned out to be difficult to deal with. We ultimately decided to permit only six values for it (8, 4, 2, 1, 0.5 and 0.25). We also conducted a sensitivity analysis on our priors on the smoothness and anisotropy parameters. However, we were at the edge of what was feasible to compute at the time, especially with respect to anisotropy.

Revisiting a topic because there is an unsatisfying aspect of previous work happens from time-to-time, and contributes to a deeper understanding of the issues. The earlier work is not necessarily wrong, just incomplete.

This paper was originally in the *Annals of Applied Statistics*, **4**, (#3), pp. 1139–1157. The Institute of Mathematical Statistics does not require permission to republish.

Published Paper

George Woodworth and Joseph B. Kadane

Abstract

We use a discrete-time proportional hazards model of time to involuntary employment termination. This model enables us to examine both the continuous effect of the age of an employee and whether that effect has varied over time, generalizing earlier work (Kadane and Woodworth, 2004). We model the log hazard surface (over age and time) as a thin-plate spline, a Bayesian smoothness-prior implementation of penalized likelihood methods of surface-fitting (Wahba, 1990). The nonlinear component of the surface has only two parameters, smoothness and anisotropy. The first, a scale parameter, governs the overall smoothness of the surface, and the second, anisotropy, controls the relative smoothness over time and over age. For any fixed value of the anisotropy parameter, the prior is equivalent to a Gaussian process with linear drift over the time-age plane with easily computed eigenvectors and eigenvalues that depend only on the configuration of data in the time-age plane and the anisotropy parameter. This model has application to legal cases in which a company is charged with disproportionately disadvantaging older workers when deciding whom to terminate. We illustrate the application of the modeling approach using data from an actual discrimination case.

Keywords and phrases: Age discrimination, thin plate spline, smoothness prior, discrete proportional hazards, semiparametric Bayesian logistic regression.

12.1 Introduction

Federal law prohibits discrimination in employment decisions on the basis of age. There are two different bases on which a case may be brought alleging age discrimination. First, in a disparate impact case, the intent of the defendant is not at issue, but only the effect of the defendant's actions on the protected class, namely, those forty or older. For example, a rule requiring new hires to have attained bachelor's degrees after 1995 would be facially neutral, but would have the effect of preventing the hiring of older applicants. For such a case, data analysis is essential to see whether the data support disproportionate disadvantage to persons over 40 years of age with respect to whatever employment practices might be in question. Those practices might include hiring, salary, promotion and/or involuntary termination. A disparate treatment case, by contrast, claims intentional discrimination on the basis of age. Malevolent action, as well as intention, must be shown in a disparate treatment case. While statistics can address the defendant's actions in a disparate treatment case, usually intent is beyond what data alone can address.

This paper uses a proportional hazards model as the likelihood (Cox, 1972). Finkelstein and Levin (1994) used such a model using as dependent variable the positive part of (age −40) as an explanatory variable. Kadane and Woodworth (2004) treat age as a continuous variable, but do not model the response as a function of calendar time. This paper models both age and time continuously. This choice enables us to examine both the effect of age of an employee on employment decisions (our example uses involuntary terminations) and whether that effect has varied over time. Hence, there are two continuous variables, time and the age of the employee. In this way, the work here generalizes our earlier work (Kadane and Woodworth, 2004) that allowed continuous time, but reduced age to a binary variable (over 40/under 40). The analysis presented here allows us to address the extent to which a pattern or practice of age-based discrimination extends over a period of time. Proportional hazards regression is particularly suited to a pattern or practice case because it concerns the probability or odds of a person of a given age being involuntarily terminated relative to that of a person of another age (or range of ages), and hence directly addresses whether an older person is disproportionately disadvantaged.

We choose to use Bayesian inference because we find that it directly gives the probability that a person of a given age at a particular time is more likely to be fired than another person of a given other age at the same time. This contrasts with sampling-theory methods that give probabilities in the sample space, even after the sample is observed (Kadane, 1990b). When combined with sensitivity analysis, Bayesian analysis permits us to assess the relative influence of the data and the model. We undertook the line of research in Kadane and Woodworth (2004) and in this paper to deal with temporally-sparse employment actions taken over a long time period. We particularly wanted to avoid the need to aggregate data into arbitrary time periods–months, quarters, years, etc.–in order to apply Cochran-Armitage type tests and the like.

12.2 Proportional Hazards Regression

The data required to analyze age discrimination in involuntary terminations comprise the beginning and ending dates of each employee's period(s) of employment, that employee's birth date, and the reason advanced by the employer for separation from employment (if it occurred). Table 12.1 is a fragment of the data analyzed in Section 12.3, below. Data were obtained for all persons employed by a firm at any time between 06/07/1989 and 11/21/1993. The tenure of the last employee shown is right censored; that is, that employee was still in the work force as of 12/31/1993, and we are consequently unable to determine the time or cause of his or her eventual separation from the firm (involuntary termination, death, retirement, etc.).

Table 12.1: Flow data for the period June 1, 1989 to December 31, 1993

Birth Date	Entry Date	Separation Date	Reason
⋮	⋮	⋮	⋮
3/1/1925	3/1/1961	6/1/1990	Vol[a]
4/9/1938	4/8/1961	8/17/1992	Vol
10/17/1934	4/5/1962	6/3/1992	Invol
12/9/1939	4/7/1962	12/18/1991	Invol
11/29/1932	5/29/1962	8/26/1989	Invol
9/5/1928	10/27/1962	6/12/1991	Vol
5/31/1941	1/12/1963	n/a	n/a
⋮	⋮	⋮	⋮

[a] "Voluntary" termination includes death and retirement.

12.2.1 Overview

The purpose of our statistical analysis is to determine how an employee's risk of termination depends on his or her age and how the risk for employees of a given age changes with time. The idea is to estimate a surface such as the one in Figure 12.1 in such a way that it balances a penalty for infidelity to the data and for a penalty for a surface that is unrealistically "rough" (Gersch, 1982). The result is a surface that is generally within the margins of sampling error but is also smooth. Smoothness, generally speaking, amounts to not having areas of high curvature (i.e., spikes, cliffs, buttes, sharp creases, etc.). The idea is to get a good fit to the data without sacrificing smoothness.

The mesh surface in Figure 12.1 is derived from a thin-plate spline model of the log odds (logit) of the probability of involuntary termination at a given time and age. The vertical axis shows the posterior median log odds ratio of termination for employees of a given age on a given date relative to the weighted average rate for employees aged 39 years or younger on the same date (the legally unprotected class often used by statistical experts as a reference class for claims of disparate impact[1]). The gray plane corresponds to odds ratios equal to 1.00, indicating no age discrimination relative to the reference class; points above this plane exhibit discrimination. Although the underlying thin plate spline is smooth, the log-odds ratio surface is locally slightly rough because the observed numbers of employees in each age bin at the time of each termination were used as weights in computing the termination rate in the reference class.

The black ribbon in Figure 12.1 is the trajectory of the log-odds ratio over time for employees aged 56-57, and the dashed ribbon is the log-odds ratio as a function of age on day 1121 (05/30/92), the date of the involuntary termination of 57-year old plaintiff W1 in Case W described in Kadane and Woodworth (2004). The height of the surface at their intersection (0.297) is the posterior median log odds on the involuntary termination of 56-57 year-old employees relative to those under 40 on that date.

Figure 12.2 shows the posterior probability of age discrimination relative to under-40 employees as a function of age and date. Points above the gray plane represent dates and ages at which there was at least 70% posterior probability of age discrimination. By itself, this would be comparatively weak evidence; however, Kadane (1990a) commenting on empirical research by Mosteller and Youtz (1990), suggests that this level of probability could, in standard usage, be said to make it "likely" that discrimination had occurred. The height of the surface at the intersection of the dashed and black ribbons (0.79) is the posterior probability that employees aged 56-57 were terminated at a higher rate compared to under-40 employees.

12.2.2 Proportional Hazards Models for Time to Event Data

We are analyzing a group of individuals at risk for a particular type of failure (involuntary termination) for all or part of an observation period. The jth person enters the risk set at time h_j (either his/her date of hire or the beginning of the observation period) and leaves the risk set at time T_j either by failure (involuntary termination), or for other reasons (death, voluntary resignation, reassignment, retirement), or was still em-

---

[1]Note, however, that Mr. Justice Scalia's majority opinion in *O'Connor v. Consolidated Coin Caterers Corp.*, 517 U.S. 308 (1996) states that "though the prohibition is limited to individuals who are at least 40 years of age, §631(a). This language does not ban discrimination against employees because they are aged 40 or older; it bans discrimination against employees because of their age, but limits the protected class to those who are 40 or order. The fact that one person in the protected class has lost out to another person in the protected class is thus irrelevant, so long as he has lost out *because of his age*."

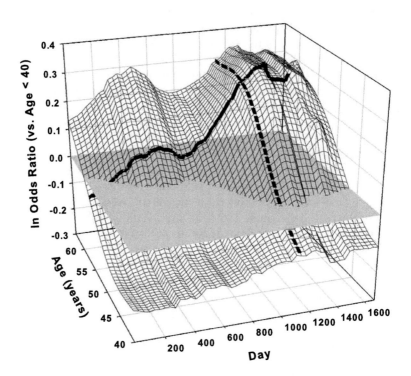

Figure 12.1: Smooth-model-derived log-odds of termination relative to under-40 employees.

ployed at the end of the observation period. The survival function $S_j(t) = P(T_j > t)$ is the probability that the jth employee is still employed at time t.

In practice, we rescale time and age to the unit interval $[0,1]$ and, to make computations tractable, discretize each to a finite grid; $0 = t_0 < t_1, < \cdots < t_p = 1$, $0 = a_0 < a_1, < \cdots < a_r = 1$. Let p_{iw} be the conditional probability that employee (worker) w is terminated in the interval $(t_{i-1}, t_i]$ given the parameters and given that s(he) was in the workforce at time t_{j-1}. The discretized data for this employee are $f_{iw}, \cdots, f_{pw}; r_{iw}, \cdots, r_{pw}$ where $r_{iw} = 1(0)$ if the employee was (not) in the work force (risk set) at time t_{i-1}, and $f_{iw} = 1(0)$ if the worker was (not) involuntarily terminated (fired) in that interval. The joint likelihood for all employees is, $\prod_{w=1}^{W} \prod_{i=1}^{p} p_{iw}^{f_{iw}} (1 - p_{iw})^{r_{iw} - f_{iw}}$, where W is the total number of employees. Letting $a_w(t)$ denote the age of employee w at time t, we use the natural parametrization $\text{logit}(\text{p}_{\text{iw}}) = \beta(t_i, a_w(t_i))$, where $\beta(t, a)$ is a smooth function of time and age.

The aggregated data n_{ij} and x_{ij} are, respectively, the number of employees with ages in the interval $[a_{j-1}, a_j)$ at time t_i and the number of those who were terminated in that interval. At this level of aggregation, the likelihood is

$$l(\beta) = \prod_{i=1}^{p} \prod_{j=1}^{r} exp\left(\beta_{ij} x_{ij} - n_{ij} \ln\left(1 + \exp\left(\beta_{\text{ij}}\right)\right)\right), \tag{12.1}$$

where $\beta_{ij} = \beta(t_i, a_j)$. We assume that the grid is fine enough and the function smooth enough that variation of β within a grid cell is negligible. Changing the grid requires

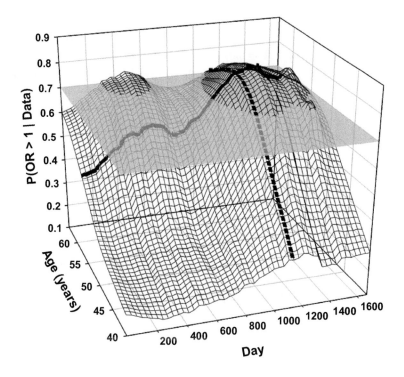

Figure 12.2: Probability of age discrimination relative to under-40 employees.

recomputing the cell counts, (n_{ij}, x_{ij}) and basis vectors defined below, which is fairly time consuming. We did a few runs with a grid roughly twice as fine (which quadrupled the run time and storage requirements) without observing substantive changes in the results; however, we focused our sensitivity analysis on varying the prior distribution of the smoothness parameter, which appeared to have much greater impact on the results. We compute the log odds ratio at time t_i for employees aged a_j relative to unprotected employees (i.e., employees under age 40) as

$$\beta_{ij} - \text{logit}\left(\sum_{\text{age}_u \leq 40} n_{iu} p_{iu} \Big/ \sum_{\text{age}_u \leq 40} n_{iu}\right), \tag{12.2}$$

where age_u is age in years corresponding to scaled value a_u, and $\text{logit}(p_{ij}) = \beta_{ij}$.

12.2.3   Thin-Plate Spline Smoothness Priors

Likelihood measures fidelity to data (the larger the better); however, it does not incorporate our belief that the hazard ratio varies comparatively smoothly with time and age; this is provided by a roughness penalty (the smaller the better) that is subtracted from the log-likelihood,

$$\frac{\lambda}{2} \iint \left[\left(\frac{\partial^2 \beta(t,a)}{\partial^2 t}\right)^2 + 2\left(\frac{\partial^2 \beta(t,a)}{\partial t \partial a}\right)^2 + \left(\frac{\partial^2 \beta(t,a)}{\partial^2 a}\right)^2 \right] dt da. \tag{12.3}$$

The smoothness parameter, λ, weights the importance of smoothness relative to fidelity to noisy data (larger values of the smoothness parameter produces smoother fitted surfaces). However, there is no reason to expect the log odds to be *isotropic*–equally smooth in time and age–and for that reason we assume that there is a rescaling $T = t/\sqrt{1+\rho^2}$, and $A = \rho a/\sqrt{1+\rho^2}$, such that the function $b(T, A) = \beta\left(T\sqrt{1+\rho^2}, A\sqrt{1+\rho^2}/\rho\right)$ is equally smooth (isotropic) in A and T. That is, the roughness penalty is

$$\frac{\lambda}{2} \iint \left[\left(\frac{\partial^2 b(T, A)}{\partial^2 T}\right)^2 + 2\left(\frac{\partial^2 b(T, A)}{\partial T \partial A}\right)^2 + \left(\frac{\partial^2 b(T, A)}{\partial^2 A}\right)^2 \right] dT dA, \qquad (12.4)$$

which reduces to the anisotropic roughness penalty,

$$\frac{\tilde{\lambda}}{2} \iint \left[\left(\frac{\rho^2}{1+\rho^2}\frac{\partial^2 \beta(t, a)}{\partial^2 t}\right)^2 + 2\left(\frac{\rho}{1+\rho^2}\frac{\partial^2 \beta(t, a)}{\partial t \partial a}\right)^2 + \left(\frac{1}{1+\rho^2}\frac{\partial^2 \beta(t, a)}{\partial^2 a}\right)^2 \right] dt da, \qquad (12.5)$$

where ρ is called the anisotropy parameter and $\tilde{\lambda} = \lambda\rho^3/(1+\rho^2)$. When $\rho = 1$ the surface is isotropic, and as $\rho \to \infty$ (or $\rho \to 0$), there is relatively less constraint on roughness in the age (or time) dimension.

It is interesting to compare this model to the earlier one of Finkelstein and Levin (1994), which is a special case of ours. In their case, our function $\beta(\cdot, \cdot)$ takes the form

$$\beta(t_i, a_w(t_i)) = (a_w(t_i) - 40)^+.$$

Since that function has zero second partial derivatives (except at 40, where they do not exist), their function imposes smoothness in our sense. One could think of this computationally as setting $\lambda = 0$.

Since the likelihood depends on the smooth function $\beta(t, a)$ only through the values β_{ij}, the roughness penalty is minimized for fixed β_{ij} when $\beta(t, a)$ is the interpolating thin-plate spline with values $\beta(t_i, a_j) = \beta_{ij}$. We have from Wahba [1990, page 31, eq. 2.4.9] that there exist coefficients c such that the isotropic thin plate spline $b(T, A)$ can be represented as

$$b(T, A) = \sum_{ij} c_{ij} H(T - T_i, A - A_j) + l(T, A), \qquad (12.6)$$

where $l(T, A)$ is an arbitrary linear function, $H(\mathbf{v}) = |\mathbf{v}|^2 \ln(|\mathbf{v}|)/(8\pi)$, and the coefficients c_{ij} satisfy the conditions: $\sum_{ij} c_{ij} = \sum_{ij} t_i c_{ij} = \sum_{ij} a_j c_{ij} = 0$. Then the isotropic roughness penalty, equation (12.4), reduces to $\lambda \mathbf{c}' \mathbf{K}_\rho \mathbf{c}$, where $\mathbf{c}$ is the vector of coefficients and $\mathbf{K}_\rho$ is the $pr \times pr$ symmetric matrix with elements of the form $k_{ij,uv} = H(T_i - T_u, A_j - A_v) = H\left(\frac{(t_i-t_u)}{\sqrt{1+\rho^2}}, \frac{\rho(a_j-a_v)}{\sqrt{1+\rho^2}}\right)$. To accommodate the constraints on vector $\mathbf{c}$, let $\mathbf{P}$ be the projection onto the linear space orthogonal to the constraints so that $\mathbf{c} = \mathbf{Pc}$.

Finally, let $\mathbf{PK}_\rho \mathbf{P} = \mathbf{U}_\rho \mathbf{\Lambda}_\rho \mathbf{U}_\rho'$ be the spectral decomposition of $\mathbf{PK}_\rho \mathbf{P}$ and define the basis vectors $\mathbf{B}_\rho$ as the nonzero columns of $\mathbf{U}_\rho \mathbf{\Lambda}_\rho^{1/2}$. It follows that the model for the vector of logits is

$$
\begin{aligned}
\beta &= \mathbf{K}_\rho \mathbf{c} + \mathbf{L}\tilde{\phi} \\
&= \mathbf{K}_\rho \mathbf{Pc} + \mathbf{L}\tilde{\phi} \\
&= \mathbf{PK}_\rho \mathbf{Pc} + (\mathbf{I} - \mathbf{P})\mathbf{K}_\rho \mathbf{Pc} + \mathbf{L}\tilde{\phi},
\end{aligned}
\qquad (12.7)
$$

where β is the matrix with ijth row β_{ij} and the ijth row of matrix $\mathbf{L}$ is $(1, t_i, a_j)$. But $\mathbf{I} - \mathbf{P}$ is the projection onto the column space of $\mathbf{L}$ and, consequently, $(\mathbf{I} - \mathbf{P})\,\mathbf{K}_\rho\mathbf{Pc}$ can be absorbed into the linear term. Therefore, the model reduces to

$$
\begin{aligned}
\beta &= \mathbf{PK}_\rho\mathbf{Pc} + (\mathbf{I} - \mathbf{P})\,\mathbf{K}_\rho\mathbf{Pc} + \mathbf{L}\tilde{\phi} \\
&= \mathbf{U}_\rho\mathbf{\Lambda}_\rho^{\frac{1}{2}}\left(\mathbf{\Lambda}_\rho^{\frac{1}{2}}\mathbf{U}_\rho\mathbf{c}\right) + \mathbf{L}\phi \\
&= \mathbf{B}_\rho\delta + \mathbf{L}\phi
\end{aligned}
\tag{12.8}
$$

where $\delta = \mathbf{\Lambda}_\rho^{\frac{1}{2}}\mathbf{U}_\rho\mathbf{c}$ and $\mathbf{B}_\rho = \mathbf{U}_\rho\mathbf{\Lambda}_\rho^{\frac{1}{2}}$. Thus, for a given anisotropy, ρ, the columns of $\mathbf{B}_\rho$ are basis vectors for the nonlinear part of the logit vector β.

The roughness penalty is, $\lambda\mathbf{c}'\mathbf{K}_\rho\mathbf{c} = \lambda\mathbf{c}'\mathbf{PK}_\rho\mathbf{Pc} = \lambda\mathbf{c}'\mathbf{U}_\rho\mathbf{\Lambda}_\rho\mathbf{Uc} = \lambda\delta'\delta$. The standard Bayesian interpretation of penalized likelihood estimation is that the penalty function is the log of the prior density of δ. Consequently, the components of that vector are a-priori independent and identically distributed normal random variables with precision λ. It follows that the prior conditional variance of β given λ, ρ and ϕ is

$$
\begin{aligned}
Var\,(\mathbf{B}_\rho\delta) &= \lambda^{-1}\mathbf{B}_\rho\mathbf{B}_\rho' \\
&= \lambda^{-1}\mathbf{PK}_\rho\mathbf{P}
\end{aligned}
$$

and, consequently, if $\mathbf{d}$ is a vector such that $\mathbf{d}'\mathbf{L} = 0$, then

$$
\mathrm{Var}\,(\mathbf{d}'\beta) = \lambda^{-1}\mathbf{d}'\mathbf{K}_\rho\mathbf{d}.
\tag{12.9}
$$

The posterior distributions of λ and ρ are not well identified by the data and it is necessary to be somewhat careful about specifying their priors. However, the regression coefficients, ϕ, of the linear component do not influence smoothness, are well identified by the data, and can be given diffuse, normal prior distributions.

Viewing both time and age as continuous variables allows a more precise and general view of a firm's policy. However, due to the comparative sparseness of the data, some constraint on or penalty for roughness is needed to avoid an unrealistically rough model, unlike that depicted in Figure 12.1. It is, of course, possible to introduce discrete discontinuities into an otherwise smooth model at time points where there is other evidence of a shift in employment practices [see, for example, Figure 6 in Kadane and Woodworth (2004), i.e., Figure 11.6 in this volume]. However, we do not think that it is appropriate to "mine" for unknown numbers of discontinuities at unknown time points in the sparse data common in age-discrimination cases. Hence, it is necessary to smooth the data. The key parameters in doing so are smoothness and anisotropy. The smoothness parameter controls the average smoothness of the surface and the anisotropy parameter controls the relative degree of smoothing in the age and time coordinates.

12.3 Case W Revisited

Over an observation period of about 1600 days the workforce at a firm was reduced by about two thirds; 103 employees were involuntarily terminated in the process. A new CEO took control at day 862, near the middle of the observation period. The plaintiff asserted that employees aged 50 and above were targeted for termination under the influence of the new CEO. Here we present a fully Bayesian analysis with smoothly time- and age-varying odds ratio. The personnel data were aggregated by status (involuntarily terminated, other) into one-week time intervals and two-year age intervals (20-21, 22-23, ..., 64-65). Figures 12.1 and 12.2 show posterior medians and posterior probabilities of age-related discrimination (i.e., of increased odds of termination relative to unprotected employees).

12.3.1 Forming an Opinion about Smoothness and Anisotropy

The anisotropy parameter ρ governs the relative smoothness in time relative to age. This is clearly illustrated in Figure 12.3, which shows the seventh eigensurface (basis function) for (a) the isotropic case where there is about one cycle in either direction in contrast to (b) the anisotropic case $\rho = 4$ in which the surface is four times rougher in the age dimension (there are about 3 half cycles in the age dimension to about 3/4 of a half cycle in the time dimension).

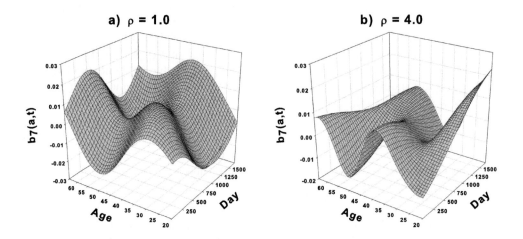

Figure 12.3: Effect of anisotropy on the 7th basis function.

In the context of employment discrimination we think that, in terms of roughness of the logit, a 3 year age difference is about equivalent to a business quarter. Recalling that we have rescaled 1600 calendar days and a 45-year age span into unit intervals, a quarter is 0.056 and a three-year age interval is 0.067 of the unit interval, corresponding to anisotropy $\rho = 1.2$. We have found empirically that doubling or halving anisotropy has a fairly modest effect on surface shape; consequently, we used the prior distribution shown in Table 12.2, which has prior geometric mean 1.4.

Table 12.2: Prior Distribution of the Anisotropy Parameter

ρ	8	4	2	1	0.5	0.25
Prior	0.08	0.16	0.26	0.26	0.16	0.08

Larger ρ-values favor smoothness in time.

As in our earlier analysis of this case (Kadane and Woodworth, 2004), we now derive a prior distribution for the smoothness parameter from our belief that the odds ratio on termination for a 10-year age difference are unlikely to change more than 15% over a business quarter. This implies that a particular mixed difference is unlikely to exceed 0.15 in absolute value; i.e., Prior $\left(\ell \left| \Delta_t^2 \Delta_a \beta\left(t_0, a_0\right)\right| \le 0.15\right)$ is large, where

$$\Delta_t^2 \Delta_a \beta\left(t_0, a_0\right) = \beta\left(t_0 + 2d_t, a_0 + d_a\right) - 2\beta\left(t_0 + d_t, a_0 + d_a\right) + \beta\left(t_0, a_0 + d_a\right)$$
$$-\beta\left(t_0 + 2d_t, a_0\right) + 2\beta\left(t_0 + d_t, a_0\right) - \beta\left(t_0, a_0\right),$$

where d_t is a rescaled half-quarter and d_a is a rescaled decade. We have from equation (12.9) above that the prior distribution of $\Delta_t^2 \Delta_a \beta\left(t_0, a_0\right)$ is normal with mean zero and conditional variance, $\mathbf{d'Hd}/\lambda = V_\rho/\lambda$, where $\mathbf{H}$ is the matrix with entries $H\left(T_i - T_{i'}, A_j - A_{j'}\right)$, $\mathbf{d}$ is the vector $(1, -2, 1, -1, 2, -1)$, $T_i = (t_0 + td_t)/\sqrt{1 + \rho^2}$, $i = 0, 1, 2$, and $A_j = \rho\left(a_0 + jd_a\right)/\sqrt{1 + \rho^2}$, $j = 0, 1$. Values of V_ρ are listed in Table 12.3.

The conditional prior distribution of the smoothness parameter given the anisotropy parameter is gamma with shape parameter and scale parameter selected so that Prior $\left(\left|\Delta_t^2 \Delta_a \beta\left(t_0, a_0\right)\right| \leq 0.15\right) = 1 - \alpha$ is large. To complete the derivation, we have, conditional on ρ, that

$$\left[\Delta_t^2 \Delta_a \beta\left(t_0, a_0\right)\right]^2 \backsim V_\rho \cdot \frac{sc_\rho \Gamma\left(0.05\right)}{\Gamma\left(sh_\rho\right)} \sim V_\rho \cdot sc_\rho \frac{1 - \beta\left(sh_\rho, 0.05\right)}{\beta\left(sh_\rho, 0.05\right)},$$

where, abusing the notation somewhat, we let $\Gamma\left(sh\right)$ denote an independent gamma-distributed random variable with shape parameter sh, and let $\beta\left(sh, 0.5\right)$ denote a beta-distributed random variable. Consequently, if

$$\text{Prior}\left(\left[\Delta_t^2 \Delta_a \beta\left(t_0, a_0\right)\right]^2 \leq 0.15^2\right) = 1 - \alpha,$$

then

$$sc_\rho = \frac{0.15^2 \beta_\alpha\left(sh_\rho, 0.5\right)}{V_\rho\left(1 - \beta_\alpha\left(sh_\rho, 0.5\right)\right)},$$

where $\beta_\alpha\left(sh_\rho, 0.5\right)$ is the αth quantile of the $\beta\left(sh_\rho, 0.5\right)$ distribution. The third column of Table 12.3 shows the values of the scale parameter, sc_ρ that we used to compute the surface in Figures 12.1 and 12.2.

Table 12.3: Prior variance$\times \lambda$ of $\Delta_t^2 \Delta_a \beta\left(t_0, a_0\right)$ and prior scale parameter of λ

Anisotropy ρ	V_ρ	sc_ρ for sh_ρ=0.5 and $\alpha = 0.05$
8	0.000383	5.04
4	0.000453	4.26
2	0.000492	3.93
1	0.000449	4.30
0.5	0.000332	5.81
0.25	0.000195	9.90

12.3.2   Computing the Posterior Distribution

To estimate this model, we included enough basis vectors in the last row of equation (12.8) to account for at least 95% of the total roughness variance a priori (i.e., we included basis vectors accounting for 95% of the sum of the eigenvalues of K_ρ). We computed the posterior distribution of the probabilities of involuntary termination, and of the odds ratios relative to under-40 employees in each time-age bin using a program written in SAS IML language. For a given anisotropy value, ρ, we used the Metropolis-Hastings within iteratively reweighted least squares algorithm proposed by Gamerman (1997) to separately update the logistic regression coefficient vectors ϕ and δ, and a Gibbs step to update the smoothness parameter, λ. Anisotropy values were chosen from the six shown in Table 12.2; where, beginning with an arbitrary initial value, we attempted a jump from the current anisotropy value to an adjacent value with transition probabilities from the 6 doubly stochastic matrix shown in Table 12.4. Letting current parameter values be δ, ϕ, λ, and ρ, we attempt a reversible jump,

$\rho \to \tilde{\rho}$. We then propose values $\tilde{\phi} = \phi$, and $\tilde{\lambda} = \rho \cdot sc/\tilde{sc}$, where sc and $\tilde{sc}$ are scale parameters from Table 12.3 corresponding to ρ and $\tilde{\rho}$, respectively. Finally, we generate a proposal for $\tilde{\boldsymbol{\delta}}$ as follows. Let $\beta = \mathbf{B}_\rho\delta + \mathbf{L} \cdot \phi$ be the current logit vector and let $\mathbf{p}$ be the current vector of termination probabilities in time-age bins [i.e., $\mathrm{logit}(\mathbf{p}) = \beta$] and let $\mathbf{q} = 1 - \mathbf{p}$. Let vectors $\mathbf{n}$ and $\mathbf{y}$ be the numbers at risk and terminated in the time-age bins. Then, $\tilde{\boldsymbol{\delta}}$ is proposed from the multivariate normal distribution with precision $\tilde{\boldsymbol{\Pi}} = [\tilde{\lambda} + \mathbf{B}'_{\tilde{\rho}}\mathbf{npq}\mathbf{B}_{\tilde{\rho}}]$ and mean $\tilde{\boldsymbol{\mu}} = \tilde{\boldsymbol{\Pi}}^{-1}\mathbf{B}'_{\tilde{\rho}}\mathbf{npq}\cdot\hat{\mathbf{y}}$ where $\mathbf{B}_\rho$ is the matrix of basis vectors corresponding to anisotropy ρ, as defined in the paragraph after equation (12.8), and $\hat{\mathbf{y}} = \mathbf{B}_\rho\delta + (\mathbf{y} - \mathbf{p})/\mathbf{pq}$. The proposal is accepted with probability

$$\alpha = \min\left[1, \frac{p(\tilde{\rho})p(\tilde{\lambda}|\tilde{\rho})p(\delta|\tilde{\lambda})\ell(\tilde{\beta})}{p(\rho)p(\lambda|\rho)p(\delta|\lambda)\ell(\beta)} \cdot \frac{p(\tilde{\rho} \to \rho)(\delta|\tilde{\lambda}, \tilde{\delta}, \phi)}{p(\rho \to \tilde{\rho})q(\tilde{\delta}|\lambda, \delta, \phi)} \cdot \frac{\partial\tilde{\lambda}}{\partial\lambda}\right]$$

$$= \min\left[1, p(\tilde{\rho})\tilde{\lambda}^{\tilde{q}/2}\exp\left(-\frac{1}{2}\tilde{\lambda}\tilde{\delta}'\tilde{\delta}\right)\ell(\tilde{\beta})\right.$$

$$\times \left|\prod\right|^{0.5}\exp\left(-\frac{1}{2}(\delta - \mu')\prod(\delta - \mu)'\right)$$

$$\left/ \left(p(\rho)\lambda^{q/2}\exp\left(-\frac{1}{2}\lambda\delta'\delta\right)\ell(\beta)\right.\right.$$

$$\left.\left.\times\left|\tilde{\prod}\right|^{0.5}\exp\left(-\frac{1}{2}(\tilde{\delta} - \tilde{\mu})'\tilde{\prod}(\tilde{\delta} - \tilde{\mu})'\right)\right)\right]$$

where $l(\beta)$ is the likelihood function [equation 12.1], q and $\tilde{q}$ are the ranks of B_ρ and $B_{\tilde{\rho}}$, and μ and Π are the mean and precision of the reverse proposal (Green, 1995).

12.3.3 Sensitivity Analysis

It is a good statistical practice to investigate whether and to what extent the results of an analysis are sensitive to the prior distribution. That means in this case investigating the influence of the prior distribution of the smoothness and anisotropy parameters. Figures 12.1 and 12.2 above are based on our preferred prior distribution as specified in Tables 12.2 and 12.3. In Figure 12.3 we compare Figure 12.1(a) with an analysis (b) in which the scale parameters in Table 12.4 are multiplied by 10, decreasing the roughness penalty by a factor of 10 and producing a substantially rougher surface. Figure 12.5 shows the effect of this variation on the probability of discrimination.

Table 12.4: Jump proposal probabilities for the anisotropy parameter.

Anisotropy	8	4	2	1	0.5	0.25
8	0.9	0.1				
4	0.1	0.8	0.1			
2		0.1	0.8	0.1		
1			0.1	0.8	0.1	
0.5				0.1	0.8	0.1
0.25					0.1	0.9

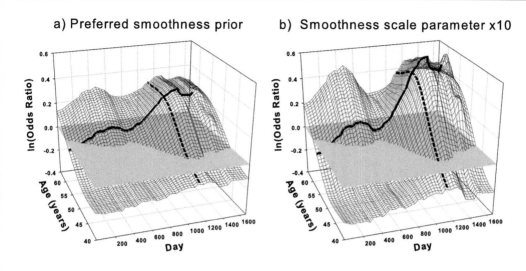

Figure 12.4: Effect of the smoothness prior on the log odds ratio

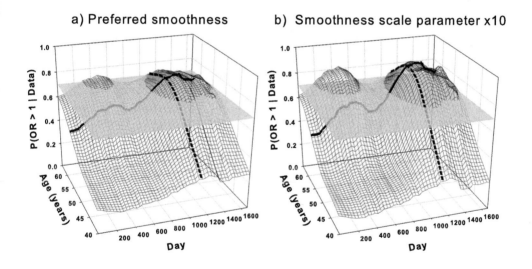

Figure 12.5: Effect of the smoothness prior on the posterior probability of discrimination

12.3.4   Identification of the Anisotropy Parameter

Table 12.5 shows the marginal posterior distribution of the anisotropy parameter for the preferred prior distribution of the smoothness parameter (Table 12.3). The posterior probability $P(\rho|Data)$ is the observed rate of sampler visits to value ρ of the anisotropy parameter in 19,000 replications, the marginal likelihood is $P(\rho|Data)/P(\rho) \propto P(Data|\rho)$, and $p_{0.025}$ and $p_{0.975}$ are nominal Monte-Carlo error bounds computed on the assumption that the observed rate has a binomial distribution.

It is clear from the marginal likelihood that the data carry information about anisotropy and, in particular, that models with large values of ρ (i.e., which are very rough in the time dimension) are disconfirmed by the data. However, high levels of smoothness in the time dimension are not disconfirmed by data and apparently must be discouraged by the prior. Because of this, we investigated the effect of a prior that forces more smoothness in the time dimension.

Table 12.5: Posterior distribution and marginal likelihood of the anisotropy parameter

ρ	Prior	Posterior[a]			Marginal Likelihood		
		$P(\rho\mid Data)$	$p_{0.025}$	$p_{0.975}$	$\propto P(Data\mid\rho)$	$p_{.025}$	$p_{.975}$
8	0.08	0.122	0.12	0.13	1.53	1.47	1.61
4	0.16	0.231	0.22	0.24	1.44	1.40	1.50
2	0.26	0.286	0.28	0.30	1.10	1.07	1.14
1	0.26	0.217	0.21	0.23	0.83	0.81	0.87
0.5	0.16	0.101	0.10	0.11	0.63	0.61	0.67
0.25	0.08	0.043	0.04	0.05	0.54	0.50	0.59

[a]$p_{0.025}$ and $p_{0.975}$ are Monte-Carlo error bounds (see text).

In Figure 12.6 we altered the prior distribution for the anisotropy parameter to favor smoothness in the time dimension (Table 12.6). In this case the prior geometric mean of the anisotropy parameter is about 4, meaning that we think that, in terms of roughness of the log odds on termination, a decade of age is about equivalent to a business quarter (see Section 12.3.1). Evidence of discrimination in the plaintiff's case (the intersection of the dashed and black ribbons) is slightly stronger for the prior that forces more smoothness in the time dimension; $P(OR > 1\mid Data)$ is about 0.79 for the preferred prior (a) and about 0.83 for the more time-smoothing prior (b).

Although the analysis in panel (b) is more favorable to the plaintiff, we think it would be less persuasive to the trier(s) of fact (judge or jury) since it does not seem to distinguish between the periods before and after the arrival of the new CEO (day 862).

Table 12.6: Alternate prior distribution of the anisotropy parameter

ρ	8	4	2	1	0.5	0.25
Prior	0.5	0.25	0.125	0.0625	0.03125	0.03125

Larger ρ-values favor smoothness in time.

12.3.5   *Previous Analyses of Case W*

The plaintiff who was between 50 and 59 years of age was one of 12 employees involuntarily terminated on day 1092. He brought an age discrimination suit against the employer under the theory that the new CEO had a pattern of targeting employees aged 50 and above for termination.

In the original case, the plaintiff's statistical expert tabulated involuntary termination rates for each calendar quarter and each age decade. He reported that, "[Involuntary] separation rates for the [period beginning at day 481] averaged a little above three percent of the workforce per quarter for ages 20 through 49, but jumped to six and a half percent for ages 50 through 59. The 50-59 year age group differed significantly from the 20-39 year age group (signed-rank test, $p = 0.033$, one sided)." The plaintiff alleged and the defendant denied that the new CEO had vowed to weed out older employees. The case was settled before trial.

In a subsequent re-analysis (Kadane and Woodworth, 2004), we employed a pro-

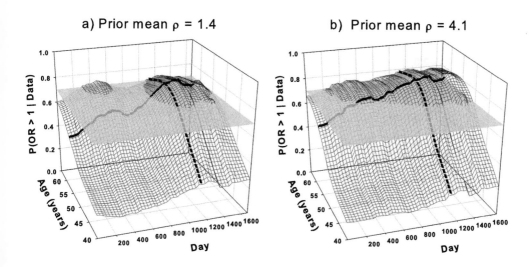

Figure 12.6: Effect of the anisotropy parameter on the posterior probability of discrimination.

portional hazards model with separate, smoothly time-varying log hazard ratios for ages 40-49, and 50-64, with ages 20-39 as the reference category. Thus the log hazard ratio was smooth over time but piecewise constant over age; Figure 12.7, is reproduced with permission from that paper. Our preferred model, represented by the solid curves, had prior mean smoothness 0.007. For this prior the posterior probability of age-discrimination in the case of Plaintiff W1 was 0.842.

The model depicted in Figure 12.7 has two explanatory variables for age, an indicator variable for age in the range 40-49 and an indicator variable for age 50 and above (there are no employees 65 and over in the data set). The likelihood model was proportional hazards regression with smoothly time-varying coefficients for the two explanatory variables. Three analyses are shown here with different prior means for the smoothness parameter, λ. The upper panel shows posterior means of the proportional-hazards regression coefficients as functions of time and the smoothness parameter. As suggested in the figure, the regression coefficients are interpretable as instantaneous log odds ratios with unprotected, under-40, employees as the reference category. The second panel presents posterior probabilities that the two regression coefficients are positive; that is, that the termination rate is higher for the protected subclasses compared to the unprotected class. For example, at the time of plaintiff W2's termination, the posterior probability exceeds 80% that employees age 50 and above had a higher risk of termination than the protected class.

A second plaintiff, W2 aged 60 terminated on day 733, also brought an age-discrimination suit on the theory that employees aged 60 and above were disproportionately targeted at the time of his termination. On that day three of eight employees (37.5%) aged 60 and up were terminated compared to 15 of 136 (11.0%) employees terminated out of all other age groups (one-sided Fisher exact test $p=0.0530$). In our re-analysis the posterior probability of age discrimination against employees aged 50-64 was about 50% but did not distinguish between employees aged 50-59 and 60-64. Our second re-analysis reported in this paper remedies that deficiency and gives a more detailed picture of the impact of age on the risk of discrimination; in particular, for our preferred prior, the posterior probability of age discrimination against

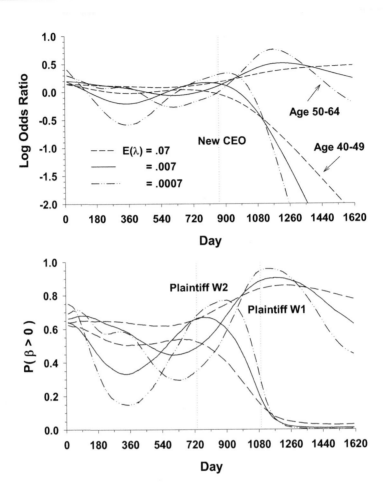

Figure 12.7: Smooth by piecewise constant proportional hazards model.

60-year old employees on day 733 is about 65% but is only about 37% for 50-year old employees.

12.3.6 *Summary*

Table 12.7 summarizes the results of the three analyses of case W for each of the two plaintiffs. In the first, classical, analyses for Plaintiff W1, it is assumed that each employee in the age groups 20-39 and 50-59 has the same chance of being involuntarily terminated (i.e., fired) in each quarter-year after day 481. The test of significance calculates the probability of obtaining data as or more extreme than that observed were it true that persons in these two age groups have the same chance of being fired in any given quarter. The classical analysis for plaintiff W2 is somewhat different, in that it focuses solely on what happened on the day that W2 was fired. It conditions on both the age distribution of the workforce at the time (eight of 144 employees 60 years old or older) and the number fired (18) and computes the probability of three or more of the eight older employees being fired, if employees were equally likely to be fired.

Table 12.7: Summary of three analyses of case W

Analysis	Method	Figure of Merit	Treatment of Age	Age × Time Interaction	Plaintiff	
					W1	**W2**
Original Expert's Report	Frequentist	*p*-value	categorical: 40-up	none	0.033	0.053
Kadane and Woodworth (2004)	Bayesian	probability of disproportional disadvantage	categorical: 40–49, 50–64	smooth	0.84	0.50
				smooth/w discontinuity at day 862	0.88	0.49
This paper	Bayesian	probability of disproportional disadvantage	smooth	smooth	0.65	0.37
Anonymous referee of this paper	Cox regression	*p*-value, OR, and 90% LCL	linear above 40	none but restricted to day 1000 up	*p*:0.041 OR: 2.04 LCL: 1.01	n/a

The second analysis is based on a model for the log-odds of being fired that is continuous in time but still assumes constancy in age categories. The analysis of this paper relaxes this latter assumption, and allows smoothness in both age and time. In both Bayesian analyses, the probability computed is that an employee of a given age was more likely to be fired at a particular time than was an employee in the unprotected 20-39 age group.

Although the classical analyses are computing probabilities in the sample space while the Bayesian analyses are computing probabilities in the parameter space, the stronger effect here appears to be that as the assumptions get less rigid, there is less certainty that these plaintiffs' cases were meritorious, as Table 12.7 shows. In view of the tendency of Bayesian analyses to draw estimates toward each other, this is perhaps not too surprising.

12.4 Discussion

In a nonhierarchical model, the effect of the prior can be isolated by separately reporting the likelihood function and the prior distribution. In particular, if the parameter space is divided into two disjoint subsets, the likelihood ratio and the prior odds suffice. However, in a hierarchical model such as this one, such a separation is not possible. For this reason, we have reported the results of changing our prior directly, in Sections 12.3.3, 12.3.4 and 12.3.5.

We have presented a global analysis of involuntary terminations that incorporates all of the data but reflects fine-grained variations over time and age of employee. The results are somewhat sensitive to assumptions about prior distribution of the smoothness parameter, although not enough to materially alter the strength of evidence supporting the plaintiff's discrimination claim in Case W. This analysis, in our view, casts new light on the apparent patterns in coarser-grained descriptive presentations that might be easier for nonspecialists to grasp.

Our intent is to develop a methodology that does not require complex assumptions about the relationship between time, age and risk of termination. Indeed, the only structural assumption is smoothness and the only prior opinion required has to do with the degree of smoothness. We have suggested how that prior opinion could be elicited by considering how rapidly the risk of termination is likely to change over a business quarter and over a decade of age. A referee described our analysis as "staggeringly complex" and "shuddered to think what a judge or jury would make of this approach."

All statistical analyses are "staggeringly complex" to most laypersons. We think our responsibility as statisticians (and experts in court) is to present our best analysis of the data, and to explain it as best as we can.

A global analysis such as this one is more powerful and more appropriate than analyzing subsets of the data, perhaps in the form of individual termination waves or individual business quarters, and more appropriate than analyzing coarse aggregations such as employees aged 40 and above compared to younger employees. The fallacy of subdividing the data is that such analyses implicitly assume that there is no continuity in the behavior of a firm and no difference in treatment of employees of different ages within the same broad age category (40 and older). We believe that the appropriate approach to possible inhomogeneities of the age effect is to incorporate them in a global model–see for example, our discussion of Gastwirth's (1992) analysis in Valentino v. United States Postal Service (Gastwirth, 1992; Kadane and Woodworth, 2004).

Finally, it has not escaped our notice that our analysis of Case W has made it clear that only a subgroup of older employees, centered around the peak at day 1275 and age 54-55, has even moderately strong statistical evidence to support a claim of age discrimination. We believe that this is precisely the information that the court needs in order to determine how an award (if any) should be distributed among members of a certified class.

Supplementary Material

Supplement A: Employment – Case W (DOI: 10.1214/10-AOAS330SUPPA;.txt). Data from two cases described in the paper "Hierarchical models for employment decisions," by Kadane and Woodworth. A constant number of days has been subtracted from each date to preserve confidentiality.

Supplement B: Code for calculations (DOI: 10.1214/10-AOAS330SUPPB;.zip).

REFERENCES

Cox, D. (1972). "Regression models and life-tables." *Journal of the Royal Statistical Society Series B*, 34, 187–220. MR034178. 229

Finkelstein, M. and Levin, B. (1994). "Proportional Hazard Models for Age Discrimination Cases." *Jurimetrics Journal*, 34, 153–171. 229, 234

Gamerman, D. (1997). "Sampling from the posterior distribution in generalized linear mixed models." *Statistics and Computing*, 7, 57, 57–68. 237

Gastwirth, J. (1992). "Employment discrimination: A statistician's look at analysis of disparate impact claims." *Law and Inequality: A Journal of Theory and Practice*, 11, 1, 151–179. 244

Gersch, W. (1982). "Smoothness priors." In *Encyclopedia of Statistical Sciences*, eds. S. Kotz, N. L. Johnson, and C. B. Read, vol. 8, 518–526. John Wiley & Sons. 231

Green, P. (1995). "Reversible jump Markov chain Monte Carlo computation and Bayesian model determination." *Biometrika*, 82, 4, 711–732. MR1380810. 238

Kadane, J. (1990a). "Comment: Codifying chance." *Statistical Science*, 5, 18–20. 231

— (1990b). "A Statistical Analysis of Adverse Impact of Employer Decisions." *Journal of the American Statistical Association*, 85, 925–933. 230

Kadane, J. and Woodworth, G. (2004). "Hierarchical Models for Employment Decisions." *Journal of Business and Economic Statistics*, 22, 2, 182–193. MR2049920, also Chapter 11 in this volume. 229, 230, 231, 235, 236, 240, 244

Mosteller, F. and Youtz, C. (1990). "Quantifying probabilistic expressions." *Statistical Science*, 5, 2–12. MR1054855. 231

Wahba, G. (1990). *Spline models for observational data*. Philadelphia: Society for Industrial and Applied Mathematics. MR1045442. 229

Epilogue

What is the scientific issue?

How can time and employee age be treated continuously in the context of a disparate treatment employment lawsuit?

Is justification given for

a) the use of the data?

The same data were used as in Chapter 11.

b) the likelihood and prior?

The methods of Chapter 11 could be used separately on time and on employee ages. The novel aspect here is anisotropy, which expresses the relative smoothness in the two continuous dimensions.

What robustness studies were done?

A variety of robustness studies are done on the anisotropy parameter.

How were the computations done?

Markov chain Monte Carlo, but were at the very edge of what we could do.

If I were doing the problem again, how would I change the approach?

I would not, despite a referee finding the method "staggeringly complex."

Was Bayesian analysis useful in this problem?

Yes, I believe it was very useful.

TEACHING SUGGESTIONS

References for theoretical ideas:

1. Thin plate spline: Wahba, G. (1990). Spline models for observational data, SIAM, Philadelphia

2. Markov chain Monte Carlo: *Principles* Chapter 10

3. Reversible jump: *Principles* Section 10.6

Exercises

1. Is it important that age, as well as time, be regarded as a continuous variable in these analyses?

2. Compare the results in this paper to those in paper 11 in this volume with respect to plaintiffs W1 and W2. To what extent are they similar, to what extent are they different? Does this paper (#12) shed new light on those cases? If so, how does it change your view, and why?

3. The paper reports the effects of changes in the prior in Sections 12.3.3, 12.3.4 and 12.3.5. If you could choose one more prior to be tested for robustness, which would it be and why?

4. A referee found the analysis "staggeringly complex." Do you agree? If you were going to use a simpler model on this data, what would it be?

Chapter 13

Error Analysis for Small Angle Neutron Scattering Datasets Using Bayesian Inference (2010)

Foreword

Sara Majetich is an experimental physicist, and a colleague at Carnegie Mellon. As I recall, we started chatting while waiting at the airport, and agreed to meet after we returned from our trips.

What she wanted was a well-based statement of uncertainty about results she was getting from SANS (small angle neutron scattering) experiments she was conducting at the National Institute of Standards. Quickly, Chip Hogg, then a physics graduate student, and Jong Soo Lee, a postdoctoral fellow in statistics, joined our discussions.

It took quite a while to get to a common language and point of view. The physicists were used to running their data through a program that was basically a black box to them, and getting answers quickly. The Bayesian statisticians wanted to know about each potential source of uncertainty, how to parameterize it, and what was reasonably known about it. But gradually we converged. Fortunately, we had a dataset that had been previously analyzed as physicists were used to doing, so we could contrast our results to the traditional ones. (See Table 13.5 and Figure 13.14).

This took us two years to complete, but it is a good example of a real and complicated system analysed Bayesianly with results that add substantively to knowledge.

Where are they now? Charles Hogg works for Google in Pittsburgh. Jong Soo Lee is an Assistant Professor in the Department of Applied Economics and Statistics at the University of Delaware, and Sara Majetich continues as Professor of Physics at Carnegie Mellon University.

This paper was originally published in *Bayesian Analysis*, (with discussion and response), **5**, 1–34. The International Society for Bayesian Analysis does not require permission to republish.

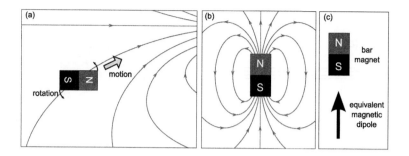

Figure 13.1

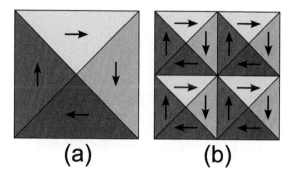

Figure 13.4

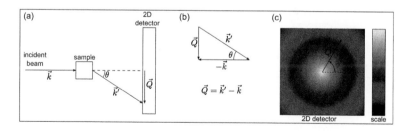

Figure 13.5

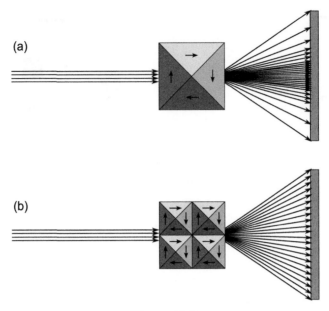

Figure 13.7

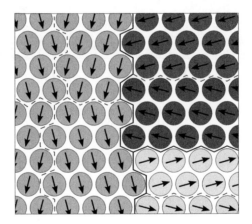

Figure 13.8

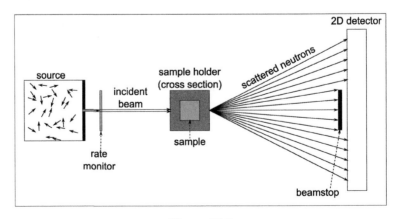

Figure 13.9

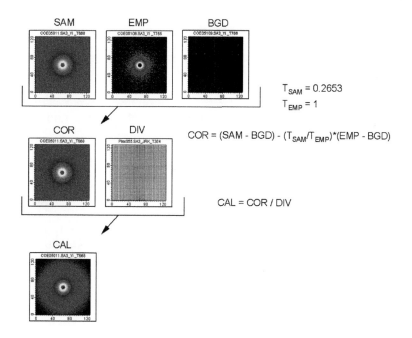

Figure 13.11

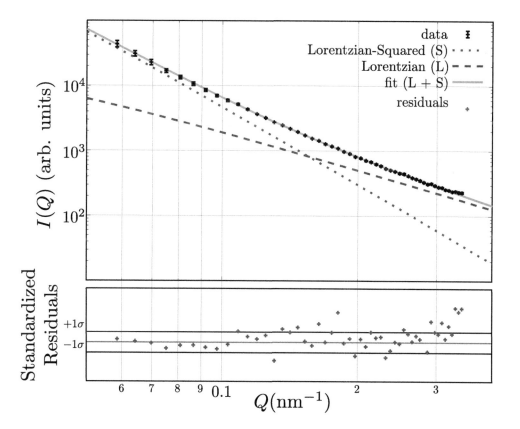

Figure 13.12

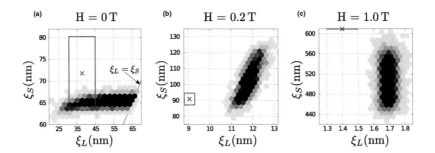

Figure 13.14

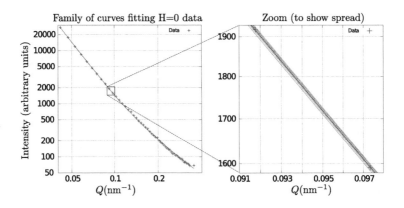

Figure 13.15

Published Paper

Charles R. Hogg, Joseph B. Kadane, Jong Soo Lee and Sara A. Majetich

Abstract

We present a Bayesian methodology for extracting correlation lengths from small-angle neutron scattering (SANS) experiments. For demonstration, we apply the technique to data from
a previous paper, which investigated the presence of dipolar ferromagnetism in assemblies
of ferromagnetic Co nanoparticles. Bayesian analysis confirms the presence of multiparticle
dipolar domains even at zero magnetic field, but higher-field correlation lengths were found
to be much smaller than previously believed, yielding new information on the maximum
lengthscale which the instrument can reliably probe. We use two complementary types of
graph to visualize the results. Plots of standardized residual distributions show quality of fit,
and guide model refinement. These principles can be applied to other types of sample, and
even to other small-angle scattering techniques.

13.1 Introduction

A bar magnet is perhaps the most familiar magnetic object. As illustrated in Figure 13.1, if placed in a magnetic field, the magnet rotates to line up with that field.
Once aligned, it moves in the direction where the field increases most rapidly. It also
generates its own magnetic field, whose pattern is shown in Figure 13.1(b). The bar
magnet is a good example of a more general class of magnetic objects, called magnetic
dipoles (Figure 13.1(c)), which behave in this way.

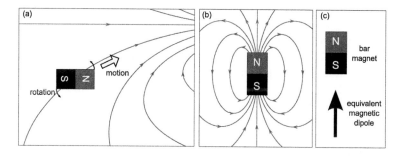

Figure 13.1: (SEE COLOR INSERT) Basic concepts relating to bar magnets and magnetic
dipoles. (a) When placed in a magnetic field (represented by the grey lines), the magnet
rotates until the lines point from the south to the north pole. It also moves in the direction
where the lines are densest, which is where the field is strongest. (b) The magnetic field of a
bar magnet. (c) A bar magnet and its equivalent magnetic dipole representation: an arrow
pointing from the south to the north pole.

Despite their familiarity, important questions remain about their behaviour when
large numbers of magnetic dipoles interact. One key goal is to learn whether, in regular

assemblies of dipoles, large regions spontaneously order to share the same direction, a phenomenon known as dipolar ferromagnetism (Luttinger and Tisza, 1946). Though a vague sense that "magnets prefer to align" might make this seem trivial, Figure 13.2 shows that this is far from true. Dipoles lined up along the axis indeed prefer to align, but adjacent dipoles prefer to *anti*-align, and the preference for dipoles at other angles can be anywhere in-between.

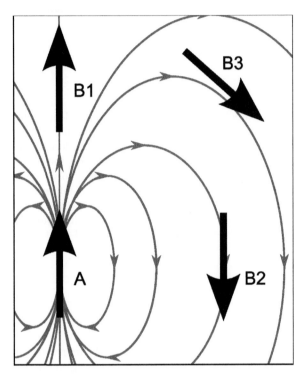

Figure 13.2: Demonstration that the preferred orientation of one dipole (B) with respect to another (A) depends on the angle between them. Dipole A is shown in the lower left, along with its magnetic field. Along A's dipole axis (position B1), the dipoles preferentially align. Perpendicular to this axis (position B2), B prefers to *anti*-align with A. At intermediate angles (e.g. position B3), the preferential alignment may be anywhere in-between.

Monodomain magnetic nanoparticles are an ideal test system to investigate this phenomenon. Each nanoparticle consists of aligned atomic dipoles so that it behaves effectively as a single giant dipole (Stoner and Wohlfarth, 1948). Additionally, their highly regular size allows them to self-assemble into ordered two- and three-dimensional structures (Murray et al., 1995; Talapin et al., 2001; Narayanan et al., 2004), as shown in Figure 13.3.

The homogeneous regions where nanoparticles are magnetized in the same direction are called *dipolar domains* (Yamamoto et al., 2008), and the size of these domains is the main quantity we are interested in. An example is given in Figure 13.4. Although both samples have zero average magnetization, the domains in (a) are twice as large as domains in (b). Instruments which measure only the total magnetization, called magnetometers, could not distinguish between these samples. However, scattering techniques can determine the average domain size.

The geometry of a general scattering experiment is shown in Figure 13.5. The

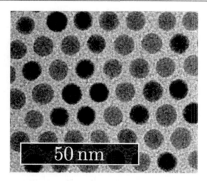

Figure 13.3: A picture of a thin cobalt magnetic nanoparticle crystal, taken with a transmission electron microscope (TEM). This particular crystal is only one monolayer thick, so that individual particles are easily distinguished.

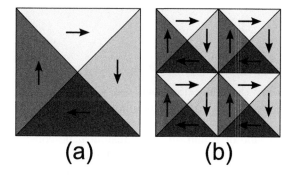

Figure 13.4: (SEE COLOR INSERT) Two hypothetical magnetic samples, identical except for the domain structure. A magnetometer would measure both to be demagnetized, but the correlation length in (a) is twice as large as in (b).

sample is placed in a beam of radiation, whose component particles[1] it deflects (or *scatters*) at an angle θ. The scattering of each individual particle is a stochastic event, whose governing distribution is determined by the size of the ordered regions within the sample. When many particles have been scattered, the intensity pattern built up on the detector can be analyzed using theoretical models, yielding information about the parameters characterizing the sample.

The connection between characteristic sizes and scattered radiation can be briefly illustrated by explaining Bragg's Law (Kittel, 2004), the most basic scattering relation. Atoms in a crystal are arranged in planes, each of which reflects a small amount[2] of the incoming radiation, as in Figure 13.6. These reflected rays undergo *interference* when they recombine at the detector, where a high intensity signal occurs only if they all have the same phase. Rays reflected from deeper planes must travel a correspondingly longer distance, $\Delta L = 2d \sin \theta$ (see Figure 13.6); accordingly, their phase is more advanced by an amount $2\pi \Delta L / \lambda$, with λ the wavelength of the radiation. Since a phase difference of 2π makes no difference, the first bright spot occurs when $\Delta L = \lambda$,

---

[1] All radiation is composed of particles, according to the "particle-wave duality" in quantum mechanics.

[2] Since only a small fraction of the incident radiation is scattered, we neglect higher-order corrections accounting for multiple scattering.

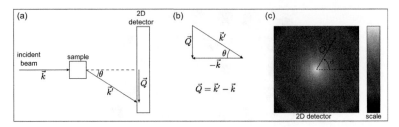

Figure 13.5: (SEE COLOR INSERT) Schematic of a general transmission-geometry scattering experiment. (a) The incident beam comes in from the left and strikes the sample, which deflects the radiation at an angle θ towards a two-dimensional detector. Here, a single scattering event is shown, but the detector records the total amount of radiation scattered into all areas, as indexed by the scattering vector $\vec{Q}$. (b) The definition of $\vec{Q}$: the wavevector $\vec{k}$ has the direction of the incident neutron, and magnitude $2\pi/\lambda$, with λ the wavelength of the radiation. (c) A sample pattern of scattered radiation which might be observed on a detector.

i.e.

$$\lambda = 2d \sin \theta. \tag{13.1}$$

Equation 13.1 shows the connection between a measured size, d, and the angle θ where radiation is strongly scattered. For many scattering experiments, λ is held constant, and the scattered intensity is measured as a function of θ (Hammouda, 2008). Since the right side of Equation 13.1 must *also* be constant, structures with larger sizes d must scatter at smaller angles θ. Though many systems exist whose scattering is not described by Bragg's law, this inverse relationship between sizes and scattering angles is quite generally true, as Figure 13.7 shows schematically.

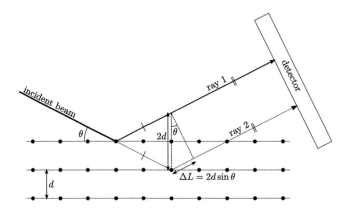

Figure 13.6: An illustration of Bragg's Law for scattering. The incident beam comes in from the left and is partially reflected from each plane of atoms. The path lengths of rays 1 and 2 differ by the amount ΔL, as shown in the figure.

13.1.1 Correlation Lengths

The sizes measured by Bragg's Law correspond to distances between nearest neighbours. By contrast, we're interested in measuring *regions* of order, which often extend

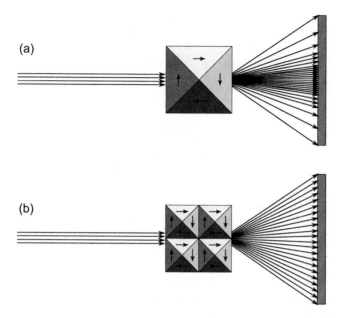

Figure 13.7: (SEE COLOR INSERT) An illustration of the relationship between the scattering angle θ and the size of ordered regions. In both cases, the sample is placed in the path of a neutron beam, and it scatters the neutrons into a detector. The sample in (a) has larger ordered regions than (b), and consequently scatters proportionately more neutrons at *smaller* angles.

across many neighbours. The size of these ordered regions is measured by a quantity known as the "correlation length". The term, 'correlation,' is well-established in both the physics and statistics communities, but the meanings differ.

In physics, correlation always refers to systems possessing some kind of order, and the *correlation length* ξ measures how large the ordered regions tend to be (Yeomans, 1992). In the case of our dipolar domains, the ordering is found in the normalized[3] dipole orientation $\vec{S}$ on different nanoparticles. This ordering is measured as a function of separation by means of the *correlation function, $G(r)$*:

$$G(r) = \langle \vec{S}_i \cdot \vec{S}_j \rangle_r \tag{13.2}$$

where the angle brackets denote averaging over all pairs of nanoparticles, i and j, separated by a distance r.

The behavior of $G(r)$ relates to ξ as follows. When $r \ll \xi$, most pairs of locations separated by r are within the same domain, so $G(r) \sim 1$. On the other hand, when the separation r is large ($r \gg \xi$), the magnetization in remote regions is just as likely to point one way as the opposite way, so $G(r) \to 0$. The correlation length ξ therefore sets the scale of how quickly $G(r)$ goes to zero, and it can be obtained by fitting to the rate of damping of $G(r)$.

Some systems, such as ours, require more than one correlation length for their complete description (Bernhoeft, 1999). Within each dipolar domain, smaller regions of inhomogeneities (Figure 13.8) are found, where clusters of nanoparticles deviate slightly from the average domain orientation (Michels et al., 2003). We denote the

---

[3]By "normalized," we mean that $|\vec{S}| = 1$.

"domain size" correlation length as ξ_S, and the "inhomogeneity" correlation length as ξ_L. These correlation lengths are the parameters of greatest interest.

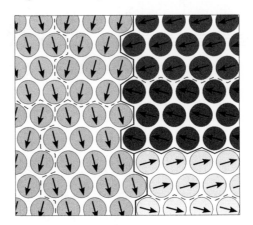

Figure 13.8: (SEE COLOR INSERT) An example configuration of dipoles in a nanoparticle array. The dipole orientation is shown both by the central arrow and the color of the nanoparticle. Here, three dipolar domains are shown, separated by thick solid lines: the downward domain occupies the left half, and the right half supports a leftward domain on top and a rightward domain on the bottom. Within each domain are shown smaller regions of inhomogeneities, bounded by thin dashed lines, where subgroups of nanoparticles deviate slightly from the average direction in the domain.

13.1.2   *Small-angle Neutron Scattering*

Neutrons have several key advantages for studies of condensed matter, particularly of magnetic materials (Hammouda, 2008; Squires, 1997). They are uncharged, which allows them to penetrate very deeply through most matter. "Slow" neutrons — those travelling less than roughly $v = 1$ km/s — have wavelengths[4],

$$\lambda = \frac{h}{mv},\tag{13.3}$$

suitable for scattering studies on structures of current interest (typically a few tens of nm, where 1 nm is one billionth of a meter). Finally, each neutron also possesses a magnetic moment, which enables it to interact magnetically with the sample.

In small-angle neutron scattering (SANS), theory predicts the relative scattered intensity as a function of the scattering vector $\vec{Q}$, which was defined in Figure 13.5(b). SANS scattering tends to be elastic, meaning that $|\vec{k}'| = |\vec{k}|$, and $|\vec{Q}|$ can be evaluated based purely on geometry:

$$|\vec{Q}| = \frac{4\pi \sin(\theta/2)}{\lambda} \approx \frac{2\pi\theta}{\lambda}\tag{13.4}$$

A key result of scattering theory is that the intensity $I(\vec{Q})$ is simply related to $G(\vec{r})$ by a Fourier transform (Van Hove, 1954). This shows the connection between $I(\vec{Q})$ (the quantity measured experimentally) and ξ (the quantity of interest).

The two types of regions discussed in Section 13.1.1 each give rise to a distinctive

---

[4]Here, m is the mass of the neutron, and h is Planck's constant.

type of scattering. The correlation function for dipolar domain-like ordering decays like $\exp(-r/\xi_S)/r$ (Sachan et al., 2008), and its Fourier transform has a Lorentzian-Squared ("S") lineshape:

$$I_S(Q) \propto \frac{1}{(\kappa_S^2 + Q^2)^2}, \tag{13.5}$$

where we define the parameter $\kappa_S = 1/\xi_S$ for convenience. Similarly, the inhomogeneities yield a correlation function like (Sachan et al., 2008) $\exp(-r/\xi_L)$, which Fourier transforms to a Lorentzian ("L") lineshape:

$$I_L(Q) \propto \frac{1}{\kappa_L^2 + Q^2}, \tag{13.6}$$

again defining $\kappa_L = 1/\xi_L$. Adding in appropriate scaling constants Σ_S and Σ_L, the total magnetic scattering at low Q becomes

$$I(Q) = \frac{\Sigma_S}{(\kappa_S^2 + Q_i^2)^2} + \frac{\Sigma_L}{\kappa_L^2 + Q_i^2}. \tag{13.7}$$

Changes in the ratio of Σ_L to Σ_S, from one run to another, indicate changes in the relative prominence of domains versus the inhomogeneities within them.

13.2 The SANS Instrument

We now describe the SANS instrument, shown in Figure 13.9, in greater detail. The workings of each major component are briefly explained, with emphasis on their contributions to uncertainty. Readers desiring a more in-depth description are referred to (Glinka et al., 1998).

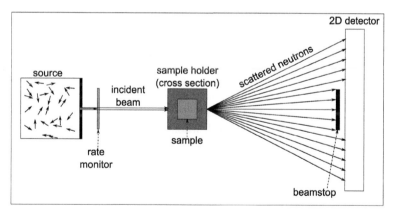

Figure 13.9: (SEE COLOR INSERT) The SANS instrument. Here, we show an abstracted view for simplicity, which includes only the conceptual parts necessary to understand our model.

13.2.1 Instrument Components

Neutron Source

The *neutron source* as we model it has two main stages: production, and moderation. Production takes place in a nuclear fission reactor, where neutrons are liberated during the splitting of heavy atomic nuclei. Moderation sets the wavelength distribution of the resulting beam, both by changing the speeds[5] of the neutrons, and by filtering out neutrons of certain speeds. The end result is that the beam has some measurable wavelength distribution $\varphi(\lambda)$ (Hammouda, 2008, Chapter 12), where $\varphi(\lambda)\,d\lambda$ is proportional to the amount of neutrons in the beam having wavelengths between λ and $\lambda + d\lambda$. Typically, this distribution is reported in terms of the peak wavelength λ_+, and a relative wavelength spread σ_λ/λ_+.

Rate Monitor

The output from the source varies, necessitating a *rate monitor* to measure it. A thin ^{235}U plate, which has a low probability to capture each passing neutron, is inserted immediately after the source. Captured neutrons are counted for a predetermined time, and the totals are recorded in a datafile. The monitor averages roughly 10^6 counts per minute.

Sample

The sample must be held in the path of the beam by a sample holder. The neutrons scattered from this assembly constitute the measured signal. Though the holder is necessary, its presence complicates data interpretation, as discussed in Section 13.2.2.

Beam Stop

Because the transmitted beam is very intense, and would quickly damage the detector, a beam stop is inserted which blocks the central portion of the detector. This unfortunately renders the lowest-Q range inaccessible, but is necessary to protect the detector. Datapoints close to the beamstop edge should be viewed with suspicion, and are typically discarded.

Neutron Detector

The two-dimensional neutron detector consists of a 128×128-pixel grid, where each pixel records the cumulative number of neutrons passing by its position. The grid is comprised of horizontal and vertical wires, immersed in a high-pressure mixture of ^{3}He and CF_4 gases. Passing neutrons have some probability to ionize this gas, and the resulting charge is detected on the nearest wires: one horizontal, one vertical. Their intersection defines the location of a pixel, whose counter is then incremented by one.

Each pixel i detects only some fraction of the neutrons which impinge upon it. This fraction, known as the *detection efficiency* η_i, must be carefully measured before the data can be quantitatively analyzed. Typically, this is done by staff scientists on a regular basis, and the latest measured efficiencies are distributed to users.

The expected number of counts also depends on the solid angle β_i which the pixel covers, i.e. the apparent size of the pixel as viewed from the sample. Since all pixels have the same area, solid angle is primarily determined by the distance from the sample to the detector. We define the detection *capacity* $\gamma_i \equiv \eta_i\beta_i$ as the product of detection *efficiency* and solid angle.

We point out that each pixel corresponds to a given scattering angle θ, determined by its displacement from the center and the detector's distance from the sample. However, the neutron count from each pixel is recorded at a specific $\vec{Q}$-value. Equation 13.4 shows that mapping θ onto Q is unique only if the wavelength λ is precisely defined. The fact that the wavelength spread σ_λ/λ_+ is nonzero means that each pixel actually contains a *probability distribution* of Q-values, an effect known as smearing.

---

[5] From Equation 13.3, the wavelength of the neutron is directly related to its speed.

13.2.2 Instrument Configurations

The sample signal is but one of three contributions to the measured $I(\vec{Q})$. By reconfiguring the instrument, the other two can be measured. We show these configurations schematically in Figure 13.10, explaining below the contributions they account for.

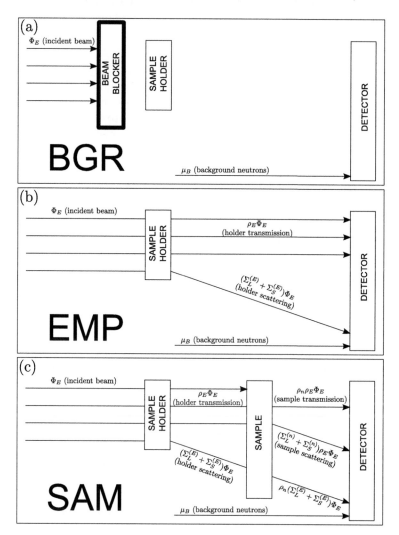

Figure 13.10: A schematic showing the three contributions to the signal, and how they are measured by including them one by one. (a) The beam is blocked, and only the background contributes. (b) Scattering and transmission are measured for the empty sample holder. (c) The sample is inserted into the holder, both attenuating the holder's signal and adding its own contribution. Neutrons scattered by both sample and holder are neglected in the single-scattering approximation. (We emphasize that this is a *schematic*; the paths show the history of the neutrons, and are *not* intended to represent trajectories.)

The experimental room contains additional sources of neutrons which are independent of the beam configuration, known collectively as the "background". This background rate is measured by blocking the beam completely (Figure 13.10(a), "BGR") and counting neutrons. An empty sample holder (Figure 13.10(b), "EMP") is next inserted, letting us account for neutrons scattered by the holder. Finally, the sample is added inside the holder (Figure 13.10(c), "SAM"), contributing both nuclear and magnetic scattering to the measured signal.

The sample transmits undisturbed only some fraction of neutrons, and the holder's contribution is smaller by this amount. This fraction can be measured in *transmission mode*, which only counts the neutrons in the transmitted beam: it is the ratio of the intensity with the sample in the holder, to that with the sample removed.

Magnetic Scattering

Accounting for the above effects permits isolation of the sample signal, which is the sum of nuclear and magnetic scattering. To separate them, note that magnetic scattering along the local magnetization direction is always zero (Squires, 1997, chap. 7). By applying a magnetic field large enough to saturate the sample, we obtain a purely nuclear signal along the field direction. Since nuclear scattering is isotropic, the remaining magnetic signal can be extracted in all directions.

13.3   SANS Error Analysis

This paper presents an alternative technique for error analysis of SANS data. We will give an overview of the traditional method, before describing how we have applied Bayesian techniques to SANS.

13.3.1   Traditional Error Analysis

Existing tools for SANS error analysis have relied upon traditional statistical methods. These tools are mature and refined through years of heavy use with a variety of users studying diverse types of systems. We illustrate using the package written by Steven Kline at NIST (Kline, 2006), where we performed our experiments.

Two separate steps are involved in analysis of SANS data: reduction, and fitting. The former involves using the configurations described in Section 13.2.2 to compensate for the undesired contributions. This procedure is inherently tied to the specific instrument where the data was taken: reduction procedures are not generic. Traditional fitting procedures, by contrast, can be quite generic, since the *reduced* data is expected to have all major instrument-specific effects accounted for.

Figure 13.11 shows a diagram of the traditional reduction process. We applied it to our data, and then converted the resulting 2-D function of $\vec{Q}$ to a 1-D function of Q, by averaging a narrow range of angles perpendicular to the applied magnetic field. We measured the nuclear signal as described in Section 13.2.2, and subtracted it off to yield the magnetic data, which we fit to the sum of a Lorentzian and Lorentzian-squared.

Data Fitting

The "best fit" is traditionally decided by minimizing the χ^2 per degree of freedom, as follows. Each datapoint y_i is assigned a standard error s_{y_i}, and associated with a coordinate x_i. The y_i are assumed to be based on a model function $f(x)$, such that the deviations $(f(x_i) - y_i)$ should be small compared to s_{y_i}. These deviations are called *standardized residuals* when normalized by s_{y_i}. χ^2 is the sum of squares of these standardized residuals,

$$\chi^2 = \sum_{i=1}^{N} \left(\frac{f(x_i) - y_i}{s_{y_i}} \right)^2, \tag{13.8}$$

and the curve which minimizes χ^2 is taken to be the "best fit" for a given model. The model itself may be checked by examining the standardized residuals and looking for

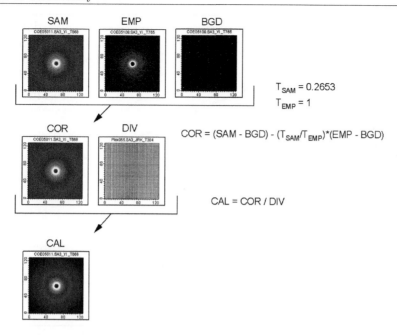

Figure 13.11: (SEE COLOR INSERT) The datafiles used in our Bayesian analysis, processed here using traditional analysis. Note the horizontal and vertical lines visible in COR, which are removed by the DIV correction.

trends. Figure 13.12 shows the results of applying this method to our data at $H = 0$; the y_i are shown in black, and $f(x)$ is the green curve.

13.3.2 *The Bayesian Alternative*

Bayesian analysis is an alternative methodology; (Lindley, 2006) gives a very readable general introduction, and (Agostini, 2003) introduces Bayesian methods from a physicist's perspective.

We distinguish two types of quantities. *Data* (denoted by Latin letters) are directly observed in the experiment, and *parameters* (denoted by Greek letters) are unobserved quantities which affect the distribution of data. The sole reason for collecting the former is to learn about the latter. We use $\vec{y}$ as shorthand for the set of all data values, and $\vec{\alpha}$ for the set of all parameter values.

The information about $\vec{\alpha}$ yielded by $\vec{y}$ is encoded in the posterior probability distribution $P(\vec{\alpha}|\vec{y})$. Bayesian analysis relates this to two other distributions through Bayes' rule,

$$P(\vec{\alpha}|\vec{y}) = \frac{P(\vec{y}|\vec{\alpha})P(\vec{\alpha})}{\int P(\vec{y}|\vec{\alpha}')P(\vec{\alpha}')\,d\vec{\alpha}'}. \tag{13.9}$$

The likelihood, $P(\vec{y}|\vec{\alpha})$, gives the probability of obtaining the observed data, given a particular set of values for the parameters. The prior, $P(\vec{\alpha})$, summarizes all knowledge of the sample before the experiment was performed. These two distributions constitute the model. When combined with the observed data $\vec{y}_0$, they contain all statistical information about the parameters $\vec{\alpha}$.

Calculations using $P(\vec{\alpha}|\vec{y})$ involve integrals in a high-dimensional space (i.e. parameter space). We performed these integrals using a Markov chain Monte Carlo (MCMC), written in the R programming language (R Development Core Team, 2008). The re-

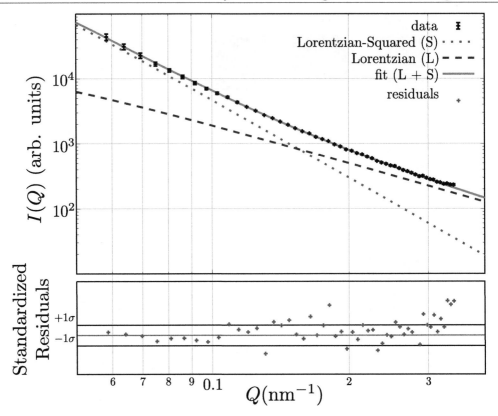

Figure 13.12: (SEE COLOR INSERT) The results of traditional fitting methods applied to data from this experiment (Sachan et al., 2008, Figure 3). The red Lorentzian-squared curve corresponds to scattering from the *dipolar domains*, and the blue Lorentzian corresponds to magnetic inhomogeneity scattering. Standardized residuals plotted at bottom show that the line of best fit agrees with most datapoints within standard errors.

sulting chain of MCMC steps was analyzed using the `boa` package, short for Bayesian Output Analysis (Smith, 2007). Both the code and the datafiles used in our analysis are available online (Hogg, 2009). We ran for 10^6 steps at each field, then used `boa` to discard steps until the remaining chain represented equilibrium. The final MCMC chains contained 4973 steps at $H = 0$ T, 2813 steps at $H = 0.2$ T, and 10987 steps at $H = 1.0$ T. Execution took roughly 4 days on our computer cluster, but recoding in `C++` could yield a significant advantage in speed.

We now describe our model in greater detail.

Data

Most data analyzed in this paper comes directly as a raw number of neutron counts in some detector. Associated with instrument configuration X, we have a count N_X^i for each pixel i of the detector, and a monitor count M_X. The different configurations are listed in Table 13.1.

The only data not in the form of a raw number of neutron counts is the detector efficiency data (Section 13.2.1). The efficiency e_i of the ith pixel is based on raw data from an isotropic scatterer, but the final values have been processed by instrument scientists. We note in passing that the posterior distribution on the detector efficiencies

Table 13.1: A list of the instrument configurations.

Abbreviation	Name	Purpose
BGR	Background	Measure background neutron rate
EMP	Empty holder	Measure sample holder scattering
SAM-n	Sample (high field) scattering	Measure the nuclear (i.e. nonmagnetic) contribution to the scattering signal
SAM	*Sample (low field) scattering*	*Contains the signal of greatest interest*
EMP-t	Empty cell transmission	Measured sample transmission ratio at different fields
SAM-n-t	Sample (high field) transmission	
SAM-t	Sample (low field) transmission	

could be measured once by instrument scientists, and distributed to users desiring to use Bayesian analysis.

Parameters

Our model requires 16 parameters to describe our system. Of these, the magnetic correlation lengths ξ_S and ξ_L are the most important. A complete list of parameters is given in Table 13.2.

Several additional parameters would be required for complete rigor, but have been approximated as constants for this preliminary version. The relative detection efficiency η_i of pixel i is not known with certainty, but assumed to be equal to the *measured* efficiency e_i. Similarly, the instantaneous reactor output during datafile v, Ω_v, is assumed to be equal to the number of monitor counts M_v. In both cases, the error introduced by these simplifications is negligible compared with the uncertainty from other sources: using Poisson statistics, it is less than 0.01 for η, and less than 0.001 for Ω. Nevertheless, it is important to verify with each new experiment that the counts are high enough to make these errors negligible compared to other sources of uncertainty.

Likelihood

We make the assumption that the data are *conditionally* independent from one another, *given* the parameters. It should be noted that this is equivalent to assuming that there are no unaccounted-for parameters that influence multiple pixels. Under this assumption, the likelihood can be decomposed into a product of likelihood functions for each individual neutron count — whether from the rate monitor, or a pixel in the two-dimensional detector.

We can simplify considerably by grouping pixels receiving the same number of incident neutrons per solid angle. Because of this assumption, each such group may be treated as a giant pixel P, whose detection capacity γ_P (Section 13.2.1) is the sum $\sum_{i \in P} \gamma_i$ of capacities of the pixels which comprise it. For example, the background neutron rate is modeled as independent of location on the detector, so we can replace the separate counts from all pixels by the single count $N_{\text{BGR}} = \sum_{i=1}^{N_{\text{pixel}}} N_{\text{BGR}}^{(i)}$. Another example is the signal at the bottom of Figure 13.11, which only depends on the pixel's distance Q from the center; here, our groups would be the rings of pixels which have

Table 13.2: A list of parameters in our model, and a brief description of the role of each

Name	Description
σ_G	Spread of the transmitted beam
μ_B	Normalized, per-pixel mean rate of background neutrons
Φ_E	Normalized rate of incident neutrons reaching the sample holder, which are either scattered or transmitted
ρ_E	Fraction of neutrons which the sample holder transmits
ρ_n	The transmission of the sample in high field
ρ	The transmission of the sample in low field
$\Sigma_L^{(E)}$	Fraction of neutrons which the sample holder scatters with a Lorentzian signal
$\Sigma_L^{(n)}$	Fraction of neutrons undergoing nuclear Lorentzian scattering
$\Sigma_S^{(n)}$	Fraction of neutrons undergoing nuclear Lorentzian-squared scattering
Σ_L	Fraction of neutrons undergoing magnetic Lorentzian scattering
Σ_S	Fraction of neutrons undergoing magnetic Lorentzian-squared scattering
κ_E	Inverse correlation length for Lorentzian scattering from sample holder
$\xi_L^{(n)}$	Nuclear Lorentzian correlation length
$\xi_S^{(n)}$	Nuclear Lorentzian-squared correlation length
ξ_L	Magnetic Lorentzian correlation length (average size of magnetic inhomogeneities)
ξ_S	Magnetic Lorentzian-squared correlation length (average size of dipolar domains)

the same Q. Subject to these reductions, the data we consider are

$$\vec{y} = \left\{ N_{\text{BGR}}; \vec{N}_{\text{EMP}}; \vec{N}_{\text{SAM-n}}; \vec{N}_{\text{SAM}}; \vec{N}_{\text{EMP-t}}; \vec{N}_{\text{SAM-n-t}}; \vec{N}_{\text{SAM-t}}; \right.$$
$$\left. M_{\text{BGR}}; M_{\text{EMP}}; M_{\text{SAM-n}}; M_{\text{SAM}}; M_{\text{EMP-t}}; M_{\text{SAM-n-t}}; M_{\text{SAM-t}}; \vec{e} \right\} \tag{13.10}$$

where $\vec{N}_{\text{EMP}}$ is shorthand for the set of all grouped neutron counts in the EMP configuration, and similarly for $\vec{N}_{\text{SAM}}$ and $\vec{N}_{\text{SAM-n}}$.

With this notation, we use our assumption of conditional independence to write the explicit form of the likelihood:

$$P(\vec{y}|\vec{\alpha}) = [P(N_{\text{BGR}}|\vec{\alpha})] \times [P(N_{\text{EMP}}|\vec{\alpha})] \times [P(N_{\text{SAM-n}}|\vec{\alpha})] \times [P(N_{\text{SAM}}|\vec{\alpha})] \times$$
$$[P(N_{\text{EMP-t}}|\vec{\alpha})] \times [P(N_{\text{SAM-n-t}}|\vec{\alpha})] \times [P(N_{\text{SAM-t}}|\vec{\alpha})] \tag{13.11}$$

Each factor in Equation 13.11 corresponds to one of the seven datafiles used in fitting. Factors corresponding to the measured detector efficiencies $\vec{e}$, or to any of the M_v, are missing because we have approximated them as constants.

Each neutron count N is modeled with an underlying Poisson distribution (Hengartner, 2008), with mean ν:

$$N|\nu \sim \frac{\nu^N e^{-\nu}}{N!} \tag{13.12}$$

Here, ν is proportional to the *normalized* mean μ, but also to the detection efficiency η, the solid angle β which the pixel covers, and reactor output Ω, i.e. $\nu = \mu\eta\beta\Omega$. The sum of independent Poisson-distributed random variables is another Poisson distribution, with the aggregate mean given by the sum of the individual means, but η, β, and Ω are the same for neutrons of all sources. Accordingly, the factor corresponding to each datafile v can be described simply by giving the form of this aggregate mean, μ_v.

The functional forms for the μ_v are complicated by an additional source of experimental uncertainty, known as *instrumental smearing*. As discussed more fully in Appendix 13.5, neutrons at a given pixel correspond not to a single Q-value, but to a distribution of Q-values. It is the *unsmeared* mean $\bar{\mu}_v$ which we model, but the *smeared* mean $\bar{\mu}_v^{(Sm)}$ which we measure, where the bar indicates that background neutrons are excluded because they are not smeared, i.e.

$$\mu_v = \mu_B + \bar{\mu}_v^{(Sm)}. \tag{13.13}$$

We now give the associated unsmeared mean $\bar{\mu}$ for each of the seven factors listed in Equation 13.11. The corresponding likelihood factor is given by:

$$P(N|\mu(\vec{\alpha}), \eta, \beta, \Omega) = \frac{(\mu(\vec{\alpha})\eta\beta\Omega)^N \exp[\mu(\vec{\alpha})\eta\beta\Omega]}{N!}; \tag{13.14}$$

here, the functions $L(Q; \kappa)$, $S(Q; \kappa)$, and $G(Q)$ are defined precisely in Appendix 13.5:

$$\bar{\mu}_{BGR} = 0$$

$$\bar{\mu}_{EMP} = \Phi_E \left[\Sigma_L^{(E)} L(Q; \kappa_E) + \Sigma_S^{(E)} S(Q; 1/L_t) \right]$$

$$\bar{\mu}_{SAM\text{-}n} = \Phi_E \left\{ \rho_n \left[\Sigma_L^{(E)} L(Q; \kappa_E) + \Sigma_S^{(E)} S(Q; 1/L_t) \right] + \right.$$
$$\left. \rho_E \left[\Sigma_L^{(n)} L(Q; 1/\xi_L^{(n)}) + \Sigma_S^{(n)} S(Q; 1/\xi_S^{(n)}) \right] \right\}$$

$$\bar{\mu}_{SAM} = \Phi_E \left\{ \rho \left[\Sigma_L^{(E)} L(Q; \kappa_E) + \Sigma_S^{(E)} S(Q; 1/L_t) \right] + \right.$$
$$\left. \rho_E \left[\Sigma_L^{(n)} L(Q; 1/\xi_L^{(n)}) + \Sigma_S^{(n)} S(Q; 1/\xi_S^{(n)}) + \Sigma_L L(Q; 1/\xi_L) + \Sigma_S S(Q; 1/\xi_S) \right] \right\}$$

$$\bar{\mu}_{EMP\text{-}t} = \Phi_E \rho_{att} \rho_E G(Q)$$
$$\bar{\mu}_{SAM\text{-}n\text{-}t} = \Phi_E \rho_{att} \rho_E \rho_n G(Q)$$
$$\bar{\mu}_{SAM\text{-}t} = \Phi_E \rho_{att} \rho_E \rho G(Q). \tag{13.15}$$

Priors

We decompose the parameters into disjoint independent subsets. The functional form of the prior on each of these subsets is given, along with a brief justification of why we believe its parameters are independent from all other parameters.

Background Neutrons

Background neutrons are completely described in our model by the parameter μ_B, the mean number of background neutrons arriving at each pixel per monitor count. We do not expect this rate to be affected by the experimental setup in any way, so the assumption of independence is well-justified. We turn to previous runs to elicit a prior: for each BGR file, the total number of neutrons detected, divided by the monitor counts for that file, gives an approximation for μ_B. We can calculate the sample mean and variance of μ_B values obtained from several such runs, and use these as the mean and variance for our prior distribution. The specific form chosen is a Gamma distribution, since its domain is the same as for μ_B: $(0, \infty)$. The results are shown in Table 13.3. The rightmost column was obtained by dividing the total number

Table 13.3: Total neutron counts, compared to monitor counts, for blocked-beam files from different runs. The first two were taken on the same day with the detector at different locations, and the third was taken almost a year later. Variation arises because the background depends on the location of the detector in the room, and also on what other neutron experiments are being run at the same time. Despite agreeing only to within an order of magnitude, the background is overall a very small effect, and minimally affects the parameters of greatest interest.

Filename	BGR Neutron Counts	Monitor Counts	Count time	μ_B Estimate
AUG07154.ASC	1486	23.91×10^6	20 min.	37.9×10^{-10}
AUG07156.ASC	8094	23.92×10^6	20 min.	206.5×10^{-10}
JUN08007.ASC	738	6.02×10^6	5 min.	74.8×10^{-10}

of neutron counts by the monitor counts for that datafile, then further dividing by the number of pixels (i.e. 2^{14}). The mean and standard deviation for our prior distribution are estimated using the sample mean and sample standard deviation of these values:

$$s_{\text{BGR}}^{\text{old}} = \sqrt{\frac{1}{N-1} \sum_{i=1}^{N} (x_i - \bar{x})^2}. \tag{13.16}$$

Values for $\mu_{\text{BGR}}^{\text{old}}$ and $s_{\text{BGR}}^{\text{old}}$, along with all other values needed to describe our priors, are found in Table 13.4.

Beam Spread

Our transmitted beam is fit to a Gaussian form (Hammouda, 2008). Since the beam is centred around $Q = 0$, only the spread σ_G is needed to characterize its shape. We expect that the transmitted beam will be insignificant outside the beamstop, whose edge Q_b should therefore be at least $2\sigma_G$ from the center. We use a Gaussian (normal) prior having mean $Q_b/2$ and standard deviation $Q_b/4$.

Independence is justified because the intrinsic spread of the beam does not depend on the sample holder, sample, or background rate.

Incident Non-absorbed Flux

We define Φ_E as the rate of neutrons incident on the sample holder, considering only neutrons which contribute to some measured signal in some way. Other incident neutrons are either absorbed or scattered at wide angles; since they have no effect on any measured signal, we exclude them from Φ_E. We have not performed an absolute calibration in this experiment, so we do not know the *magnitude* of Φ_E. To express this, we choose a prior which is uniform in log-space, subject to a cutoff X representing the maximum order of magnitude we will probe:

$$P(\Phi_E) = \frac{1}{\Phi_E} \Theta \left(X - |\log_{10}(\Phi_E)| \right), \tag{13.17}$$

where the theta-function $\Theta(x)$ is 1 if its argument is positive and zero otherwise.

All other parameters relating to the sample or holder are expressed as *fractions* of the flux incident upon them; hence, we may treat Φ_E as an independently adjustable measure of this flux.

Partitioning of Neutrons for Sample Holder Alone

Consider all neutrons incident on the bare sample holder which are either scattered at small angles or transmitted. The relative fractions transmitted and scattered are intrinsic properties of the holder, and hence independent of all other parameters. Calling the fraction transmitted ρ_E, the fraction undergoing Lorentzian scattering $\Sigma_L^{(E)}$, and the fraction undergoing Lorentzian-squared scattering $\Sigma_S^{(E)}$, we have

$$\rho_E + \Sigma_L^{(E)} + \Sigma_S^{(E)} = 1, \tag{13.18}$$

since we have disregarded all other neutrons. Because this constraint leaves only two free parameters, we only explicitly specify ρ_E and $\Sigma_L^{(E)}$. Our prior on these parameters is a Dirichlet distribution, governed by the hyperparameters $A_\rho^{(E)}$, $A_{\Sigma_L}^{(E)}$, and $A_{\Sigma_S}^{(E)}$.

Partitioning of Neutrons for Sample (both high- and low-field)

These parameters partition the neutrons incident on the sample according to the type of interaction they experience (i.e. magnetic Lorentzian-squared scattering, undisturbed transmission, nuclear Lorentzian scattering, etc.). We divide them into three groups: nuclear scattering, SAM, and SAM-n. Our strategy is to first specify the prior for the nuclear scattering, which contributes to both SAM and SAM-n configurations. Parameters in the remaining two groups are independent of each other, *given* values for the nuclear scattering parameters, so we can specify these two groups separately. All of these parameters are intrinsic properties of the sample, justifying our assumption of independence from all other parameters.

The prior for the nuclear scattering parameters is Dirichlet, governed by $A_{\Sigma_L}^{(n)}$, $A_{\Sigma_S}^{(n)}$, and $A^{(n)}$. The remaining two priors are *scaled* Dirichlets, on the domain $(0, F)$, where we define $F = 1 - (\Sigma_L^{(n)} + \Sigma_S^{(n)})$ for convenience. Conservation of neutrons is expressed for SAM-n as

$$\Sigma_L^{(n)} + \Sigma_S^{(n)} + \rho_n < 1, \tag{13.19}$$

and for SAM as

$$\Sigma_L^{(n)} + \Sigma_S^{(n)} + \rho + \Sigma_L + \Sigma_S < 1. \tag{13.20}$$

The total prior for these sample partitioning parameters is thus

$$
\begin{aligned}
P(\Sigma_L^{(n)}, \Sigma_S^{(n)}, \rho_n, \Sigma_L, \Sigma_S, \rho) = &D(\Sigma_L^{(n)}, \Sigma_S^{(n)}, F; A_{\Sigma_L}^{(n)}, A_{\Sigma_S}^{(n)}, A^{(n)}) \times \\
&D(\rho_n/F, 1 - \rho_n/F; A_\rho^{(n)}, A_\delta^{(n)}) \times \\
&D(\Sigma_L/F, \Sigma_S/F, \rho/F; A_{\Sigma_L}, A_{\Sigma_S}, A_\rho).
\end{aligned}
\tag{13.21}
$$

Sample Holder Correlation Lengths

We now turn our attention to correlation length-describing parameters. The normalization described in Appendix 13.5 means that each of these should be *a priori* independent of its corresponding Σ, and we have only to consider prior knowledge on any possible relationship among the correlation lengths.

The prior for κ_E should be uniform in $\xi_L^{(E)} = 1/\kappa_E$, since any correlation length is as likely as any other; hence,

$$P(\kappa_E) = \frac{1}{\kappa_E^2}. \tag{13.22}$$

We simulate the inverse length κ_E because that is what appears directly in $L(Q)$.

The sample holder also has a Lorentzian-squared signal which is important at lower Q. Because the holder is made from highly crystalline aluminum, we expect this correlation length to be longer than this SANS instrument can probe. This limitation is the transverse coherence length L_t. Setting $\xi_S^{(E)} = L_t$ saves computation time without compromising accuracy, as we verified by checking the fits at low Q.

Nuclear Correlation Lengths

The nuclear correlation lengths $\xi_S^{(n)}$ and $\xi_L^{(n)}$ describe the positional arrangement of the elements in our sample. The nuclear data is known to be well-fit by the sum of a Lorentzian and Lorentzian-squared, and that like any other correlation lengths they are constrained to be less than L_t. Accordingly, the prior for each is uniform within the region $(0, L_t)$.

Magnetic Correlation Lengths

The magnetic correlation lengths are similar to their nuclear counterparts, except that we identify ξ_L as the size of magnetic inhomogeneities within dipolar domains of size ξ_S (Michels and Weissmuller, 2008). This implies that $\xi_S > \xi_L$ always. Additionally, because our nanoparticles are single-domain, the domains can never be smaller than the diameter d_{NP} of a single nanoparticle. This allowed region roughly has the shape of a triangle with the bottom corner snipped off, as shown in Figure 13.13. We choose our prior to have uniform probability density inside this region and zero outside.

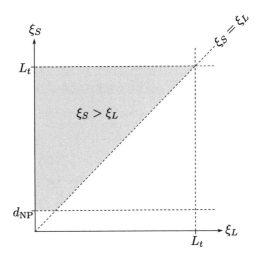

Figure 13.13: Probability distribution for the length scales of the Lorentzian and Lorentzian-squared terms, ξ_L and ξ_S. L_t is the transverse coherence length of the beam, here 1000 nm; correlation lengths larger than this cannot be distinguished by the instrument. $D_{particle}$ is the diameter of a single particle, here 8 nm. The probability distribution is flat within the shaded region, and zero outside.

These are the parameters of greatest interest.

13.4 Results and Discussion

The data we fit are identical to those in (Sachan et al., 2008). The same datafiles were used in both cases. Pixels have been grouped according to sector averaging within

Table 13.4: List of hyperparameters which characterize our experimental setup or govern the shape of our prior distributions, along with the values used in our analysis.

Category	Hyperparameter	Value	Description
Experimental setup	Q_b	0.04 nm^{-1}	Q-value of the edge of the beamstop
	λ	0.5 nm	Mean wavelength of incident neutrons
	L_t	1000 nm	Transverse coherence length of neutron beam
	ρ_{att}	0.0003	Transmission ratio of attenuator (inserted during transmission mode)
	d_{NP}	8 nm	Diameter of a single Co nanoparticle
Priors	$\mu_{\text{BGR}}^{\text{old}}$	106×10^{-10}	Prior mean of μ_B
	$s_{\text{BGR}}^{\text{old}}$	89×10^{-10}	Prior standard deviation of μ_B
	X	10	Cutoff order of magnitude for Φ_E
	$A_{\Sigma_L}^{(E)}$	2	Dirichlet portion for Lorentzian scattering from sample holder
	$A_{\Sigma_S}^{(E)}$	2	Dirichlet portion for Lorentzian-squared scattering from sample holder
	$A_\rho^{(E)}$	16	Dirichlet portion for transmission through sample holder
	$A_{\Sigma_L}^{(n)}$	2	Dirichlet portion for nuclear Lorentzian scattering from sample
	$A_{\Sigma_S}^{(n)}$	2	Dirichlet portion for nuclear Lorentzian-squared scattering from sample
	$A^{(n)}$	6	Dirichlet portion for neutrons not nuclearly scattered
	A_{Σ_L}	3	Dirichlet portion for magnetic Lorentzian scattering from sample
	A_{Σ_S}	3	Dirichlet portion for magnetic Lorentzian-squared scattering from sample
	A_ρ	4	Dirichlet portion for neutrons transmitted by sample in low field
	A_δ	2	Dirichlet portion for remaining neutrons in low field (absorbed, high-angle scattered, etc.)
	$A_\rho^{(n)}$	4	Dirichlet portion for neutrons transmitted by sample in high field
	$A_\delta^{(n)}$	8	Dirichlet portion for remaining neutrons in high field (absorbed, high-angle scattered, etc.)

Table 13.5: Traditional fit results ("T.A.") presented alongside new Bayesian results ("B.A."). Bayesian uncertainty estimates represent one standard deviation of the posterior distribution.

Parameter	Method	$H = 0$	$H=0.2$ T	$H=1.0$ T
$\xi_L/$nm	T.A.	37 ± 8	9.1 ± 0.3	1.4 ± 0.1
	B.A.	50 ± 10	11.8 ± 0.4	1.68 ± 0.04
$\xi_S/$nm	T.A.	72 ± 9	91 ± 4	1000
	B.A.	64 ± 1	102 ± 10	504 ± 34

a $\pm 5°$ range around the given direction: horizontal for the pure nuclear signal, and vertical for the mixed nuclear-plus-magnetic signal. These pixels were subsequently binned to match the Q-values from (Kline, 2006), with the center of each Q-bin placed at the corresponding Q-value from the traditional analysis.

The general picture which emerges is qualitative reproduction of general trends, with significant quantitative differences. For direct comparison, Bayesian analysis can easily reproduce the traditional style of uncertainty reporting, where the parameter mean is given along with standard deviations. However, the richness of information available in $P(\vec{a}|\vec{y})$ enables novel forms of presentation, capable of conveying deep insight into uncertainty and correlation at a glance.

Among the parameters listed in Table 13.2, ξ_S and ξ_L are the two of overwhelmingly greatest interest. Henceforth, our discussion concerns not the full posterior $P(\vec{a}|\vec{y})$, but the marginal posterior $P(\xi_L, \xi_S|\vec{y})$, with all other parameters integrated out.

13.4.1 *Separate Marginal Distributions on ξ_L and ξ_S*

Table 1 of (Sachan et al., 2008) gave values for four different field configurations. Because the final two gave very similar results, we focus on the first three. We calculated uncertainty estimates of one standard deviation based on our MCMC results. For ease of comparison, the results from the original paper ("T.A.", for "traditional analysis"), are presented alongside the updated uncertainties ("B.A.", for "Bayesian analysis"), in Table 13.5.

The agreement is best at $H = 0$, which is the configuration of greatest interest for proving the existence of domains. Here the Bayesian results overlap the traditionally obtained values, but with significantly smaller uncertainty for ξ_S. The fact that $\xi_S(H = 0) \gg d_{\mathrm{NP}}$ indicates magnetic correlations extending over multiple particles, providing strong supporting evidence for the presence of dipolar domains.

At higher fields, the agreement is more qualitative, and only the general trends in $\xi_S(H)$ are reproduced. In particular, correlations in the apparently-saturated sample are closer to 500 nm than the nominal limit of 1000 nm. This shorter correlation length may indicate that the sample is not fully saturated, but we feel this is unlikely, because (Sachan et al., 2008) shows negligible change from 1 T to 5 T. A more likely explanation is that the limit of what SANS can probe (i.e. the transverse coherence length L_t is lower than we previously believed).

13.4.2 *Joint Posterior Distribution on (ξ_L, ξ_S)*

A plot of the full joint posterior distribution $P(\xi_L, \xi_S|\vec{y})$ is perhaps the most informative way to present data. We used the `hexbin` package (Carr, 2008), without smoothing, to estimate the posterior density by counting the number of MCMC steps within each bin. The results are shown in Figure 13.14.

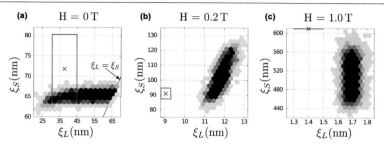

Figure 13.14: (SEE COLOR INSERT) The joint posterior distribution $P(\xi_L, \xi_S | \vec{y})$, plotted for (a) $H=0$, (b)$H=0.2$ T, (c)$H = 1.0$ T. The red × marks the location of the best fit according to traditional analysis, and the box represents the region within one standard deviation of the traditional fit. The diagonal line in (a) represents the constraint $\xi_S > \xi_L$; recall that the prior is uniform above and to the left of this line. Note that in (c), the red bar has been moved down from its actual location of $\xi_S = 1000$ nm, for ease of visualization.

	$H = 0$	$H=0.2$ T	$H=1.0$ T
$\mathrm{Cor}(\xi_L, \xi_S)$	0.384	0.781	0.031

Table 13.6: Measured correlations between ξ_L and ξ_S at different applied field strengths.

The most probable regions are darker. Moreover, correlations which are not straightforward to obtain in traditional analysis are readily apparent in these plots. For instance, there is a high positive correlation between ξ_S and ξ_L at 0.2 T: in this regime, larger domains are particularly likely to be found containing larger inhomogeneous regions. This qualitative visual observation is supplemented by Table 13.6, which lists the calculated correlation between the parameters at each field.

If we were to represent *traditional* uncertainty graphically, summarizing the two separate means and standard deviations, it might take the form of a box, with side lengths given by the standard deviation. Depending on the number of standard deviations included, we would be more or less "confident" to find the true parameter values within the box, and more or less surprised to find them outside. It should be noted, however, that the confidence bounds in the traditional analysis are frequency proportions of a procedure, implemented in only a single instance. Thus their correct interpretation is that, "repeating the procedure used to calculate these bounds many times, 68% of the time the bounds calculated as these were would contain the parameter value." Additionally, reporting parameters separately from one another always implies an assumption of independence, and this traditional method therefore cannot capture the correlations which are so evident in, say, Figure 13.14b.

Note that Bayesian analysis has done more than simply refine the uncertainty estimates. As Figure 13.14 starkly shows, it has shifted the estimates of the parameters, to the point that the traditionally obtained values do not overlap for $H > 0$. In part, this may be due to neglecting high-Q datafiles in the present work: ξ_L is always shifted in the same direction, and the missing datafiles contain a Q-range which strongly constrains the Lorentzian. But the main reason they differ is that a proper accounting of uncertainty can have profound effects on the parameter values extracted from experimental data.

13.4.3   Representing Fits Graphically: "family of curves" and Standardized Residual Distributions

Though the joint posterior plots of Figure 13.14 are informative, they give no indication of how well these parameters fit the data, only that they fit better than the others which were explored. We consider the traditional method of representing variation in graphs, then present an attractive Bayesian alternative.

Traditionally, datapoints are plotted along with error bars of one standard deviation, which represent the variation one might expect if the experiment were repeated numerous times. Automated fitting routines then determine the "best fit" values of the parameters, and the curve described by these parameters is plotted with the data, hopefully passing nearer each datapoint than its associated error bar. Two things are peculiar here. First, plotting a single curve gives no indication when other parameter values might fit just as well. Second, associating uncertainty with data is misplaced, since it inevitably refers to quantities which *might* have been observed, but in fact were not. (If the experiment is repeated, all repetitions may be analyzed as part of the data. If not, then statements about uncertainty should depend only on what was *actually* observed.)

Bayesian analysis assigns no uncertainty to datapoints. Instead, variation may be shown by taking a random subset of MCMC steps, plotting the curves corresponding to each, and plotting the datapoints on top. As a bonus, correlations between *datapoints* are automatically accounted for. (By contrast, two adjacent datapoints with errorbars implies they are just as likely to vary oppositely as together, which is generally untrue.)

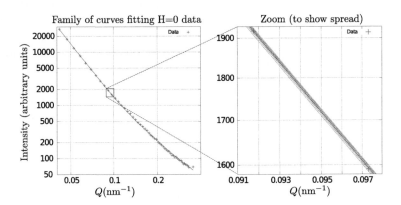

Figure 13.15: (SEE COLOR INSERT) The "family of curves" corresponding to a randomly chosen subset of 16 MCMC steps from the chain. In this case, the difference between curves is indistinct when the plot is fully zoomed out, so a central portion has been expanded to show the variation. (Note that in contrast to Figure 13.12, these data include contributions from nuclear scattering, background, and the sample holder, making direct comparison difficult.)

In this case, we see that the shape of the curve is quite tightly constrained, giving no visual indication of the degree to which the parameters vary. Significant magnification is required before the curves can be distinguished, suggesting the need for alternative plots to show goodness of fit.

Standardized residuals fit this role, and can also show all MCMC steps simultaneously, like the joint posterior plots of Figure 13.14. The residual Δ_i^s for pixel i at MCMC step s is $(N_i - \nu_i^s)$, where N_i is the observed number of neutrons, and ν_i^s the

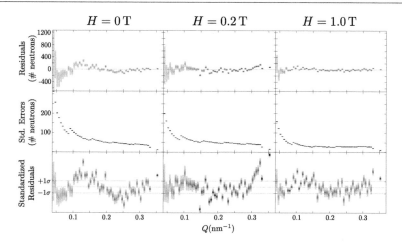

Figure 13.16: Residual distributions at each field. Each distribution is binned, with darker bins having higher density, and black representing the most populous bin for each plot. The top row shows a distribution at each Q of non-normalized residuals, i.e. the difference between the number of neutrons observed and the number expected for each MCMC step. The expected variation is plotted in the middle row as the square root of the fit function at each step. (Discontinuities correspond to changes in the number of grouped pixels.) The bottom row plots distributions on *standardized* residuals, equivalent to dividing the top row by the middle row.

number expected based on the parameter values at s. Considering all MCMC steps leads to a residual *distribution* at each Q, shown in Figure 13.16.

The residual distributions at all fields exhibit wide variation at low Q, and become narrow at higher Q. This trend is a consequence of the higher counts at low Q. The variation expected from Poisson statistics, $\sqrt{\nu_i^s}$, is plotted in the middle row of Figure 13.16. Dividing each residual (top) by the expected variation (middle) yields the *standardized residuals* (bottom), $\delta_i^s = (N_i - \nu_i^s)/\sqrt{\nu_i^s}$. These plots are the closest Bayesian analogue to the bottom of Figure 13.12, but we caution against *direct* comparison, because different data are being fit: traditional analysis processes the data first, while Bayesian analysis models all contributions and fits the unaltered data.

The zero-field data lie within 2σ of most fits, but display clear systematic trends as a function of Q. We attribute these trends to the extra contributions, and suggest that refining the models for nuclear and holder scattering may mitigate these effects. At intermediate field ($H = 0.2$ T), only the last several points disagree significantly. The fits systematically and increasingly underestimate the data, but since data near the detector edges are inherently less trustworthy, we expect the inclusion of higher-Q datafiles to improve agreement in this region. The datapoints at the highest field ($H = 1.0$ T) agree well all around, generally within 1σ of most fits. Note that at all fields, the residual distributions widen at lowest Q, even *after* standardization.

13.5 Conclusions

In conclusion, we have applied Bayesian analysis to data from a recently published SANS paper (Sachan et al., 2008). Our analysis supports the main conclusions, that dipolar domains existed in a Co colloidal crystal even at zero field, and grew larger as higher fields were applied. Our new approach has put our uncertainty analysis on firmer footing and yielded quantitative results.

More broadly, small-angle neutron scattering datasets can be analyzed using a Bayesian approach, which yields the conditional posterior probability $P(\vec{a}|\vec{y})$. Correlations between parameters can be made obvious by a glance at a plot of this posterior distribution. Furthermore, since the MCMC explores all of parameter space, it often finds possibilities in obscure regions, which traditional analysis might easily miss. Modeling the system in detail requires eliciting reasonable priors for the parameters, and often reveals important details about the system or key gaps in knowledge even before the MCMC is run. Bayesian analysis is more computationally intensive than conventional forms of data fitting, due to the need to run a Monte Carlo simulation. Finally, the lack of a mature, versatile analysis package constitutes an additional barrier to scientists who might otherwise make use of Bayesian analysis. We hope this work will serve as the first step to the creation of just such a tool.

Appendix A. Normalization Conventions

Our Σ parameters are intended to represent the total scattering from a given functional form (i.e. Lorentzian or Lorentzian-squared). It is therefore important to normalize these functional forms, much more so than for traditional fitting, where no model gives meaning to the magnitudes of the relative scaling factors.

We begin by considering the Lorentzian function; the discussion for the Lorentzian-squared is similar. When we say that the Lorentzian $L(Q;\kappa)$ should be *normalized*, we mean that it should represent the stochastic scattering pattern for an *individual* neutron. In other words, since the neutron must be scattered with some $\vec{Q}$, integration over all allowed $\vec{Q}$-values should yield unity:

$$\int_R L(Q;\kappa)\,d\vec{Q} = 1, \tag{13.23}$$

where R stands for the region of integration.

This equation is required to hold for all κ. The integral of the non-normalized Lorentzian,

$$\tilde{L}(Q;\kappa) = \frac{1}{Q^2 + \kappa^2}, \tag{13.24}$$

typically depends on κ; hence, the normalization factor must be some function of κ and of the region R of integration, i.e.

$$L(Q;\kappa) = F_L(\kappa;R)\tilde{L}(Q;\kappa) = \frac{F_L(\kappa;R)}{Q^2 + \kappa^2}, \tag{13.25}$$

where F_L is the normalizing factor for the Lorentzian function.

Since SANS is an elastic technique, we normalize over all elastically scattered vectors. This region takes the form of a sphere of radius $2\pi/\lambda$, whose center is displaced from the origin by this same amount. For radiation of wavelength λ scattered at an angle θ, we have

$$Q_{\text{elastic}} = \frac{4\pi \sin(\theta/2)}{\lambda}. \tag{13.26}$$

In order to turn our integral from $d\vec{Q}$ into dQ, we must weight the integrand by the amount of $\vec{Q}$-space available at each value of Q. The amount of $\vec{Q}$-space available on the sphere at an angle θ is proportional to $(4\pi^2/\lambda)\sin\theta$. Solving the geometry to express everything in terms of Q, we find that the Q-dependent weighting factor is

$$W(Q) = 2\pi Q\sqrt{1 - \left(\frac{Q\lambda}{4\pi}\right)}, \tag{13.27}$$

Note that this reduces to $2\pi Q$ at small angles, as it must, before the curvature of the sphere distorts this factor.

Putting it all together, we find

$$\int_R L(Q;\kappa)\,d\vec{Q} = \int_0^{4\pi/\lambda} \frac{W(Q)F_L(\kappa;R)}{Q^2+\kappa^2}\,dQ = 1, \tag{13.28}$$

which implies that

$$F_L(\kappa;R) = \left[\int_0^{4\pi/\lambda} \frac{W(Q)\,dQ}{Q^2+\kappa^2}\right]^{-1}. \tag{13.29}$$

After carrying out this integration, along with a similar one for the Lorentzian-squared $S(Q;\kappa)$, we find the following normalized forms of the functions, defining the dimensionless variable $\tilde{\kappa} = \kappa\lambda/4\pi$ for convenience:

$$L(Q;\kappa) = \left(\frac{1}{2\pi\left[(1+\tilde{\kappa}^2)\operatorname{arcsinh}(\tilde{\kappa}^{-1})-1\right]}\right)\frac{1}{Q^2+\kappa^2}$$

$$S(Q;\kappa) = \left(\frac{8\pi\sqrt{1+\tilde{\kappa}^2}}{\lambda^2\left[\tilde{\kappa}^{-2}\sqrt{1+\tilde{\kappa}^2}-\operatorname{arcsinh}(\tilde{\kappa}^{-1})\right]}\right)\frac{1}{(Q^2+\kappa^2)^2} \tag{13.30}$$

It is these forms which we have used in our simulation.

Appendix B. Smearing Corrections

Equation 13.4 makes the connection between the scattering vector $\vec{Q}$, used in theory, and the deflection angle θ which is experimentally measured. This connection is one-to-one as long as only neutrons of a single wavelength are used. However, no single wavelength gives enough neutrons to yield a detectable signal in a reasonable amount of time; in other words, SANS is a *flux-limited* technique. In practice, we are forced to allow a distribution of wavelengths, which means that each deflection angle θ corresponds to a *distribution* of Q-values. This effect is known as smearing, and it distorts the measured signal.

Traditional analysis uses one of two methods to account for smearing. The first is to "desmear" the data, by attempting to invert the function. Desmearing has the advantage that it only needs to be performed once, thus saving computation time. However, smearing is not strictly invertible.

The alternative is to smear the model function before fitting it to the measured data. Smearing at every step incurs a considerable computational cost, but leaves the experimental data inviolate. This latter option is very commonly done in traditional analysis; in Bayesian analysis, it is the *only* option.

The technique for smearing correction is outlined in (Kline, 2006). The fit function, $I(Q)$, is a continuous function determined by the values of its associated fit parameters (i.e. ξ_L, ξ_S, ...). To calculate the *smeared* intensity $I_s(Q_i)$, at the ith Q-value, one takes a weighted average of the unsmeared intensity,

$$I_s(Q_i) = \int_0^\infty R(Q,Q_i)I(Q)\,dQ \tag{13.31}$$

where $R(Q,Q_i)$ is the resolution function of the instrument at the point Q_i. This resolution function is well approximated as a Gaussian

$$R(Q, Q_i) \equiv \frac{f_s}{\left(2\pi\sigma_Q^2\right)^{1/2}} \exp\left[\frac{-\left(Q - \bar{Q}\right)^2}{2\sigma_Q^2}\right],$$ (13.32)

characterized by a mean $\bar{Q}$, standard deviation σ_Q, and a parameter f_s which represents the fraction not shadowed by the beamstop (typically, $f_s = 1$ for all but the lowest-Q points). Each of these parameters varies with the nominal Q (i.e. the angle θ), and these values are measured by the instrument scientists and provided to the users.

To improve execution time, we have replaced the integral in Equation 13.31 by a sampled Riemannian sum. A series of Q-values is generated, consisting of the original Q-values plus F more between each pair. The unsmeared fit function is evaluated at each Q-value in this new series. To calculate the *smeared* intensity at the original Q-values, a cutoff C is supplied by the user, such that only points between $(\bar{Q}_i - C\sigma_Q)$ and $(\bar{Q}_i + C\sigma_Q)$ are considered. These points are averaged according to

$$I_s(Q_i) = K_i \sum_{j;|Q_j - \bar{Q}_i| < C\sigma_Q} I(Q_j) exp\left[\frac{-\left(Q_j - \bar{Q}\right)^2}{2\sigma_Q^2}\right],$$ (13.33)

where the normalizing factor

$$K_i = f_s \left[\sum_{j;|Q_j - \bar{Q}_i| < C\sigma_Q} exp\left[\frac{-\left(Q_j - \bar{Q}\right)^2}{2\sigma_Q^2}\right]\right]^{-1}$$ (13.34)

ensures that the weights sum to f_s.

The results presented in this paper correspond to $F = 5$ and $C = 3$.

REFERENCES

Agostini, G. D. (2003). *Bayesian Reasoning in Data Analysis: A Critical Introduction.* World Scientific Publishing Company. 259

Bernhoeft, N. (1999). "Geometrical effects in diffraction analysis." *Acta Crystallographica. Section A, Foundations of Crystallography*, 55, 2, 274–288. 253

Carr, D. (2008). "hexbin: Hexagonal Binning Routines." *R package version 1.18.0*, ported by Nicholas Lewin–Koh, and Maechler, M. 268

Glinka, C. J., Barker, J. G., Hammouda, B., Krueger, S., Moyer, J. J., and Orts, W. J. (1998). "The 30 m Small-Angle Neutron Scattering Instruments at the National Institute of Standards and Technology." *J. Appl. Cryst*, 3, 430–445. 255

Hammouda, B. (2008). "The SANS Toolbox." http://www.ncnr.nist.gov/staff/hammouda/the/_SANS/_toolbox.pdf. 252, 254, 256, 264

Hengartner, N. (2008). "Statistical Analysis of Neutron Scattering Experiments." *5th LANSCE Neutron School 2008*. 262

Hogg, C. R. (2009). *Bayesian SANS MCMC.* stat-lib. http://lib.stat.cmu.edu/modules.php?op=modload&name=Downloads&file=index&req=viewdownloaddetails&lid=931&ttitle=SANS. 260

Kittel, C. (2004). *Introduction to Solid State Physics.* 8th ed. Wiley. 251

Kline, S. R. (2006). "Reduction and analysis of SANS and USANS data using IGOR Pro." *Journal of applied crystallography*, 39, 895–900. 258, 268, 273

Lindley, D. V. (2006). *Understanding Uncertainty*. 1st ed. Wiley-Interscience. 259

Luttinger, J. M. and Tisza, L. (1946). "Theory of Dipole Interaction in Crystals." *Physical Review*, 70, 954. 250

Michels, A., Viswanath, R. N., Barker, J. G., Birringer, R., and Weissmuller, J. (2003). "Range of Magnetic Correlations in Nanocrystalline Soft Magnets." *Physical Review Letters*, 91, 26, 267204. 253

Michels, A. and Weissmuller, J. (2008). "Magnetic-field-dependent small-angle neutron scattering on random anisotropy ferromagnets." *Reports on Progress in Physics*, 71, 6, 066501. 266

Murray, C. B., Kagan, C. R., and Bawendi, M. G. (1995). "Self-Organization of CdSe Nanocrystallites into Three-Dimensional Quantum Dot Superlattices." *Science*, 270, 5240, 1335–1338. 250

Narayanan, S., Wang, J., and Lin, X. M. (2004). "Dynamical Self-Assembly of Nanocrystal Superlattices during Colloidal Droplet Evaporation by in situ Small Angle X-Ray Scattering." *Physical Review Letters*, 93, 13, 135503. 250

R Development Core Team (2008). *R: A Language and Environment for Statistical Computing*. ISBN 3-900051-07-0. Vienna, Austria.: R Foundation for Statistical Computing. 259

Sachan, M., Bonnoit, C., Majetich, S. A., Ijiri, Y., Mensah-Bonsu, P., Borchers, J. A., and Rhyne, J. J. (2008). "Field evolution of magnetic correlation lengths in epsilon-Co nanoparticle assemblies." *Applied Physics Letters*, 92, 15, 52503–3. 255, 260, 266, 268, 271

Smith, B. J. (2007). "boa: An R Package for MCMC Output Convergence Assessment and Posterior Inference." *Journal of Statistical Software*, 21, 11, 1–37. 260

Squires, G. L. (1997). *Introduction to the Theory of Thermal Neutron Scattering*. Dover Publications. 254, 258

Stoner, E. C. and Wohlfarth, E. P. (1948). "A mechanism of magnetic hysteresis in heterogeneous alloys." *Philosophical Transactions of the Royal Society of London. Series A, Mathematical and Physical Sciences (1934-1990)*, 240, 826, 599–642. 250

Talapin, D. V., Shevchenko, E. V., Kornowski, A., Gaponik, N., Haase, M., Rogach, A. L., and Weller, H. (2001). "A New Approach to Crystallization of CdSe Nanoparticles into Ordered Three-Dimensional Superlattices." *Advanced Materials*, 13, 24, 1868. 250

Van Hove, L. (1954). "Correlations in Space and Time and Born Approximation Scattering in Systems of Interacting Particles." *Physical Review*, 95, 1, 249. http://link.aps.org/abstract/PR/v95/p249. 254

Yamamoto, K., Majetich, S. A., McCartney, M., Sachan, M., Yamamuro, S., and Hirayama, T. (2008). "Direct visualization of dipolar ferromagnetic domain structures in Co nanoparticle monolayers by electron holography." *Applied Physics Letters*, 93, 8, 82502–3. 250

Yeomans, J. M. (1992). *Statistical Mechanics of Phase Transitions*. USA: Oxford University Press. 253

Comment

Nick Hengartner
Los Alamos National Laboratory, Los Alamos, NM
mailto:nickh@lanl.gov

The authors are to be congratulated for a well writing introduction to the analysis of Small Angle Neutron Scattering (SANS) experiments datasets. These experiments provide a powerful tool to explore the ferromagnetic properties of thin films and nano-particles. The presented modeling framework for joint calibration data and experimental data is timely. It represents a paradigm shift from current established analysis practices and proposes a more principled approach to extract signal in SANS datasets. Better analysis methods are needed by experimentalists vying to measure signals ever more obscured by noise. As such, this papers answer Rutherford's call for better experiments to alleviate the need of statistics[†] by offering better statistics to analyze an existing experiment.

There are three aspects of SANS data analysis worth further comments: the need to model the signal in the space of the observations, ongoing calibration of the instrument, and a look at designing future SANS experiments.

Modeling. Raw SANS experimental data consist of pixel counts $N_{x,y}$ in the xy-plane, whose intensity is related to the scattering vector $\vec{Q}$ (see Figure 5 in Hogg et al. (2010)). Standard analysis (see Kline (2006) for example), transforms the xy-plane into $\vec{Q}$ before fitting the model by minimum χ^2. A better approach, advocated in this paper, is to transform the model defined as a function of $\vec{Q}$ into an expectation counts $\lambda_{x,y}$ in each pixel in the xy-plane.

There are several advantages to bringing the model into the space of observable data. First, it enables either a Bayesian or maximum likelihood type analysis that take advantage of the Poisson assumption for the raw pixel counts. Second, it makes possible to graphically explore the goodness-of-fit of the estimated model by displaying the residuals

$$R_{x,y} = \sqrt{N_{x,y}} - \sqrt{\hat{\lambda}_{x,y}}.$$

Finally, bootstrap samples for the data at hand are easily generated by drawing, for each pixel, the random variables

$$M_{xy}|N_{xy} \sim \text{Binomial}(N_{xy}, p),$$

for some $p \in (0,1)$. Since marginally M_{xy} is Poisson distributed with attenuated intensity $p\lambda_{xy}$, one can analyze that data in the same way as the original counts. And since $N_{xy} - M_{xy}$ is Poisson distributed with mean $(1-p)\lambda_{xy}$, independent of M_{xy}, this opens the door to Bayesian model checking using the inferred predictive distribution for $N_{xy} - M_{xy}$.

Calibration. The calibration of measurement instruments is an integral part of many modern experiments in the physical sciences. It involves characterizing the systematic effects arising from the measurement process, slowly varying effects, called drifts, that occur over the course of the experiment, and sample to sample random effects. The traditional approach to calibrate SANS experiments first estimates the baseline, and then uses that estimate to correct subsequently the data from the sample. The presented framework has many nice features, one of which I will elaborate on.

It is important to realize that calibration of an instrument is an ongoing process, and hence estimation of the baseline should not be undertaken *de novo* each time an experiment is performed. The Bayesian framework makes it possible to accumulate knowledge about the baseline of an instrument from periodic calibration experiments by viewing the posterior for the calibration parameters as the prior of these parameter for the next experiment.

Such an approach requires one to divide the systematic effects into fixed effects (for

---

[†] "If you need statistics, you ought have done a better experiment", Barron Rutherford

example the flux absorber, if it is fixed to the detector) and into random effects (for example the sample holder, if its position is changed from one experiment to the next). While the resulting analysis becomes more complex, it enables the accumulation over time of information about the baseline that results in more informative priors.

Design. Magnetization of a sample can be explored using polarized SANS experiments (Fitzsimmons et al. 2007). These experiments aim at measuring subtle differences in the scattering of *spin up* and *spin down* polarized neutrons. The framework presented in this paper is easily adapted to these experiments. However, since we seek to compare the response of the same sample to different beams, we have the opportunity to design experimental protocols that yield better paired comparisons. One such technique is to alternate during the course of the experiment the polarization of the beam. The second technique, still experimental (Fitzsimmons 2010) is to split the beam. These two techniques are not the approaches to control known sources of experimental variations. But they point the way that it is possible to estimate very small signals in SANS experiments. It is my hope that continued collaborations between statisticians and experimentalists will not only improve the analysis of SANS datasets, but impact the underlying experimental protocols, and to ultimately improve our ability to do science using small angle neutron scattering experiments.

In conclusion, the authors of this paper are to be commended for introducing statisticians to a fascinating topic in experimental physics, and physicists to modern data analysis methods.

REFERENCES

Fitzsimmons, M.R. (2010). Personal communication.

Fitzsimmons, M.R., Kirby, B.J., Hengartner, N.W., Trouw, F., Ericsson, M.J., Flexner, S.D., Kondo, T., Adelmann, C., Palmistry, C.J., Crowell, P.A., Chen, W.C, Gentile, T.R., Borchers, J.A., Majkrzak, C.F. and Pynn, R. (2007). "Suppression of nuclear polarization near the surface of optically pumped GaAs." *Phys. Rev. B*, 76: 1–6.

Hogg, C.R., Kadane, J.B., Lee, J.S. and Majetich, S.A. (2010) "Error analysis for small angle neutron scattering datasets using Bayesian inference." *Bayesian Analysis*, 5: 1–34.

Kline, S.R. (2006). "Reduction and Analysis of SANS and USANS Data Using IGOR Pro." *J. Appl. Crust.*, 39: 895–900.

Comment

John Skilling
Maximum Entropy Data Consultants, Kenmare, Ireland
skilling@eircom.net
and Devinder Sivia
St. Johns College, Oxford, UK
devinder.sivia@sjc.ox.ac.uk

This is a beautifully illustrated and clear account of a particular data analysis problem in the physical sciences. It is particularly helpful to see this sort of problem in the literature of statistics, whose techniques can serve any of the sciences.

Different sciences import different outlooks. To oversimplify, social science data is "soft" and modelled by smooth distributions, physical science models are tightly defined with the data defining a likelihood function that can be arbitrarily digital and rough, while biological sciences are nowadays dominated by size and complexity. Statistics used to be oriented towards the social sciences, with physical sciences being an almost trivial (usually frequentist and wrong) aside. That has changed, and it's valuable that statisticians be exposed to the differing needs. The particular topic of neutron scattering measurement of magnetism is specific, but the authors' approach is general. And it raises basic points.

Theory suggests a model for magnetism in solids, described by a 4-parameter function of radial separation r;

$$G(r) = \sum_L \exp(-r/\xi_L) + \sum_S r^{-1} \exp(-r/\xi_S)$$

Neutron scattering measures the Fourier transform of G, being the intensity scattered sideways as a beam traverses the magnetised solid. Of course, matters aren't quite so simple when instrumentation is involved, and the data finally involve 16 partially known parameters, not 4. And minor complexity is added because the sample is embedded in magnetic fields H of three different strengths (0, 0.2 and 1 Tesla), so there are three cases to consider. Welcome to the real world.

Bayesian analysis demands careful attention to priors as well as to likelihood, but the prize is that "the richness of information available [in the posterior] enables novel forms of presentation, capable of conveying deep insight into uncertainty and correlation at a glance". Quite so!

Yet there remains scope for improvement. All too often, Bayesian computation remains expensive, but that may be due to algorithm inefficiency more than intrinsic difficulty. Eyeballing these results suggests that posterior parameters are here located to a few percent accuracy, and there are only 16 of them, so the prior-to-posterior compression is no more than a factor $30^{16} = 2^{80}$. A good algorithm, compressing geometrically, should not need more than 80 iterates to accomplish this. Then, having a seed point, 100 random samples from the posterior should be more than enough to acquire any chosen property, along with its uncertainty, each needing a few MC proposals from the seed. So 1000 or so iterates should suffice. Yet the authors use a million, which takes 4 days and seems to be inefficient by 3 orders of magnitude. Better off-the-shelf algorithms please!

More fundamentally, and this is a distressingly common omission, there is no mention of the evidence (a.k.a. marginal likelihood) value. Bayesian inference produces this fundamental number as well as the posterior. As a matter of courtesy, that number should always be calculated and stated. Otherwise, researchers with a different model or a different prior are forced to reproduce this calculation as well as performing their own before they can reach the Bayes factor that guides the decision as to which model is better. Evidence please! But let us not seem churlish by applying future standards to present practice. We like the paper.

Rejoinder

We thank the discussants for their valuable commentary on our paper. A common theme was the value in making modern statistical methods more widely known in the physical sciences. Below, we comment on specific issues raised by the discussants.

Algorithm Efficiency

Skilling and Sivia rightly point out the poor efficiency of our MCMC algorithm. We've continued to attack the speed problem, and are pleased to report significant progress.

The main culprit was the proposal strategy for bounded parameters. We wanted distributions which vanish outside the allowed region, since this greatly simplifies correcting for unequal proposal probabilities. The scaled Beta fits nicely; moreover, there are simple analytic expressions for the parameter values which give a target mean and variance,

$$\alpha = \left[\frac{\mu(1-\mu)}{\sigma^2} - 1\right]\mu$$

$$\beta = \left[\frac{\mu(1-\mu)}{\sigma^2} - 1\right](1-\mu),$$

(13.35)

as long as $\alpha > 0$ and $\beta > 0$.[6] However, these formulae are non-unimodal when $\alpha < 1$ or $\beta < 1$, exhibiting proposal probabilities which diverge near the boundaries. This caused a computational instability, since the most extreme values were the most often proposed. We circumvented this by requiring both α and β to be greater than one, yielding a unimodal distribution.

More seriously, our original approach is suboptimal even without this numerical instability. The support of the distribution covered the entire domain, leading to huge proposed jumps when near the boundaries. We eliminated this problem with a new paradigm for bounded proposals. Pick a "jump" distance J: the limit is either J, or the boundary, whichever is closer. Explicitly, we generate candidates X' from current value X as follows:

$$\frac{X' - (X - JA)}{J(A+B)} \sim \text{Beta}(\alpha = A+1, \beta = B+1)$$

(13.36)

with A the maximum allowed negative jump, and B the maximum allowed positive jump, both as fractions of J. This new approach eliminates extreme proposals which waste computation, while still respecting the boundaries of parameters.

We found further room for improvement with strongly correlated parameters. Originally, we proposed changes to parameters one at a time, and made the accept/reject decision before generating the next parameter's proposals. We now generate simultaneous proposals for correlated parameters, empirically reducing the number of steps to equilibrium by a factor of 2. Moreover, the steps themselves are considerably quicker, since multiple accept/reject decisions are condensed into one. We expect our algorithms could converge still more quickly, either with proposals skewed towards the direction of correlation, or by reparameterizing the correlated parameters.

In addition to algorithmic improvements, we reduced the computation time by recoding our MCMC loop in C++ instead of R. We output the chain to a textfile, then use boa to analyze the results just as in the previous case.

Bayes factors

It is worth noting that unlike posterior distributions, likelihood functions are not probability distributions over the parameter space. In order to interpret them, some prior distribution must be assumed.

We think, however, that Bayes factors are overemphasized. In the very special case in which there are only two possible "states of the world", Bayes factors are sufficient. However in the typical case in which there are many possible states of the world, Bayes factors are sufficient only when the decision-maker's loss has only two values: 0 if the decision is correct and 1 otherwise. Thus the use of Bayes factors involves the

---

[6] These conditions can always be met by requesting a smaller target variance.

rather unsatisfactory idea that if I decide that a parameter $\theta = 0$ and I am wrong, it doesn't matter how wrong I am: $\theta = e^{17}$ and $\theta = e^{-17}$ have the same loss for me. Few situations in any science satisfy this criterion (see Kadane and Dickey (1980)).

However, we take the issue of robustness seriously. Prior robustness is rather simple in the MCMC context. An MCMC sample can be reweighted by the ratio of the prior of interest to the prior used in the MCMC, whether the prior incorporates independence or dependence among parameters.

Modeling, Calibration, Design

We also thank Nick Hengartner for his constructive thoughts about how to use hierarchical Bayesian models flexibly. We agree that further collaboration between physicists and statisticians could push the field forward. Unlike in Rutherford's day, machine time is precious, so efficient use of the data produced seems well worthwhile.

REFERENCES

Kadane, J.B. and Dickey, J.M. (1980). "Bayesian Decision Theory and the Simplification of Models." In Kmenta, J. and Ramsey, J. (eds.), *Evaluation of Econometric Models*, NBER Chapters, 245–268. National Bureau of Economic Research, Inc. http://ideas.repec.org/h/nbr/nberch/11704.html

Epilogue

What is the scientific question addressed?
        To give well-based estimates and measures of uncertainty (in our case, posterior distributions) for correlation lengths from small-angle neutron scattering (SANS) experiments.
Is justification given for
        a) the use of the data?
        The data were collected from SANS experiments from the background (using the beam blocker), the empty sample holder, and the sample.
        b) the likelihood and prior?
        These are described extensively in the paper.
What robustness studies are performed?
        The main comparison is with an already-published traditional analysis of the same data (see Table 13.5).
How were the computations done?
        Markov chain Monte Carlo.
If I were doing the problem again, how would I change the approach?
        I would not.
What do I see as the contribution of the paper?
        To give physically meaningful measures of uncertainty. We also found that at higher fields, SANS is more limited than had previously been thought.
Was Bayesian analysis useful in this problem?
        I believe it is critical to the success of the effort.

TEACHING SUGGESTIONS

References for theoretical ideas:

1. Hierarchical modelling: *Principles* Chapter 9

2. Markov chain Monte Carlo: *Principles* Chapter 10

3. Poisson distribution: *Principles* Section 3.9

Exercises

1. In this application, what are the advantages of Bayesian analysis over traditional chi-squared analysis? What are the disadvantages?

2. Why is it important to model the background and the sample holder?

3. The paper claims that Bayesian analysis permits "novel forms of presentation, capable of conveying deep insight." Really? What are they? Why can't a traditional analysis do the same?

Chapter 14

Impacts of Beliefs about Tropical Cyclone Detection on Conclusions about Trends in Tropical Cyclone Number (2011)

Foreword

One of the purported consequences of the increased release of carbon dioxide into the air due to the industrial revolution is an increase in the number and/or intensity of hurricanes in the North Atlantic. To examine the extent to which this is the case, one looks to data on North Atlantic hurricanes in the last 150 years, and this does indeed show an increase. However, the criteria for recording a hurricane in the standard database are strict, and it is obvious that our ability to detect hurricanes has increased enormously. Where once we relied on reports of ship captains and landfall, we now have satellites that plausibly detect every tropical disturbance. Accordingly, it is necessary to model the extent to which detection capabilities have improved in order to assess whether hurricanes have increased.

This paper proposes such a model. By changing one of the priors in the detection model with a seemingly small variation, we obtain increasing, constant, or decreasing numbers of hurricanes over the period. The consequence is that the historical record is ambiguous. This does not mean that climate change is not a serious matter, or that human activity is not responsible for a large part of it. Rather it simply means that we do not know, and are not likely to know, whether hurricanes in the North Atlantic have increased. This is an example in which uncertainty has important strategic implications for science: study climate change, certainly, but do not look to hurricanes in the North Atlantic for evidence either way.

This paper is an outcome of Anne-Sophie's Advanced Data Analysis project. Surya Tokdar and I were her advisors in the Statistics Department. Her subject-matter experts were Iris Grossmann and Mitchell Small from the CMU Department of Engineering and Public Policy.

Where are they now? Surya Tokdar is Assistant Professor in the Department of Statistical Science, Duke University. Iris Grossmann is Research Scientist at the Center for Climate and Energy Policy, Department of Engineering and Public Policy, Carnegie Mellon University, Anne-Sophie Charest is Assistant Professor in the Department of Mathematics and Statistics, University of Laval, Montreal, and Mitchell J. Small is H. John Heinz III Professor of Environmental Engineering, Department of Engineering and Public Policy, Carnegie Mellon University.

This paper was published in *Bayesian Analysis*, **6**, (#5), pp. 547–572. The International Society for Bayesian Analysis does not require permission to republish.

Published Paper

S.T. Tokdar[1], I. Grossmann[2], J.B. Kadane[3], A.-S. Charest[4] and M.J. Small[5]

Abstract

Whether the number of tropical cyclones (TCs) has increased in the last 150 years has become a matter of intense debate. We investigate the effects of beliefs about TC detection capacities in the North Atlantic on trends in TC numbers since the 1870s. While raw data show an increasing trend of TC counts, the capability to detect TCs and to determine intensities and changes in intensity has also increased dramatically over the same period. We present a model of TC activity that allows investigating the relationship between what one believes about the increase in detection and what one believes about TC trends. Previous work has used assumptions on TC tracks, detection capacities or the relationship between TC activity and various climate parameters to provide estimates of year-by-year missed TCs. These estimates and the associated conclusions about trends cover a wide range of possibilities. We build on previous work to investigate the sensitivity of these conclusions to the assumed priors about detection. Our analysis shows that any inference on TC count trends is strongly sensitive to one's specification of prior beliefs about TC detection. Overall, we regard the evidence on the trend in North Atlantic TC numbers to be ambiguous.

Keywords: Atlantic tropical cyclones, HURDAT, tropical cyclone data, tropical cyclone detection.

14.1 Introduction

Whether anthropogenic global warming may be impacting tropical cyclones (TCs) has become a matter of intense debate (Knutson et al., 2010; Grossmann and Morgan, 2011). Raw data from the North Atlantic show an increasing trend of annual TC counts in the region (Vecchi and Knutson, 2008; Holland and Webster, 2007). A similar observation holds for the number of high-intensity TCs (Webster et al., 2005). The difficulty of interpretation is that the capability to detect TCs and to determine intensities and change in intensity has also increased dramatically over the same period (e.g. Landsea et al., 2004, 2006; Landsea, 2007). Consequently there is a relationship between what one believes about the increase in detection capability and what one believes about trends in TC activity. This paper investigates the effects of beliefs about TC detection capacities in the North Atlantic on trends in Atlantic TC numbers.

The inference on the trend of tropical cyclone counts shares common elements with other statistical problems in trend analysis with missing observations, particularly where there is systematic bias in observations over a portion of the temporal

[1] Department of Statistical Science, Duke University, Durham, NC, st118@stat.duke.edu
[2] Climate Decision Making Center, Carnegie Mellon University, Pittsburgh, PA, irisg@andrew.cmu.edu
[3] Department of Statistics, Carnegie Mellon University, Pittsburgh, PA, kadane@stat.cmu.edu
[4] Department of Statistics, Carnegie Mellon University, Pittsburgh, PA, acharest@stat.cmu.edu
[5] Department of Engineering and Public Policy, Carnegie Mellon University, Pittsburgh, PA, ms35@andrew.cmu.edu

or spatial domain (Coles and Sparks, 2006; Cornulier et al., 2011; Kéry and Royle, 2010). An effective approach for dealing with nonrandom missing data is to include a representation for the observation process (or the missing data mechanism) as part of the overall statistical model (Little, 1995; Zeger and Liang, 1996; Ibrahim et al., 2001; Tingley and Huybers, 2010). Missing data are then imputed as part of the parameter estimation process, resulting in a joint distribution for the model parameters and the missing observations (Rubin, 1996; Allison, 2001; Honaker and King, 2010).

The dataset used for studies on North Atlantic TC trends is the "best track" dataset of the National Hurricane Center (HURDAT) (Jarvinen et al., 1984). HURDAT includes observed positions, maximum wind speeds, and some central pressure measurements for TCs dating back to 1851. The North Atlantic is widely regarded as having the most reliable TC data and the longest TC time series. Trend detection in all basins, in particular the North Atlantic, is complicated by natural variability on several time scales, including the multidecadal (Klotzbach and Gray, 2008; Vecchi and Knutson, 2008). Consequently, long historical coverage is essential for trend analysis. However, Atlantic TC records from the earlier period prior to the availability of reconnaissance aircraft and satellites rely on sparsely populated coasts and limited ship tracks (Landsea et al., 2004, 2006), with the consequence that some TCs likely did not get recorded. Thus, an increasing trend of the observed counts might be attributed entirely to improvements in detection technology (Landsea, 2007).

The extent of data quality issues in HURDAT has been the subject of intense discussions (Landsea, 2007; Holland and Webster, 2007; Vecchi and Knutson, 2008; Chang and Guo, 2007; Mann et al., 2007; Bengtsson and Hodges, 2008; Landsea et al., 2010), with some studies suggesting that the Atlantic TC record can be regarded as reasonably reliable back into the late 19th century because ships could not be warned off from approaching TCs (Mann and Emanuel, 2006; Holland and Webster, 2007). A number of recent studies aim at interpreting the HURDAT records by augmenting it with estimates of year-by-year missed TC counts. These studies can be categorized into three groups based on the principles they employ to estimate missed TCs. One group matches satellite-era TC tracks with earlier ship tracks and land points (Chang and Guo, 2007; Vecchi and Knutson, 2008). A second group analyzes time trends of the proportion of TCs possessing certain characteristics, such as TCs making landfall, which can be argued to have enjoyed good detection even in the earlier times (Solow and Moore, 2000, 2002; Landsea, 2007; Nyberg et al., 2007; Elsner and Bossak, 2006). A third group predicts TC counts by modeling their relationship to other climate variables with more accurate historical records (Mann et al., 2007; Solow and Beet, 2008).

Building on these studies, our analysis investigates the sensitivity of conclusions about trends in TC numbers to the assumed priors about detection. Our goal is to encourage climate researchers to use the platform we develop, possibly in conjunction with other trend models, and to draw their attention to the extremely important issue of carefully quantifying one's beliefs about detection probabilities. To illustrate this latter point, we first develop a belief quantification that produces estimates of missed TC counts that match the numbers reported in Vecchi and Knutson (2008), thus recapturing their conclusion of an increasing trend of yearly TC counts since the 1870s. We then show that seemingly minor changes to this belief quantification result in either roughly constant or negative trends. This sensitivity of the inference to the prior input is not a negative feature of our approach, rather a simple reminder of the inherent ambiguity of the HURDAT records caused by missing observations. Our analysis shows that any inference on TC count trend is strongly sensitive to one's specification of prior beliefs about TC detection.

In Section 14.2, we begin by reviewing changes in TC detection methods and

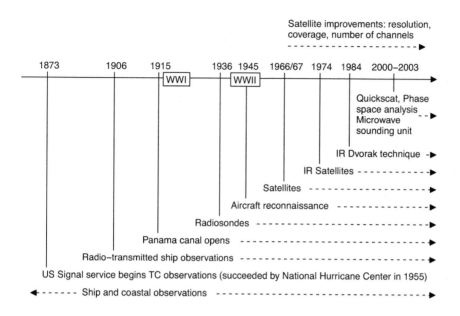

Figure 14.1: A timeline of Atlantic TC observation cataloging main changes in observation technology along with other major events that may have impacted TC recording.

technologies over time. We then briefly discuss the assumptions that had to be made by different previously published approaches for the estimation of missed Atlantic TCs. Section 14.3 explains the data and methods. Our results in Sections 14.4 and 14.5 show the strong sensitivity to the assumptions made on TC detection capacities and highlight the resulting ambiguity in the trend of TC numbers. In Section 14.6 we present possible ways to resolve this ambiguity.

14.2   TC Detection and Recording over the Years

Tropical cyclones are warm-core low pressure systems with a closed circulation over tropical or subtropical oceans. The weakest form of a TC is called tropical depression. TCs with wind speeds of 35 knots or more are called tropical storms, TCs with speeds of 65 knots or more are called hurricanes; the latter range from the less intense category 1 to the very intense category 5 (Simpson, 1974). Trend analysis of TC numbers considers "named storms", that is, TCs of tropical storm strength or greater. Two criteria determine whether wind speed observations of tropical storm strength or greater are recorded as tropical cyclones within HURDAT (Landsea et al., 2008). First, evidence of a closed circulation and the non-frontal character of the system are required to distinguish the cyclone from an extratropical or subtropical cyclone. Second, at least two wind speed measurements or estimates by independent observers are required (Landsea et al., 2008). Thus, the reasons leading to a TC not being recorded in HURDAT are twofold: first, an actual lack of observations of the TC in question, and second, a lack of information to classify the observed wind anomaly as a tropical cyclone. Figure 14.1 gives a timeline of how TC observation technology has changed over the years, along with the occurrences of the major events that may have impacted our ability to record TCs.

The US Signal Service has been observing Atlantic TCs since approximately 1873 (Sheets, 1990; Fernández-Partagás and Diaz, 1996). Several forecast offices were established in the 1930s, followed by the designation of the Miami forecast office as National Hurricane Center in 1955 (Sheets, 1990). Satellite observations have been available since 1967, aircraft reconnaissance since 1945. Prior to 1945, TC records relied entirely on ship and coastal observations. In parts of the US, insufficient coastal density and limited reporting in the early part of the century may have led to a failure to detect landfalling TCs that had not been reported by ships (Landsea, 2007; Landsea et al., 2008; Sheets, 1990, Figure 1). This is illustrated by the recent addition of four new landfalling storms to the 10-year period from 1911-20 in the course of the ongoing reanalysis of the HURDAT records (Landsea et al., 2008).

Ships may not have sighted and reported all TCs that occurred due to insufficient coverage with regular ship routes, insufficient observation equipment, and possibly conscious avoidance of an approaching storm. Until radio became available in 1905, TC observations relied on ship reports after the ship returned to port. TC observations were evaluated with the Beaufort scale, which specifies differences in waves and the ocean state up to category 1 hurricanes, and with marine barometers if available (Landsea et al., 2004). In 1900, approximately one quarter of ships were equipped with marine barometers; by 1930, most had barometers (C. W. Landsea, personal communication, 2007). Prior to the opening of the Panama Canal in 1915, ship routes were concentrated in the northern and eastern parts of the basin and near the US East coast. The opening of the Panama Canal significantly increased the likelihood of observation of TCs south of 32°N (Vecchi and Knutson, 2008). Methods to detect approaching TCs prior to recording gale force winds were available although it is unclear to what extent mariners made use of these methods to avoid contact with approaching TCs (Bowditch, 1841; Piddington, 1860; Bowditch, 1995).

Both limited coverage by ship tracks and the possible conscious avoidance of TCs may have resulted in missed TCs. Evidence of a closed circulation usually relied on weather maps or multiple observations of the same TC. With the limited coverage and limited quality of observations, such evidence was not always available, likely resulting in the omission of several TCs from HURDAT during this era. Aircraft reconnaissance has been used sporadically since 1944, and more regularly since 1956 after the devastation caused by several New England hurricanes (Dorst, 2007). Until the 1960s, reconnaissance flights were typically dispatched to investigate TCs that had already been detected; in addition, regular patrols covered the route from Bermuda to east of St. Croix, St. Croix to Miami and back to Bermuda (Dunn and Miller, 1960). Flights generally did not travel beyond 55°W. Dunn and Miller (1960, page 155), report that about half of all TCs were initially detected by ships until the 1960s. While some TCs were probably first detected by aircraft, this leaves a large number of TCs to be initially detected by islands or coastal areas, implying that at least some of those TCs that remained at a reasonable distance from islands and coasts were likely missed altogether.

During the early satellite era beginning in 1967, TC observations relied on a combination of visible satellite imagery and aircraft reconnaissance (Neumann et al., 1999). Nighttime observations became possible only with the launch of infrared (IR) satellites in 1974 and the adoption of a Dvorak-scheme for the interpretation of IR imagery in 1984 (Dvorak, 1984). Further significant changes were gradual improvements in coverage and resolution (Sheets, 1990; Landsea et al., 2006), and the addition of the Advanced Microwave Sounding unit (Brueske and Velden, 2003), the Quick Scatterometer, or "QuikSCAT" (Atlas et al., 2001) and the Cyclone Phase Space analysis tool (Harper and Callaghan, 2006), during the years 2000 to 2003 (Landsea, 2007).

Two types of systems might be underrepresented to some extent prior to these more recent improvements. First, TCs with very short lifetimes could have been missed (Landsea et al., 2010), in particular due to a lack of nighttime IR imagery and due to viewing gaps. Knapp and Kossin (2007) find that in the 1980s, satellite observations were not available during 5.5% of all 6-hour periods during which a TC was present in the North Atlantic; during the 1990s and 2000s this was reduced to 1.6% and 0.5%, respectively. Second, storms may have been detected but not classified as TCs as they exhibited tropical characteristics or tropical storm strength for only a short period of time. The capacity to classify storms that were tropical only for short time periods has also improved dramatically over time; in fact Landsea (2007) suggests that capacities may have become adequate only in recent years with the help of new tools. The original Dvorak developmental sample (Velden et al., 2006) did not include subtropical systems – storms that exhibit both tropical and extratropical characteristics and that might or might not become fully tropical at some stage of their lives.

Approaches that estimate missed TCs necessarily rely on assumptions about detection capacities, and in some cases, aspects of TC activity and the presence or absence of changes in TC activity over time. Matching ship tracks with satellite era TC tracks requires the assumption that the spatial distribution of satellite era TC tracks is similar to the distribution during earlier time periods (Vecchi and Knutson, 2008). However, tracks may not be static in time if they respond to shifts in atmosphere-ocean conditions such as the recent warming of the eastern Atlantic (Holland, 2007).

A second type of assumption made by approaches using ship tracks is that the number of recorded TCs during the satellite era matches the number of TCs that actually occurred. This assumption is problematic given the insufficiency of observational capacities for the correct classification of short-lived or weak tropical storms until very recently (Landsea, 2007; Landsea et al., 2010). Models using climate variables are affected by a similar problem, as the assumed relationship between TCs and climatic variables has to rely on data over a certain time period (or time periods) to estimate the parameters in the model. However, available observation technologies and interpretation schemes continued to undergo significant changes and improvements during the satellite era, with likely effects on the completeness of TC records (Landsea, 2007; Landsea et al., 2010). Hence even the satellite era records are likely not to be complete.

A third type of assumption made by approaches that consider ship tracks concerns observation and detection capacities and practices. Available studies assume land points to be perfect storm detectors. This means, first, that coasts were populated at sufficient density to detect TCs, which may not have been the case in the first two or three decades of the century (Sheets, 1990; Landsea et al., 2006). Second, it is assumed that land points everywhere were sufficiently equipped to observe and correctly classify TCs (Vecchi and Knutson, 2008; Chang and Guo, 2007). It is further assumed that ships did not alter their course to avoid encounters with TCs before tropical storm force winds and in particular evidence for a closed circulation could be reported (Vecchi and Knutson, 2008). If TCs were avoided, this should have caused the record of observed TCs to be even more incomplete. It is also assumed that observation by one (Chang and Guo, 2007) or two (Vecchi and Knutson, 2008) observers always led to a storm being recorded. The additional requirement that evidence of the storms' tropical characteristics be available has not been incorporated into available studies (Vecchi and Knutson, 2008).

14.3 Combining Detection Probability with Raw Counts

Let n_i denote the raw TC counts in the HURDAT records corresponding to calendar year y_i, $i = 1, 2, \cdots, N$. We cover the period from $y_1 = 1871$ through $y_N = 2008$ with

$N = 138$. Let m_i denote the missed TC counts for these years, and $t_i = n_i + m_i$ the actual total TC counts. Our aim is to infer about the trend of t_i's. We achieve this within a Poisson trend model (Solow, 1989; Elsner and Kara, 1999):

$$t_i \quad \sim \quad \text{Po}(\lambda_i), \quad t_i\text{'s are independent across } i, \tag{14.1}$$

$$\log \lambda_i \quad = \quad \eta_1 + \eta_2 \frac{y_i - \bar{y}}{N - 1} + \phi_1 \cos\left(\pi\left\{\phi_2 + \phi_3 \frac{y_i - y_1}{y_N - y_1}\right\}\right) \tag{14.2}$$

where $\bar{y} = \frac{1}{N}\sum_i y_i = 1939.5$ denotes the "central year" for the period under study. In (14.2), $\eta_1 + \eta_2 \frac{y_i - \bar{y}}{N-1}$ reflects a linear trend (in log scale) of the total TC counts: e^{η_1} gives the mean TC count in the central year and $e^{\eta_2} - 1$ gives the relative change in mean counts over the N years with respect to year 1. The important parameter here is the slope η_2. A positive, zero or negative value of η_2 indicates an increasing, flat or decreasing trend of the total TC counts. The cosine term in (14.2) is introduced to allow for multidecadal oscillation in TC frequency (Klotzbach and Gray, 2008; Elsner and Jagger, 2006; Goldenberg et al., 2001; Vecchi and Knutson, 2008; Knutson et al., 2007). Here, ϕ_1 encodes the amplitude of this oscillation; ϕ_2 encodes a phase shift, $\phi_2 = 0$ makes year 1 coincide with a peak (positive or negative depending on the sign of ϕ_1) of this oscillation; ϕ_3 encodes the number of oscillation cycles within the period of study.

For the j-th TC in the i-th year, let the detection probability be π_{ij}, $j = 1, 2, \cdots, t_i$, $i = 1, 2, \cdots, N$. We let π_{ij} depend both on the detection technology available in year i and a scalar z_{ij} denoting some measure of strength of the TC being detected. The latter is included to reflect the notion that for any given detection method, a stronger TC was more likely to be detected than a weaker one. This measure of strength can be defined in various ways and a vector of multiple measures could also be considered. For our illustration, we consider a simple measure where z_{ij} denotes the time (in hours) the corresponding TC had wind speed in category 1 or higher. We specify

$$\pi_{ij} = \Phi(\gamma_i + \beta z_{ij}) \tag{14.3}$$

where the scalar parameter γ_i gives the contribution of the i-th year's detection technology, and the scalar parameter β gives the influence of TC strength on its detectability; $\Phi(x) = \int_{-\infty}^{x} (\sqrt{2\pi})^{-1} \exp(-z^2/2) dz$ denotes the cumulative distribution function of the standard normal distribution. In principle, one can replace β with a year dependent β_i, but we shall stick to a constant β to maintain simplicity.

Note that z_{ij} is unobserved for every TC that went undetected. This requires a probability distribution to describe what these missing measurements could have been, with parameters underlying the distribution that can be learned from the z_{ij} that were actually recorded. Toward this, we define $z_{ij} = \max(0, v_{ij})$ with $v_{ij} \sim \text{N}(\mu_i, \sigma_i^2)$ independently of each other. This definition reflects that each z_{ij} is non-negative and can equal zero with probability $1 - \Phi(\mu_i/\sigma_i)$. The year specific means μ_i and variances σ_i^2 allow year to year variation in the overall strength of the North Atlantic TC season. Although other models for z_{ij} could be considered, we prefer the truncated normal model because it leads to simple computations for learning its parameters within a Bayesian setting with a conjugate prior specification.

The unknown parameters in our model are η_1, η_2, ϕ_1, ϕ_2, ϕ_3, $\{\mu_i\}_{i=1}^N$, $\{\sigma_i^2\}_{i=1}^N$, $\{\gamma_i\}_{i=1}^N$ and β. For our illustrations, we fix the detection parameters β and $\{\gamma_i\}_{i=1}^N$, partly to emphasize that the inference on the other parameters, particularly η_2, is quite sensitive to the choice of these parameters. Specific choices are given in the next section. Prior beliefs about each of the remaining parameters are specified by choosing an appropriate probability distribution as described in Table 14.1. These parameters

Table 14.1: Prior distributions on model parameters (except for detection probability parameters).

Parameter	Prior	Related TC characteristic	TC characteristic median (95% CI)
η_1	$N(2,1)$	Mean TC count in central year: e^{η_1}	7 (1, 52)
η_2	$N(0, 0.7^2)$	Percentage change over N years in mean TC count relative to year 1: $e^{\eta_2} - 1$	0% (-75%, 294%)
ϕ_1	Discrete uniform on $\{-.5, -.475, \cdots, .5\}$	Percentage change from minimum to maximum mean TC count due to oscillation: $e^{2|\phi_1|} - 1$	65% (3%, 165%)
ϕ_2	Discrete uniform on $\{-.5, -.4, \cdots, .5\}$	Oscillation phase shift: $\pi\phi_2$	0 ($-\pi/2$, $\pi/2$)
ϕ_3	Discrete uniform on $\{2, 2.2, \cdots, 8\}$	Number of oscillation cycles: $\phi_3/2$	2.5 (1, 4)
$(\mu_i, \sigma_i^2)_{i=1}^N$	$\mu_i \vert \sigma_i^2 \sim N(25, \frac{\sigma_i^2}{100})$, $\sigma_i^{-2} \sim Ga(50, 50 \cdot 10^4)$, independent over i	A. Fraction of years with 40% or more non-hurricane TCs: $\frac{\#\{i: \ \Phi(-\frac{\mu_i}{\sigma_i}) \geq .4\}}{N}$	51% (43%, 60%)
		B. Fraction of years with 1/6-th or more TCs staying category 1 or higher for 5 or more days: $\frac{\#\{i: \ \Phi(\frac{120-\mu_i}{\sigma_i}) \geq 1/6\}}{N}$	57% (49%, 64%)

are taken to be *a priori* independent of each other, i.e., the joint prior distribution on all these parameters is simply the product of the marginal prior distributions that appear in Table 14.1. The entries in Table 14.1 are chosen as follows. For each parameter, we look at model features (usually one) that are directly influenced by the parameter. Then a prior distribution is chosen to provide reasonable values for the *a priori* midpoint and range for each of these model features. All prior distributions are chosen from simple exponential family distributions or discrete distributions. A normal-inverse-gamma prior for the (μ_i, σ_i^2)'s is chosen because of its conjugacy properties.

14.4 Illustration

To specify the detection probability parameters β and $\{\gamma_i\}_{i=1}^N$, we first split the study period into 10 sub-periods. The separation points are chosen to reflect significant changes in detection technology over the years as well as some other global events that are likely to have affected TC recording. These ten sub-periods are shown on the first column of Table 14.2, with the events determining the onset of these sub-periods described in the second column. The γ_i values for all years within a sub-period are taken to be identical.

Table 14.2: Choice of detection probability parameters γ_i and β for experiments E1, E2 and E3.

		E1	E2	E3
y_i	Comments	γ_i	γ_i	γ_i
1871-1872	Beginning of study	-3.5	-3.5	-3.5
1873-1905	US Signal Service	-2.75	-3.25	-3.25
1906-1916	Ships with radio	-0.75	-1.5	-1.5
1917-1920	US in WWI & after-effects of WWI	-1.5	-2.25	-2.25
1921-1940	Post WWI	0.5	-1.25	-1.25
1941-1945	US in WWII	-2.5	-2.5	-2.5
1946-1966	Post WWII & aircraft	0.5	0.5	0.5
1967-1973	Early satellite era	1.5	1.5	1.5
1974-2001	Infrared satellites; better resolution & coverage	2	2	2
2003-2008	New tools (QuikSCAT, Microwave Sounding Unit, Cyclone Phase Space Analysis)	2.5	2.5	2.5
		β	β	β
		0.02	0.02	0.01

In our first experiment (E1 hereafter), we consider values of γ_i and β as given in the E1 column of Table 14.2. The detection probabilities in E1 were chosen to obtain a posterior summary of missed TC counts similar to that of Vecchi and Knutson (2008). For this choice, detection probabilities of 7 hypothetical TCs are shown in the top-left panel of Figure 14.2. These 7 TCs correspond to 7 different levels of strength, starting from a TC that never reached category 1 windspeed, to one that was category 1 or more for 10 days. For each sub-period, the detection probabilities of the 7 storms are shown by 7 dots in the middle. Detection probabilities are flat within a sub-period; the lines joining dots from one sub-period to the next are purely for visual assistance.

Once the detection probabilities are specified, we learn about other model parameters from data through their joint posterior distribution as determined by the likelihood function and the prior. We use a reversible jump Markov chain Monte Carlo (Green, 1995) to sample from the joint posterior of the model parameters plus the missing observations m_i and z_{ij} (for unobserved TCs). A Metropolis update with Gaussian increment is used for each of η_1 and η_2, with increment size chosen to achieve an acceptance rate close to 45%. Gibbs updates are used for ϕ_1, ϕ_2, ϕ_3, and the block $\{(\mu_i, \sigma_i^2)\}_i$. The conditional posterior distribution of each of these parameters assumes a simple form thanks to either discreteness or well-known conjugacy properties of the normal-inverse-gamma prior.

The missing observations $\{(m_i, \{z_{ij}\}_{j=n_i+1}^{n_i+m_i})\}_{i=1}^N$ are updated via reversible jump Metropolis. For a randomly chosen year, an "addition" or a "deletion" is proposed with equal probability. In the case of addition, a missing TC, with z_{ij} generated from the prior, is proposed to be added to that year's TC count. For deletion, a TC from that year's list of missing TCs is chosen randomly and is proposed to be removed. These proposals are complementary to each other and lead to simple calculations of acceptance probabilities that preserve detailed balance. For a year with no missing TC currently imputed, only the addition proposal is made. We use 50 addition-deletion moves per iteration of the MCMC. Additionally, we update the z_{ij} values of all imputed TCs by a Gibbs update which is available due to our formulation of $z_{ij} = \max(0, v_{ij})$ with a normal prior on the v_{ij}'s.

Posterior sampling is done through two parallel runs of the Markov chain, with starting points overdispersed with respect to the imputed TC counts. One run starts with zero imputation ($m_i = 0$) for all years while the other run starts with m_i's generated from $\mathsf{Po}(\lambda_i(1 - \Phi(\gamma_i)))$ distributions. Each run is 20,000 iterations long. Convergence takes place within a few hundred iterations (see supplementary materials). The first quarter of each chain is discarded, the rest is thinned and the two chains are then pooled together to form a sample of 6000 draws from the posterior distribution.

	E1	E2	E3
$\mathsf{P}(\eta_2 > 0 \mid \text{data})$	0.98	0.81	0.31
$\mathsf{E}\,(e^{\eta_2} - 1 \mid \text{data})$	25%	11%	-4%

Table 14.3: Posterior inference on the trend of mean TC count under experiments E1, E2 and E3.

The bottom-left panel of Figure 14.2 shows the posterior distribution over missed TC counts m_i under choice E1. The posterior means of m_i are shown by the gray line. Overlaid on this is the black line showing the missed TC counts reported by Vecchi and Knutson (2008). The detection probabilities in E1 were chosen to obtain a posterior summary of missed TC counts similar to that of Vecchi and Knutson (2008). The top and middle panels on the right show posterior densities of η_1 and η_2. The posterior mean total TC count in the central year is approximately 10. The posterior places an overwhelmingly large probability (98%) on the slope η_2 being positive. Thus the assumptions of E1 strongly support the conclusion of increasing TC activity. The posterior mean of $e^{\eta_2} - 1$, the change in TC counts over the N years (relative to beginning of the study) is 25%. On top of this linear growth, the posterior also supports additional fluctuation in annual TC counts through multidecadal oscillation (bottom-right panel) with a mean of 2.3 (95% interval $= (2.1, 2.5)$) oscillation cycles ($\phi_3/2$) over the entire period. The oscillation alone accounts for an average 49% (95% interval $= (28\%, 82\%)$) relative change from minimum to maximum mean TC counts ($e^{2|\phi_1|} - 1$). Posterior summaries of several model parameters are provided in the supplementary materials.

14.5 Sensitivity to Prior Quantification

We consider two other choices of detection probability parameters, as given in the E2 and E3 columns of Table 14.2, to illustrate how the posterior trend critically depends on these choices. E2 is similar to E1, except for the years 1878 through 1940. E1 assigns very high detection probabilities ($\approx 80\%$ or more) even to tropical storm strength TCs in the period 1921-1940, when measurements were based on ship and land records only. E2 (Figure 14.3) presents a somewhat less optimistic view, where the detection probabilities are more than 50% only for TCs that were category 1 or stronger for at least 3 days. E2 also lowers detection probabilities for 1878-1920, to maintain the same relative patterns in the 1878-1940 period as given by E1. E3 (Figure 14.4) is exactly the same as E2 except for the value of β which is halved.

Experiments E2 and E3 lead to substantially different inferences on the TC count trend relative to E1 (Table 14.3). Under E2, the posterior probability of η_2 being positive is less overwhelming (81%) than that under E1. The posterior mean of total percentage increase reduces to 10%. E3 presents a different picture, where the posterior probability of $\eta_2 > 0$ drops down to 31% and the mean trend is negative, with about a 4% drop in TC counts over the study period. Both E2 and E3 support multidecadal

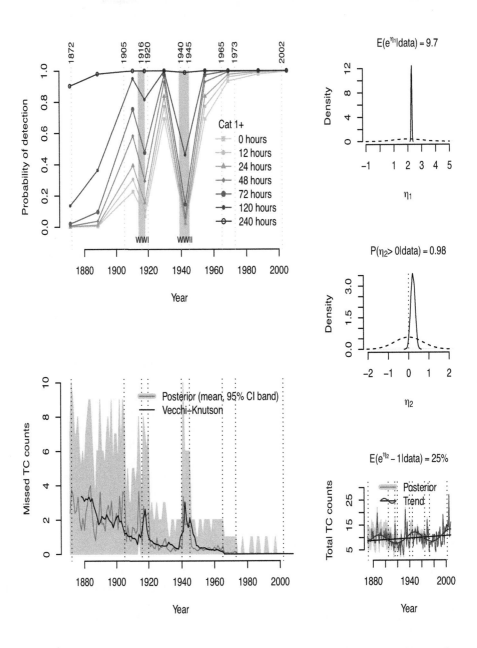

Figure 14.2: A visual summary of experiment E1. Top-left panel shows chosen detection probabilities across years for a set of 7 hypothetical TCs of various strength, measured by the hours each TC was a category 1 or higher. The vertical dotted lines mark the end of detection sub-periods as described in Table 14.2. Bottom-left panel shows posterior mean and range (95% equal-tail credible interval) for missed TC counts across years, overlaid with missed TC counts reported in Vecchi and Knutson (2008). Posterior (solid) and prior (broken) densities of η_1 and η_2 are shown on the top and middle panels on the right. Bottom-right panel shows posterior mean and 95% credible band of annual TC counts (observed + imputed).

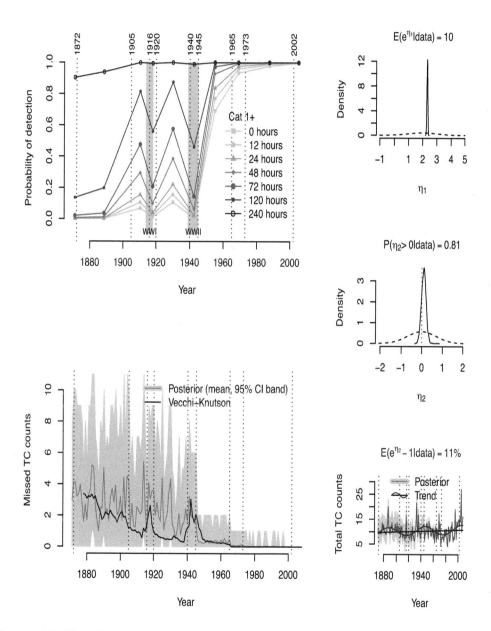

Figure 14.3: Visual summary of experiment E2. Conclusion of a positive trend is much weaker than that in E1.

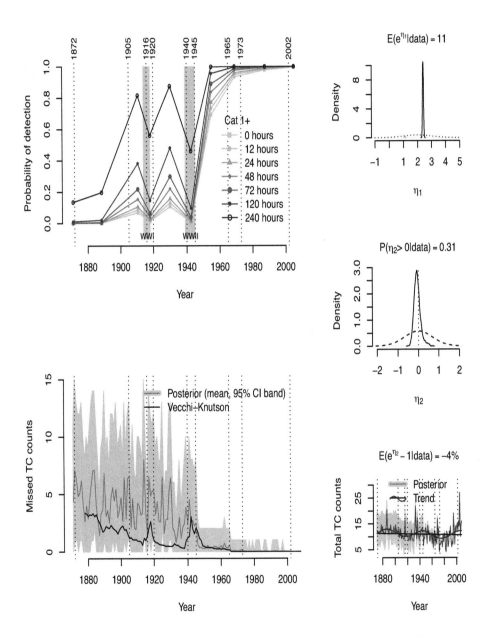

Figure 14.4: Visual summary of experiment E3. The posterior assigns 70% chance of a negative trend, with a mean drop of 4% in average TC counts across the period of study.

oscillation similar to E1, with an average 2.3 oscillation cycles, but with reduced amplitudes.

14.6 Concluding Remarks

14.6.1 *Resolving Ambiguity with Further Studies*

Our three experiments point to significant ambiguity present in the historical tropical cyclone occurrence records, with the assessment of TC counts trend clearly linked to assumptions regarding historic detection probabilities. Can we draw any reasonable conclusions about the trend despite this ambiguity? We feel the answer is yes, but it would involve using beliefs about detection probabilities that are deemed reasonable by the scientific community.

First, formal elicitation could be conducted with experts on past tropical cyclone detection to derive expert-specific detection probability formulation. This can be achieved by an extension of the statistical framework presented here. The main vehicle for this extension is the probability detection plot that appears on the top-left panel of Figures 14.2, 14.3, and 14.4. This plot provides an interface between our statistical model and quantities that can be elicited from a climate expert.

The expert would be required to generate her version of this plot by quantifying her belief about detection probabilities of a collection of TCs of various intensities, durations, tracks, etc. across different eras starting from the mid nineteenth century. These elicited quantities would be used to identify a suitable detection probability function (14.3) with z_{ij} possibly reflecting a multitude of TC characteristics and Φ possibly replaced with a different distribution function. It might also be necessary to use a non-trivial prior distribution on the parameters in (14.3) to accommodate the expert's uncertainty about them. Once a suitable detection probability function is found to match the expert's belief, the rest of the modeling, computing and summarizing can proceed in exactly the same manner as in the examples presented here.

Ideally, such a study would be carried out with many different experts, generating a catalog of conclusions about TC trend based on current expert opinions. Whether any kind of scientific consensus might result from this remains to be seen.

14.6.2 *Sensitivity to Formulation*

In incorporating an expert's quantified belief, it is important to ascertain how sensitive the results will be to the particular choice of the formulation of (14.3). In particular, if an expert's quantified beliefs are well represented by two different formulations of (14.3), will the conclusions about trend depend on which formulation is used? While such a question cannot be addressed in full generality, we report below additional experiments that suggest the conclusions are indeed robust to moderate variations in the choice of (14.3).

We consider three additional experiments, E1*, E2* and E3* in which (14.3) is specified as

$$\pi_{ij} = F_3(\gamma_i^* + \beta_i^* z_{ij}) \tag{14.4}$$

where F_3 denotes the cumulative distribution function of the Student-t distribution with 3 degrees of freedom. We continue with our 10 sub-periods split of the study period (Table 14.2) and assign a common value to γ_i^* for all years i within a sub-period. The same is done for β_i^*.

In experiment E1*, we choose γ_i^*'s and β_i^*'s to match the "quantified beliefs" of E1 as displayed on the top-left panel of Figure 14.2. For the 7 (hypothetical) TCs displayed on that panel, with strengths $z_1^h = 0, z_2^h = 12, \cdots, z_7^h = 240$, we record their detection probabilities $\pi_{1k}^h, \pi_{2k}^h, \cdots, \pi_{7k}^h$ for all sub-periods $k = 1, \cdots, 10$, as specified under E1. Next we find $\hat{\gamma}_k$ and $\hat{\beta}_k$ for $k = 1, \cdots, 10$, by minimizing

$$f(\gamma_1, \cdots, \gamma_{10}, \beta_1, \cdots, \beta_{10}) = \left[\frac{1}{70} \sum_j \sum_k \{\pi_{jk}^h - F_3(\gamma_k + \beta_k z_j^h)\}^2 \right]^{1/2} \tag{14.5}$$

and set $\gamma_i^* = \hat{\gamma}_k$ and $\beta_i^* = \hat{\beta}_k$ for all years i within sub-period k. This minimization is done numerically by using the `optim()` routine of R and the minimum value equals 0.0091, which suggests a reasonably good fit. The rest of the model is kept as before. Posterior summaries are generated by the reversible jump Markov chain sampler as discussed earlier with a suitable modification to reflect the change from (14.3) to (14.4). Experiments E2* and E3* are similar in design, but with "quantified beliefs" coming from E2 and E3, respectively. The minimum value of $f(\gamma_1, \cdots, \gamma_{10}, \beta_1, \cdots, \beta_{10})$ equals 0.0101 for E2* and 0.0102 for E3*.

	E1*	E2*	E3*
$P(\eta_2 > 0 \mid \text{data})$	0.98	0.83	0.34
$E(e^{\eta_2} - 1 \mid \text{data})$	24%	12%	-3%

Table 14.4: Posterior inference on the trend of mean TC count under experiments E1*, E2* and E3*.

Table 14.4 shows conclusions about trend under E1*, E2* and E3*. Full graphical summaries, as in Figure 14.2 etc., are included in the supplementary materials. Despite the differences in (14.3) and (14.4), the conclusions about trend in these new experiments are virtually indistinguishable from the conclusions drawn in, respectively, E1, E2 and E3.

It is possible to obtain different conclusions than E1 etc. by replacing F_3 in (14.4) with a function that is more dissimilar to Φ. In fact, with F_1 instead of F_3, the minimum value of $f(\gamma_1, \cdots, \gamma_{10}, \beta_1, \cdots, \beta_{10})$ undergoes about a 3-fold increase to values of 0.0247, 0.0259 and 0.0275 for E1*, E2* and E3* respectively, suggesting a less satisfactory fit. The conclusion about η_2 is different, but not by a big margin (supplementary materials). Equation (14.4) with F_1 instead of F_3 does not provide as good a fit to the "quantified beliefs" of E1 and so the difference in conclusion is not worrying. However, determining lack of fit to an expert's quantified beliefs is a nontrivial task and should be based upon both graphical plots of detection probabilities and numerical values of f.

14.6.3 Toward a Flexible Formulation

Both (14.3) and (14.4) are limited in their ability to encode an expert's quantified beliefs. A slightly richer formulation, of which both (14.3) and (14.4) are special cases, can be obtained by taking $\pi_{ij} = F_\nu(\gamma_i^* + \beta_i^* \cdot z_{ij})$ where the degrees of freedom parameter ν is also to be included in the minimization of $f(\gamma_1, \cdots, \gamma_{10}, \beta_1, \cdots, \beta_{10}, \nu) = [\frac{1}{70} \sum_j \sum_k \{\pi_{jk}^h - F_\nu(\gamma_k + \beta_k z_j^h)\}^2]^{1/2}$. Here z_{ij} is taken to be a vector of strength measures which would possibly include summaries of duration, size and trajectory. This vector is to be decided upon in consultation with the expert to characterize the variation in TCs she chooses as the examples for her belief quantification.

14.6.4 Incorporating Climate Models

The proposed analysis could be extended further by combining expert knowledge with climate model projections of North Atlantic TC activity. Climate model studies have investigated how TC intensity, frequency and tracks may change in a warmer climate both globally and in individual basins such as the North Atlantic. Global climate models that are used to project temperature increases resulting from increased CO_2 levels have low resolution (Knutson et al., 2010) and consequently are limited in their ability to simulate TCs. Recent approaches have combined the output from global models with regional higher-resolution models that are able to simulate more realistic TCs (Emanuel et al., 2008; Knutson et al., 2010, 2008).

Ideally, the results of such models would be used to specify priors for the vector z_{ij}, where this vector includes a multitude of TC characteristics such as intensity, duration, seasonal variation, and geographic distribution of tracks. This would allow the experts to focus on the detection probabilities during the elicitation process. However, despite the improvements in model resolution, currently available models remain somewhat limited in their capacity to simulate realistic distributions of these TC properties. In particular, projections of TC frequencies in individual basins and changes in tracks and duration are regarded as rather unreliable at present as is evident, for instance, in the disagreement on the sign of changes in these parameters (Knutson et al., 2010; Grossmann and Morgan, 2011). A recent model driven by annual observed North Atlantic ocean temperatures and atmospheric parameters over the 27-year period 1980-2006 was able to simulate North Atlantic TC activity that agreed remarkably well with observed activity. However, this model first had to be calibrated to the observed basin-inwide TC counts, the very dataset that is sought to be corrected. This introduces a circular problem. We also note that this kind of study cannot be extended to the period prior to 1980 because the required detailed atmospheric parameters are only available from 1980 onwards (Kalnay et al., 1996).

Acknowledgements

We thank the referees and an Associate Editor who reviewed this paper for helpful comments and suggestions. The second author was supported by the Climate Decision Making Center created through a cooperative agreement between the National Science Foundation (SES-0345798) and Carnegie Mellon University.

REFERENCES

Allison, P. D. (2001). *Missing Data*. Thousand Oaks, CA: Sage. 286

Atlas, R., Hoffman, R. N., Leidner, S. M., Sienkiewicz, J., and Yu, T.-W. (2001). "The effects of marine winds from scatterometer data on weather analysis and forecasting." *Bulletin of the American Meteorological Society*, 82, 1965–1990. 288

Bengtsson, L. and Hodges, K. I. (2008). "Comment on "Is the number of North Atlantic tropical cyclones significantly underestimated prior to the availability of satellite observations?" by EKM Chang and Y Guo." *Geophysical Research Letters*, 35, doi:10.1029/2007GL032251. 286

Bowditch, H. I. (1841). *Memoir of Nathaniel Bowditch*. James Munroe and Company. 288

Bowditch, N. (1995). *The American Practical Navigator*. United States Government. 288

Brueske, K. F. and Velden, C. S. (2003). "Satellite-based tropical cyclone intensity estimation using the NOAA-KLM series Advanced Microwave Sounding Unit (AMSU)." *Monthly Weather Review*, 131, 687–697. 288

Chang, E. K. M. and Guo, Y. (2007). "Is the number of North Atlantic tropical cyclones significantly underestimated prior to the availability of satellite observations?" *Geophysical Research Letters*, 34, doi:10.1029/2007GL030169. 286, 289

Coles, S. G. and Sparks, R. S. J. (2006). "Extreme value methods for modeling historical series of large volcanic magnitudes." In *Statistics in Volcanology*, vol. Special Publication of IAVCEI, 1, 47–56. London: Geological Society. 286

Cornulier, T., Robinson, R. A., Elston, D., Lambin, X., Sutherland, W. J., and Benton, T. G. (2011). "Bayesian reconstitution of environmental change from disparate historical records: hedgerow loss and farmland bird declines." *Methods in Ecology and Evolution*, 2, 86–94. 286

Dorst, N. M. (2007). "The National Hurricane Center research project: 50 years of research, rough rides, and name changes." *Bulletin of the American Meteorological Society*, 88, 10, 1566–1588. 288

Dunn, G. E. and Miller, B. I. (1960). *Atlantic hurricanes*. Louisiana State University Press. 288

Dvorak, V. F. (1984). "Tropical Cyclone Intensity Analysis Using Satellite Data." NOAA Technical Report NESDIS 11, 47pp. 288

Elsner, J. B. and Bossak, B. H. (2006). "Hurricane landfall probability and climate." In *Hurricane and typhoons - past, present and future*, eds. R. J. Murnane and K.-B. Liu, 333–353. Columbia University Press. 286

Elsner, J. B. and Jagger, T. H. (2006). "Prediction Models for Annual U.S. Hurricane Counts." *Journal of Climate*, 19, 2935–2952. 290

Elsner, J. B. and Kara, A. B. (1999). *Hurricanes of the North Atlantic: climate and society*. New York: Oxford University Press. 290

Emanuel, K. A., Sundararajan, R., and Williams, J. (2008). "Hurricanes and global warming: Results from downscaling IPCC AR4 simulations." *Bulletin of American Meteorological Society*, 89, 347–367. 299

Fernández-Partagás, J. and Diaz, H. F. (1996). "Atlantic hurricanes in the second half of the nineteenth century." *Bulletin of the American Meteorological Society*, 77, 2899–2906. 288

Goldenberg, S. B., Landsea, C. W., Mestas-Nuñez, A. M., and Gray, W. M. (2001). "The recent increase in Atlantic hurricane activity: Causes and implications." *Science*, 293, 474–479. 290

Green, P. J. (1995). "Reversible jump Markov chain Monte Carlo computation and Bayesian model determination." *Biometrika*, 82, 711–732. 292

Grossmann, I. and Morgan, M. G. (2011). "Tropical cyclones, climate change, and scientific uncertainty: what do we know, what does it mean, and what should be done?" *Climatic Change*, doi: 10.1007/s10584–011–0020–1. 285, 299

Harper, B. A. and Callaghan, J. (2006). "On the importance of reviewing historical tropical cyclone intensities." 27th Conference on Hurricanes and Tropical Meteorology. American Meteorological Society: April 23-28, Monterey, CA. 288

Holland, G. J. (2007). "Misuse of landfall as a proxy for Atlantic tropical cyclone activity." *Eos*, 88, 36, 349–356. 289

Holland, G. J. and Webster, P. J. (2007). "Heightened tropical cyclone activity in the North Atlantic: natural variability or climate trend?" *Philosophical Transactions of the Royal Society A*, 365, 1860, 2695–2716, doi:10.1098/rsta.2007.2083. 285, 286

Honaker, J. and King, G. (2010). "What to do about missing values in time-series cross-section data." *American Journal of Political Science*, 54, 561–581. 286

Ibrahim, J. G., Chen, M. H., and Lipsitz, S. R. (2001). "Missing responses in generalized linear mixed models when the missing data mechanism is nonignorable." *Biometrika*, 88,

551–564. 286

Jarvinen, B. R., Neumann, C. J., and Davis, M. A. S. (1984). "A tropical cyclone data tape for the North Atlantic basin, 1886-1983: contents, limitations, and uses." NOAA Technical Memorandum NWS HHC 22, Coral Gables, FL, 21 pp. Available online at `http://www.nhc.noaa.gov/pdf/NWS-NHC-1988-22.pdf`. 286

Kalnay, E., Kanamitsu, M., Kistler, R., Collins, W., Deaven, D., Gandin, L., Iredell, M., Saha, S., White, G., Woollen, J., Zhu, Y., Leetmaa, A., Reynolds, R., Chelliah, M., Ebisuzaki, W., Higgins, W., Janowiak, J., Mo, K. C., Ropelewski, C., Wang, J., Jenne, R., and Joseph, D. (1996). "The NCEP/NCAR 40-Year Reanalysis Project." *Bulletin of the American Meteorological Society*, 77, 437–471. 299

Kéry, M. and Royle, J. A. (2010). "Hierarchical modelling and estimation of abundance and population trends in metapopulation designs." *Journal of Animal Ecology*, 79, 453–461. 286

Klotzbach, P. J. and Gray, V. M. (2008). "Multidecadal variability in North Atlantic tropical cyclone activity." *Journal of Climate*, 21, 3929–3935. 286, 290

Knapp, K. R. and Kossin, J. P. (2007). "New global tropical cyclone data from ISCCP B1 geostationary satellite observations." *Journal of Applied Remote Sensing*, 1, 13505–13510. 289

Knutson, T. R., McBride, J. L., Chan, J., Emanuel, K., Holland, G., Landsea, C., Held, I., Kossin, J. P., Srivastava, A. K., and Sugi, M. (2010). "Tropical cyclones and climate change." *Nature Geoscience*, 3, 157–163. 285, 299

Knutson, T. R., Sirutis, J. J., Garner, S. T., Held, I. M., and Tuleya, R. E. (2007). "Simulation of the recent multidecadal increase of Atlantic hurricane activity using an 18-km-grid regional model." *Bulletin of American Meteorological Society*, 88, 1549–65. 290

Knutson, T. R., Sirutis, J. J., Garner, S. T., Vecchi, G. A., and Held, I. M. (2008). "Simulated reduction in Atlantic hurricane frequency under twenty-first-century warming conditions." *Nature Geoscience*, 1, 359–364. 299

Landsea, C. W. (2007). "Counting Atlantic tropical cyclones back to 1900." *Eos*, 88, 18, 197–202. 285, 286, 288, 289

Landsea, C. W., Anderson, C., Charles, N., Clark, G., Dunion, J., Fernández-Partágas, J., Hungerford, P., Neumann, C., and Zimmer, M. (2004). "The Atlantic hurricane database reanalysis project: Documentation for the 1851-1910 alterations and additions to the HURDAT database." In *Hurricanes and Typhoons: Past, present and future*, eds. R. J. Murname and K. B. Liu. Columbia University Press. 285, 286, 288

Landsea, C. W., Glenn, D. A., Bredemeyer, W., Chenoweth, M., Ellis, R., Gamache, J., Hufstetler, L., Mock, C., Perez, R., Prieto, R., Sanchez-Sesma, J., Thomas, D., and Woolcock, L. (2008). "A renalysis of the 1911-1920 Atlantic hurricane database." *Journal of Climate*, 21, 2138–2168. 287, 288

Landsea, C. W., Harper, B. A., Harau, K., and Knaff, J. A. (2006). "Can we detect trends in extreme tropical cyclones?" *Science*, 313, 452–454. 285, 286, 288, 289

Landsea, C. W., Vecchi, G. A., Bengtsson, L., and Knutson, T. R. (2010). "Impact of duration thresholds on Atlantic tropical cyclone counts." *Journal of Climate*, 23, 2508–2519. 286, 289

Little, R. J. A. (1995). "Modeling the dropout mechanism in repeated-measures studies." *Journal of the American Statistical Association*, 90, 1112–1121. 286

Mann, M. E. and Emanuel, K. A. (2006). "Atlantic hurricane trends linked to climate change." *Eos*, 87, 24, 233–244. 286

Mann, M. E., Sabbatelli, T. A., and Neu, U. (2007). "Evidence for a modest undercount bias in early historical Atlantic tropical cyclone counts." *Geophysical Research Letters*, 34, doi:10.1029/2007GL031781. 286

Neumann, C. J., Jarvinen, B. R., and McAdie, C. J. (1999). "Tropical cyclones of the North Atlantic Ocean, 1871-1998." NOAA Historical Climatology Series 6-2. 288

Nyberg, J., Malmgren, B. A., Jury, A. W. M. R., Kilbourne, K. H., and Quinn, T. M. (2007). "Low Atlantic hurricane activity in the 1970s and 1980s compared to the past 270 years." *Nature*, 447, 698–702. 286

Piddington, H. (1860). *The sailors horn-book for the law of storms*. Williams and Norgate. 288

Rubin, D. B. (1996). "Multiple imputation after 18+ years." *Journal of the American Statistical Association*, 91, 473–489. 286

Sheets, R. C. (1990). "The National Hurricane Center – Past, present and future." *Weather and Forecasting*, 5, 2, 185–232. 288, 289

Simpson, R. H. (1974). "The hurricane disaster potential scale." *Weatherwise*, 27, 169–186. 287

Solow, A. R. (1989). "Statistical modeling of storm counts." *Journal of Climate*, 2, 131–136. 290

Solow, A. R. and Beet, A. R. (2008). "On the incompleteness of the historical record of North Atlantic tropical cyclones." *Geophysical Research Letters*, 35, doi:10.1029/2008GL033546. 286

Solow, A. R. and Moore, L. (2000). "Testing for trend in a partially incomplete hurricane record." *Journal of Climate*, 13, 3696–3699. 286

— (2002). "Testing for trend in North Atlantic hurricane activity, 1900-1998." *Journal of Climate*, 15, 3111–3114. 286

Tingley, M. and Huybers, P. (2010). "A Bayesian Algorithm for Reconstructing Climate Anomalies in Space and Time. Part 1: Development and applications to paleoclimate reconstruction problems." *Journal of Climate*, 23, 2759–2781. 286

Vecchi, G. A. and Knutson, T. R. (2008). "On estimates of historical North Atlantic tropical cyclone activity." *Journal of Climate*, 21, 3580–3600. 285, 286, 288, 289, 290, 292, 293, 294

Velden, C., Harper, B., Wells, F., Beven, J. L. I., Zehr, R., Olander, T., Mayfield, M., Guard, C., Lander, M., Edson, R., Avila, L., Burton, A., Turk, M., Kikuchi, A., Christian, A., Caroff, P., and McCrone, P. (2006). "The Dvorak tropical cyclone intensity estimation technique." *Bulletin of the American Meteorological Society*, 10, 1195–1210. 289

Webster, P. J., Holland, G. J., Curry, J. A., and Chang, H. R. (2005). "Changes in tropical cyclone number, duration and intensity in a warming environment." *Science*, 309, 1844–1846. 285

Zeger, S. L. and Liang, K. Y. (1996). "Longitudinal data analysis for discrete and continuous outcomes." *Biometrics*, 42, 121–130. 286

Epilogue

What is the scientific issue addressed?

Whether the records of tropical cyclones (hurricanes) in the North Atlantic support conclusions about increases in frequency over the last 150 years.

Is justification given for

a) the use of the data?

The question of how storms come to be in the data base is the focus of the paper.

b) the likelihood and prior?

These center on possible trends in the detection probability over the last 150 years.

What robustness studies were done?

The heart of the inference is robustness with respect to the prior. A small change in the prior for one variable in the detection model leads to increasing, constant or decreasing trends in numbers of tropical cyclones.

How were the computations done?

The computations were done by Markov chain Monte Carlo.

If I were doing the problem again, how would I change the approach?

I would not.

What do I see as the contribution of the paper?

The contribution of the paper is that it shows that the trend in numbers of tropical cyclones in the North Atlantic is ambiguous (and is likely to stay that way).

Was Bayesian analysis useful in this problem?

Bayesian analysis was critical to the application.

TEACHING SUGGESTIONS

References for theoretical ideas:

1. Poisson distribution: *Principles* Section 3.9

2. Normal distribution: *Principles* Section 6.9

3. Missing data: *Principles* Section 9.2

4. MCMC: *Principles* Chapter 10

5. Reversible jump: *Principles* Section 10.6

Exercises

1. Why does detection matter in investigating whether the frequency of tropical cyclones in the North Atlantic has increased? Why not just plot the number of tropical cyclones against time?

2. Why does the exact specification of the prior distribution matter for this analysis? Don't most robustness studies show that priors can be changed without substantially changing the results?

3. The paper reports results from three main experiments E1, E2 and E3, and three subsidiary ones, E_1^*, E_2^* and E_3^*. If you were to design further experiments, what would they be? How would your experiments shed further light on the subject?

Chapter 15

The Number of Killings in Southern Rural Norway, 1300–1569 (2013)

Foreword

I have been in a room with Ferdinand Næshagen only once, when he was visiting a mutual friend at CMU. He outlined his question, which was how to estimate how many killings there might have been in medieval Norway, based on the numbers that appear in the written record.

The project went through several phases, in which I proposed it to various people, who helped get the data in shape but did not analyze them. Finally, I decided that if the analysis was going to happen, I would have to do it myself. Over the years, Ferdinand and I became Internet friends.

There are several aspects of the analysis that deserve mention. The first (see paper #1) is again that the phenomenon occurs only once. Never again will Norway experience the years in question. Technically, this is a dual systems estimate. With only two systems, a dual systems model perforce requires the assumption of independence between the systems. In this application the two systems are: (1) survival of at least one of five official documents sent to the killer as part of the legal process and (2) mentions of the killing in other surviving documents from the period, such as bishopric records, personal letters, etc. Third, model checking is done against what I take to be the most problematic aspect of the model, the binomial distribution for the number of surviving letters to a given killer. I prefer this kind of targeted model checking to the more general sort against a very general and vague alternative. This model checking required the use of a somewhat novel distribution, the Conway-Maxwell binomial distribution.

As with many collaborations, together we wrote something that neither of us could have written alone.

Other readings:

Kadane, J. and Næshagen (2014). Homicide Rates in southern rural Norway, 1300–1569. *Scandinavian Journal of History*, 39 (3), 287–298. http://dx.doi.org/10.1080/03468755.2014.822270

Kadane, J.(2015). Sums of Possibly Associated Bernoulli Variables: The ConwayMaxwell-Binomial Distribution, *Bayesian Analysis*, to appear. Advance Publication, 14 May 2015. doi: 10.1214/15-BA955. http://projecteuclid.org/euclid.ba/1431607821

Where are they now? Ferdinand Næshagen is retired, and writing a book, in Southern rural Norway.

This paper was originally published in the *Annals of Applied Statistics*, **7**, (#2),

Published Paper

Joseph B. Kadane and Ferdinand L. Næshagen

Abstract

Three dual systems estimates are employed to study the number of killings in southern rural Norway in a period of slightly over 250 years. The first system is a set of five letters sent to each killer as part of the legal process. The second system is the mention of killings from all other contemporary sources. The posterior distributions derived suggest fewer such killings than rough demographic estimates.

Key words and phrases. Dual systems, com-binomial distribution, integrated likelihood

15.1 Norwegian Homicide Law and the Documentary Evidence

This paper studies the number of killings in Norway in the period 1300–1569, that is, the last fifty years of Norway's High Middle Age, through the Late Middle Ages, and a generation or so into the Early Modern Age. The extant written data about such killings, is of course, only a fraction of the documents issued.

Certain homicides (and some other crimes) were "non-compensation crimes" (*ubotemal*), which means that they, unless the king decided otherwise, were atoned for by capital punishment or outlawry and confiscation of the criminal's property. Noncompensation homicides would, for instance, be the killing of a man in his own house, the killing of a kinsman, or a killing on a holy day. A study of the documents issued in such cases shows that King Magnus the Lawmender's National Law of 1274 was systematically set aside in such cases, for good economic reasons. There would be no compensation to the victim's next of kin, and it might even be a loss to the king's district officer (*sysselmann*, the equivalent of an English sheriff) if he had to pay an executioner the equivalent of a craftsman's monthly pay for decapitating a pennyless youngster. With, however, an economic atonement for the killing (*botemal*), the victim's heirs would get their compensation, and the king's district officer would get the fine [strictly speaking, two fines, a recently introduced one for depriving the king of a subject (*tegngilde*) and an older one for the king's pardon (*fredkjop*), similar to the continental Germanic *fredus*] nominally due to the king, which was about fifty percent of the normal compensation. In case of noncompensation killings the fine would be relatively higher, one regular fine for a killing, to which would be added another one for the killing of a brother, a second if it took place in his own house, and a third if it took place on a holy day. As we can see from some documents, family members would help to pay even though their legal obligation to do so had been abolished in 1260. The loss of a family member, cherished or not, would weaken the family. Some may have contributed in money or species, others may have guaranteed as securities as some documents show. Furthermore, there was some opportunity for haggling and the period before the compensation or fine was fully paid might on occasion be considerably longer than the year specified in the letter of pardon.

This process had five documents as its outcome. The killer, who was left at large

Table 15.1: Two-way classification of records of killings.

		Number of letters from killer's archive						
		0	1	2	3	4	5	Total
Mentioned in other sources?	No	n	162	20	5	3	0	$190 + n$
	Yes	143	3	0	1	0	0	147
Total		$143 + n$	165	20	6	3	0	$337 + n$

and indeed might be said to be the prosecutor, had first to go to the King's Chancellor in Oslo to get a protection letter (*gridsbrev*) which both gave him a temporary protection against avengers and also was an order to the king's district officer to hear the case so as to find whether the killer had fulfilled the obligation of taking public responsibility for the killing and also whether he had sureties for the payment of compensation and fine. In accordance with this the district officer held a hearing with witnesses and the parties present and issued an evidence letter (*provsbrev*) summing up the relevant facts, including what might make this one or several ubotemal. With this provsbrev the killer had once more to travel to the King's Chancellor who then issued a permanent pardon (*landsvist*, right to stay in the country) which also stated the amount to be paid in fine, and the condition that compensation and fine were to be paid within a year. As we can see, practice did at times give the killer several years respite before these sums were paid, but when paid they resulted in one receipt from the king's district officer and one from the victim's heirs. These five letters were all preserved in the killer's archive as part of a farm archive together with deeds, inheritance divisions etc. until fire, wetness or some overly tidy daughter-in-law put an end to the existence of the large majority.

Supplementary materials (Kadane and Næshagen, 2012) is an index of the documents that did survive, showing evidence of 337 killings in this time period. Of these, 194 are documented from the killer's archive, 143 are only from other sources and 4 are mentioned both in the killer's archive and in other sources. The other sources are quite varied, but include local officials, the King's Chancellor, regional potentates, church officials, and private letters and diaries. The data used in this paper are summarized in Table 15.1.

The purpose is to find a distribution for n and hence for $337 + n$, the total number of killings in the period.

15.2   Demographic Evidence about the Number of Killings

During this period Norway (like other European countries) underwent dramatic demographic changes. There is, furthermore, some disagreement about absolute numbers in given years during this period, but the most recent text book authors agree that when the plague first hit Norway in 1349 its population may have been 500,000 and perhaps slightly lower in the preceding half century. The recurrent plague epidemics reduced the population to its lowest point ca. 1450 to 1500, ca 200,000 or perhaps less (Moseng et al., 2007, pp. 233–236, 294 and 295). After this population started growing again and, in spite of recurrent epidemics, grew to 440,000 in the 1660s, the first really reliable assessment. These estimates concern Norway as it was then, before the country had lost almost ten percent of its territory and population due to Danish military misadventures. The data used here are, for the sake of comparison, only taken from present-day Norwegian territory, so about ten percent should be deducted from population estimates.

With two exceptions there is no conspicuous geographic bias in the data. Telemark, which both in the Middle Ages and later had a reputation for violence, is very well represented in these data. Due to the cases where the scene of the homicide is geographically localized, or that of the person paying for receiving compensation or fine, or their provenience (come to an archive from a rural district) is, and the fact that family archives are preserved in rural districts, as farm archives while similar urban archives are unknown, we can be fairly sure that scarcely any of these documents had an urban origin–which means that they reflect the situation in the countryside, not in the much more violent cities and towns. This may account for the discrepancy between the homicide estimates for the mid-sixteenth century (10–15 per 100,000) made from another type of data (accounts of fines and confiscations) by Næshagen (2005), and the somewhat lower estimates this study yields. Only about 3 percent of the population lived in the three larger cities, Bergen, Trondheim, and Oslo, but their population showed an extreme inclination to homicide. Thus, Bergen, Norway's largest and most heterogenous city, with a population of 6,000 had from 1562 to 1571 a homicide rate of 83 per 100,000 (Sandnes, 1990, pp: 72–74). Thus, with these rural data one should expect a somewhat lower estimate than Næshagen's 10 to 15 per 100,000 from the mid-sixteenth century which includes cities (2005).

Central Norway (Trøndelag) and Northern Norway with, respectively, 13 and 11 percent of the population (Dyrvik, 1979, page 18) seem not to be represented among these documents. Judging from the mid-sixteenth-century lists of fines and confiscations, homicides may have been rarer in Central Norway than in the rest of the country, while Northern Norway does not distinguish itself in any way (Næshagen, 2005, p. 416), and later data support the conclusion about Central Norway (Sandnes, 1990, p. 79).

So supposing that the population of Norway as it was then was 500,000 in the period from 1300 to 1350, and roughly 200,000 in the period from 1350 to 1569, we must deduct 10% to account for the territory lost. This yields 450,000 in 1300 to 1350, and 180,000 for the later period. Additionally, we deduct 24% (13% in Central Norway, 11% in Northern Norway) for rural areas not covered, and another 3% for the cities, yielding a deduction of 27%. Thus we estimate rural southern Norway to have had a population of 330,000 in the period from 1300 to 1350, and 130,000 from 1350 to 1569. It should be emphasized that these are rough estimates only.

The next set of estimates concerns the rate of killings. Accepting the estimates from somewhat later of 10 to 15 per hundred thousand per year overall, but a much higher rate (83 per hundred thousand) for the 3% of the urban population suggests a rate of 8 to 13 per hundred thousand per year in rural southern Norway.

Applied to the 50 year period before the plague and the 219 years after the plague, this yields a range of 3600 to 5850 for the number of killings in rural Southern Norway during the period in question.

15.3   Models of the Data

Problems of missing data are ubiquitous; indeed, every parameter not known with certainty can be regarded as "missing data" in some sense. In biostatistics, survival analysis can be regarded as a method for dealing with missing time-of-death data for patients still alive. But these problems are especially acute in history, geology, the interpretation of fossils, astronomy and archeology. In one instance, Kadane and

Hastorf (1988), [Chapter 1 in this volume] the authors assumed known preservation probabilities for different kinds of burnt seeds in an archeological site in Peru.

While the methods used here bear a relationship with problems of estimating the number of species (see Bunge and Fitzpatrick (1993) for a review), the more closely related literature is that of dual systems estimators, growing out of the early work of Petersen (1896) and Lincoln (1930), and applied to the problem of census coverage by Wolter (1986).

A. Simple dual systems

The simplest treatment of data of this kind is to amalgamate all mentions in the killer's archive together, resulting in the following 2×2 Table 15.2.

Table 15.2: Reduced data

| | | Killer's Archive? | | |
		No	Yes	Total
Mentioned in other sources?	No	n	190	$190 + n$
	Yes	143	4	147
Total		$143 + n$	194	$337 + n$

To establish notation for this case, let the numbers in Table 15.2 be represented as shown in Table 15.3.

Table 15.3: General notation for Table 15.2.

| | | Killer's Archive? | | Total |
		No	Yes	
Mentioned in other sources?	No	n_{00}	n_{01}	n_{0+}
	Yes	n_{10}	n_{11}	n_{1+}
Total		n_{+0}	n_{+1}	n_{++}

Note: $n_{00} = n$.

The data can be taken to be multinomial, with probabilities p_{ij}, and hence likelihood

$$L = \binom{n_{++}}{n_{00}, n_{01}, n_{10}, n_{11}} \prod_{\substack{i=0,1 \\ j=0,1}} p_{ij}^{n_{ij}}. \tag{15.1}$$

A key assumption is that of independence, which would mean that whether a killing is known from the preservation of a letter from the killer's archive has no bearing on whether it is known from the other sources. In this application, such an assumption seems entirely reasonable. So if p is the probability a killing is mentioned in other sources and q is the probability a killing is known from at least one letter from the killer's archive, the assumption of independence can be written as

$$p_{ij} = p^i \bar{p}^{\bar{i}} q^j \bar{q}^{\bar{j}} \quad i = 0, 1; j = 0, 1 \tag{15.2}$$

where $\bar{x} = 1 - x$.

Substituting (15.2) into (15.1) yields

$$L = \binom{n_{++}}{n_{00}, n_{01}, n_{10}, n_{11}} p^{n_{1+}} \bar{p}^{n_{0+}} q^{n_{+1}} \bar{q}^{n_{+0}}. \tag{15.3}$$

The parameters p, q and n are all that matter here, and n is the parameter of interest. Any reasonable prior distribution (i.e., one that is not strongly opinionated) for p and q will lead to the same inference, given the values of n_{0+}, n_{1+}, n_{+0} and n_{+1} in this data set. Hence we accept independent uniform priors for p and q. In view of the material in Section 15.2, the prior of interest on the total number of killings, $n + 337$, is uniform $(337, 5850)$. However, for the first computation reported here we use a much broader uniform prior on n in order to show the uncertainty inherent in the likelihood.

Using the well-known integration result,

$$\int_0^1 x^n (1-x)^m dx = B(n+1, m+1) = \frac{\Gamma(n+1)\Gamma(m+1)}{\Gamma(n+m+2)} = \frac{n!m!}{(n+m+1)!}, \quad (15.4)$$

the integrated likelihood is

$$\binom{n_{++}}{n_{00}, n_{01}, n_{10}, n_{11}} \frac{n_{1+}!n_{0+}!n_{+1}!n_{+0}!}{[(n_{++}+1)!]^2}. \quad (15.5)$$

Now $n_{01}, n_{10}, n_{11}, n_{+1}$ and n_{1+} do not depend on n. Hence, these factors do not matter for the integrated likelihood, yielding an integrated likelihood proportional to

$$\frac{(n_{0+})!(n_{+0})!}{n_{00}!(n_{++}+1)(n_{++}+1)!} = \frac{(n+190)!(n+143)!}{n!(n+338)(n+338)!}. \quad (15.6)$$

Figure 15.1 plots, as a probability distribution, the quantity $n + 337$, the total number of killings. Implicitly the prior on n used in this calculation is uniform with an upper bound of at least 25,000, which is much higher than we find credible. Nonetheless, for display purposes, we show it.

The quantiles of the data in Figure 15.1 are reported in Table 15.4. Together Figure 15.1 and Table 15.4 suggest substantial uncertainty about the total number of killings; the middle 80% of the distribution lies between 3337 and 10,837, a gap of 7500 killings; the median of the distribution is 5837.

Table 15.4: Quantiles for Figure 15.1

Quantile	3337	3837	4337	4837	5837	6337	7337	8337	10,837
probability	0.1	0.2	0.3	0.4	0.5	0.6	0.7	0.8	0.9

This suggests the desirability of making more use of the data in Table 15.1, and in particular the data on the number of letters found in each killer's archive.

B. Dual systems binomial model

To do so, we now establish general notation for Table 15.1, in Table 15.5.

Let $\mathbf{n} = (n_{00}, n_{01}, n_{02}, \ldots n_{05}, n_{10}, n_{11}, \ldots n_{15})$ and $\mathbf{n!} = \prod_{i=0}^{5} \prod_{j=0}^{1} n_{ij}!$.

Then the multinomial likelihood can be written as

$$L = \frac{n_{++}!}{\mathbf{n}!} \prod_{\substack{i=0,1 \\ j=0,\ldots 5}} p_{ij}^{n_{ij}}. \quad (15.7)$$

Again imposing independence, we have

$$p_{ij} = r_j s^i \bar{s}^{\bar{i}} \quad j = 0, \ldots, 5; \; i = 0, 1, \quad (15.8)$$

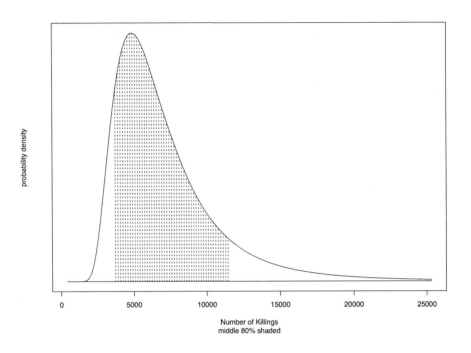

Figure 15.1: Simple dual systems integrated likelihood

where r_j is the probability of j surviving letters in the archive and s is the probability of being mentioned in other sources.

Substituting (15.8) into (15.7), we obtain

$$L = \frac{n_{++}!}{\mathbf{n}!} \prod_{j=0}^{5} r_j^{n+j} s^{n_{1+}} \bar{s}^{n_{0+}}. \tag{15.9}$$

A simple model to impose on $\mathbf{r} = (r_o, r_1, \ldots, r_5)$ is binomial $(5, p)$ where p is here the probability that each letter in a killer's archive survives (this assumption is revisited in subsection C, ahead). With the binomial assumption,

$$r_j = \binom{5}{j} p^j \bar{p}^{5-j}, \quad j = 0, \ldots, 5. \tag{15.10}$$

Table 15.5: Notation for Table 15.1

		Number of letters in Killer's archive						
		0	1	2	3	4	5	Total
Mentioned in other sources?	No	n_{00}	n_{01}	n_{02}	n_{03}	n_{04}	n_{05}	n_{0+}
	Yes	n_{10}	n_{11}	n_{12}	n_{13}	n_{14}	n_{15}	n_{1+}
Total		n_{+0}	n_{+1}	n_{+2}	n_{+3}	n_{+4}	n_{+5}	n_{++}

Then

$$\prod_{j=0}^{5} r_j^{n+j} = \prod_{j=0}^{5} \left(\frac{5}{j, 5-j} \right)^{n+j} p^{\sum_{j=0}^{5} jn_{+j}} \bar{p}^{\sum_{j=0}^{5}(5-j)n_{+j}}. \tag{15.11}$$

Let $S_1 = \sum_{j=0}^{5} jn_{+j}$. Then $\sum_{j=0}^{5}(5-j)n_{+j} = 5n_{++} - S_1$.

Hence

$$\prod_{j=0}^{5} r_j^{n+j} = \prod_{j=0}^{5} \left(\frac{5}{j, 5-j} \right)^{n+j} p^{S_1} \bar{p}^{5n_{++} - S_1}. \tag{15.12}$$

The first term on the right can be written for our data as

$$\prod_{j=0}^{5} \left(\frac{5}{j, 5-j} \right)^{n+j} = \left(\frac{5!}{0!5!} \right)^{n+143} \left(\frac{5!}{1!4!} \right)^{165} \left(\frac{5!}{2!3!} \right)^{20} \left(\frac{5!}{3!2!} \right)^{6} \left(\frac{5!}{4!1!} \right)^{3} \left(\frac{5!}{0!5!} \right)^{0}. \tag{15.13}$$

Only the first term has an exponent that depends on a parameter, and that term is 1 raised to a power, so the entire product is constant with respect to the parameters, and can be dropped. Similarly, in the terms for **n**! only the first, $n!$, depends on the parameters, and the others can be dropped:

$$L \propto \frac{(n_{++})!}{n!} p^{S_1} \bar{p}^{5n_{++} - S_1} s^{n_{1+}} \bar{s}^{n_{0+}}. \tag{15.14}$$

Again, using (15.4) and independent uniform distributions on p and s, the integrated likelihood for n is

$$\frac{(n_{++})!}{n!} \frac{(S_1)!(5n_{++} - S_1)!}{(5n_{++} + 1)!} \frac{(n_{1+})!(n_{0+})!}{(n_{++} + 1)!}$$
$$= \frac{S_1!(5n_{++} - S_1)!(n_{1+})!(n_{0+})!}{n!(5n_{++} + 1)!(n_{++} + 1)}. \tag{15.15}$$

Finally S_1 and n_{1+} also do not depend on n, so those terms can be dropped as well, yielding the integrated likelihood proportional to

$$\frac{(5n_{++} - S_1)!(n_{0+})!}{n!(5n_{++} + 1)!(n_{++} + 1)}. \tag{15.16}$$

Figure 15.2 plots the posterior distribution for $n + 337$ whose quantiles are given in Table 15.6. Here the median is 1155.

Table 15.6: Quantiles for dual systems posterior distribution under the binomial model

Quantile	978	1037	1076	1116	1155	1195	1234	1293	1372
Probability	0.1	0.2	0.3	0.4	0.5	0.6	0.7	0.8	0.9

Thus this model suggests remarkably fewer killings than those suggested by the simple dual systems estimate reported in Figure 15.1 and Table 15.6.

C. Com-binomial model

The binomial model implies that the survival of a document from a killer's archive is an event independent of the survival of other documents from the same killer's archive. Since all five letters are addressed to the same person (the killer), it is likely that they

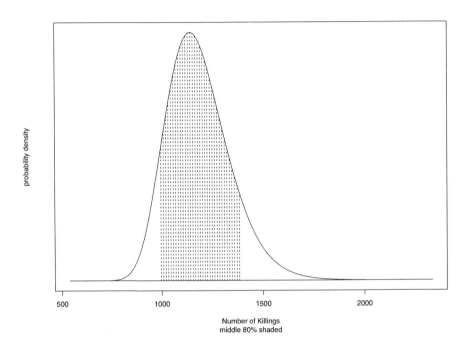

Figure 15.2: Binomial dual systems posterior distribution. Note that Figure 15.1 has a wider scale of the number of killings.

would tend to be stored together. Hence, it seems prudent to expand the model to allow for positive correlation among the events of survival of letters addressed to the same killer. [A referee suggests that an overly tidy daughter-in-law may have kept only one letter, leading to negative correlation. While that may have happened in a few instances, we think that joint physical destruction (fire and water) is far more likely, and hence expect positive correlation in the survival event of documents from a killer's archive.]

One model that allows for such correlation is the com-binomial distribution (Shmueli et al., 2004). The pdf for this distribution is given by

$$P\{X = j | p, \nu\} = \frac{p^j (1-p)^{m-j} \binom{m}{j, m-j}^\nu}{\sum_{k=0}^{m} p^k (1-p)^{m-k} \binom{m}{k, m-k}^\nu}, \quad j = 0, 1, \ldots, m. \tag{15.17}$$

When $\nu = 1$, this distribution reduces to the binomial distribution, and hence to independence of survival of the documents sent to a given killer. For $\nu > 1$, the survival would be negatively correlated. For $\nu < 1$, the survival would be positively correlated. In this application, the latter is expected. As $\nu \to \infty$, the probability would become concentrated on a single point. As $\nu \to -\infty$, it would become concentrated on 0 and m.

Because this distribution is unfamiliar, it is perhaps useful to look at some examples, displayed in Figure 15.3 for the case $m = 5$, which is the value of m in this application. In this figure, looking across rows, as ν increases, the probability tends to concentrate on a single point (except at $p = 1/2$, where symmetry leads to two dominant points, 2 and 3).

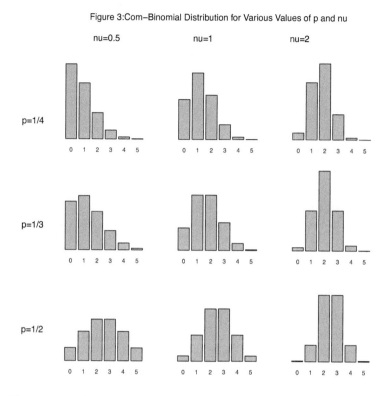

Figure 3:Com–Binomial Distribution for Various Values of p and nu

Figure 15.3: Com-binomial distribution for various values of p and nu

As alluded to above, values of ν above 1 do not make sense in this application. Therefore, the analysis to be presented imposes the condition $\nu \leq 1$ as a hard constraint, by using a prior that put zero probability in the space $\nu > 1$.

To incorporate the com-binomial distribution into the model, r_j in (15.10) is replaced by the expression in (15.17). This yields the likelihood

$$
\begin{aligned}
L &= \frac{n_{++}!}{\mathbf{n}!} s^{n_{1+}} \overline{s}^{n_{0+}} \prod_{j=0}^{5} r_j^{n_{+j}} \\
&= \frac{n_{++}!}{\mathbf{n}!} s^{n_{1+}} \overline{s}^{n_{0+}} \prod_{j=0}^{5} \left[\frac{p^j (1-p)^{m-j} \binom{m}{j,m-j}^{\nu}}{\sum_{k=0}^{m} p^k (1-p)^{m-k} \binom{m}{k,m-k}^{\nu}} \right]^{n_{+j}} .
\end{aligned}
\tag{15.18}
$$

It is convenient to divide the numerator and denominator in the product term by the factor $(1-p)^m (m!)^{\nu}$, yielding

$$
\frac{p^j (1-p)^{m-j} \binom{m}{j,m-j}^{\nu}}{\sum_{k=0}^{m} p^k (1-p)^{m-k} \binom{m}{k,m-k}^{\nu}} = \frac{\theta^j / [j!(m-j)!]^{\nu}}{\sum_{k=0}^{5} \theta^k / [k!(m-k)!]^{\nu}},
\tag{15.19}
$$

where $\theta = p/(1-p)$.

It is further convenient to rewrite (15.19) as follows:

$$\theta^j / \left\{ [j!(m-j)!]^\nu \left(\sum_{k=0}^{5} \theta^k / [k!(m-k)!]^\nu \right) \right\}$$

$$= e^{j \log \theta - \nu \log[j!(m-j)!]} / Z(\theta, \nu) \tag{15.20}$$

where $Z(\theta, \nu) = \sum_{k=0}^{5} \theta^k / [k!(m-k)!]^\nu.$

Substituting (15.20) into (15.18) yields:

$$L = \frac{n_{++}!}{n!} s^{n_1 +} \bar{s}^{n_0 +} e^{s_1 \log \theta - s_2 \nu} / (Z(\theta, \nu))^{n_{++}}, \tag{15.21}$$

where $s_1 = \sum_{j=1}^{5} j n_{+j}$ and $s_2 = \sum_{j=0}^{5} n_{+j} \log(j!(5-j)!).$

Once again s can be integrated with respect to a uniform prior, yielding the integrated likelihood

$$\frac{n_{++}!}{n!} \frac{(n_{1+})!(n_{0+})!}{(n_{++}+1)!} e^{s_1 \log \theta - s_2 \nu} / Z(\theta, \nu)^{n_{++}}. \tag{15.22}$$

Finally, factors not involving θ, ν and n can be eliminated, yielding

$$\frac{(n_{0+})!}{n!(n_{++}+1)} e^{s_1 \log \theta - s_2 \nu} Z(\theta, \nu)^{-n_{++}}. \tag{15.23}$$

In order to have results comparable to those in Figure 15.2, proper account must be taken of the transformation from p to θ. The differentials are related by

$$dp = \frac{d\theta}{(1+\theta)^2}, \tag{15.24}$$

so p uniform on $(0,1)$ is equivalent to θ having the density $1/(1+\theta)^2$ on $(0, \infty)$. Thus, the form of likelihood used here is (15.23) multiplied by (15.24), that is,

$$\frac{(n_{0+})!}{(n_{++}+1)n!} e^{s_1 \log \theta - s_2 \nu} \frac{Z(\theta, \nu)^{-n_{++}}}{(1+\theta)^2}. \tag{15.25}$$

Using a grid method to integrate (15.25) with respect to θ and ν yields the posterior distribution in Figure 15.4, with quantiles given in Table 15.7. The median for this model is 1143, about the same as for the binomial model.

Table 15.7: Quantiles for dual systems integrated likelihood under the com-binomial model

Quantile	959	1021	1051	1113	1143	1174	1235	1265	1357
probability	0.1	0.2	0.3	0.4	0.5	0.6	0.7	0.8	0.9

The results of the com-binomial in Figure 15.4 are very similar to those of the binomial in Figure 15.2. The reason for this is that the likelihood for ν strongly indicates a preference for $\nu = 1$. Glancing back at the data in Table 15.1, the data are strongly piled up at 0 and 1 letters from a killer's archive; there are no killings at all for which all five letters have survived. Therefore, the data looks much more like it would at $\nu = \infty$, which makes no substantive sense in this problem. Given that the hard constraint $\nu \leq 1$ has been imposed, the integrated posterior puts most weight on the largest ν permitted, that is, $\nu = 1$; the results therefore resemble those of the binomial model reported in Figure 15.2. While the generalization afforded by the com-binomial did not lead to a substantially different integrated likelihood, it was important to see whether positive correlation in the survival of letters sent to the killer was a dominant feature of the data. This turned out not to be the case.

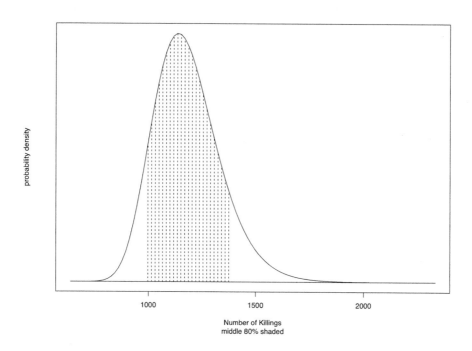

Figure 15.4: Com-binomial posterior distribution. Note that Figure 15.1 has a wider scale for the number of killings.

15.4   Conclusion

An assumption underlying our model is that every killing resulted in the five letters being sent to the killer. It is possible that this is not true, and possible that the propensity to send the requisite letters varied by geography. It is also possible that some geographical areas were more prone to document destruction by fire, flood, etc., and such areas might be those less carefully administered. We leave these possibilities for further exploration.

This paper presents three analyses of the number of killings in rural Norway during the period in question. The first (Table 15.4 and Figure 15.1) used only the presence or absence of a mention in the killer's archive, and found huge uncertainty in the number of killings. The latter two, reported, respectively, in Table 15.6 and Figure 15.2, and in Table 15.7 and Figure 15.4, are so similar that substantively they are the same. The distribution reported indicates that perhaps rural Norway was more peaceful in this period than had previously been thought.

Acknowledgments

The authors thank their good friend Baruch Fischhoff for introducing them and suggesting that this problem might interest us both. Sarah Brockwell did much to clean the data, and Anthony Brockwell helped with the data structure. Jong Soo Lee also contributed to the data handling. Conversations with Rebecca Nugent, Howard Seltman and Andrew Thomas about R were also very helpful. A referee was very helpful in correcting our rough demographic estimates of the numbers of killings.

SUPPLEMENTARY MATERIAL

Criminal homicides in Norwegian letters 1300 to 1569 (DOI:10.1214/12AOAS612SUPP;.pdf). A list of letters found in Norway concerning killings during the period of 1300 to 1569.

REFERENCES

Bunge, J. and Fitzpatrick, M. (1993). "Estimating the Number of Species: A Review." *JASA*, 88, 1, 364–373. 310

Dyrvik, S. (1979). "Jordbruk og folketal 1500–1720." In *Norsk økonomisk historie 1500–1970, Band 1 1500–1850*, eds. S. Dyrvik, A.B. Fossen, T. Grønlie, E. Hovland, H. Nordvik, and S. Tveite. Universitetsforlaget, Bergen. 309

Kadane, J. and Hastorf, C. (1988). "Bayesian Paleoethnobotany." In *Bayesian Statistics III*, eds. D. L. J. Bernardo, M. DeGroot and A. Smith, 243–259. Oxford University Press. (This volume, Chapter 1). 309

Kadane, J. and Næshagen, F. (2012). "Supplement to 'The Number of Killings in Southern Rural Norway, 1300–1569'." 10.1214/12-AOAS612SUPP. 308

Lincoln, F. (1930). "Calculating waterfowl abundance on the basis of banding returns." *United States Department of Agriculture Circular*, 118, 1–4. 310

Moseng, O., Opsahl, E., Pettersen, G., and Sandmo, E. (2007). *Norsk Historie 750–1537*, 2. Utgave. Oslo: Universitetsforlaget. 308

Næshagen, F. (2005). "Den kriminelle voldens U-kurve fra femtenhundretall til natid (The U-curve of criminal violence from the sixteenth century to the present)." *Historisk Tidsskrift*, 84, 411–427. 309

Petersen, C. (1896). "The yearly immigration of young plaice into the Limfjord from the German sea." *Report of the Danish Biological Station (1895)*, 6, 5–84. 310

Sandnes, J. (1990). *Kniven, ølet og æren*. Oslo: Universitetsforlaget. 309

Shmueli, G., Minka, T., Kadane, J., Borle, S., and Boatwright, P. (2004). "A Useful Distribution for Fitting Discrete Data: Revival of the COM-Poisson." *Journal of the Royal Statistical Society C*, 54, 127–142. 314

Wolter, K. (1986). "Some coverage error models for census data." *Journal of the American Statistical Association*, 81, 338–346. 310

Epilogue

What is the scientific issue addressed?

To find an estimate (probability distribution) for the number of killings in southern rural Norway in the period 1300–1569.

Is justification given for

a) the use of the data?

The data consists of all known extant records of killings in the area and period in question, both from letters to the killers and all other records.

b) the likelihood and prior?

The likelihood is a dual system. The inference is not very sensitive to the prior, but see below.

What robustness studies were done?

The principle threat to the inference is whether the number of surviving letters to the killer can be regarded as independent. The material in Section 15.3.C is a robustness analysis showing that independence is not contra-indicated by the data.

How were the computations done?

On a grid.

If I were doing the problem again, how would I change the approach?

I would not.

What do I see as the contribution of the paper?

It shows that a reasonable posterior distribution can be given for the number of killings in the area and period.

Was Bayesian analysis useful in this problem?

Bayesian methods are essential to the analysis.

TEACHING SUGGESTIONS

References for theoretical ideas:

1. Dual systems: McCrea, R.S. and Morgan, B.J.T. (2014). Analysis of Capture-Recapture Data, Chapman & Hall, Boca Raton

2. Missing data: *Principles* Section 9.2

3. Multinomial distribution: *Principles* Section 2.9

4. Beta integral: *Principles* Section 8.9

Exercises

1. This paper compares the results of the binomial dual systems model to those of a more general com-binomial dual systems model. Is this a legitimate way to examine a model for goodness of fit? In what ways might it be better (or worse) to compare against a very general model?

2. The analysis in part C puts zero prior, and hence zero posterior, on the space $\nu > 1$, although the data favor $\nu > 1$. Does this invalidate the results? What are the arguments in favor of, and against, this prior assumption?

3. What accounts for the big difference between the result of part A and the results of parts B and C? Which analysis do you think is more likely to be correct? Why?

Epilogue

When I do applied work (as in the papers in this volume), my commitment is to the applied problem. My preferences about statistical philosophy and technique are secondary. Thus the question is fairly put in this collection of papers: to what extent were my Bayesian preferences a help (or a hindrance) to successfully contributing to the application? That is the issue I hope readers will ask themselves as they peruse this volume.

In the epilogues to each chapter I have given my "report card" for the research reported. But the evaluation that counts is not mine, it is yours.

Epilogue

Index

Index of Names

For Product Safety Concerns and Information please contact our EU
representative GPSR@taylorandfrancis.com Taylor & Francis Verlag GmbH,
Kaufingerstraße 24, 80331 München, Germany

Printed and bound by CPI Group (UK) Ltd, Croydon, CR0 4YY

08/05/2025

01864344-0001